Popular Science

HOMEOWNER'S ENCYCLOPEDIA

FULLER & DEES

TIMES MIRROR

New York • Los Angeles • Montgomery

© Fuller & Dees MCMLXXIV
3734 Atlanta Highway, Montgomery, Alabama 36109

Library of Congress Cataloging in Publication Data
Main entry under title: Popular Science Homeowner's Encyclopedia

1. Dwellings — Maintenance and repair — Amateurs' manuals. 2. Repairing —
Amateurs' manuals. 3. Do-it-yourself work. I. Title: Homeowner's encyclopedia.
TH4817.3.P66   643'.7'03   74-19190
Complete Set ISBN 0-87197-070-8
Volume IV ISBN 0-87197-074-0

Popular Science

HOMEOWNER'S ENCYCLOPEDIA

Pecan Wood

Pecan wood is a type of hickory widely used for furniture making. It is medium to reddish brown with an attractive grain that is further enhanced by a variety of finishes. Pecan is harder than any of the other commonly used commercial hardwoods, and it shrinks and swells less than other heavy hardwoods such as beech or hard maple. For these reasons, pecan is ideal for flooring in public places. Pecan wood produces a superior veneer that compares favorably with more expensive hardwoods and is a favorite for fine furniture, wall paneling, and television and phonograph cabinets. *SEE ALSO WOOD IDENTIFICATION.*

Peeling Paint

Peeling paint consists of scales and chips of paint that have broken loose from the surface to which the paint was applied. Peeling paint can be caused by improper priming or no primer, paint applied to old wood, excessive heat and impurities or moisture not removed from the surface before the application of paint.

Before a new surface can be applied, peeling paint must be removed. A scraper or wire brush will remove the loose particles. After removing as much paint as possible, sand the edges of the remaining pieces of paint until the edges blend with the bare surface. This will produce a smooth appearance after the surface is painted. Next, repaint the area. Primer or special paints may be needed according to the type of surface to be covered. Most paint stores have a complete list of what is needed for the various types of material to be painted. *SEE ALSO PAINTS & PAINTING.*

Pegboard

Pegboard is perforated hardboard usually $1/8$ inch thick. It is available in panels and can be cut by a table or hand saw to any size.

Designed as a space saver, pegboard has interchangeable self-locking metal hangers that will hold heavy or light objects. It can be painted.

Installation is simple. The only precaution necessary is to use framing or furring strips thick enough to provide for hanger clearance in the back. A clearance of $3/8$ inch is needed for $1/8$ inch thick pegboard. If the board is to be attached to studs or walls, nails can be used. *SEE ALSO STORAGE & STORAGE AREAS; WORK-SHOPS.*

Penetrating Finish

Penetrating finishes are entirely in the wood, not on it. The resins harden to make the wood more durable and wear-resistant. To wear off this finish, the wood must also be worn off.

These finishes are excellent on large areas such as furniture, cabinets, paneling and floors. They perform better on open-pore woods than on fine-grained woods.

Applying a penetrating finish to a floor is easy. After the floor has been sanded and dusted, brush or swab on a full coat of finish. During the next 30 minutes, watch for dull spots. If some appear, apply more finish on those areas.

At the end of the half hour, wipe the excess off. If desired, wait three hours and repeat the application. Wipe the surface dry. *SEE ALSO WOOD FINISHING.*

Penetrating Resin

Penetrating resin is one of the most durable wood finishes and is the easiest to apply. It is clear, but darkens the wood slightly. The finish sinks into the surface and the resin hardens between the fibers of the wood. The wood will be harder and will withstand ordinary household damage.

Penetrating resins are resistant to almost any damage, including water, scratching, alcohol, heat and most household chemicals. This finish is not meant for outdoor use. This type of finish is best for large areas such as wall paneling and floors and is recommended for large furniture pieces. Best results will be achieved on open-pored woods such as oak, walnut, chestnut, pecan and mahogany.

To apply the finish, pour the resin thickly on the wood. Your hands, a very fine steel wool pad, rags or a brush can be used to spread the finish and work it into the wood. Depending on the particular brand of penetrating resin being used, keep the surface wet from 30 minutes to one hour. If dull spots appear in that time, this means the resin has soaked in and more should be applied.

Use rags to wipe all the surface liquid off after the wood will not take any more. Do not leave any trace of the liquid on the surface.

If the wood is porous, a second application may be advisable. Wait approximately three hours, but do not wait until the first coat has hardened completely. The second coat should be brushed or swabbed on and kept wet for 30 minutes or longer. Then wipe it off.

Once this coat has hardened, the wood may be waxed, but this may clog the pores and detract from the beauty of the finish. *SEE ALSO RESINS.*

Penny (d) Nails
[SEE FASTENERS.]

Pentachlorophenol

Pentachlorophenol is the main ingredient of a very effective wood preservative. Often called

Penta, it is diluted in oil for easy spreading and quick penetration. Pentachlorophenol may be brushed on the wood surface or used in a large pail for soaking cut ends of posts and boards. It can be painted over with most outdoor paints.

Permit, Building
[SEE BUILDING PERMIT.]

Philippine Mahogany

Philippine mahogany is an exotic hardwood used for medium-priced furniture, boat building and as a surface veneer on plywood paneling and flush doors. It is an open-pored, middle-toned, inexpensive wood that may be finished with or without stain. Philippine mahogany is commonly referred to as lauan wood. *SEE ALSO WOOD IDENTIFICATION.*

Phillips Screw

A Phillips screw has two slots crossing at the center of its head. Made for use with a Phillips screwdriver, the head of this screw prevents the blade from slipping out of the slot and gouging the work. *SEE ALSO FASTENERS.*

Phillips Screwdriver

The driving end of the Phillips screwdriver is designed to fit Phillips screws. These screwdrivers are numbered according to their size, with numbers one, two, three and four covering most sizes of Phillips screws. When the screw size is zero to four, use a number one screwdriver; five to nine screw sizes can be driven with a number two; number three fits Phillips screws in sizes from 10 to 16; screw sizes 18 to 24 should be driven by a number four

Phillips screwdriver. *SEE ALSO HAND TOOLS.*

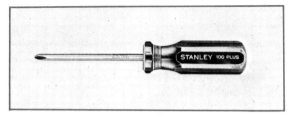

Courtesy of The Stanley Works.

Phillips Screwdriver

Photo Darkroom
[SEE PHOTOGRAPHY.]

Photoelectric Controls

Photoelectric controls are devices for controlling the operation of electric appliances and fixtures. The controls are activated by a light-sensitive switch called a photoelectric cell. When a certain light intensity strikes the photoelectric cell, it activates the appliance. Photoelectric controls may be used to turn outdoor lights on and off, turn on interior lights when no one is present and similar activities. *SEE ALSO AUTOMATION.*

Photography

Selecting a camera was once a simple matter. If one was interested primarily in sunny Sunday afternoon snapshots and did not want to spend a lot of money, he bought a *box camera*. These had an average shutter speed of about $1/_{40}$ second and an average lens speed fixed at about f/11. This combination yields reasonably sharp pictures of average subjects, not closer than six feet, in average light. For a few dollars more, a folding roll-film camera, which Eastman named *Kodak*, because the word was odd, easy to remember and sounded "like the click of a shutter," could be purchased. It had multispeed shutters, faster

lenses with variable settings and provision for selective focus.

The development of modern cameras and camera technology was hastened by constant improvement in photographic film. If film had not been so greatly improved and color had not been developed, we might still be using cameras much like those of 1935. But, film has improved and diversified. So, today we need cameras capable of more accurate exposure control, greater lens speed and higher mechanical precision. The camera has lenses that focus and form the image in an expanding cone of light on a light-sensitive surface. An iris controls the volume of light that can pass. It opens wide or closes down to admit more or less light depending on the illumination of the subject. On many of today's better models, the camera's iris adjusts automatically. The lens, the iris and the surface on which the image is formed are housed in a light-tight chamber in the camera. The image is formed on the light sensitive surface of a film, where it is instantly captured in the form of a latent image, later to be made permanent. A camera is more efficient at a moderate light level; too much is blinding and too little provides inadequate information. Since the film is sensitive to *any* exposure to light, it must see only what is to be photographed. This is accomplished with

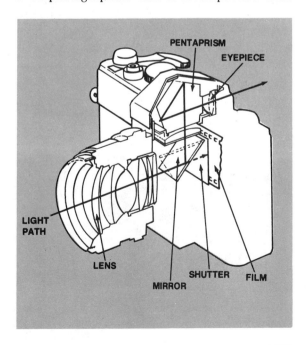

the shutter mechanism that shuts out light from the camera at all times, except for the brief instant when an exposure is made. Then the shutter closes again, the film is advanced and the camera is ready for the next shot.

Quality and conveniences are the reasons there are so many different cameras from which to chose. Lenses alone can cost from pennies to hundreds of dollars, the film advance mechanism, shutter speed range, accuracy of the control of the lens opening or iris — whether manual, fully or semi-automatic and the general workmanship all affect the cost of a camera.

FAMILY CAMERAS

The casual picture-taker is well served by any of the many models of easy-to-use, small and reasonably priced cartridge-loading *Instamatic* cameras originated by Kodak. These cameras use size 126 film cartridges that contain the film supply and the takeup spool. Simply drop in the cartridge, take the pictures and, after the last shot, take it out.

Pocket Instamatic is a slim camera that easily slips into a pocket or purse. The drop-in, cartridge-loading concept remains the same, but since the camera is so much smaller, approximately 5 x 1 x 2$^1/_2$ inches, the film size was reduced. These Pocket Instamatic cameras, available from a number of manufacturers, vary in complexity from the simplest aim-and-shoot camera to the better models that have automatic shutter and/or aperture controls and a coupled range-finder, a small area in the middle of the viewfinder which gives a double image until the

camera is properly focused and the two images merge into one.

Pocket Instamatics, like most other cameras, can take flash pictures. Some models accept *Magicubes,* a cube that contains four expendable flash bulbs, while others accept small, clip-on electronic flash units or have the flash unit built into the camera.

One of the smallest, lightest and easiest-to-use ultra-miniature precision cameras is the *Minox.* Less than four inches long, $^5/_8$ inches thick and only slightly more than one inch wide, this camera has an automatic built-in exposure meter, variable shutter speed ($^1/_2$ to $^1/_{1000}$ second) and is instantly loaded with a film cartridge. The shutter is cocked and the film advanced via a single *push-pull* motion of the camera.

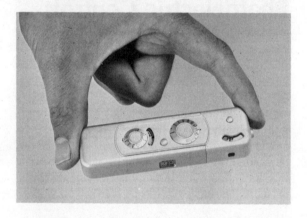

The *Keystone 60 Second Everflash Instant* picture camera has a built-in battery-operated electronic flash and produces *instant* Polaroid pictures. Exposure is automatically controlled for flash and existing light photography.

There is an endless variety of 35mm cameras from which to choose. The family name is derived from the size of film all these cameras use. The 35mm miniature camera is a direct descendant of the professional motion-picture camera that uses 35mm film, which is about 1$^3/_8$ inches wide. The 35mm film, edged-perforated and without paper backing, is usually supplied in metal cassettes or magazines that are themselves loaded into the camera. After exposure, the whole length of the film, normally 20 or 36 exposures, is rewound into the cassette for subsequent processing.

The typical 35mm camera using a range finder, is small and light. Once the camera is set to the proper film speed, as specified on the film box or instruction sheet packed with the film, its operation is fully automatic. The photocell in the top center of the lens assembly senses illumination and automatically adjusts the f/stop for correct exposure.

For flash pictures that can be taken with a matching clip-on electronic flash, the correct lens aperture is automatically set as focus is made through the range-finder. The lens opens wide when focused on distant subjects and closes down for closer subjects.

Single-lens reflex (SLR) cameras allow the photographer to look at the scene to be taken *through the same lens* used to expose the film. This eliminates *parallax,* the difference between what is seen through the viewfinder of the non-SLR camera and what the film is recording. A mirror reflects the light up into the eyepiece through a five-sided prism, *pentaprism,* which turns the picture around the right way. When the shutter release is pressed, the mirror springs out of the way an instant before the shutter opens to let the light reach the film.

There are several major advantages of this system. Shots are composed more accurately because what is seen in the eyepiece is the exact image that will appear on the film.

Focusing is easy and accurate. Instead of measuring or guessing the distance to a subject and setting this on the lens, simply look through the eyepiece and turn the focus control until the image is sharply focused.

Lenses are interchangeable. If the lens to a telephoto type, for example, is changed, what will appear on the film is still seen exactly in the eyepiece without having to make any adjustment.

SINGLE-LENS REFLEX CAMERAS

Some cameras have two lens systems: one through which the light reaches the film to make the photograph and a separate one, the viewfinder, through which the picture is composed. This means that however well the two are matched, it is unlikely that what is seen in the viewfinder will be *exactly* what appears on the film, especially in close-up shots.

This is through-the-lens-metering. Most better 35mm SLR cameras have a built-in light meter that works through the lens that takes the picture, so there is less chance of it measuring unwanted light. And, if a filter is being used over the lens, its effect on light entering the camera is automatically taken into account.

Many cameras have automatic exposure control. Once the shutter speed is set, changes in light conditions cause no problems. The aperture is set automatically by the light meter. The film speed is simply set according to the film that was being used when the camera was loaded.

Many automatic SLR cameras have an aperture setting of the match-needle type. Once a shutter speed is chosen, a ring controlling the aperture should be turned until the moving light meter needle which is seen in the eyepiece, is lined up between two markers. Alternatively the aperture can be chosen and the shutter speed adjusted until the needle is lined up.

Some cameras measure the light coming through the lens at full aperture, but allow for the fact that the picture is going to be taken at a preselected smaller aperture. This makes the image in the viewfinder always as bright as possible. Focusing becomes much easier than with a darker image. Others have a meter requiring that it be closed down to working aperture to get the appropriate meter reading. Once done, the aperture can be opened again to compose and focus a shot.

Cameras which meter at full aperture have a particular advantage if quick shots in changing light conditions are to be taken. Some camera metering systems measure the light coming from all parts of the scene. This is called *whole field metering*. Others measure only the light coming from the center of the field of view. This is called *spot metering*. Spot metering gives better results in situations such as a portrait against a bright sky or where a bright light at the edge of the picture might distort the reading. Whole field metering is useful in telephoto photography where the major area of interest is rather small.

With a 35mm SLR camera 36 pictures or frames can be shot before there is a need to reload. This, coupled with the low cost of the film and the ease with which it is handled, allows several pictures of a subject to be taken from a different

angle or at a different exposure setting, to insure at least one picture that will please. Frequently the *insurance shot,* the one that was taken as an after-thought, turns out to be the choice shot for printing and enlarging.

The standard image size of the 35mm camera is 24 x 36mm (about 1″ x 1³/₈″). Obviously prints of that size are of little use, except for test prints. Enlargement is normal procedure and 35mm positives, especially color, are naturals for projections, as slides, onto a screen for group viewing.

LENSES

One of the great pleasures of single-lens 35mm reflex photography is the ease with which any one of dozens of interchangeable special-purpose lenses can be put into service. No accessory viewfinder is needed, as on other cameras when accessory lenses are used. A telephoto lens added to a camera enables the photographer to take distant objects that may be difficult or impossible to come near, full frame photos of people without being on top of them or other subjects too distant for the standard 50mm lens usually bought with the camera.

A zoom lens is more expensive than a good, single-focal-length telephoto lens, but it is so versatile that the creative photography opportunities which such a lens affords will compensate for the extra cost.

A wide range of interchangeable lenses add to the versatility of the 35mm Single Lens Reflex camera. They range from 28mm wide angle lens to the versatile automatic zoom lens.

With the zoom lens the size of an image is adjusted from a stationary position. Stand still and make the picture size change by simply sliding or turning an adjustment on the lens. There is no need to move back and forth to vary the dimensions of the image size. Since there is no way to crop color slides *after* the shutter is clicked, and cropping color negatives and prints is not as easy as with black and white, an infinitely adjustable lens can add a totally new dimension to 35mm SLR photography.

The wide-angle lens makes it possible to photograph a larger area of a scene without stepping back, which makes it ideal for shooting in confined locations or crowded places.

The normal 50mm lens has a 45 degree angle of view. A 25mm wide-angle lens has half of its focal length and takes in an arc of 90 degrees. The most popular wide-angle lens is the 35mm which covers 64 degrees.

Because of their short focal length, wide-angle lenses offer considerable depth of field which allows *zone focusing*. The photographer can preselect a lens opening that yields good depth of field and be assured of properly focused pictures over a wide range of distances. For example, with a 35mm lens set at f/8 and 15 feet on the footage scale, everything from 8 feet to infinity will be in focus.

A wide angle lens exaggerates or distorts objects which are close in the foreground, and also distorts spherical objects at the extreme ends of the picture. Therefore, be careful not to include this shape object so that oval-shaped heads or other equally unusual shapes will not result.

The lens is attached to the camera either by a screw thread, often referred to as a *Praktica* thread or a *Pentax* thread, or with a bayonet fitting which is quicker and easier to use. Each manufacturer uses a slightly different system, so different brands of lens are not necessarily interchangeable without special adapters.

Good performance at full aperture makes lenses expensive. However, this will probably be needed only rarely, when in poor light conditions or for special effects which need a shallow depth of focus such as a portrait against a blurred background.

F/STOP SETTINGS

Behind the camera's lens is a set of overlapping metal leaves called an *iris diaphragm* which can be set to close down or to enlarge the opening through which light enters the camera. The opening is called the aperture and its various settings are referred to as *f/stops*. They appear on the lens in a series that runs 2, 2.8, 4, 5, 6, 8, 11, 16 and 22, plus or minus a setting at either end.

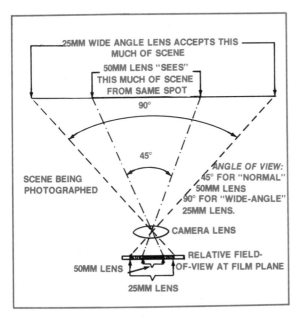

Wide-angle lens accepts larger picture area than "normal" lens when picture is taken from the same camera location.

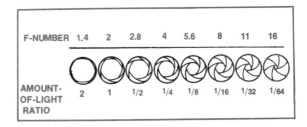

F-NUMBER	1.4	2	2.8	4	5.6	8	11	16
AMOUNT-OF-LIGHT RATIO	2	1	1/2	1/4	1/8	1/16	1/32	1/64

The amount of light that is allowed to enter the camera and strike the film is controlled by the iris diaphragm. Relative size of the opening (or aperture) is indicated by the use of f/stops. The larger f/stop number the less light admitted. Thus f/16 admits less light than any other lower number f/stop.

The amount of light that passes through the lens is determined by the f/stop number. The larger the f/stop number the smaller the aperture. Thus, half as much light can enter the camera at f/16 than at f/8. The f/stop number of a typical quality camera's lens starts at f/2, where maximum light is admitted, and goes to f/16, the smallest, in steps that are fixed so the light ratio between adjacent stops is 2:1.

The actual size of the aperture at each f/stop is the result of simple mathematics. The equation used is:

$$\frac{1}{f} = \frac{aperture}{focal\ length}$$

Thus, an f/stop of 4 on a 50mm lens means that, at that setting, the actual aperture through which light enters the camera measures 12.5mm in diameter. This is how the equation works:

$$\frac{1}{4} = \frac{aperture}{50mm}$$

$$\frac{50mm}{4} = aperture$$

$$12.5mm = aperture$$

Similarly, an f/stop of 4 on a 200mm lens represents an actual aperture size of 50mm.

Apertures are represented as f/stops rather than as real measurements to allow for standardization of exposures. Shots made at f/4 with a 50mm lens and at f/4 with a 200mm lens at the same shutter speed produce equivalent exposures on the film. The 200mm shot needs a larger physical aperture, admitting more light because, once admitted, the light must travel further down the barrel of the longer lens and its intensity is diminished along the way.

DEPTH OF FIELD

The zone of sharpness in a picture is called the depth of field. Its limits depend on three factors: the f/stop setting, the distance focused on and the focal length of the lens in use.

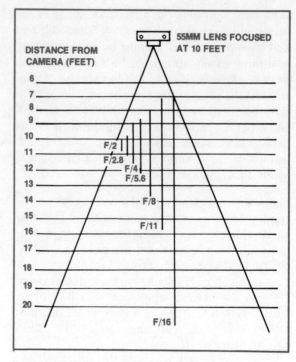

Depth of Field obtained at various f/stop settings. Lines indicate the area in focus when a 55mm Lens is focused on a subject 10 feet from the camera.

Small apertures (high f/numbers) yield photos with a great deal of in-focal area. Large apertures (small f/numbers) give pictures with a shallow in-focus area. Depth of field diminishes when the camera is focused on a close subject. Long focal length lenses have substantially less depth of field at any given f/stop and focusing distance than a normal lens focused at the same distance and set at the same f/stop, while short focal length lenses have more.

SHUTTER SPEED

The speed of whatever action or subject is being photographed is the prime consideration in choosing a shutter speed. Shooting sports or any fast moving subject requires a fast shutter to freeze the action. A subject moving parallel to the camera, across the field of view, is displaced much more in the view and on the film. It will be blurred, requiring a faster shutter speed than the oncoming or withdrawing subject. Thus, subject speed, the camera-to-subject distance and the direction of travel all must be considered when choosing an action-stopping shutter speed.

A camera's shutter-speed selector controls the length of time that light is permitted to enter the camera and strike the film. The shutter-speed dial on a camera indicates the number of seconds or fractions of a second for which the shutter can be made to open and close. The sequence usually runs from one or one-half second through $1/_{500}$th or $1/_{1000}$th second in a direct arithmetical progression. Most settings are fractions of a second (1/shutterspeed). By changing speed from $1/_{25}$th to $1/_{50}$th of a second, exposure time can be cut in half. The shutter speed is the complement of the f-stop (aperture). Together, these two settings establish the correct exposure for a given film type and lighting situation.

POLAROID SX-70 LAND CAMERA

Like other SLR cameras, the SX-70 also uses a mirror that flips out of the way the instant the shutter button is pressed. But, this camera instantly and automatically ejects a picture from the camera that is sheathed in unscratchable plastic and starts to *develop itself,* in daylight, less than two seconds after the shutter button is pressed. No processing is required. The camera itself can be folded to a thickness of about one inch and, unlike other SLR cameras, can be readily carried about in a man's suit pocket or a woman's handbag.

CAMERA-HANDLING TECHNIQUE

No matter what camera is used, proper camera handling is important to assure the sharpest possible pictures. Even slight camera movement can result in blurred photographs. To hold a 35mm SLR camera properly, support the camera/lens combination with most of the weight resting in the palm of the left hand, while applying the right hand to the camera's side. Transport the slim advance lever with the right thumb and squeeze the release button gently and smoothly, using the cushion not the tip of the index finger. The aperture ring, focusing ring and shutter speed ring are arranged to make possible operation with your left fingers right up to the moment the shutter is released.

Tips for the Photographer

A   Hold your breath at the moment of shutter release.

B   When holding the camera horizontally, keep both elbows close to the body.

C   For vertical shooting, keep one elbow close to your body and press the camera tightly against your forehead.

D   Steady yourself against any nearby firm support such as a tree, fence or wall, whenever possible.

E   When handholding a telephoto lens, camera shake is magnified as the focal length increases. Always try to use the fastest possible shutter speed lighting conditions will allow.

F   When shooting under $1/_{30}$ of a second, using a stable platform or tripod, a cable release is recommended. This eliminates the possibility of jarring the camera and is particularly important with telephoto lenses. If you have no cable release, use the self-timer that flips the mirror up before the shutter is clicked. This minimizes camera bounce at the instant of picture taking.

A camera should always be preset so that it will be ready for the *perfect* picture. If a non-automatic camera is used, an exposure meter reading should be taken, the general area needed to be in focus should be determined and the diaphragm and footage scale preset. With a 55mm lens set at f/8 and 10 feet on the distance scale, for example, everything from eight feet to 13½ feet will be in focus. With a 35mm wide angle lens set at f/5.6 and 15 feet on the distance scale, everything from about nine feet to 42 feet will be in focus. The shutter speed is then adjusted to the existing light.

AUTOMATIC ELECTRONIC FLASH

An electronic flash unit almost guarantees success in photography. The electronic flash or *strobe* contains an energy storage component called a *capacitor* that is slowly filled with an electrical charge supplied by self-contained batteries or household current. The instant the camera's shutter button is pressed, the stored energy is applied to a transparent tube filled with pressurized gas, called a *flashtube*. The gas immediately ionizes and converts the surge of electric current into a brilliant, short-duration burst of high-intensity light.

Because the light is so intense, the camera's aperture can be shut way down. This reduction in f-stop, coupled with lightning-speed exposure, produces sharp pictures with good depth of field. Distance miscalculations and slight mistakes in focusing are rectified, and movement of the subject is cancelled with the electronic flash.

Shutter speed and f-stop settings for electronic flash photography depend on the film, which always comes packed with an information sheet that gives appropriate ASA or guide number data for proper camera settings.

Light intensity hitting the subject to be photographed varies with flash-to-subject distance. At eight feet the light is only a fourth as bright as it is at four feet and only 1/16 as bright as at two feet. To get a consistent exposure, a different camera f-stop setting must be calculated every time the shooting distance is changed. Some cameras automatically adjust the lens opening for varying subject-to-camera distances, but that setting is good for only a particular electronic flash unit.

The latest refinement in electronic flash photography is a method of automatically controlling the light intensity of the flash. This eliminates the problem of distance computations usually associated with flash photography and assures perfect flash pictures. Simply focus the lens, frame the picture and shoot.

The instant that the shutter button is pressed, the flash goes off. Light from the subject photographed is bounced back into the flash unit's electronic light monitoring device, an electric eye. As soon as this sensor measures enough light exposure, a built-in energy-saving electronic calculator circuit goes to work. The circuit uses a special type of transistor called a *thyristor,* a device that acts just like an on/off switch, in that it can instantly halt the flow of electrical energy to the flash tube. This stops further light output from the flash tube, once there is sufficient light on the subject, to assure perfect exposure. In addition, the energy storage capacitor is not fully depleted after each flash. Instead, it retains the unused energy so many more automatic flashes can be made from each fresh or freshly charged battery than from electronic flash units that use up all of the energy stored in the capacitor for every flash. All this happens automatically, in 1/1000 of a second or less.

TRIPODS

There is a limit to the shutter speed at which one can hand-hold a camera without noticeable blurring of the image. Most people cannot make satisfactory hand-held exposure with a modern small camera at slower than 1/60th of a second without getting some blur. With longer-focal-length, telephoto lenses, the limit is likely to be 1/100th of a second or higher. With a single-lens-reflex (SLR) camera and its vibration-producing mirror and shutter, blurring may be encountered at even faster shutter speeds. Thus, a good quality tripod *is* a necessity for close-up work, long distance photography and slow speed or time exposures.

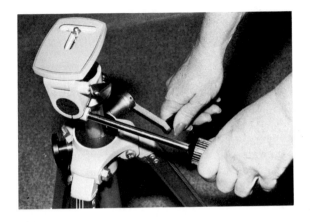

A tripod is also most useful in portraiture, even if a relatively fast shutter speed is used. It holds the camera in position while the photographer moves around adjusting other variables like focus, lights, pose or subject, background, etc. A remote shutter release can then be used to make the exposure at the precise desired moment.

A tripod is clearly helpful for still life photos requiring critical focusing, such as extreme closeups of flowers, and when shooting with available light.

Shooting in dim light without flash attachments often necessitates slow shutter speeds to get the right exposure. If shots are made at night under available light, exposure times of 30 seconds to several minutes are not unusual. Camera movement at slow speeds can ruin a picture so a sturdy tripod is needed to give the camera the firm support necessary for good available light photographs.

A tripod is essential for high-quality movie work. It is virtually impossible to handhold a movie camera steady, whether one is following action or taking a static scene.

The camera mounts on the camera platform at the top of the tripod with a mounting screw that fits into the tripod socket on the bottom of the camera. Tripods extend vertically by means of their telescopic legs and the centerpost or elevator which moves up and down at the top of the leg assembly. The pan head which can turn from side to side, *panning*, or up and down, *tilting*, sits on top of the centerpost and is used to aim the camera. A camera can be locked into the ap-propriate position for a still photo or a static movie scene, or either the pan and tilt functions or both can be left unlocked to allow the photographer to follow the action.

Choosing A Tripod

A quality tripod is rigid, stable and easy to set up and adjust. The centerpost should raise and lower smoothly. The legs must be sturdy and lock quickly and securely. The bottom of the legs should have foot pads to keep the tripod from sliding or scratching the floor. Some tripods have retractable spikes, useful for working outdoors.

It is a good idea to take along any cameras that may have to be mounted when you are buying a tripod. Try them out to be sure that everything fits together with no difficulty.

PICTURE MAKING

Picture *taking* is only half the fun of photography. There's a real thrill in picture *making* too. Whether it's a simple snapshot, a favorite landscape or a portrait of your children, what you create in the darkroom is one of the most enjoyable aspects of photography.

When you develop and print your own pictures, you can correct defects in the original shot, bringing out what you want and subduing what is less important. With only a little practice, you can create moods and expressions the camera may have missed and add entirely new dimensions to your work.

Remember that a finished photograph is a blend of many things: your skill as a photographer, the quality of your camera, the lens you choose, the film's characteristics and the processing steps taken.

COMPOSITION

The art of composition lies in the meaningful arrangement of the components of the subject matter, choice of camera angle and selection of lighting.

Diagonal lines and unequal masses create a strong, forceful effect. Textures ranging across the full monochrome gray scale enhance the solidity of a subject.

SUPPLIES AND EQUIPMENT

Many things essential to a well-equipped darkroom cannot be found in camera shops, nor in any shops specializing only in photographic materials. A vacuum cleaner can hardly be called "photographic" equipment, but since dirt and dust are serious threats to all photographic processes, a vacuum's cleaning and dusting capabilities are important to good darkroom work. A tank type vacuum is ideal for maintaining darkroom cleanliness. Fitted with an extra-long hose, the tank itself may be left outside the darkroom, where its high-velocity exhaust cannot stir up dust inside that would defeat cleanup efforts.

A large dust cloth, chemically treated to hold dust until it can be shaken clean outside the darkroom, is a necessity. Ordinary household sponges and spongemops make counter or floor spills quick to clean up; and speed is important as fixer spills, in particular, quickly dry to a fine powder that easily becomes airborn. Wherever the chemical dust particles settle on exposed film or paper, development will not take place. White specks will appear on paper, and clear "pinholes" on film.

Drug stores sell small, cotton-tipped swabs, as well as bottles of carbon tetracloride and isoprople alcohol. A swab dipped in carbon tetracloride and squeezed almost dry on a paper towel will remove oily finger smudges from negatives without damage to either base or emulsion. (Caution! Do not inhale fumes from carbon tet!)

Alcohol cleans exposed surfaces of enlarging lenses, which tend to develop a thin film from atmospheric moisture and chemical fumes. Use just a drop or two on a swab, and wipe the lens carefully. Alcohol also removes some types of water spots from emulsion and base surfaces of negatives.

Do not overlook the value of ordinary soap or detergent for keeping hands and utensils clean — but rinse thoroughly after use. Soap residue is alkaline, will accelerate the action alkaline solu-tions (such as developer) and reduce the effectiveness of acidic solutions.

Photographic Equipment and Supplies

Photographic chemicals, film paper and equipment are best bought only from camera shops or photographic specialty shops. Such suppliers know how to handle and store sensitized materials properly to keep stocks fresh. Their personnel can supply helpful information on recent improvements in materials and demonstrate equipment.

Camera shops market three products especially useful in the fight against dust. One is often referred to as "canned air;" another is a soft, chemically neutral, absorbent paper towelette; the third, a plastic funnel with built-in fine wire mesh stainless steel filter.

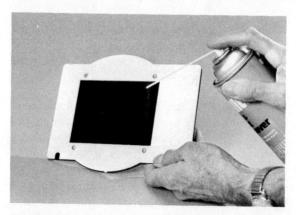

Canned "air" delivers a sharp blast through a nozzle to dislodge dust from negatives, lenses, filters.

Brands of "air" may differ in the inert gas compressed aerosol cans, but none dispense any mist or liquid. Only a burst of air, concentrated through a long nozzle, comes out when button or trigger is pressed. Dust flecks instantly disappear from negatives, filters, enlarging lenses, developing reels and condensers when cleaned with canned air.

The special paper wipes can be used safely for cleaning condensers, proofing glass, the base-side of negatives and enlarging lenses. Yet they are strong enough when wet for use anywhere in the darkroom.

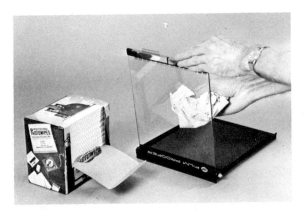

Special soft and lintless paper towelettes clean all glass surfaces in darkrooms safely.

Filter-funnels eliminate sediment and dust particles from re-usable solutions, if used routinely when returning liquids to storage bottles. (Filter paper, such as that used by chemists and in some coffee makers removes even smaller particles, but passes liquids slowly.) Electrostatic air

Funnels with built-in, very fine steel mesh remove solids and dust from solutions as they are returned to storage bottles.

cleaners, some costing less than a hundred dollars, can eliminate airborn dust from closed rooms.

Avoiding Darkroom Mistakes

Nearly all disappointments and failures in photographic processing are caused by errors easily eliminated. Failure can be the result of using the wrong solution, using it at the wrong time, at an improper temperature or for too-long or too-short a time. Any material or equipment that improves indentification, controls sequence, temperature or time, is valuable as a mistake eliminator.

Self-adhesive labels in many sizes and shapes are available in office supply stores. Use fiber-tipped waterproof ink pens on such labels to identify all bottles, trays, tongs, tanks and lids. Such pens also write directly on plastic or glass.

If any solution must sometimes be found quickly in the dark, it should have a lid easily identifiable by feel alone. Phosphorescent tape that glows in the dark can be cut into distinctive shapes, or into numbers, to prevent the possibility of using processing solutions out of sequence. This tape will not fog even the fastest film unless it is left in direct contact with the emulsion. Small dots of tape make timers, switches, hot and cold water faucets easy to locate in total darkness.

Thermometers often become inaccurate from the minor shocks and bumps unavoidable with fre-

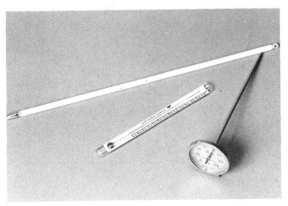

Laboratory quality, finely-calibrated thermometer (top) should be used to check accuracy of alcohol and dial-type thermometers, especially if latter have been jarred or dropped.

quent use. Buy a laboratory-quality, finely-calibrated mercury thermometer and use it carefully to check other thermometers suspected of inaccuracy. A tank or tray thermometer may become inaccurate in some temperature ranges, remain accurate in others; or it may consistently be wrong by several degrees. So long as errors are known through checks against the "master" thermometer, an inaccurate thermometer can remain useful. Keep the master mercury thermometer in a foam-lined box or rigid tube away from regularly-used work areas.

Thermostatic water-mixing valves control and monitor running water to within one-half degree of any pre-set temperature, but they are rather expensive. Other electronically controlled units attach to the sides of deep trays and heat water to within one-tenth degree accuracy, keeping all bottled solutions at identical temperature.

Simple and inexpensive temperature-monitoring devices can be attached directly to any mixing

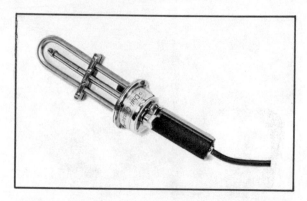

Simple emersion-type heater often is satisfactory for heating and maintaining temperature of processing solutions.

faucet. They will accommodate any standard dial-type thermometer and permit mixing water to any desired temperature as it leaves the faucet. In darkrooms that are usually too cool, ordinary emersion heaters may provide satisfactory solution temperature control.

Light-proof *paper safes*, some with lids that close automatically as a sheet of enlarging paper is removed, will eliminate paper fogging caused by white light striking an improperly closed box or envelope.

Courtesy of Eastman Kodak Company

Thermostatically controlled water mixing valves can deliver running water to within one-half degree of any pre-set temperature.

Courtesy of Spiratone, Inc.

Paper safes hold several grades or surfaces of paper in a light-tight box and eliminate constant opening, closing and re-wrapping paper boxes.

Enlarging meters quickly repay their cost by reducing or eliminating the need to make test prints. All are capable of indicating not only correct exposure at any degree of enlargement, but correct paper grade (or variable-contrast filter). Greater cost usually indicates more precise measuring capability.

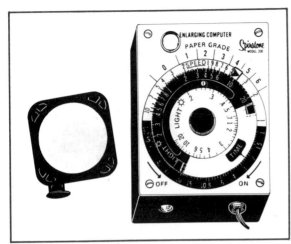

Courtesy of Spiratone, Inc.

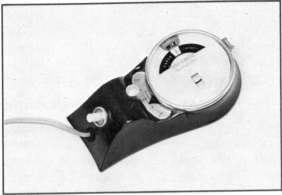

Courtesy of the Kinnard Company

Three types of inexpensive enlarging exposure meters.

Correct print exposure will not necessarily occur, even when displayed by an accurate meter, unless exposure time is controlled by an accurate timer. Most can be pre-set so the enlarger turns on and off automatically when a button is touched, then immediately is re-set for another identical exposure.

Most turn off the safelight as the enlarger lamp goes on, to make dodging or burning easier to see, then turn on the safelight again as the enlarger lamp goes off. Some timers can be set to intervals accurate to one-tenth second, but exposure increments of one second are satisfactory for all but the most delicate color print exposures.

Double-duty timers are standard in many professional darkrooms. These have dinner-plate-size luminous dials, with two luminous sweep hands, one marking off seconds, the other minutes. Most models may be pre-set, but some workers prefer to monitor time visually while controlling exposure and safelight with a two-way foot switch, leaving both hands free for dodging or burning.

Recently available is a timer with no dial at all. Plugged into an outlet, it emits one click each second. For those accustomed to adjustable automatic interval timers, this may seem a strange way to work, but timing *by ear* can have distinct advantages. If an enlargment, for example, requires a ten-second exposure; but one area should be dodged for three seconds, and another burned in for five additional seconds, any number of identical prints may be made just by counting clicks. Turn on the enlarger on the beat of one click, dodge during any three clicks before the tenth click, then burn in for five more clicks and turn off the enlarger. Eyes never need to leave the image on the easel to check a sweep second-hand; the mind never need wonder how much of the total exposure time has already elapsed via electronic interval timer, nor must the timer be re-set for shorter intervals to make dodging or burning-in times accurate.

Print permanence depends upon thorough washing, so all prints should be tested for residual fixer before they are dried. Conveniently, the

Print wash indicator, battery operated, indicates presence of fixer when prints are incompletely washed.

electrical conductivity of water is closely related to its salinity and trace-mineral content. Once a base level of conductivity for any tap water is established, the presence of fixer in water drained from *washed* prints will show increased conductivity in milliamperes. Battery-operated print wash indicators are not expensive, and a meter needle deflection beyond the base level mark provides instant visible evidence of insufficient washing time.

Variation in the voltage supplied to enlarger lamps often explain why an enlarging meter may seem inconsistent or erratic. If voltage varies, the effective amount of light reaching enlarging paper also varies in intensity; therefore, print density is affected.

An ordinary incident light exposure meter can reveal voltage fluctuations due to intermittent use of heavy appliances on the same house circuit, or because of hour-to-hour variations in the load on power supplies to a city.

Place the meter face up on the enlarger baseboard, put an empty negative carrier in the enlarger, open the lens wide and turn on the lamp. Note the exact position of the meter needle when all safelights are off. Leave the meter in place, and return every hour or so to again turn on the enlarger and check the meter needle position. If the needle indicates exposure differences as little as one-eighth stop, consistently accurate print exposures will be unlikely.

A voltage stabilizer plugged into a wall outlet, with both enlarger and enlarging timer plugged into the stabilizer, will eliminate voltage fluctuations and the resulting print density variations. If such units seem too expensive, an exposure meter check before each printing session will allow you to estimate how much exposures should be increased or decreased from normal to compensate for abnormally low or high line voltage. Be sure the enlarger is always the same height above the baseboard, and the enlarging lens always wide open, so only voltage changes will cause differences in exposure meter readings.

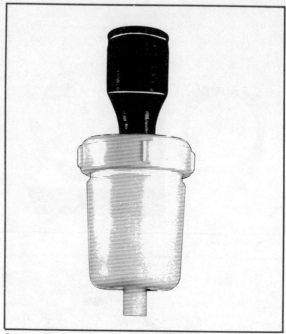

Courtesy of Beseler Photo Marketing, Inc.

Water filter fastens onto faucet, traps sediment and algae, contains cartridge cleaned by reverse flushing.

Most public water supplies deliver potable water, but may nevertheless contain minute particles of suspended solids. If negative emulsions contain dust that cannot be removed, and glossy prints have tiny imperfections that cannot be eliminated, suspended solids in the wash water usually are the cause. Solve the problem with a water filter that can be easily attached to the faucet. Camera stores can supply such filters, elements that are either easily replaced or quickly cleaned by reverse flushing.

Focusing magnifiers enlarge a segment of the negative image several diameters when placed on the easel. Some permit focusing an aerial image of the actual grains of silver that form emulsions. Any magnifier will guarantee prints sharper than those focused by the naked eye.

Other Darkroom Aids

Thin cotton gloves keep finger marks off negatives as rolls are cut into strips and put into glassine envelopes. If they cannot be found at camera shops, makeup gloves from drug stores and pall bearer's gloves used by morticians are

Courtesy of Beseler Photo Marketing, Inc.

Multiple-reel film washer frees developing tanks for immediate re-use.

nearly identical, and may be cheaper. All come in several sizes.

Multiple-reel film washers often do a quicker and more efficient job of washing roll film negatives than do developing tanks, and they free processing tanks for re-use when many rolls are to be developed. (Be sure, though, that tanks are well rinsed and dried before re-use, and use dry spare reels. Tanks and reels dried with hot air must be allowed to cool before use, or solution temperatures will be affected.)

A wall-mounted 35mm film cartridge opener costs only a few dollars and eliminates finger cuts that can occur when using a bottle opener in total darkness.

Fiber-tipped, waterproof-ink pens are a necessity when using resin coated paper. Ordinary pencil will not mark the back of such paper, and crayon or china marking pencil marks often rub off during washing or print handling.

A utility knife used with a metal-edged or steel ruler trims dry prints neatly; but a paper cutter

Courtesy of Seal, Inc.

Dry mount press permits easy mounting of prints much larger than actual size of heat platen. Presses are made in many sizes.

works faster, and prints will have square corners and parallel edges almost automatically.

Drymount presses come in many sizes. They make print mounting simple on almost any surface not damaged by heat. Any well-designed drymount press will mount a print four times the size of its heated surface if the print is mounted one section at a time. A large, heavy-duty professional press may be only faster, not better.

Aerosol cans of matte spray dulls even highly glossed prints to a matte finish. Such sprays can be found in art supply stores as well as camera shops and may prove an economical way to achieve two kinds of print surface from one box of paper.

Dichroic enlargers simplify color printing. They eliminate color-compensating filters, which are likely to fade and change color as they age. Dichroic filters are fade-proof, and permit filtration changes far more subtle than can be achieved with individual CC filters.

Because dichroic enlargers (or dichroic replacement heads available for older enlargers) contain both yellow and magenta filters, they may be used successfully for black and white enlargements on multi-grade papers. Cyan filtration is set at zero, and the yellow and magenta

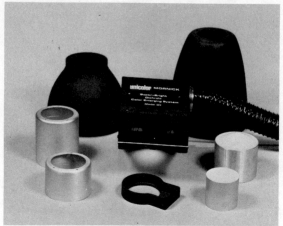

Courtesy of Unicolor Division, Photo Systems, Inc.

Dichroic light source conversion kits are available for many older enlargers.

filtration adjusted to produce contrasts corresponding to individual filters normally used with multi-contrast papers. *In between* filtration is naturally very easy to achieve. Exceptionally flat negatives, one with extreme contrasts, may require that a deep magenta or yellow filter be added to supplement the dichroic filtration of units with limited range.

Courtesy of Unicolor Division, Photo Systems, Inc.

Many manufacturers offer a broad line of processing products: chemicals, tanks, timers, thermometers, papers, filters. Most brands are compatible with other brands.

Scratches on negatives that sometimes seem to appear out of thin air do not necessarily mean that enlargements made from them will be hopelessly marred. Most scratches occur on the base side of negatives, and they will disappear magically if the scratch is filled. Your camera shop has tiny half-ounce bottles of solution with the same refractive index as film base. A small brush, barely moistened with this liquid, makes scratches disappear and a half-ounce will last a busy photographer for years.

DARKROOMS

An all-purpose darkroom requires an area that (1) can be made completely lightproof at least for a few hours at a time, (2) has hot and cold running water available, (3) has at least two grounded electrical outlets, (4) will not be permanently damaged by minor spills and (5) will not become very warm or cold in summer or winter.

Developing Roll Film

Only the first step in the process of developing roll film requires absolute darkness, and the dark place can be a very small one. A clothes closet or storeroom that can be made lightproof will provide enough room to load the exposed film onto the developing reel, put the reel in the tank and close the lid. Once the tank is loaded, all subsequent steps in film processing can be done under normal room light in the kitchen or bathroom. A light trap in the tank lid allows pouring liquids into and out of the tank without danger of fogging the film.

To be certain that the film loading room is really dark, you must stay inside for at least twenty minutes until your eyes have become fully adapted to the dark. An astonishing amount of light leaks into any windowless room under and around the door, through or around heating vents and sometimes even between baseboards and floors. Today's high speed films can be fully exposed in a camera by light coming through a hole the diameter of a matchstick for one one-thousandth of a second, therefore any light your eyes can detect is too much.

Most doors can be made light-tight with inexpensive weather stripping available at hardware stores. Do not overlook the keyhole if there is one, and be sure the door can be locked from the inside (many closet doors cannot be). It can be a real disaster if someone should open the door as you are loading film.

Unfortunately, clothes closets and storerooms are seldom free of dust and lint, and if dust clings to the film emulsion as it is loaded onto the reel, the developed negatives will be full of undeveloped clear specks and thread-like squiggles that will produce black marks on all prints made from them.

Basic film developing equipment and materials: 3 plastic bottles; graduate and stirring rod; tank and film reel; thermometer and funnel; canned powdered developer, liquid stop bath concentrate and liquid fixer concentrate; photo-grade cellulose sponge; film clips; scissors; interval timer.

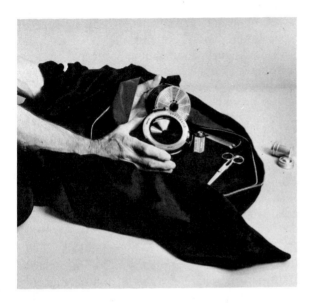

Changing bag permits light-proof film reel and tank loading anywhere. Film and loading equipment are sealed inside bag by double zippers. Elasticized arm holes allow entrance and exit of hands without fogging film.

An alternative to lightproofing a loading room is the changing bag (also referred to as a *dark bag* or *loading bag*) available at camera stores. These bags are made of two layers of black cloth, the inner layer rubberized. A zipper to close each layer is at one end and elasticized arm holes at the other. With the bag zipped closed, and your arms, scissors, film, reel and tank inside, you can load the film into the tank while comfortably seated at a table under normal room light. The bags are lintless, easily kept clean (just turn inside out and shake vigorously) and they last for many years.

In addition to the reel, tank and a place to load it, film developing requires: (1) a darkroom thermometer, (2) a graduate or kitchen measuring cup made of glass or plastic, (3) film clips or spring-type clothes pins, (4) three glass or plastic bottles with tight-fitting lids, (5) a glass or plastic funnel, (6) a photographic-quality cellulose sponge, (7) a pair of scissors, (8) a darkroom interval timer or an accurate kitchen timer (9) three chemical solutions: developer, stop bath and fixer and (10) a stirring rod.

Kits containing all the equipment needed to develop roll film are offered by many manufacturers. Some supply even the chemicals and an opener to pry open 35mm film cartridges.

Contact Printing And Enlarging

Considerably more space is needed for making prints than just for developing film. Kitchens and bathrooms fulfill most of the basic requirements, and many are provided with exhaust fans, an extra sure to be appreciated after the first half-hour or so of working in a tightly closed room.

Windows are the awkward problem, since weather stripping will make most doors lightproof. Even if you plan to work only at night, windows must be tightly covered with opaque black Visqueen or heavy black twill,

Bathtub converted to darkroom using corrugated fiberglass to support trays. Holes drilled along valleys to drain spills.

carefully fitted and securely fastened all around the edges with black masking tape. Otherwise, moonlight, or stray light from streetlamps or automobile headlights will fog prints.

To make a bathtub serve as a darkroom sink, build a wooden slatted rack to cover the whole tub. A rectangular garden trellis from a garden supply store can do the job, but it may need some reinforcement to prevent sagging. Another option is a length of heavyweight corrugated fiberglass cut to fit over the tub, with holes drilled at frequent intervals along the valleys to permit drainage.

A small table, or the vanity, will serve to support the printer or enlarger. Even better, a cabinet

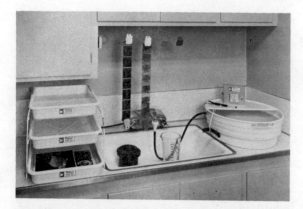

Kitchen as a film developing and print processing lab.

with enclosed shelves underneath can serve both as a work table and as storage space for solutions and supplies when the bathroom is serving its more normal function.

The kitchen is another satisfactory spot for printing as counters are an ideal working height and photographic chemicals are unlikely to stain kitchen work surfaces if they are wiped up promptly. Several layers of newspaper under tanks and trays should be used, however.

All darkrooms, whether improvised or specially constructed, must have separate wet and dry areas, or much film and paper will be ruined. Keep liquids and chemicals only in or near the sink; and work with photographic paper, film printing and enlarging equipment as far away from the sink as possible. For washing the developed film and prints and for cleaning equipment after use, plastic hoses with slip-on fittings for faucets of almost every type — including Y connections for mixing water from separate hot and cold water faucets — are available at most camera stores. Such hoses let you direct water flow where you want it and greatly reduce splashing.

Portable free-standing safelights and safelights that can be screwed into existing ceiling or drop fixtures are readily available. Interchangeable filters are provided so that you may use the color of filter that is exactly suited to each type of film and paper. The information sheet packed with each roll of film and box of paper states specifically which filter is to be used when processing that product. It also specifies what wattage of bulb to use, and how far away from the sensitized material the safelight must be. Fogged film and paper will surely be the result if these instructions are ignored.

A safelight that will not fog today's fast panchromatic or color films must be very dim and far away, and it may be turned on for just a few seconds only after the film is more than half-developed. Experienced darkroom workers seldom use a safelight at all when developing film, preferring to load their daylight-type tanks in total darkness and develop by time and temperature in normal room illumination.

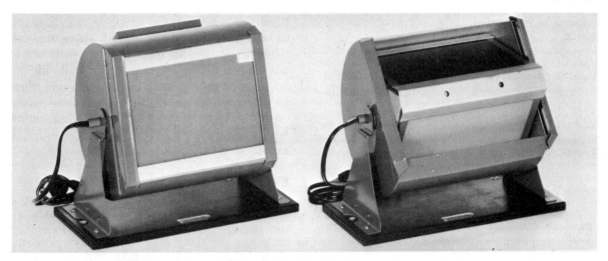

Free-standing safelight holds three filters. Proper filter for film, contact or enlarging paper is easily rotated into position.

Even if you hope to develop cut film or film packs in open tanks, *development by inspection* is an emergency procedure usually done only in professional laboratories by experts with years of experience.

Building A Darkroom

Building a room that is permanently light-tight and ready for use at a moment's notice is well worthwhile to the serious photographer. It can be comfortable to work in as well as efficient, easy to clean with places to keep equipment and supplies safe and under proper storage conditions when not in use.

Choosing the location for a darkroom is perhaps the single most important consideration. An attic, even a well insulated one, is usually a poor choice because of temperature fluctuations. A walled-off section of the garage, whether attached or detached, can make an excellent darkroom if the laundry area with its water supply and drain, is nearby. An enclosed area of a basement often is the ideal location as year-around temperatures are usually quite stable, if sometimes a bit cooler than desirable. However, raising the temperature of a relatively small enclosed area is easy and inexpensive. Concrete floors solve the problem of chemical spills whether you choose to build in the garage or in the basement.

If you can build in a corner (away from the furnace) two of the four necessary walls are already built.

The ideal solution, though, is literally to build a room within a room; all four walls and a ceiling. Walls and ceiling should be covered on both sides of the studs and rafters, with insulation bats between. Do not use existing basement walls if they show evidence of dampness or water seepage. Build new walls inside them and be sure to include a vapor barrier in the new walls. If you use existing garage walls, insulate them especially well if they are exterior walls.

The outside surface of darkroom walls can be of almost any material. They need not be neatly finished unless appearance is important.

Interior darkroom walls, and the ceiling as well, should have smooth surfaces so that dust is unlikely to cling to them. They should be virtually waterproof so that they may be wiped down easily with a damp sponge. Sheetrock taped, sanded and painted with glossy or semi-gloss enamel is quite satisfactory. Flat wall paint is more likely to absorb stains. Other good choices are smooth-surfaced particle board (also painted), sheetrock with one pre-finished vinyl-clad surface or a hard-surfaced particle board product such as marlite. Self-adhesive vinyl shelf and wall covering, available in rolls 18 and

36 inches wide, also makes an excellent wall finish.

Concrete floors with a smoothly trowelled finish are easy to keep clean, but are dangerously slippery when wet. Cover the floor, laying linoleum or a vinyl-asbestos tile with enough texture so its surface will provide good footing when wet but will be smooth enough for easy cleaning.

Some caulking may be necessary to eliminate light leaks where the walls and floor meet, since few concrete floors are truly flat. Use a non-chalking caulking compound before resurfacing the floor.

No darkroom need be gloomy. "Dark" in the word darkroom refers only to unwanted extraneous light. The color of walls and ceiling may be as light as you wish, since only safelights of the proper color will be reflected from them. Dark-colored walls are not necessary, and can become oppressive.

Long before actual darkroom construction is begun, important decisions must be made. What equipment is to go inside (now and in the future)? Where should equipment be placed so that work can be done efficiently?

How much space is really needed, and what shape should the room be?

Electrical outlets should be higher than they are usually found; 10 to 12 inches above the dry bench area, even higher above the wet bench to put them out of splash range. It is vitally important that all outlets be grounded. You will often be working with wet hands and may be standing on a wet floor. Such a situation, in combination with ungrounded electrical outlets or switches can cause a lethal electric shock.

Plan carefully the location of electrical switches. The white-light switch, in particular, must be put where it cannot be turned on accidentally by brushing against it. Many professional darkrooms have the white room-light switch in a position deliberately difficult to reach, such as under the edge of a bench or on a wall only a foot below the ceiling. The print inspection light over the tray of fixer (a daylight blue bulb shielded by a reflector), can be controlled by a pull-chain switch or a foot switch.

The long, narrow darkroom plan has a full-depth splash barrier to separate the wet and dry benches. For maximum splash protection, the barrier should be at least 24 to 36 inches high. It can be an asset rather than a nuisance if it supports narrow shelves for small items that would otherwise clutter work benches. Small hooks can be put on both sides so that print tongs, thermometer and stirring rod can be hung on the wet side; dodging tools and negative-dusting brush on the dry side, all within easy reach but out of the way when not in use.

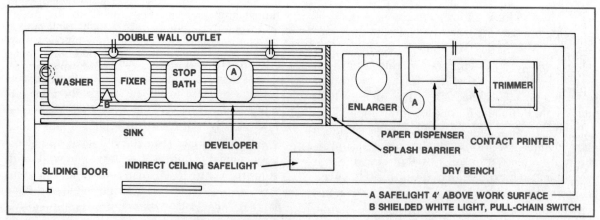

One-man darkroom with door in corner, storage space for bottled solutions, trays, etc. beneath sink. Storage for equipment and materials below dry bench and at eye level. Place faucets over sink near wash area for maximum convenience.

The wet bench, where developing, chemical mixing and washing will be done, should have shelves underneath for the storage of packaged chemicals, bottled solutions and processing tanks and trays. A cabinet above it will keep reels, funnels, graduates, sponges and film clips dust-free when not in use.

The dry bench, for printing, enlarging and film-reel loading, should have a shelf over it near eyelevel but not where it will interfere with the enlarger column. This shelf can hold the timer focusing magnifier, printing filters and anything else that need not take up space on the workbench. A generously deep cabinet beneath the dry bench (with sliding doors that cannot bang knees and shins) is a good storage place for reserve paper supplies, spare enlarger and safelight bulbs, filters, extra negative carriers, spare pencils and marking pens and — if it is cool and dry — even negative files.

It is no oversight that the darkroom plans include no space for a print dryer. Most print drying equipment is a source of heat and moisture, both of which are injurious to sensitized materials and can make the darkroom too warm and humid.

A smooth, easy-to-clean surface on work areas is essential. Plastic laminate counter tops are excellent for both wet and dry work areas, but a surface covering of heavy linoleum or hard-surfaced particle board is entirely satisfactory. Inexpensive self-adhesive vinyl shelf and wall covering material is smooth and astonishingly durable, even on wet bench areas if the joints are properly overlapped and it is applied free of wrinkles. (A print roller makes wrinkle-free application easy.)

Faucets over the sink should be high enough for easy rinsing and filling of tall bottles and large trays. Slip-on flexible hoses can lower the water outlet level and reduce splashing during normal use.

Darkroom Sinks

Sinks made of tough plastic or type 316 (chemical resistant) stainless steel are available in many sizes, but they are expensive. Kitchen or laundry sinks are more suitable for negative and print washing than heavy, all-around use. Anyone with modest skills in the use of hammer and saw can build a wooden sink to run the full length of one darkroom wall. The entire wet bench area then has a sink under it for maximum convenience and spill-safety.

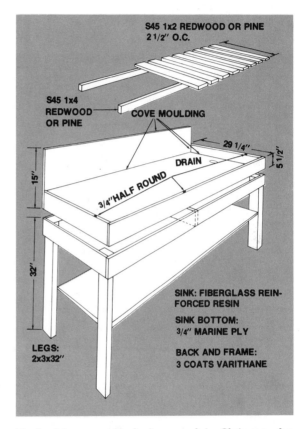

Typical homemade darkroom sink. Sink may be made any length. Add legs at 5 foot intervals, frame cross members and 2¹/₂ foot intervals. Bring fiberglass and resin up, over and down sides and splashboard. Cove molding at all inside joints, and half-round on top of edges prevents fiberglass from lifting when bent at right angles.

Resin coating materials used by boatbuilders can be used to make a simple wooden sink leak-proof and almost indestructible. When in place, the sink should slope about one quarter inch to the foot toward a drain in the low end. Inside the sink, about an inch below the rim, put a wooden rack that runs its full length. Developing trays, tanks, print washers, bottles and graduates can

Photography

be used, rinsed and then left to drain dry on the rack when work is finished. Include a splash board which extends about a foot up the wall behind the sink.

Ventilation

Vapors from processing solutions are relatively nontoxic, but may become unpleasant unless the darkroom has adequate ventilation. Special lightproof darkroom exhaust fans are available, but a ceiling or wall-mounted kitchen exhaust fan will work well if properly light-baffled both inside and outside the room. Simple *U* or *S* shaped baffles work fine if all inside surfaces are painted flat black. Black spray paint on the fan blades may be necessary.

Courtesy of Spiratone, Inc.

Darkroom exhaust fan. It should be mounted through the wall high over the wet bench area where fumes originate.

An ordinary roof gable vent from a building supply store will serve as an air intake. Paint it flat black and mount it through a wall opposite the exhaust fan near floor level. A simple box baffle for the intake may be necessary on one side of the wall.

If the darkroom requires heating, thermostat-controlled, electric baseboard heaters are best. Portable or wall-mounted, fan-forced electric space heaters can be used only while printing or enlarging since their red glow will fog undeveloped film. The fan also may circulate unwanted dust.

The ultimate in darkroom climate control is a wall-mounted heat pump. Such units automatically supply a flow of warmed or cooled air by thermostatic control, and filter and dehumidify the air as well.

Equipment

Basic equipment for an all-purpose darkroom includes a contact printer or printing frame and an enlarger; an enlarging easel and focusing magnifier; a timer; several graduates; two safelight fixtures with film and paper filters; a tank and tray thermometer; at least four trays; a paper trimmer; an antistatic brush or cloth; a stirring rod; a print washer or tray siphon; funnels; a photographic cellulose sponge; a cleanup sponge; film clips; print tongs; plastic or glass bottles in pint, quart and half-gallon sizes and several lintless hand towels.

Other useful items are a photographic paper dispenser (*paper safe*), a paper towel dispenser, a third white-light safelight with an opal glass *filter* for inspecting developed negatives, an intercom and an extension telephone.

Equipment needed outside the darkroom are a print dryer, blotter roll, ferrotype plates and a print roller for glazing glossy prints.

DEVELOPING FILM

Developing film is neither difficult nor expensive; and with careful processing, negatives will have the full range of tones necessary for high quality prints. Photo finishers who supply developing printing services to drugstores and small camera shops cannot give individual attention to each roll of film. Dozens of rolls go together into large tanks of universal developer. Such devel-

Courtesy of Unicolor Division Photo Systems, Inc.

One manufacturer's line of liquid concentrate film processing products: film developer, stop bath, fixer, hypo eliminator, wetting agent. Tank and reel in center; predevelopment "speed booster" solution for Tri X film in box.

opers are potent enough to make some sort of printable image from even badly underexposed amateur snapshots.

Some film developers are sold as bottled liquid concentrates and are simply diluted with water before use, but those most commonly used come in powdered form. All are carefully balanced formulae, and each must be mixed exactly to manufacturer's instructions for optimum results. Most stop bath solutions are bottled 28 percent acetic acid, which need only be further diluted with water for use. Liquid fixer concentrates are slightly more expensive than those sold in powdered form; but they are quickly diluted for immediate use, and any unused concentrate will keep indefinitely in the bottle. Many liquid types are of the *quick-fix* variety, and work in two or three minutes rather than the usual five to fifteen.

All fixers should contain a hardener. Hardener toughens the light-sensitive emulsion on film or paper so it will not *frill* at the edges when handled wet, nor scratch easily when sponged dry. Hardener is premixed into some liquid concentrates. Others come with a separate container of chemicals, liquid or powder, to be added after the fixer is diluted or dissolved.

Many manufacturers offer replenisher solutions for their developers. These are formulae specially balanced to replace that portion of each ingredient exhausted during the development process. Adding a specified amount of replenisher for each roll of film developed will maintain the original volume and potency of the developer for months.

So-called "one-shot" developers usually are concentrated liquids intended to be diluted heavily with water, used once, then discarded. Nearly all developers are offered in quantities to make a pint, quart or gallon of working solution. The number of rolls that can be processed in each quantity appears on the label.

Mixing Chemicals

Three glass or plastic bottles, a graduate for measuring and mixing, a darkroom thermometer and a glass or plastic stirring tool are needed to prepare the chemistry for film developing. (A funnel and a photographic sponge will be needed later, as will film clips for hanging film to dry.)

Be sure all bottles, the graduate and stirring rod are clean. Put a length of white adhesive tape near the top of each bottle, and a small piece on each lid. Use a fiber-tip pen with permanent ink to identify the bottles as developer, stop bath and fixer. Mark lids *D, S* and *F*.

Everything necessary for developing negatives. (Above, left to right:) Graduate for mixing and pouring; stirring rod; three high-density plastic bottles with contents labeled; deep tray for stabilizing temperature of all solutions with water bath. (Below, left to right:) Developing tank with reel, cover, agitation tool; film clips; tank or tray dial-type thermometer; photo quality cellulose sponge, funnel.

Identification is important. If during a future developing session the lid to the developer bottle is accidentally put on a bottle of fixer or stop bath, no harm is done. But if the bottle of developer is sealed with the lid to fixer or stop bath, the developer will be contaminated and its life shortened.

A second strip of tape on the developer bottle will provide a place to note the date it was mixed and to record the number of rolls processed. Nonreplenishable developers have limited capacity. Developing times must be increased, according to instructions, with each successive roll developed; so it is important to record the number of rolls processed.

Even replenisher-type developers must be replaced eventually. Mix new developer when the amount of replenisher added has equalled the volume of developer mixed originally. Record each ounce of replenisher used, so developer replacement time will not pass unnoticed.

Most manufacturers assume their developers will be dissolved in tap water, and formulate them accordingly. Industrial chemical residues found in many public water supplies may impair the performance of some. Use distilled water if your nose or palate suggests that tap water is suspect. Stop bath and fixer are less sensitive, and can be mixed with any clean water.

Dissolve powdered developer in water at a temperature within the range allowed by the instructions. If the water is too cool, some of the ingredients may not dissolve completely. Water too hot can cause discoloration and oxidation that degrade developer performance and shorten its life.

When developer is to be used immediately, mix it in water of the temperature designated as ideal for processing. Warmer water will dissolve chemicals more quickly, but the solution must then be cooled before use. This applies also to mixing stop bath and fixer solutions.

Some developers are panthermic (may be used throughout a wide range of temperatures), but it is important that stop bath and fixer solutions,

and wash water as well, be within a degree or two of developer temperature.

Temperature variations among solutions can produce grainy negatives. Instructions for using panthermic developers include tables or graphs showing proper developing times for each kind of film at any permissible temperature. Follow instructions carefully, or the developed negatives will be either too thin and flat, or too dense and contrasty.

Most developers are balanced for use at room temperatures: 68 to 70 degrees. When solutions must be warmed or cooled, mix hot and cold water in a deep tray (or dishpan) until the thermometer shows a temperature a few degrees cooler than developer.

Stand the bottles in this water for about half an hour. Then open the lid to the developer bottle, dip the thermometer inside and check the temperature. When the right temperature is reached, leave all bottles in the water to keep their temperatures stable until used.

Use the *fill and dump* method when there is no practical way to control and monitor the temperature of running water for film washing. Mix hot and cool water to make enough of the correct temperature to fill the film tank eight times. Fill the tank with some of the water, let it sit for five minutes, then dump and fill again. Repeat this seven more times at five-minute intervals, and the film will be free of fixer and ready to dry.

Roll Film Developing Tanks

Roll film can be developed in darkness by unrolling it and *see-sawing* it lengthwise through trays of developer, stop bath and fixer. Wet film is slippery and will scratch easily against the sides or bottom of trays.

A light-proof tank will protect the film and make developing easier. Both stainless steel tanks and those made of high-impact plastic work well. Each type and brand has its own special kind of reel. Spiral stainless steel wire reels are made in fixed sizes to fit each width of film. Most plastic reels are adjustable from 35mm to 2¹/₄ inches in

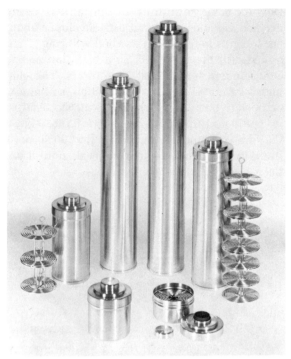

Courtesy of Spiratone, Inc.

Stainless steel tanks, single and multiple-reel, for 35mm or 2¹/₄ inch film. Reels for both sizes of film have same diameter and may be mixed in multiple-reel tanks.

width, and will accept film 60 inches long (the length of 35mm 36 exposure rolls). Some have ratchet-like self-loading features that save time and fumbling in the dark. All popular tanks come in single roll and multiple roll sizes. Extra reels, of course, are needed for multiple roll sizes.

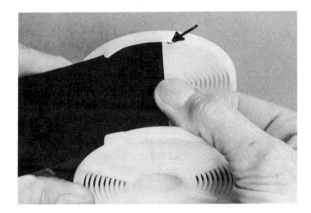

Plastic film reel with ratchet-type semiautomatic loading feature.

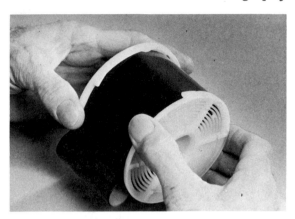

Film feeds into spiral grooves automatically as flange of reel is rotated back and forth.

Before buying a tank, take an old roll of uncut film, developed or undeveloped, to a camera shop. Try loading various types of reels first with your eyes open, then with them closed. Choose the type of reel you think will be easy to load in the dark. Check, also, to see whether the tank itself can be opened easily and closed securely.

All reels must be absolutely dry before film can be loaded successfully. Hands must be clean and dry to prevent film damage from finger marks.

Developing the Film

With all solutions at the correct temperature, an interval timer preset to the recommended development time and film on the reel, processing can

When all processing solutions are of right temperature, begin development by pouring measured amount of developer while simultaneously activating timer.

1175

Agitate film reel in developer by rolling protruding rod between thumb and forefinger. Agitate for five seconds eight or ten times during development.

begin. Measure only enough developer into the graduate to fill the tank. Then pour the developer into the tank with one hand and simultaneously activate the timer with the other. Begin agitating the film immediately according to the tank maker's instructions, and continue agitation for a full thirty seconds. Fast-working developers (four or five minutes) require five seconds of agitation at thirty-second intervals. With slower-acting developers, agitate once a minute. The general rule is to agitate at eight or ten equally-spaced intervals during development. Between agitation periods, place a clean funnel in the mouth of the developer bottle, rinse the graduate with clean water, and fill with the correct amount of stop bath.

Have premeasured amount of stop bath in graduate, and begin emptying tank of developer 10 seconds before timer is to ring. Development will continue until tank is filled with stop bath and agitated as in development, for 30 seconds.

Development continues as the tank is being drained, so start draining it of developer about ten seconds before the timer bell will ring. Then quickly fill the tank with stop bath and agitate continuously for at least 30 seconds. The stop bath terminates all developer action, so there is no need to hurry when returning the stop bath to its bottle and filling the tank with fixer. Agitate the film continuously during its first 30 seconds in the fixer; then at regular intervals until it has been fixed for the specified time.

Pour premeasured amount of fixer into tank and activate timer.

Agitate thoroughly for first 30 seconds in fixer, then every half-minute until timer indicates fixing is complete.

Now open the tank and carefully lift out the reel. Let surplus fixer drain from the reel into the tank, and then examine the film carefully. If the fixer has been used several times, the film may have a milky appearance. If so, this indicates the fixer is partially exhausted, and additional fixing time is required.

Milkiness will be most apparent in the clear spaces between frames and along the edges of the film. When all trace of milkiness is gone, fix several more minutes for good measure. (Film left in fixer a half-hour or more will not be damaged.) Then empty the tank of fixer and begin washing the film. Run water through a hose into the center of the reel as it sits in the tank, so the flowing water will flush out the fixer. Thirty minutes of washing in briskly moving water is considered the minimum necessary to prevent images from staining and fading in later years due to residual fixer in the emulsion.

A hypo eliminator or hypo clearing agent, used for two or three minutes before washing, can reduce washing time by more than half. The use of such solutions may soften film emulsion (especially if the fixer and its hardener are partially exhausted) so the film must be handled gingerly. Use care as you remove the film from the reel, hang it up to dry, and gently sponge excess water from both sides.

Film can be dried free of water spots without sponging if a few drops of wetting agent are added to a tankful of clear water after washing. Soak the reel of film in the wetting solution for about a minute before hanging.

After the film has dried, carefully cut it into strips to fit negative envelopes. Glassine envelopes (negative preservers) are available for all film sizes. Avoid using ordinary paper envelopes, since many papers contain sodium thiosulphate, the same hypo you have carefully washed from negatives.

Importance of Agitation

Agitation during development is essential. Chemical molecules in direct contact with film emulsion soon become exhausted and must be replaced frequently with fresh ones for development to continue. Inadequate or improper agitation is the most common cause of poor negatives. Agitate gently at regular intervals so exhausted chemical molecules will be replaced uniformly over all of the emulsion surface. Developing times specified by the manufacturers who compound developers presuppose that agitation instructions for each type of tank will be followed exactly and that agitation will be done at proper intervals.

Without enough agitation, negatives will be underdeveloped, weak and mottled. Continuous or violent agitation is even worse than too little. Negatives will then be overdeveloped, dense and harsh. They often are streaked and darker near the edges of the film than in the center. Improper agitation shows worse in the large, even-toned areas of a negative, such as a clear sky. When such areas are mottled, streaked or darker at the edges than in the center, reread and follow agitation instructions supplied with the tank.

How to Agitate

A spillproof tank with tight-fitting lid should be held in the hand and agitated by tipping it first to one side and then the other. Then gently rotate the tank about one-half turn clockwise and counter-clockwise. Both rocking and turning motions should total only about five seconds. Put the tank down between agitation periods so warmth from your hand does not raise solution temperature.

When a metal tank has been filled and capped, immediately give it a sharp tap on a hard surface to dislodge any bubbles that may have formed and clung to the film emulsion; then begin the initial 30 seconds of agitation, using the motions described above.

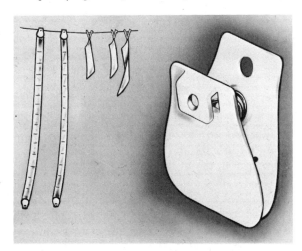

Hang film in clean place to dry. Clip at bottom of roll keeps film from curling as it dries.

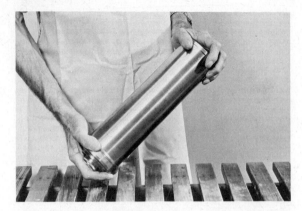

Agitate film in multiple-reel tanks by inverting, one hand securing lid.

Then roll tank back and forth one revolution for first thirty seconds. Repeat rolling motion for five seconds at proper agitation intervals. Stand tank upright between agitation periods.

Tanks without spillproof lids are supplied with a notched stirring tool to engage the reel when inserted through the center hole in the tank top. Some plastic tanks have reels with permanently attached stirring shafts that protrude through the center hole. With either kind of tank, agitate properly by rolling the stirring tool between thumb and forefinger as the tank sits on a level surface. Gently rotate the reel a half-turn to the left and right. Rotate it back and forth twice during each agitation period. Do not spin the reel vigorously, but during the initial 30 second agitation period reverse direction abruptly to dislodge bubbles that may have formed when the tank was filled. Thereafter, reverse the turning motion gently to prevent foaming and streaking.

Resist the temptation to agitate between specified intervals when using any tank. Only consistently proper agitation done at regular intervals will produce consistently fine negatives.

When processing in multiple-reel leakproof tanks, use only enough solution to cover the number of reels being developed. Begin agitation as though it were a single-reel tank. During later agitation periods use both hands to lift and invert the tank once, with one hand holding the lid firmly in place. Then lay the tank in the sink or on a work surface and gently roll it back and forth one or two revolutions. Stand the tank upright until time to agitate again.

Developing Color Film

Color film chemistry is more complex than black and white because three separate emulsion layers must be processed simultaneously in perfect balance. Developer temperature must be accurate to within one-half degree. Reversal color films require two developing steps, and the temperature of both solutions is critical. Minor temperature variations may be permitted with other solutions in the process. Incorrect developer temperature may not always seriously distort density or contrast, but it is sure to modify color balance.

Nevertheless, anyone who can repeatedly process black and white negatives of good quality is capable of developing both negative and reversal color films. Color chemistry kits are available, both in liquid and powder form, containing everything needed for processing most color films. Some kits may be used with several kinds of film. Precise step-by-step instructions are supplied for mixing and using each solution.

More empty bottles to hold additional solutions may be needed for processing some kinds of color film. Be sure to identify the contents of each bottle accurately and clearly. Number them sequentially in the order they are to be used.

A white-light reexposure step in processing reversal color film requires using either steel wire or translucent plastic reels. Any clean reel is satisfactory for color negative processing. A second interval timer is useful in developing those films requiring many processing steps.

Time for the next step may be preset between agitation periods of a prior step. Resetting a timer, activating it and simultaneously pouring solutions is a difficult job that can result in inaccurate processing times. Basic processing techniques are the same for color and black and white. Good work habits, consistently used, will guarantee success with both.

Variations from normal temperatures or processing times should not be attempted with color films unless unusual results are desired. Instructions for the use of color processing kits may include directions for *push processing* some films to a higher film speed. Some may suggest ways to alter contrast or color saturation for special effects. If not, assume that neither can be accomplished successfully.

Nearly all photographic chemicals, color processing solutions in particular, will stain clothing. Wear old clothes or a plastic apron while developing, or when mixing chemicals. Color processing chemicals are considerably more caustic than those used for black and white, so wear a pair of tight-fitting rubber gloves with nonskid fingertips when working with those chemicals. Gloves are especially important for those with sensitive skin or skin allergies.

Since the temperature at which any one color film can be developed is not flexible, neither is the time it can be left in any solution. To take advantage of this inflexibility, some photographers record every step of the process on a tape cassette exactly to time, then simply play back the tape as they work. Each kind of color film requires its own recorded cassette, because the number of processing steps and the time for each step varies according to film type.

Use an AC adaptor for both recording and playback to insure maximum tape speed accuracy.

Developing Sheet Film

Although light-tight sheet film developing tanks are on the market, few photographers use them because effective agitation is difficult in such tanks. Open-tank processing in a properly light-proofed darkroom is more practical.

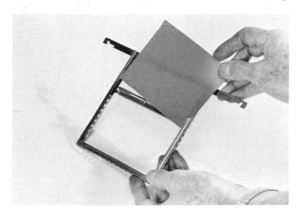

Sheet film is loaded into hanger by sliding it into open-ended steel channels. Top channel is hinged, closed after film is inserted to prevent film from coming out of hanger when emersed.

Equipment for developing sheet film: film hangers; four tanks with lids, (all identified to prevent contamination from intermixing); large tray to stabilize all solutions at proper temperature; thermometer. Agitate film during all processing steps by lifting hangers and draining them from alternate corners.

Four tanks are needed for black and white work; three for solutions, and one for washing. Tank size depends upon film size and the number of sheets to be processed at one time. As many as seven or eight tanks may be required for certain color films.

Stainless steel film hangers are available in all sheet film sizes. Each hanger holds one sheet of film, keeps it separate from other sheets and below the surface of the solution. The hangers extend over the sides of the tanks and may be lifted out or put in without getting hands wet. All hangers are simultaneously transferred from one tank to another as each processing step is completed.

To agitate sheet film lift the hangers out of a solution and tilt them to drain back into the tank from one corner of the film. Then re-dip and drain them from the opposite corner. Do this carefully and at regular intervals, as with all film agitation.

Ideally, (and really essential for color processing), all tanks should sit in a large tray of water so all solutions will be of the same temperature. Water should be deep enough to cover two-thirds the depth of the tanks. Tight-fitting lids, to retard oxidation and prevent contamination, are available for most sheet film tanks.

Oxidation and evaporation can be reduced nearly to zero with floating lids that fit beneath tank covers. A floating lid to fit any tank can be made by filling the tank with cold water, and pouring in about a half-inch of melted paraffin. Imbed and hold a small wooden spool or drawer pull in the center of the paraffin until it congeals enough to support the "handle."

In an hour or so, the paraffin is hard, and the lid can be lifted by its handle. Such lids will be impervious to chemicals and will last indefinitely. Remember, however, to identify each lid to avoid chemical contamination. Since floating lids come in direct contact with large surface areas of solution, intermixing them can cause immediate chemical damage.

CONTACT PRINTING

Contact printing is an important photographic process, even though the small cameras now prevalent require that most prints be made with an enlarger. Proof sheets from both roll and sheet film are contact printed. Experienced photographers often make enlarged *dupe* negatives from hard-to-print miniature negatives. All dodging, burning-in and distortion correction is incorporated into the enlarged negative. The new negative can then be contact printed quickly and inexpensively hundreds of times.

Wallet-sized prints from larger roll-film sizes often are contact printed. In fact, most enlargers (except for professional models) cannot produce prints less than two or three times larger than the original negative.

Contact Printing Equipment

Contact prints are made with a simple printing frame, a simple or complex printing box or with an enlarger by using a proofsheet making device. A flat sheet of glass, to hold the negative and paper in close contact, works well for contact printing under an enlarger.

Contact printing frame. Negative is placed on glass emulsion side up, printing paper on negative emulsion side down. Both spring clips rotate to close frame, holding negative and paper in tight contact.

A printing frame looks much like an ordinary picture frame, with glass. The back, however, is removable. It is hinged to fold in the center, the underside is padded with felt, and each half has a rotating spring clip to hold film and paper in firm contact.

Use a printing frame by first cleaning the glass and brushing the negative free of dust particles. Put the film emulsion-side up on the glass, cover it with sensitized paper emulsion-side down, set the back in place and rotate the spring clips so they engage the metal tabs or slots that hold them taut. Do this, of course, by safelight illumination. Then turn the glass side toward any convenient

Courtesy of Eastman Kodak Company

Simple contact printer. Light in a box, glass top for negative, hinged over to hold paper and negative in contact, switch for exposure.

white lamp bulb, turn the lamp on long enough for correct exposure, turn it off and remove the paper for development.

A simple contact printer is little more than a printing frame with a box underneath containing an exposing lamp. The center-hinged cover also is hinged to the rear edge of the box. It is held down or locked down during exposure. A sheet of frosted or opal glass between the lamp and printing glass distributes light evenly over the negative.

Professional contact printers contain many lamps, each of which may be switched on or off individually.

Any area of a negative may be dodged by turning off the lamp directly beneath it, thereby lightening that part of the print. Many professional models provide a sheet of clear glass just underneath the glass that supports the negative. Bits of tissue paper placed on the lower glass can lighten sharply localized areas of a print.

Contact print-makers in professional laboratories often place a full sheet of tissue paper directly on the negative, and apply black crayon heavily or lightly over specific areas. Then the tissue is put on the lower glass and carefully aligned with the negative, so that crayoned areas lighten matching negative areas.

Elaborate contact printers have hinged front panels, so the clear glass can be taken out for

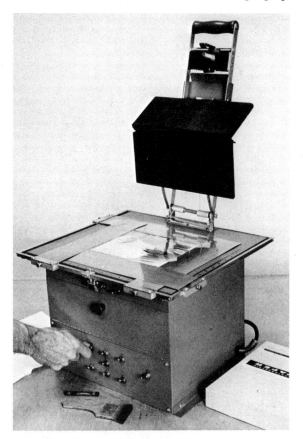

Professional contact printer. Six individually-switched exposure lamps, plus switches for red and amber lamps. Exposure lamps turn on when top is closed and locked. Adjustable border-masking metal strips cover edges or negative on top glass. Upper half of printer opens for access to diffusing and dodging glasses, or for insertion of large multi-contrast filter sheets.

easier tissue handling. Inside the printer is an individually-switched low-wattage lamp so the operator can see where to apply crayon on the tissue. On the top glass supporting the negative, there are thin metal masking strips, adjustable so prints may have narrow or wide borders. A ruby lamp inside the printer allows exact placement of sensitized paper over the negative without danger of fogging it.

Contact Printing Materials

Sensitized paper used in printing frames or on contact printers is much slower than enlarging paper. If it were not, exposures would be uncontrollably short. Because the paper is so slow, darkrooms may be illuminated with amber-colored light so bright as to astonish anyone who has used only enlarging paper.

Developers, stop baths and fixers are identical to those used for enlarging. Enlarging paper may be used on contact printers, but only if the normal print lamps are changed to lamps of extremely low wattage. However, this often is done so that a single kind of paper may be used for all printing, whether by contact or enlargement. Filter sheets large enough to cover the diffusing glass of any contact printer are available, so even multi-grade enlarging paper may be used successfully.

Contact Printing With an Enlarger

Darkrooms equipped with an enlarger already contain the basic equipment needed for contact printing. Printing can be done on enlarging paper, with the enlarger serving as the light source, by using a film proofer or a sheet of glass to hold negative and paper in close contact. When using sheet glass, put a piece of rubber or polyurethane foam under it to insure perfect contact. The foam need not be thick, but should be as large as the glass, or larger.

The same dodging and burning-in techniques used in making enlargements (but not distortion correction) can be applied to contact printing, with identical results.

PRINT DRYING

Double weight photographic papers are among the easiest to dry; but if hung by one corner, or laid face up on blotters, they will always dry badly curled. Either method allows prints to dry

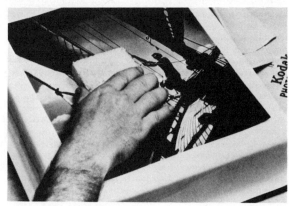

Courtesy of Eastman Kodak Company

Before drying prints in a blotter roll, remove excess water from both sides of the prints with a sponge.

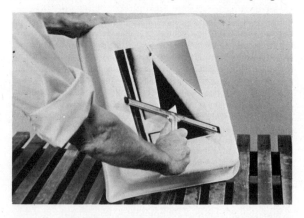

Use an ordinary window squeegee and the bottom on a clean tray as a convenient flat surface for sponging or squeegeeing.

A piece of foam supports enlarging paper (emulsion side up) and negative (emulsion side down). Sheet of glass covers both to insure good contact. Empty negative carrier in enlarger produces rectangle of light. Diaphragm of enlarging lens controls amount of light.

Place prints face down between the two layers of blotting paper in the blotter roll.

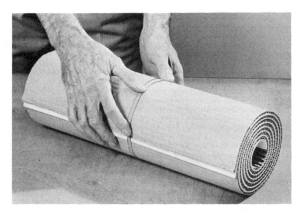

A blotter roll has three surfaces: two of blotting paper, one of single-corrugated cardboard. Close the blotter roll snugly with a rubber band, and lay it on its side so air can circulate freely through corrugations in the cardboard.

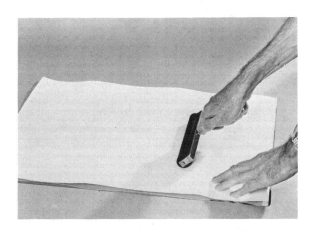

After dripping-wet glossy prints have been placed face down on a clean ferrotype plate, soak up excess water by passing a rubber roller over the sheet of blotting paper put over the plate.

more quickly along their edges than in the center; and the wet emulsion shrinks more than the paper base as it dries. A photographic blotter roll neatly solves both shrinking and curling problems. Sponge or squeegee excess moisture from both sides of the print, and place it face-down between the two layers of blotting paper. Roll the three layers up and use rubber bands to keep the roll tight while the prints dry.

Put the blotter roll on its side in a well-ventilated area, so that air may flow freely through the corrugations between blotter layers. When dry, prints will have a slight reverse curl, but the curl disappears soon after prints are removed from the roll. Having dried evenly from both sides, under moderate pressure, the prints will be flat and smooth.

Prints made on glossy paper will not dry to a high gloss if left to air-dry or put in a blotter roll. To obtain a high gloss, they must be dried in perfect contact with a highly polished surface. To glaze glossy prints, you need ferrotype plates, or tins, a sturdy rubber print roller and a smooth hard surface where prints can be rolled tightly onto the plates.

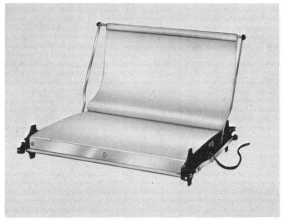

Courtesy of Bogen Photo Corporation

Platten-type electric print dryers provide uniform heat to ferrotype plates laid on surface. Canvas, tightly stretched over plate (placed face up on platten) prevents prints from lifting before completely dry; eliminates "oyster shell" ridges on glossy prints caused when edges of prints dry faster than the center. Most electric dryers have two heated plattens, can dry matte prints face up directly on plattens with canvas stretched taut over prints.

The plates must be absolutely clean before each use. Wash them with plain water and a sponge. Do not let buttons, rings or watch bands come in contact with the chrome surface, and make sure the sponge is free of grit. Any scratch made on the chrome will appear on every print rolled over it, and prints often will stick to scratched plates when they are dry.

Prints should be dripping wet when laid face-down on the plates. Leave about an inch of open space between prints. When all are in place, cover the entire plate with a sheet of photographic blotting paper. Use the roller with moderate pressure on the blotter so all surplus water is absorbed from the prints and plate. Remove the blotter and again run the roller back and forth over the back of each print several times. Bear down firmly with the roller so every inch of each print is in firm contact with the plate.

Ferrotyped prints may be left to air-dry naturally on the plates; but again, edges are likely to dry more rapidly than the center, resulting in "oyster shell" ridges on the surface of dry prints. A dry blotter laid over the plate and prints may help achieve print flatness; but the ideal solution is to have an electrically-heated surface in contact with the back of the plate, as a tightly-stretched canvas covers the polished side.

Many manufacturers make glossy print dryers designed this way. Some have two heated drying surfaces, and can be turned over so that a second plate may be prepared and fastened under canvas as prints on the first plate are drying. These dryers come in many sizes, and most also may be used to dry matte prints by following instructions supplied with the dryer.

A motorized drum dryer is worth considering if many glossy prints must be dried frequently. The surface of the drum is seamless chrome-plated steel. An electric heating element inside the drum warms the chrome surface uniformly, and a motor rotates it in contact with a canvas apron. The apron surrounds the drum except for an area in front, where it extends to provide a flat area where wet prints are laid face up. Underneath the canvas, spring-tensioned rubber rollers automatically squeegee prints from the apron onto the surface of the revolving drum. In one revolution of the drum, prints are dry and fall off the surface into a catch-basket as more prints are fed continuously onto the apron.

Drum dryers are available in widths to accommodate even 16 by 20 inch prints. Most of them also will dry matte prints if they are put on the apron face down. However, unless there is a way to release pressure from the squeegee rollers, matte prints may show a canvas texture from high-pressure contact with the apron.

Dull spots on glossy prints mean that air has been trapped between print and drying surface. Such spots are usually circular. Tiny "flecks" in the glossy surface may be caused by minute solid particles in wash water, or result from imperfect contact with the polished drying surface. Close inspection with a magnifier will indicate which is the problem. Tiny specks of grit always can be seen in flecks if dirt has caused them. Blemishes caused by poor contact will seem to have appeared for no reason, and they will have irregularly shaped edges.

Resoak flecked prints. Under running water, gently rub the emulsion with your fingers (supporting the print by first laying it on a piece of glass or the bottom of a tray) until dirt flecks are removed. If the flecks were not caused by dirt particles, put the resoaked prints on ferrotype plates again and apply more pressure with roller.

If even great roller pressure does not eliminate contact-fleck problems, prints have been over-hardened. Mix new fixer, and use the smallest amount of hardener that permits washing and handling prints without emulsion damage. Be sure prints are not left in fixer longer than necessary, or prints will be difficult to ferrotype even when minimal hardener is used.

Resin Coated Papers

Do *not* use regular drying methods or equipment with resin coated paper. Moisture in the emulsion cannot escape through the base of such paper, and too much heat will easily melt or blister the print's surface. Remember that although water may cling to both sides of the paper, only the emulsion side gets thoroughly wet. To dry RC prints, just use a squeegee or squeezed-out sponge to remove excess water from both surfaces. Then allow prints to dry, face up, on a clean blotter or towel. Or, lay prints on a home-made wooden frame over which plastic window screening has been stretched taut.

The degree of "shinyness" obtainable on glossy RC paper depends upon how quickly it can be dried with warm air. An ordinary hand held hair dryer, aimed at the print emulsion from a few inches away and kept gently moving, does an excellent job in two or three minutes.

All prints, glossy or matte, regular base or resin coated, benefit from the use of a solution such as Pakosol or Super Flat. Prints soaked for about five minutes in such solutions will adhere better to ferrotype plates and drums, will dry flatter and be more supple when dry.

Essentially, print flatting solutions accomplish results by making print emulsions hydroscopic. Ambient moisture in the air enters the emulsion, expands it slightly, and thereby counteracts the tendency of emulsions to shrink and curl as they dry. Even the heavy inward curl produced by hot glossy drum dryers will disappear from treated prints laid out on any flat surface for a few minutes.

Naturally, the strength of flattening solution necessary to make prints lie flat depends upon the normal humidity of your climate. Instructions on the bottle will suggest what proportion of solution-to-water should be sufficient. Although flattening solutions may seem expensive, a little goes a long way; and the dilute solution, so long as it is kept clean, may be used over and over until exhausted.

It is important to be aware that inadequately washed prints will contaminate flattening solutions, blotters, dryer aprons and all other equipment used for print drying. Once contamination occurs, it will be transferred to all subsequent prints dried with the same materials or equipment. Competent professional workers are so acutely concerned about this that dirty prints, processed on a "crash-rush" basis, are dried with separate equipment in a special area where fully-washed prints are never allowed to stray.

PRINT MOUNTING

Photographs for exhibition or display need rigid support to prevent curling and cracking.

Portrait Mounts

A simple metal frame, with glass front and heavy cardboard backing, is usually an ideal choice for the traditional picture. A more informal free-standing print display is the slip-in portrait folder or easel. Most camera stores can supply these in all normal print sizes through eight-by-ten inches, but the print should be fastened securely to the mount so the emulsion will not buckle or curl with changes in humidity. Quick-drying portrait mounting cement (similar to model-building cement) is effective when applied sparingly in a proper pattern; but dry mounting both the print and cut-out matte to the base of the folder or easel will improve appearance and increase rigidity.

Be sure prints are thoroughly dry; then use dabs of quick-setting mounting cement in this pattern on portrait folders or easels. Prints should be put under weight until cement is completely dry, to insure flatness.

Dry Mounting

Dry mounting is accomplished by the application of heat and pressure to a thin sheet of thermoplastic, wax-like, or shellac-like tissue placed between photograph and mounting surface. A print dry mounted with wax or thermoplastic impregnated tissue usually may be removed successfully from its mount through reheating and careful lifting. Prints mounted with shellac-like tissue become bonded so firmly to the mount that print removal without severe damage is all but impossible.

Photographs may be dry mounted to any smooth surface that will withstand temperatures of 200 to 275 degrees (the melting temperature of dry mounting tissues). Large display prints often are mounted on Masonite because of its dimensional stability, high density and rigidity. Photographic mounting board, available in art supply stores and camera shops is the usual choice for prints 16 x 20 inches or smaller.

Courtesy of Seal, Inc.

Small dry mounting press with only 8¹/₂'' x 11¹/₂'' platen can mount 16' x 20' print on 24' x 28'' mount board by pressing one 8 x 10'' area at a time.

Put a thin cardboard insert inside the matte opening. Then cover print and folder with heavy kraft paper or thin cardboard before dry mounting. Cool mounted prints under weight.

To dry mount portraits in folders or easels, position the print under the cut-out opening of the matte, and slip a sheet of dry mount tissue under the print almost as large as the matte. Then cut a piece of thin cardboard slightly smaller than the matte opening. Place the cardboard over the print, cover the entire face of the matte with heavy paper and mount. The cardboard insert provides uniform pressure and heat transfer to both print and matte.

A display print may be mounted bleed (all print edges flush with the mount edges) or may be centered on mounting board several inches larger in both dimensions than the print, providing a matte effect. Mattes with ready-cut openings in many sizes and colors are stocked by art supply stores.

Ideally, dry mounting is done with one of the many dry mount presses offered commercially. Most are made of cast metal, are heavy and must be supported by a solid table. The lower part of the press has a flat, but padded, upper surface. The hinged top has a smoothly polished electrically heated metal plate on its lower surface. A thermostat can be preset to control the temperature of the heating plate, and the hinge, or jaw, of the press can be adjusted to accommodate mounting materials of various thicknesses.

An ordinary electric hand iron, such as normally used to press clothes, also can do a satisfactory job of dry mounting. The iron must have a thermostat, and a Teflon-coated sole plate is advantageous. A steam iron may be used, but must be

Begin dry mounting with hand iron by placing iron in center of print; apply pressure and move iron in slowly widening circles until all of protective cover placed over print has been given about fifteen seconds of heat and pressure.

empty. A thermostat setting midway between "wool" and "silk" or "synthetic" should provide proper dry mounting temperature. Too much heat, whether with hand iron or dry mount press, may melt the gelatin base or photographic emulsions. Too little heat will not produce a proper bond between print, tissue, and mount.

Be sure the heated surface, whether press platten or hand iron, is perfectly clean and smooth. All mounting surfaces must be free of dust and grit. Small particles clinging to the platten or iron will make pits or scratches in the print emulsion; particles on the mount will produce lumps or pimples.

Promptly place mounted print under weight so it cannot warp while cooling.

A warped or badly curled print cannot be dry mounted successfully. Rewet the print, and dry overnight in a blotter roll. Make sure the print is completely dry before attempting to mount it. Preheat the print with press or iron between several sheets of paper to drive out any residual moisture. Then, use a tacking iron or the tip of a hand iron to attach a sheet of dry mount tissue to the back of the print in the center. If a hand iron is used, make a swipe three or four inches long with the tip, then lift the iron immediately so it will not stick to the tissue. Sticking is unlikely to occur with a Teflon-coated tacking iron or hand iron.

Trim the print and tissue simultaneously to the desired size, using a paper trimmer. Or, use a metal straight edge and sharp knife. Use a ruler to position the print on the mount. When it is properly centered, hold the print in place; then gently lift each of the four corners and lightly tack the tissue to the mount. With the print attached to the tissue in the center, and the tissue attached to the mount at each corner, all will stay in proper alignment when bonding is done under heat and pressure.

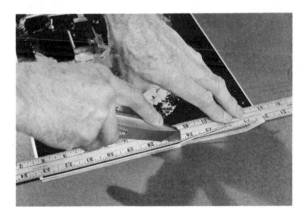

Trim print and dry mount tissue together, after tacking in center of print, with metal ruler and sharp knife.

Bonding With a Hand Iron

Dry mount press manufacturers caution the user to put a covering of thin cardboard or heavy kraft paper between the heated platten surface and the print, to avoid marring the emulsion. It is even more important to do so when a hand iron is used, since the iron must be moved as pressure is applied.

Dry mount with a hand iron on a sturdy table with a smooth surface. Be sure the paper or cardboard cover is large enough to cover the print and any part of the mount the iron might touch.

Place the iron in the approximate center of the print and begin a slow, circular motion, bearing down with considerable pressure. Keep the iron moving as you work from the center toward the edges of the print, and keep the pressure as constant as possible. Working from the center outward eliminates the possibility that bubbles may form from air trapped between print and mount.

On mounting board, heat and pressure must be applied to all areas of the print for about fifteen seconds to produce a good bond. Heavier mounts, such as Masonite, or the use of an unnecessarily thick cardboard cover, may require as much as a full minute.

When you think bonding is complete, remove the cover paper or cardboard and quickly flex the mount once in each direction. If you hear a crackling noise as the mount is flexed, heat is required for additional time, or with more pressure, or both.

When bonding is tight, cover the entire mount with a substantial weight — heavy books, or several heavy ferrotype plates. If the mounted print is held flat as it cools, it will remain flat. If allowed to warp while still warm, the warp is likely to be permanent. If close examination of the cooled print reveals poorly bonded edges, reapply heat and pressure to those areas, and again allow the mounted print to cool under weight.

Prints to be mounted on Masonite, metal or wood must be made slightly oversized; since print, mounting tissue and mount cannot easily be trimmed simultaneously without special equipment. Such heavy mounting materials should be precut to correct size, and all edges sanded smooth, but not chamferred. After

mounting the print, trim the overhang with a sharp blade, using a downward shearing motion.

If a heavier-than-normal mount is advisable (as is the case with bleed-mounted prints) but you have neither the tools nor the experience to work with Masonite, good results can be achieved with mounting board. Use heavy-gauge board, and laminate two pieces with dry mount tissue prior to mounting the print. If the two surfaces of the board are different, laminate the pieces back-to-back, so that any tendency to curl will be self-cancelling. Allow the laminated mount to cool under weight before mounting the print.

Although several passes with a sharp blade will be necessary, it is not difficult to trim prints on laminated cardboard with a combined thickness of three-sixteenths of an inch. Hide the laminate and give the finished print a neat appearance by drawing a broad-tipped felt pen carefully along all edges.

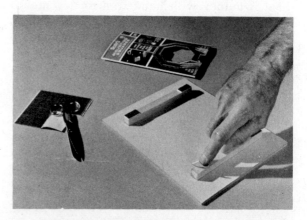

Cement balsa wood rails to back of bleed-mounted print to make stand out blocks. Then apply pressure sensitive two-faced mounting tape at each end of both rails.

Bleed-mounted prints are often hung slightly away from a wall surface to add a three-dimensional quality. Do this with "stand-out blocks."

Cut ½ by ½ inch or 1 by 1 inch balsa wood rails about two inches shorter than the print is wide. Cement the rails to the back of the print mount, then put about one inch of two-faced pressure sensitive mounting tape at the end of each rail. Simply press the mounted print in place on any surface, and it will adhere.

Mounting Resin Coated Papers

Photographic papers coated with resin require special handling when dry mounting. Heat in excess of 230 degrees will blister and melt the emulsion of such paper; and since the paper base is not porous, air bubbles or steam caused by traces of moisture cannot escape through it.

Although ordinary dry mount tissue and techniques may sometimes produce satisfactory results, special mounting materials are marketed specifically for resin coat mounting. Once proper press temperature has been determined by one of the temperature-test strips included with these materials, the mounting tissue must first be heat-mounted to the back of the print. A special nonstick paper put on top of the tissue prevents it from adhering to the hot platten. After the print has cooled, it is then returned to the press in position on the mounting board, this time with nonstick paper protecting the emulsion from platten damage.

One manufacturer offers a hand-operated tool combining rollers with a thermostatically controlled heat platten. The combination of accurate temperature control with a rolling motion is designed to eliminate trapped-air blisters and emulsion damage.

Other Mounting Methods

Ordinary rubber cement produces only a semi-permanent bond. Coatings on both mount and print should be allowed to dry until tacky before joining. In time, however, oxidation of the cement will cause prints to stain, and eventually edges of the print will lift from the mount.

Modern spray adhesives in aerosol cans seem to produce a bond stronger than rubber cement, with less tendency to stain; but they have not yet been in use long enough to establish whether the bond is truly permanent. Resin coated papers would seem more likely to result in a permanent bond, since no oxidation can occur through the paper. A bond limited in durability only by the permanence of the adhesive itself will result if resin coated paper is mounted on a nonporous surface.

ENLARGING

Small cameras have become basic tools in modern photography primarily because the enlarger has made film size relatively unimportant. Fine-grain, high-speed film emulsions and camera lenses of vastly improved quality, have made invaluable contributions; but without the enlarger, miniature cameras would still be only fascinating toys.

With an enlarger, the photographer can make any size print from a small negative, or from any part of it. He is free to decide how light or dark each area of the print shall be, which information in the negative he shall emphasize or subdue. Through enlarging, the photographer has full control of his print.

Mechanically and optically, an enlarger is much like an ordinary slide projector. But for enlarging, the projector is mounted vertically on a rigid column, so it can be raised or lowered to vary print size.

Enlargers can be divided into two groups: diffusion-type and condenser-type. (A few are hybrids combining certain elements of each.) The two types may often have identical light sources (usually an opalized tungsten lamp), but their systems for illuminating the negative are quite different.

Diffusion enlargers use a sheet of opal glass below the lamp to distribute uniformly and diffuse the light before it reaches the negative. This produces a soft, smooth light which minimizes imperfections and minute detail in the negative. Diffusion enlargers are the choice for portrait negatives.

Condenser enlargers employ lenses below the lamp to form the light into parallel rays before it passes through the negative. These condensing lenses produce a uniformly distributed circle of light at the negative plane only slightly larger than the negative itself. Condensed light is more intense than that from a diffusion enlarger, and because it is sharply focused, it produces crisp finely-detailed images.

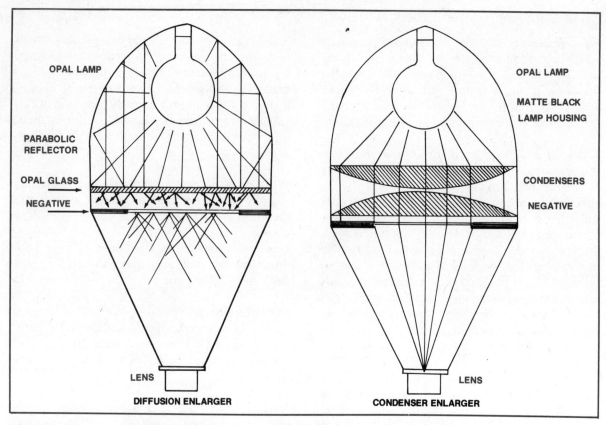

OPAL LAMP

PARABOLIC
REFLECTOR

OPAL GLASS

NEGATIVE

LENS

DIFFUSION ENLARGER

OPAL LAMP

MATTE BLACK
LAMP HOUSING

CONDENSERS

NEGATIVE

LENS

CONDENSER ENLARGER

**Diffusion-type and condenser-type enlarger light sources. Diffusion-type produces *soft*
light, minimizes minor negative imperfections and portrait retouching. Condenser
illumination is more intense, sharply reproduces fine detail (including dust and negative
scratches).**

Courtesy of Omega Division of Berkey Marketing, Inc.

**Condenser enlarger for 35mm and 2¹/₄″ square nega-
tives. Interchangeable lenses, additional condensing
lens to alter focus for second lens.**

Condensing lenses of different focal lengths,
however, are needed to make circles of light of
the correct diameter for negatives of different
sizes. Inexpensive condenser enlargers are
designed to illuminate efficiently only one negative size. More expensive models may have interchangeable condensers for two or more negative sizes. Professional models often use a third
movable condenser to vary the size of the circle
of focused light to cover negatives of many sizes.

All enlargers have an image forming lens below
the negative and a focusing knob or helicoid tube
to produce a sharp image of any size on the
baseboard. The lens contains an iris diaphragm
to regulate the amount of light passing through it.

Enlarging lenses, like camera lenses, must be
matched in focal length to negative size. Condenser enlargers that can accommodate two or

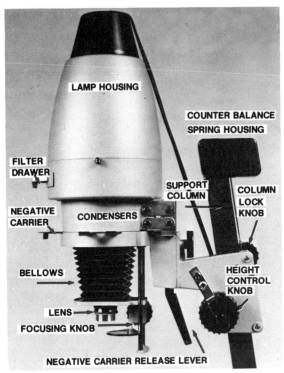

Courtesy of Bogen Photo Corp.

Basic parts of a condenser enlarger.

more negative sizes should have interchangeable condensing lenses with focal lengths correlated to each enlarging lens. Any mismatch of enlarger lens, condenser lens and negative size is immediately apparent on the baseboard, because the negative image is not uniformly illuminated. A bright *hot spot* may appear in the center or the corners may be dark or rounded. Check the illumination uniformity of any enlarger by focusing the edges of the rectangle of light formed by an empty negative carrier on a sheet of white paper.

An enlarging lens too short in focal length for the size of negative placed in a diffusion enlarger will produce illumination less obviously uneven at the baseboard; but with a negative in the carrier, the image will be out of focus near the edges and unusably dim.

Enlarging lenses differ from camera lenses. They are seldom *fast* since they need not cope with moving subjects. Even relatively fast f:2.8 enlarging lenses are intended for use wide open only for easier focusing, and reach peak performance when brought down two or three stops.

Courtesy of Omega Division of Berkey Marketing, Inc.

Professional enlarger with three-lens turret and variable focal-length condensers. Accommodates negatives from 16mm to 4 x 5 inches.

Most importantly, enlarging lenses must be capable of focusing a perfectly flat plane (the negative) onto another flat plane (enlarging paper on the baseboard). And, their optimum performance must be at short distances. Camera lenses, designed to photograph three-dimensional subjects at long distances, perform poorly when used on enlargers.

Courtesy of Omega Division of Berkey Photo Marketing Co. Inc.

Array of lenses in many focal lengths specially formulated for enlarging to produce flat image with corner-to-corner sharpness.

Courtesy of Omega Division of Berkey Photo Marketing, Inc.

Enlarging easel with all four border-masking blades adjustable. Accepts three sizes of paper: 5 x 7", 8 x 10", 11 x 14".

Automatic re-set synchronous-motor driven electric timer, with electrical outlets for safelight and enlarger.

Dodging and diffusing tools made from straightened paper clips; burning-in card from grey cardboard; black net diffuser on embroidery hoop; anti-static brush.

Enlarging Equipment

In addition to the enlarger, the following are necessary for making enlarged prints: enlarging paper (much more sensitive than contact paper), a safelight filter compatible with the paper chosen (Series OA for single-grade papers, series OC for multi-grade papers), an enlarging easel to hold paper flat, adjustable for prints of various sizes, a timer, or timers, for controlling the duration of exposure and for timing print development, three trays and a print washer, or four trays and a trap syphon (glass or ceramic ovenware can serve for trays), developing solution, stop bath and fixer solutions, a quart-size graduate, a tray thermometer, two print tongs, an anti-static cloth or brush, dodging and burning tools, a focusing magnifier and a contact-sheet proofer or a 9 x 12 inch piece of clear glass (preferably plate glass).

Enlarging Papers

There are two basic kinds of enlarging paper; single-grade and multi-grade. Single-grade papers may be numbered from 0 to 6, but most brands range from 1 to 4. Grade number two is considered *normal, i.e.* will produce a full range of tones from black to white, when used with negatives that also have a full range of tones. Lower-numbered grades are *softer* for use with unusually contrasty negatives, while higher-numbered grades are *harder* for printing thin or flat negatives.

Multi-grade, or variable-contrast papers, are not graded. Their emulsions are made of two layers; one sensitive to yellow light, the other to magenta. Contrast is controlled by a graduated series of filters, numbered to correspond to the grades of single-grade papers, placed either above the negative or below the lens during exposure. Some filter sets have half-grades between whole numbers. A number two filter allows approximately equal amounts of yellow and magenta light to strike the paper, producing normal contrast. Lower-numbered filters become more yellow or entirely yellow, and result in softer prints. Higher-numbered filters become more magenta or entirely magenta, and produce more prints with more contrast.

(top) Large filters for multi-contrast papers for use above negative in enlargers have filter drawers. (bottom) Set of below-the-lens filters, with filter holder and relative-speed filter dial.

Sets of multi-contrast filters may seem expensive; but if they are handled with reasonable care, they are a one-time expense, and a full range of negative contrasts can be printed on paper from a single box. With practice, it is practical to expose one section of a print through a low-contrast filter, another section through a high-contrast filter, and thereby obtain a balance and range of tones impossible to achieve with any single-grade type of paper.

Filters for use below the enlarging lens (usually supplied with an adjustable holder to clamp on the lens) are relatively small and perfectly flat so they will not distort light rays passing through them. Filters large enough to fit filter drawers of enlargers so equipped are available in several sizes. Unlike below-the-lens filters, these need not be optically flat. They color the light before it passes through the negative, so small irregularities or minor damage from handling does not effect image quality. It is important, however, that all filters, whether above or below the enlarging lens, be large enough so no white light spills around their edges to dilute color.

Most paper manufacturers now give their products an *ANSI number*. This number establishes the speed of any paper relative to a fixed standard. ANSI numbers progress arithmetically. Paper with a speed of 400 is twice as sensitive as a paper rated at 200 and therefore requires an exposure only half as long. Paper rated at 100 is

only half as fast, so needs an exposure twice as long.

Most enlarging paper comes in two thicknesses: single-weight (light) and double-weight (heavy). Double weight is more durable but is more difficult to wash free of fixer and takes longer to dry. Single weight paper usually is used when a print is intended for publication. It can be washed and dried quickly, is less expensive to mail and costs less per sheet than double weight.

Paper emulsions are made in a variety of surfaces, ranging from a mirror-bright gloss to that of heavily-textured canvas. Camera shops have sample books of surfaces offered by each manufacturer, so that both surface and weight may be examined, compared and chosen to suit negatives to be enlarged.

Glossy paper is preferred for magazine or newspaper publications because it produces the greatest possible range of tones, from a pure black to white. Matte surface papers reflect more light from their black areas, thereby shortening tonal scale, but they are usually preferred for display because they are free of distracting reflections.

Resin coated paper (often abbreviated RC on box labels) is a relative newcomer to enlarging. Such paper is coated on both sides with waterproof resin, and the light-sensitive emulsion is put over the resin on one side. Since developer and fixer penetrate only the emulsion, prints will wash completely in four minutes and dry very quickly.

Resin coated papers may be double weight or medium weight, about half-way between single and double weight. Although the number of surfaces available is more limited than that of other papers, RC papers can be either single-grade or multi-grade. Multi-grade types use the same filters as non-coated papers of the same brand.

Chemistry for Enlarging

All black and white photographic processing demands three basic solutions: developer, stop bath and fixer. Paper developers, whether for enlarging or contact papers, act much more quickly than film developers. Development usually is complete in two or three minutes, sometimes less.

All three chemicals are offered both as powders and as liquid concentrates. Powdered developers are mixed with water into a concentrated *stock* solution and bottled. A few ounces of stock solution are mixed with still more water to produce a *working* solution for print developing. When working solution is exhausted (yellowish and murky), it is discarded and a new batch mixed from stock solution and water.

Many fixer concentrates are packaged with a separate bottle hardener, so that the proportion of hardener to fixer may be varied. In hot weather, when all solutions—especially the wash water—may be warmer than is ideal, the maximum allowable amount of hardener usually is required to prevent paper emulsion from becoming so soft it is easily scratched or even partially detached from the paper base.

Hypo eliminator, or Hypo clearing agent solutions, used after prints are fixed, conserve water by reducing washing time 50 per cent or more. Such solutions cancel the fixer by chemical action and further shorten washing time by making the paper more permeable to water. Mix all chemicals exactly according to instructions, and wear old clothes or a darkroom apron as you work. Label each bottle clearly.

Print tongs are used to keep hands dry, so paper and negatives may be handled without damage from moisture. Label one pair of tongs *stop-fix* and the other *developer* with waterproof ink. Fixer and stop bath are compatible, so the stop-fix tongs can be used in both solutions. Stop bath or fixer dripped into the developer will quickly destroy it, so never put stop-fix tongs into the developer. (Fixer and stop bath both are acidic and therefore will neutralize developer, which is always alkaline.)

In a graduate, mix a convenient amount of developer into working solution according to instructions, and pour it into one tray. Use a tray thermometer to be sure the solution is no cooler than

65 degrees or warmer than 78 degrees. Put stop bath in a tray beside the developer and fixer in a tray beside the stop bath. Always work in a single direction, transferring the print from solution to solution toward a tray of water, or print washer, where prints may be accumulated for subsequent washing.

Making an Enlargement

Enlarging one negative actually involves processing three separate prints: a proof sheet, a test print and the final enlargement.

First make the proof sheet. Cut the roll of film into strips so that all negatives will fit on one eight-by-ten inch sheet of paper. Do this in room light, using a piece of paper of proper size as a guide. Then darken the room and turn on the enlarger. Insert the empty negative carrier in the enlarger head, then lift it until the rectangle of light on the baseboard is two or three inches larger than the paper. Lift the paper by one corner and mark the approximate center of the rectangle on the baseboard with a felt-tip pen or small piece of masking tape. Turn off the enlarger.

Be sure hands are absolutely dry. Use grade No. 2, or a No. 2 variable contrast filter, and arrange strips of film and the paper in a film proofer according to manufacturer's instructions. Or, place the enlarging paper emulsion side up on the

Using a sheet of glass to make proof sheets under the enlarger. Place enlarging paper emulsion-side up; negatives emulsion-side down; cover with glass and expose.

baseboard (using the mark to center it), lay the strips of film on the paper emulsion side down and cover both with a piece of clean glass. Set the enlarger lens at f:8, and expose the paper for fifteen seconds. If the negatives are of normal density, this should be about the right exposure time with most enlargers.

Develop proof sheet by rocking tray, using tongs to hold the print under the developer. Time development, using interval timer, or ordinary electric clock with sweep second-hand.

Carefully remove the paper from under the negatives; and slide it, face up, beneath the surface of the developing solution. Keep the paper moving in the tray with the developing tongs, or hold the paper down with tongs while gently rocking the tray. In about one and one-half minutes, spaces between negatives and along the film edges should be jet black, and the images themselves should contain a full range of tones.

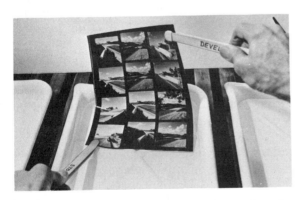

Remove the proof from the developer. Slip it into the stop bath, pulling it under with the stop-fix tongs. Agitate the proof in the stop bath for about 30 seconds.

Lift the proof by one corner with the developer tongs, and drain it into the tray for about ten seconds. Then slip into the stop bath, pulling it under the surface and agitating it there with the stop-fix tongs. If developing tongs should accidentally touch the stop bath, do not return them to the developing tray. Put them aside and continue agitating the proof in the stop bath for about fifteen seconds, then remove the print and put it in the fixer.

Agitate the proof in the fixer occasionally with the stop-fix tongs.

Keep the proof moving gently in the fixer for about thirty seconds if it is quick-fix type, or for one to two minutes in regular fixer, before turning on room lights. If the developer tongs were contaminated, rinse them promptly and thoroughly under running water and dry them, so they will be ready to use again. Leave the proof in the fixer for the recommended time, occasionally agitating it gently; then drain and transfer it into the water tray.

If the proof looks too dark or too light in normal room illumination, make another and give it a shorter or longer exposure. Beginners should keep a small notebook in the darkroom, and record the correct exposure time, f-stop and development time. With this information, and the enlarger head always returned to the same height, making properly exposed proofs will soon become nearly automatic except in unusual circumstances or when using a different brand of paper.

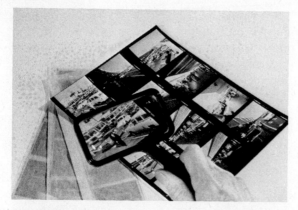

Dry the proof sheet, and use a magnifying glass to check for sharpness and to choose frames to be enlarged.

With experience, a proof sheet can be evaluated while still wet, but it should nevertheless be washed fully, dried and filed with the negatives as a permanent record. All prints look darker when dry, so beginners will learn more from a dry proof sheet.

Look at each frame on the sheet with a magnifying glass. Choose the sharpest and most interesting for enlarging. Since the proof was made on No. 2 paper, its appearance will indicate whether the enlargement from any frame chosen should be made on softer or harder paper. Good judgement here comes with experience.

The Test Print

Determine correct exposure for the final enlargement by making a test print. Hold the chosen negative by its edges and gently brush each side with an anti-static brush, or wipe each side lightly with an anti-static cloth. The base

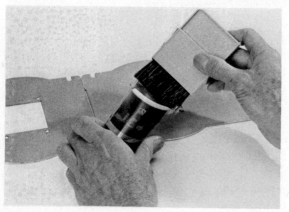

(shiny) side of the negative is the more likely to have a static charge that must be neutralized so it will not attract airborn dust.

Place the negative carefully in the negative carrier, emulsion side down. Then turn on the enlarger and open the lens wide. Hold the negative carrier at an angle in the light under the lens, and examine it for dust. If you see whitish specks, flick them off with the brush; then insert the negative carrier in the enlarger.

Set the enlarging easel margins to accommodate the size of enlarging paper being used. Put a sheet of ordinary white paper in the easel, and turn off room lights. Raise the enlarger head on its column until the negative image, or that section of it to be enlarged, fills the white paper. Then, using a magnifier, focus the center of the image sharply on the paper. Being sure hands are dry, put a sheet of enlarging paper, emulsion side up, in the easel. (Most photographic paper curls slightly toward the emulsion side, making identification easier.)

Set the enlarging timer for five seconds. Cover four-fifths of the paper with a piece of cardboard, and expose the uncovered portion for five seconds. Move the cardboard to uncover two-fifths of the paper, and expose again for five seconds. Continue in this way until the entire sheet of paper has been uncovered, and the total exposure has reached twenty-five seconds.

Now develop the test print in the same way and for the same length of time as the proof sheet. *Be sure the box of unexposed enlarging paper is tightly closed before turning on a white light to examine the test!* Unless the negative is exceptionally thin or dense, one segment of the test print should be correctly exposed, or so nearly correct that adding or subtracting a second or two will give correct exposure.

If the correctly-exposed segment is the one exposed longest, open the enlarger lens one stop before making a final print and halve exposure time. If the shortest exposure looks best, close the lens one stop and double the exposure time. Exposures ranging from ten to fifteen seconds are ideal.

Check the contrast of the correctly-exposed test segment. If it looks too harsh, or too gray and lifeless, make another test print on a softer or harder grade of paper. Single-grade papers vary in speed from grade to grade, so a new exposure time must be determined. Multi-grade paper may not require a new test print if filters are changed to alter contrast. Most are supplied with a calculator dial, or a list of ANSI speed numbers, for each filter, so correct exposure through any one filter can be converted to the right exposure through any other.

The Final Print

Set the enlarging timer for the exposure time judged correct. Before putting a sheet of paper in the easel, use a medium-soft pencil (press lightly) to note exposure time, f-stop and developing time on the back of the paper. After exposure, develop the print for exactly the same time as the test, rinse it in stop bath, fix, wash and dry it.

Instructions for the use of most developers and enlarging papers quote a "useful range" of developing times. If ideal developing time is given as two minutes, the useful range of time may be from one minute to three. This flexibility in the permissible developing time is valuable as a means of rescuing prints that have been slightly under or overexposed. However, it cannot compensate for gross errors. Murky and mottled dark tones, and greyed highlights, will be the result if developing time is too short. Prolonged overdevelopment will never bring a badly underexposed print to normal density, and will probably fog or stain it.

Evaluating the Print

Dry prints look somewhat darker than wet ones. For this reason alone, you may decide to make a second print and give it less exposure. Or, you may decide that the print, as a whole, is the right density and contrast, but you would like to see some dark areas lighter, and some highlight area a bit darker.

Dodging and *burning* tools make this possible. They can be bought ready-made or made easily from wire and cardboard. Straightened paper

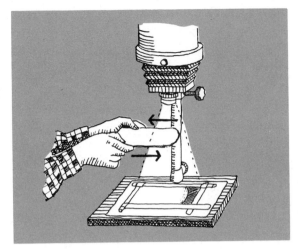

Reprinted with permission from Kodak publication, "Enlarging."

Dodging tools should be kept moving to diffuse the edges of areas dodged.

clips, with various sizes of cardboard ovals fastened to one end with masking tape, work well. Sheets of thin cardboard, with different-sized roughly circular holes in them, are fine for darkening small areas of a print while keeping light off the remainder.

Use a dodging tool during about one-quarter of the total print exposure. Keep it several inches above the print so it will cast moderate shadow, and always keep it moving slightly so the dodged area will blend smoothly.

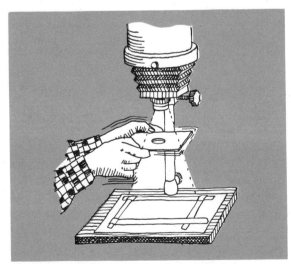

Reprinted with permission from Kodak publication "Enlarging."

Burning-in card also should be kept moving so darkened area will blend smoothly.

Use a burning-in card after the basic exposure is complete. Re-set the timer for 25 to 30 per cent of the original exposure, use the card several inches above the print with the hole over the area to be darkened, and keep it moving slightly in a circular motion until the timer turns off the enlarger lamp. Use grey cardboard rather than black. It reflects the entire image well enough to make finding the too-dense negative areas easy. White cardboard can reflect enough enlarger light toward ceiling and walls to fog the print.

Modern camera lenses are so sharp that enlarged close-ups of people are often unflattering. Diffusing the image part of the time during enlarging exposure usually solves this problem. Crumple a piece of cellophane, smooth it out, then hold it a few inches below the enlarger lens during half the exposure. Keep it moving slightly. Or, stretch a piece of fine black netting on an embroidery hoop and use it in the same way. Crumpled cellophane also works well to diffuse small areas of a print in which sharpness is a distraction. Cut a small piece and fasten it with clear cellophane tape to the end of a wire. Use it as though it were a dodging tool. Any diffusion material will absorb or reflect some light from the lens, so it may be necessary to increase exposure by five or ten per cent when diffusion is employed.

Buildings photographed with miniature cameras seem to fall over backward because the camera is pointed upward. This distortion can be corrected when enlargements are made. Raise one end of the easel with books or boxes until vertical lines of the building are parallel. Refocus the lens so the image is sharp at a point one-third the distance below the high edge of the print. Then stop the lens down as far as it will go before exposing. Remember that exposure time must be doubled for each stop below normal, i.e. f:22 requires eight times—2 x 2 x 2—more exposure than f:8. Some enlargers permit tilted easel and so do not require very small lens stops when correcting distortion.

Washing Prints

Light will not darken or damage thoroughly fixed prints, but a fixed print is by no means a permanent one. Fixing solutions dissolve and remove unexposed silver bromine from the emulsion, leaving only the developed (darkened) metallic silver image. As fixer works, it produces sulfur compounds. If fixer is allowed to remain in the print, the sulfur compounds will tarnish and stain the silver image, just as the sulfur in egg yolk tarnishes silverware. Ultimately, sulfur-stained images may simply fade away completely in the presence of atmospheric moisture.

Because these sulfur compounds are soluble in water, washing all traces of fixer from the print will give it permanence. A single print on double weight paper may require a full hour of washing in running water to achieve archival permanence. (The silver image on an archival-quality print will outlast the paper on which it rests.) For a print life of even ten or twenty years, washing time cannot be substantially reduced.

When several prints are washed at one time, it is vitally important that moving fresh water flow over both surfaces of every print as they wash. Well-designed print washers keep prints separated and in motion relative to each other by water-jet action, mechanical action, physical separation or some combination of the three.

Remember that all chemical action is accelerated by heat. Do not wash prints in hot water (the emulsion will melt), but expect prints washed in 50-degree water to require more time if washed at 70 degrees.

If no print washer or tray siphon is available, use a generous-sized tray of water and turn each print over separately under the surface of the water. When each print has been turned over twice, lift all prints from the tray, dump the water and refill with fresh water. Repeat the turn-twice-and-dump procedure until prints test fixer-free. Since fixer is heavier than water, it settles to the bottom of the tray. Prints will wash faster if the water is dumped than if a continuous stream of fresh water flows into the tray as prints are agitated. Even the best washers may sometimes allow groups of prints to *pack* or *clump*. When this happens, prints must be separated or *shuffled* by hand at frequent intervals during wash cycle, or some of the prints will not wash thoroughly no matter how long washing is continued.

Single weight prints tend to sink in water. Double weight prints float. Sometimes washing the two together helps prevent packing. When this is done, however, all prints must be washed as long as is needed to clean the double weight prints. Single weight prints require less washing time than double weights; but when washed together, the heavier prints will continue to release sulfur compounds into the water, contaminating single weight prints which would theoretically be clean if washed alone.

A fixer-neutralizing solution (hypo clearing agent) used prior to washing makes prints easier to wash in less time. Rinse fixed prints briefly in running water to remove surface fixer, and soak them for two or three minutes, with agitation (according to print weight and manufacturer's instructions) in the neutralizing solution and then wash. Camera shops sell chemical test solutions which quickly prove or disprove the presence of fixer in prints when washing is assumed to be complete. Such test solutions are inexpensive insurance against print deterioration.

Picket Fence
[SEE FENCES & GATES.]

Picture Molding

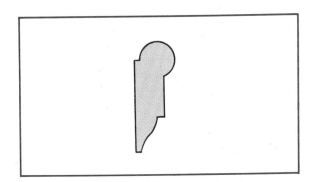

Picture molding has a rounded extension that is designed to hold heavy-duty picture hooks. It is nailed close to the ceiling and is used for hanging pictures and mirrors. With the rounded extension used for finger grips, picture molding also makes excellent drawer or door pulls. *SEE ALSO MOLDING & TRIM.*

Pier Blocks

Pier blocks are rectangular, concrete blocks that are used in foundation work. Pier blocks have three separate cores running from side to side through the center. Unlike some blocks, piers have flat ends and sides so they cannot be placed next to different style blocks and maintain a continuous pattern. *SEE ALSO FOOTINGS & FOUNDATIONS.*

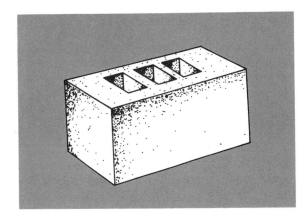

Pier Block

Piers, Boathouses, Docks & Floats

A float, dock, or pier can add immeasureably to the fun of a shoreside home or summer place. And, fortunately, you can build any one of them yourself from readily available materials. The size of the units depends on the way you plan to use them and the load they will have to support.

The type of flotation depends on your budget and the availability of the flotation material or units in your area. Old style flotation can cut your costs, but modern flotation can simplify the job and provide almost unlimited service life. The drawings show you how each of the common forms of flotation for floats can be used. As to docks, you can buy a readymade type, ready to assemble, through your nearest large marine supplier, or you can build your own from standard size lumber and plumbing materials.

TYPES OF FLOTATION

There are several major forms of flotation. The old familiar type, 55 gallon drums, is likely to be the lowest in cost. These are a little under 23 inches in diameter and approximately 35 inches long. Each one can support about 385 pounds in

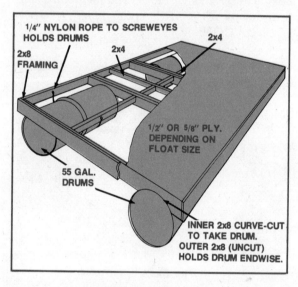

1/4" NYLON ROPE TO SCREWEYES HOLDS DRUMS

2x8 FRAMING

2x4

2x4

1/2" OR 5/8" PLY. DEPENDING ON FLOAT SIZE

55 GAL. DRUMS

INNER 2x8 CURVE-CUT TO TAKE DRUM. OUTER 2x8 (UNCUT) HOLDS DRUM ENDWISE.

addition to the weight of the drum itself. *Important:* be sure the screw-in plug to fit the opening in the drum is with the drum (or in the drum opening) when you buy. It should then be tightened in place after coating the threads with pipe compound. As an added precaution, the opening in the drum should be at the top, above the expected waterline, when the drum is set in place. If the drum was originally used as a container for a petroleum product like automotive lubricant, the residue will usually provide good inside protection. The outside of the drum should be protected by a good exterior oil base gloss enamel.

Foam flotation, such a styrofoam, is the more modern choice. It cannot leak like a drum because it is a solid mass of tiny sealed air cells. Even if you drive a pole through it the loss of buoyance is relatively minor. You only lose the flotation of the portion actually removed. All the rest of the foam retains its buoyancy. Styrene type foam, however, can be broken down by gasoline and oil. If your float is to be used where excessive spillage of these materials is likely, a protective skirt extending below the waterline should be used.

The newest of the flotation types is the plastic float drum. This is available in low cost hollow form or in foam-filled form, either of which is unaffected by gasoline or oil, and is free from rust or corrosion. The foam-filled form, too, is unsinkable even if punctured and never requires painting.

The drums are made with a mounting flange around them to permit easy installation in a float frame. Each float will support 260 pounds when submerged to a little less than two inches below this flange.

CONSTRUCTING A FLOAT

As floats can be built in any reasonable size, the drawings show only an average float in an average size. The important point is the method of construction. Standard size lumber is used throughout. The use of 1/2 or 5/8 inch plywood decking reduces the weight appreciably, though 2 x 6 decking boards spaced 3/16 inches apart may be substituted. The advantage of plywood is its greater live load capacity. It can hold more people on deck with the float at the same waterline. If you use plywood, paint it with a long life marine deck paint and imbed a nonskid material such as the mineral granules made for the deck paint while the paint is still wet.

Be sure to plan a method of putting your float in the water. If the job must be done by two people it may be wise to build the float in two half-sections that can be bolted together after they are put in the water. The logical way to decide: try lifting the materials (in a batch) that will go into your float. If two people cannot lift them, plan for a two-section float to be bolted together after launching. A typical method of doing this is shown in the drawing.

When the float is used as a boat landing, the simplest arrangement for anchoring consists of eye bolt and rod hinges at each end. In windy weather you can add reinforcing cables. Concrete block anchors can be used although weight for weight, mushroom anchors have much greater holding power. In shallow water, however, there is a chance that the shank of a mushroom anchor may be lifted by excessive pull in rough water. If you use this type of anchor, connect the shank to the midpoint of the float so boats docking at the outer edge water do not have to pass over the anchors. The shank of a mushroom anchor in a near upright position can cause considerable hull damage if struck by a moving boat.

PIERS OR DOCKS

Where the water level is relatively constant, as in many lakes, a pier with supporting legs resting directly on the lake bottom may be your best bet. You can buy metal types, ready to assemble, with adjust-length supports, such as the Aqua-Matic pier made by Aqua-Matic Piers, Inc. These can be assembled in various forms, such as straight, or L-shaped. To get the length required, join the 8-foot sections. If you prefer to build your own pier, use dock-size lumber and pipe legs.

To simplify construction when you build your own pier you can measure the depth of the water at the points where the supporting legs will be, and have your pipe cut and threaded to hold the pier deck at the desired height above the water. Flanges are used to bolt the legs to the wood deck assembly and also as feet at the bottom. Naturally, this type of support requires a firm lake bottom and the inner end of the pier must be very solidly anchored to the ground. By building the pier in sections, it can be removed by simply dismantling at the end of the season. This is advisable where winters are cold enough to ice over the water. Depending on local conditions, ice may damage the pier by shifting, or even lift-

ing the legs from the bottom (with rising water level) and possibly breaking it free at the ground end.

BOATHOUSES

The serious boatowner who has a considerable investment in his power boat may want to provide permanent protection for his boat. If he is fortunate enough to own water front property, he can built what is, in essence, a garage for his boat.

In stable waters, the boatowner may want to simply build a U-shaped float with a simple flat roof supported by metal posts. To allow for easy exits a deck of approximately 24 inches should be built around the perimeter of the opening.

For even greater protection, the boater can build his boathouse on the bank and by use of a ramp and winch, take the boat completely out of the water.

Some enterprising boatowners use the trailer as a means of transporting the boat from the water into the boathouse.

For added convenience, the boathouse should contain storage facilities for essential equipment such as life preservers, sports and fishing equipment.

Pigments

Pigments are a powdery matter used to color paint. The pigments more commonly used in paint manufacturing are white, yellow, blue, green, red, brown, black, inert and metallic powders, with white being the most popular. Pigments may be obtained either from the earth or by mixing chemicals. Different types of paints will contain various pigment counts. Enamels and gloss paints have a low pigment concentration, while flat paints and primers are approximately 50 to 75 per cent pigment. Pigments are manufactured differently according to their source but should always be in a powdered form before combining with liquids in paint making. *SEE ALSO PAINTS & PAINTING.*

Pigmented Wiping Stains

Pigmented wiping stains are a penetrating oil stain with pigments stirred into them. Because the pigments are suspended, not dissolved, in the solution, almost constant stirring is necessary to maintain an even color. Dyes may be dissolved in the stain to add color, but the majority of the coloration is done by the pigments. *SEE ALSO WOOD FINISHING.*

Pigtail Splice

The pigtail splice is necessary in making a continuous run in the wiring circuit. For instance, a pigtail splice is advisable when joining the wires leading from the ground terminal of a fuse box to the wires of a grounding rod. The splice is made by stripping about two inches of insulation from the ends of both wires. With the wires side by side, twist the bared ends together about five turns. Twist the rest of the wire back onto the

splice, solder and tape. *SEE ALSO ELECTRICAL WIRING.*

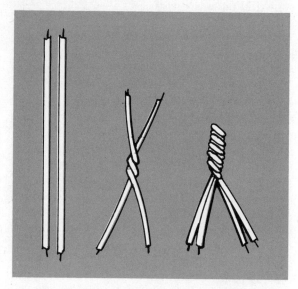

The Three Steps in Forming a Pigtail Splice

Pilaster

A pilaster is an architectural support that is vertically adjacent to a wall. Although it functions as

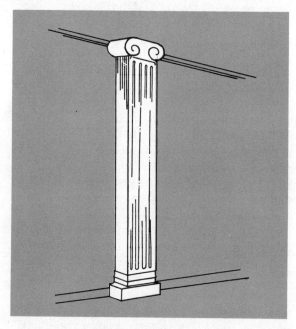

A Pilaster

a brace, it is usually disguised as a pillar or column. *SEE ALSO WALL & CEILING CONSTRUCTION.*

Pile

A pile is a heavy beam of concrete or metal that is driven into the ground to support a dock or bridge, or to act as a supporting member in laying a floor. *SEE ALSO FOOTINGS & FOUNDATIONS.*

Pilot Hole

A pilot hole is a starting hole which receives the threaded part of the screw. Pilot holes are needed for screws to help keep the fibers of two joined boards connected tightly. Since only a small starting hole is needed in softwoods, either make the pilot hole half as deep as the threaded section of the screw or just make a small indentation. For hardwoods, the depth of the pilot hole should be as long as the screw. Both the pilot hole and the screw shank should be equal.

Pilot Light

A pilot light is a small, permanent flame which ignites gas for burners, such as in pot-type or vaporizing burners, and generates electric current by heating a thermocouple, a device that changes the heat to electric current. This current holds an electrical valve open in the main gas line which supplies heat. Pilot lights can be found in furnaces, gas driers and gas ranges.

When the pilot light or flame goes out, it causes the thermocouple to cool off, the electric current to stop and the supply valve to close, preventing gas from escaping. Until the pilot flame is relighted, the burner cannot be operated. Before attempting to relight the pilot light, be sure the combustion chamber has been aired out completely and that the gas valve has been turned off. The pilot flame can be relighted by the homeowner by following the directions which are printed in the plate or tag connected to the unit. If unsure of the procedure, the homeowner should not relight the pilot light. The local utility company can be notified in advance to have someone demonstrate the proper way to do the job, or the serviceman who relights the pilot light can give instructions.

To relight a furnace pilot light, the room thermostat should be set to the lowest temperature. The switch controlling current that comes to the furnace should be turned off. The gas supply leading to the furnace should be turned off, but the gas leading to the pilot light should be left on. Then light the pilot, turn the current on, open the main supply valve and set the thermostat on the proper temperature. After this procedure, if the pilot flame does not burn, shut off the gas valves and contact a serviceman.

Normally, there is little trouble with pilot lights. The color of the flame can help indicate if the pilot flame is functioning properly. If the inner flame is a blue-green color, the pilot is working properly. If more than half of the flame is yellow, it indicates that there is not enough oxygen. A very dark blue inner flame indicates that there is too much oxygen. Be sure to have the flame adjusted properly. Surface burner pilots on ranges should have flames about $1/8$ inch high and the oven should have flames about $1/2$ inch high. If the gas pilot is constantly going out, there could be improper ventilation or there may be a faulty thermocouple. Have a serviceman check it.

Pine Finishes

Pine, one of the most useful and versatile woods, can be finished in many ways.

A penetrating resin finish emphasizes the grain and intensifies the colors. It makes the wood more durable. The color will darken naturally over time.

A spatter finish is applied with a base coat of woodtone brown, and then spattered with another color. This type of finish gives the impression of one color from a distance.

Stains of green, blue or other hues are often used on pine. Sometimes wall paint is used for the stain rather than enamel because it is easier to handle.

Fruitwood stain is a type of pigmented wiping stain. It has red and brown hues. An ebony stain will make pine black. Pieces such as wall brackets, small furniture and shelves look ebony and onyx when stained black. When these are given a semigloss or flat varnish, they lose their shine and look their best.

When pine is stained with potassium permanganate, it turns a unique shade of brown. It should be given a topcoat of varnish, lacquer or shellac.

A black swirl finish is a built-up finish that involves the use of plaster of paris.

A propane torch or other flame is used to obtain a scorched finish. After the pine surface is blackened, a wire brush is used to remove the charcoal. Then varnish or lacquer the surface. *SEE ALSO WOOD FINISHING.*

Pine Wood

Pine wood has a uniform texture, resists shrinking, swelling and warping, works easily and finishes well. It is usually straight grained with resin canals appearing as brown flecks. The two major categories are soft and hard. Soft pines have a soft, close-grained wood with a thin, white sapwood. Soft pines include woods such as sugar, nut, foxtail, limber, Mexican white and whitebark pine. Hard pines have heavy, coarse-grained wood with a dark colored heartwood

and pale sapwood. Woods included are jack, shortleaf, Virginia, sand, longleaf, loblolly, ponderosa and slash pine.

Pine wood is usually used for house construction, paneling, interior and exterior trim, furniture, crates, boxes, millwork, foundry patterns, moldings and toys. Tar and turpentine are extracted from pine wood. *SEE ALSO WOOD IDENTIFICATION.*

Pin & Groove

Pin-and-groove is a guiding technique used in folding door construction. The inside vertical piece contains the guide pin which moves in a groove in the lower case in smaller openings, and in both the top and bottom case in larger projects. A track may also be installed in the top case to support the door. The door, which contains a T-shaped pin, is actually hung from this track. In smaller openings, one pin acting as a guide is sufficient. In longer openings, however, a pin should be placed at the top of every other piece to accomodate the folding motion. *SEE ALSO FOLDING DOORS.*

Pinking Shears

Pinking Shears

Pinking shears are cutting instruments much like a pair of scissors that provide a ravel-resistant edge and seam finish to materials. The teeth of the shears are triangular to produce the pinked finish. Besides being excellent for preventing raveling, pinking shears are also used to provide a decorative finish. *SEE ALSO HAND TOOLS.*

Pin Punch

The pin punch is used for finishing work in wood or metal projects. Its generally round body tapers at one end to a sharp point so that it resembles one variety of center punch, except that the pin punch is smaller in size. *SEE ALSO HAND TOOLS.*

Pin Punch

Pipe

A pipe is a hollow cylinder which allows matter to flow through it to a desired location. Divided into two major divisions, pipe is generally classified as transmittal and dispersal systems.

TRANSMITTAL SYSTEM

There are four general types of a transmittal system used for a variety of tasks.

Available in rigid or flexible form, copper pipe and tubing does not require threading. Joints are formed by soldering the connection or flaring the end of the pipe to accommodate a fitting.

Galvanized steel is durable and more often available than copper. When pipes are exposed and subject to being accidently struck, such as in a workshop, galvanized steel is used. It is commonly found in lengths of 21 feet. Short sections of galvanized steel available in lengths up to six feet are called nipples. Steel pipes are durable and most often used for drainage.

Cast-iron is one of the more durable pipes. Widely used for drainage, cast-iron pipe joints use molten lead poured over oakum to seal a connection.

Plastic pipe is available in rigid and flexible form. Although quite adaptable for well use, plastic pipe has not been used widely for household plumbing because it is not suitable for extremely hot temperatures. Plastic pipe is used more for drainage than supply systems. This pipe is light-weight, easy to assemble, resistant to many corrosive elements and inexpensive.

DISPERSAL SYSTEM

A dispersal system has four major divisions. Used for drainage, each type of pipe is spaced $1/8$ to $1/4$ inches apart to allow the liquid flowing through it to seep into the soil around the pipe. Placing tar or roofing paper over the spaces prevents soil from filling the gaps.

Concrete or cement tile is the least expensive of the pipes. Better grades of vitrified pipe are made with coal-tar elements and available with small, evenly spaced holes in the side. Fiber pipe is reddish-brown pipe often seen stacked in building supply yards. Yellowish or red in color, clay tile is kiln hardened. *SEE ALSO PLUMBING MATERIALS.*

Pipe Cutter

A pipe cutter makes a right-angle cut around pipes or tubes which is important for threading and making pipe connections. Besides being easy to use, this cutter does a better job than a saw. Contained in the cutter head are small rollers, which press against the pipe's surface, and an extremely sharp, hard wheel which cuts steel. The cutter is placed on the pipe with the cutting wheel on the measured line. To force the cutting wheel into the pipe's surface, tighten the screw handle. Make deeper cuts by tightening the handle before each turn until the pipe has been cut through. To ease the job and lengthen the cutter's life, apply thread-cutting oil to the pipe and cutter when in use. A tube cutter which is like the pipe cutter, but lighter, may be used when working with copper pipe or tubing. *SEE ALSO PLUMBER'S TOOLS & EQUIPMENT.*

Pipe Cutter

Pipe Fittings

Since each type of pipe has its own characteristics, pipe fittings are designed to accommodate the unique qualities of each. Each fitting is classified according to the type of pipe, with copper pipe fittings having two classifications (sweat and flare) according to the method of securing the fitting to the pipe.

COPPER PIPE FITTINGS

A copper fitting slips over a pipe end. Straight run fittings include the coupling and slip coupling. To attach a steel or cast-iron pipe, a steel pipe or cast-iron pipe adapter can be used. Joining pipes at an angle to one another may be accomplished with a $1/2$ inch, $1/8$ inch or closet bend. A street elbow rather than a bend is used if one of the pipes has internal threads. Sanitary tee and a sanitary tee with side inlet are used to join straight runs with a branch entering at a right

angle. A Y-branch is used for pipes entering a straight run at angles other than 90 degrees. The drum trap allows fluid to enter the straight run portion and exit the smaller side inlet. A closet flange attaches the toilet bowl securely to the closet bend, which is located at floor level.

COPPER TUBE FITTINGS

A copper tube sweat-type fitting is secured to the pipe by *sweating* the joint. Sweat soldering is done by first polishing the inside of the fitting and the outside of the pipe with a fine abrasive or steel wool. Next, the polished areas are coated with soldering flux before twisting the pipe into the fitting to spread the flux. The fitting and pipe are then heated with a torch. Without touching the flame to the soldering wire, allow the wire to melt into the seam created by the fitting and tube. Remove the flame as soon as the solder has filled the seam completely.

A copper tube sweat-type fitting that slips into a tube to seal the end is a *cap*. Straight-run joints are formed by a coupling or a union. A union has an outer rim used to secure the two ends of the fitting on to the pipe. Straight runs with a branch entering at a right angle are formed by a regular tee or a reducing tee. The regular tee joins a straight run of the same sized pipe, while a reducing tee joins different diameters of pipe. Two pipes entering at an angle to one another are usually joined by 45 or 90 degree bends. A stop-and-waste valve is connected to a pipe to aid in draining the line from the fitting to an outside faucet. This fitting is particularly useful when working on pipes and when clearing liquid from the pipe and faucet during freezing weather. A brass cap on the side of the valve allows air to enter the pipe. The male and female copper-to-steel adapters are used to change a plumbing system from copper tube to steel. The male adapter has external threading on one end and a slip end on the other. The female adapter has one end which slips into the pipe while the other end has internal threading that receives the external threading of the male adapter.

A copper tube flare fitting is joined to a tube by enlarging the end of the tube with a flanging tool so that the fitting will be secured tightly on the tube. A union is used to join a straight run while a regular tee is used to join a straight run and a pipe entering at a right angle. Two tubes entering at an angle to each other are joined with an elbow. Male and female adapters are used to join copper tubes.

GALVANIZED STEEL FITTINGS

Most all galvanized steel pipe fittings are threaded since the pipe ends are also threaded. A few fittings simply slip over the ends to accommodate cut pipe.

Straight runs of same diameter pipes are joined by a coupling, hose adapter or a union. A coupling slips on the pipe. While both have an outer rim to secure the ends of the fitting, the hose adapter has external threading and the union has internal threading. Straight runs with different diameter pipes use a reducer or a bushing. A reducer has internal threading on both ends while the bushing has internal threading on one end and external threading on the other end. Straight runs with a branch entering at a right angle are joined by a regular tee or reducing tee. The reducing tee allows different diameter pipe to be joined in the straight run portion.

Use elbows to join pipes entering at an angle to each other. While it is most commonly found with internal threading with either 45 or 90 degree angles of curvature, the street elbow has one end with internal and one end with external threading. To seal the ends of a galvanized steel pipe, either a cap or a plug can be used. A plug screws into the pipe flush with the end while a cap screws over the end of a pipe.

PLASTIC PIPE FITTINGS

Plastic pipe fittings may be joined to the pipe by clamping the fitting on the pipes or by solvent welding. Solvent welding involves coating the pipe ends with a plastic cement and pushing it into the fitting with a slight twisting motion to spread the cement. The solvent in the cement fuses the fitting and the pipe.

Straight runs with same diameter pipes are formed with a coupling while different diameter plastic pipes use a reducer. A tee forms a straight

run and joins a branch entering at a right angle. Two pipes meeting at angles to each other are connected by an elbow. A straight run formed by a plastic pipe and a steel pipe are joined by the steel pipe adapter. A joint clamp is placed around the end of the pipe and is secured by tightening the screws on the side of the clamp.

FIBER PIPE FITTINGS

Fiber pipe fittings are secured to the fiber pipe by forcing the pipe end into the fitting. The friction created by the force will fuse the elements of coal tar in the fiber pipe to the fitting. Straight runs are formed by a joining sleeve, coupling or a snap coupling. The snap coupling simply *snaps* around the pipe. A coupling slips over the ends while a joining sleeve is long enough to accommodate the tapered ends of uncut fiber pipe. A cross joins four pipes meeting at right angles forming two straight runs.

While it usually forms a straight run, a tee can also join a branch entering at a right angle. The Y-branch connects a straight run and a pipe entering at an angle. A bend usually the 1/4 and 1/8 size, joins two pipes meeting at an angle. When a fiber pipe and a cast-iron soil pipe are to be joined, a cast-iron pipe adapter is used.

STEEL PIPE DRAINAGE FITTINGS

Steel pipe drainage fittings are usually threaded. A tee branch joins a straight run and a pipe entering at a right angle. The 90 degree long turn Y also connects a straight run and a pipe entering at a right angle. The difference is that the tee branch joins the pipe midway to the fitting and at a right angle, whereas the long turn Y has the pipe entering at a right angle nearer to one end of the fitting. The regular Y simply joins a straight run and a branch entering at some angle.

Two pipes meeting at an angle are connected by an elbow. Elbows are commonly found with 45 and 90 degree angles of curvature. A long turn elbow has a more slender curve between the ends of the fitting. While the other elbows have internal threading at both ends, a street elbow has internal at one end and external on the other end. A p-trap was designed to collect articles dropped into a drain and to eliminate pipe odors.

The U-shaped part of this fitting contains a water barrier to inhibit the back-passage of air. A cleanout is usually located at the bottom of the U. This fitting provides easy access to the inside of the pipe to remove clogs or lost articles.

CAST-IRON SOIL PIPE FITTINGS

Cast-iron soil pipe fittings are secured to the pipe by centering the pipe in the fitting and packing oakum firmly in the remaining space. Next, molten lead is poured in the space up to the rim and allowed to cool. When the lead has hardened, a caulking iron is driven into the lead. The chipped lead is then packed against the pipe and the fitting to form a better seal. This last step of the procedure is repeated until all traces of a gap between the lead, the pipe and the fitting are completely filled. A joint runner, a piece of fat asbestos rope with a clamp to hold the ends together, is used for a horizontal joint. When the lead is cool, chisel off the bump left by the clamp.

A bend connects cast-iron soil pipes meeting at angles to each other. The $1/4$ inch, $1/8$ inch and the long $1/8$ inch bend with inlet, which has an additional opening at the curve of the fitting, are common cast-iron soil pipe fittings. A sanitary tee joins a straight run with a branch entering at a right angle while the test tee has a plug in the inlet for the branch. A sanitary tee has two inlets for branches entering at right angles. A 45 degree Y-branch connects a straight run and a branch entering at a 45 degree angle.

Both forming straight runs, a reducer joins pipes having different diameters, while a caulking spigot joins same sized pipes. A vent increaser is used to enlarge the diameter of a vent pipe at roof level. Similarly, a hub-vent fitting allows an adaption to a larger diameter pipe at roof level.

A soil p-trap collects articles that fall into drains and acts as a water barrier to inhibit the back-passage of air to stop pipe odors. A floor drain has a slotted metal disc to prevent objects from falling into the drain. This disc is located at the wide horizontal opening on a soil p-trap. It has a small outlet running from the disc level to a portion of the pipe on the other side of the U to act as an overflow passage. A cleanout ferrule is located either at the bottom of traps or at the end of a pipe to provide easy access to the inside of the pipe.

For more information and illustrations check each individual category as well as the entries on the individual pipe fittings. *SEE ALSO PLUMBING MATERIALS.*

Pipe Joints

Pipe joints, which are used on copper, plastic, vitrified and vertical or horizontal cast iron, fuse two pipes together to form a continuous length. Different procedures of fusing are employed for all four types of pipe joints.

For the copper pipe joint, use a fine abrasive cloth to rub the outside end of the pipe and the inside of the fitting until they become shiny. Using a toothbrush, spread the soldering flux, a thick paste, over the cleaned areas and slip the pipe and fitting together. No force will be needed. A propane torch or gas welding outfit may be used to heat the joint so that solder-flow temperature will be reached. Play the torch flame on the pipe, close to the joint, but do not point it directly on the joint. When the joint is hot enough, solder will melt at the tip of the soldering wire and flow into the space between the pipe and the joint. Keep pushing the wire against

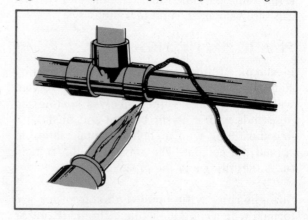

Copper Pipe Joint

the hot joint until a gleam of solder can be seen all around the seam. Since the heat will stay in the joint for a while, wipe away any extra solder with a rag instead of the fingers. After allowing the joint to cool for a few minutes, water may be poured over it to aid in the cooling process. Test the joint by running water through the pipe.

If working with flexible plastic pipe, simply slip a metal joint clamp on the end of it and push the end of the pipe as far as it will go on the fitting. Clamp it securely. Rigid plastic pipe, however, may use threaded fittings or the solvent welding system. When using the solvent welding system, coat the end of the pipe with special plastic cement and push it into the fitting with a slight twisting motion to spread the cement. The solvent in the cement fuses the pipe and the fitting, forming a tight joint. When using this process, be sure the cement is formulated specifically for the type of pipe being used.

Cast-iron pipe joints can be made either vertically or horizontally. Since cast-iron pipe has a larger diameter hub at one end and a slight ridge called a spigot at the other end, the spigot will fit inside the hub with room to spare. After centering the pipe within the hub, wrap the oakum around the pipe loosely and pack it by banging with a yarning iron to within $3/4''$ to $1''$ of the hub. Next, pour molten lead on top of the oakum in the hub with an iron ladle. As soon as the lead has hardened, caulk with a caulking iron by banging the sharp edges into the lead and spreading the chipped lead with the caulking tool. The inside iron of the caulking tool packs lead against the inside pipe, while the outside

Vertical Cast-Iron Pipe Joint

iron packs lead against the hub. Repeat this caulking procedure several times.

To form a horizontal joint, use an instrument called a joint runner, a fat asbestos rope with a clamp, to hold the rope ends together. After the joint has been packed with oakum, wrap the rope around the pipe and clamp. Once the joint is filled, lead will rise into the top part of the clamp which serves as a funnel. As soon as the lead cools, chisel off the bump left from the clamp and caulk as done in the vertical joint.

Horizontal Cast-Iron Pipe Joint

A vitrified pipe joint is made like a cast-iron pipe joint except cement is used instead of molten lead. *SEE ALSO PLUMBING MATERIALS.*

Pipe Leaks

Pipe leaks are easily fixed unless they occur at a badly rusted old fitting that will break if wrench pressure is applied. Unless the worker has ample time to replace pipes in such a case, a plumber should be called. All other leaks can be taken care of simply and easily.

Straight-run pipe leaks are easily fixed with a pipe leak clamp that matches the pipe's diameter. Join the two pieces of the clamp around the pipe so that the rubber lining is over the leak and tighten the screws on its side.

By snugly wrapping rubber electrician's tape around the place of seepage, drain-pipe leaks are repaired simply. Be sure to overlap the edges of the tape.

Cast-iron drainage pipe leaks occurring at the leaded joint are fixed by spreading the lead from the joint around the joint itself. A flattened nail head sharpened at the end to form a flattened end like a chisel can be used to spread lead instead of a caulking tool. Tapping the joint to form small cuts, smooth the lead from the cuts against the pipe joint surfaces. This procedure will stop the leak.

Rusty cold-water pipes that have not yet developed leaks may be given a coating of rust-inhibiting paint to prevent pinhole leaks. *SEE ALSO PLUMBING EMERGENCIES.*

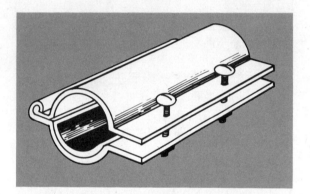

Pipe Leak Clamp With Rubber Lining

Pipe Measuring

Pipe measuring is essential in estimating the amount of piping required for a job. Measure the distance from the mouth of the opening into which the pipe fits to the next point where a fitting will be placed. This is called face-to-face measuring. Having determined this measurement, calculate the distance the pipe goes into all of the fittings and add this distance to the first measurement.

The next step is to figure how much space the fittings add to the pipe length. There are some elbows and bends that are longer than others. This amount is subtracted from the total.

If the handyman does not like to use the above arithmetic method, he can measure from the point at which the pipe connection will begin to the point where a fitting will be located. Placing the fitting at the spot it will be attached to the pipe, measure to the next location. Finally, add on the screw-in distance. Pencil marking the location of the fittings may prove to be a useful means of keeping a more accurate method of counting.

The chart gives screw-in distances and fitting dimensions for the more common water and drain pipe sizes. *SEE ALSO PLUMBING.*

Distance Pipe Is Screwed Into Fitting		
Pipe Size	Standard Fitting	Drainage Fitting
1/2″	1/2″	—
3/4″	1/2″	—
1 ″	5/8″	—
1 1/4″	5/8″	5/8″
1 1/2″	5/8″	5/8″
2 ″	3/4″	5/8″
3 ″	—	7/8″
4 ″	—	1 ″

Pipe Reamer

A pipe reamer removes the burr or rough edge on the inside of a cut pipe. To use this tool, first hold the pipe firmly with a pipe vise or removable pipe jaws. Securely mount the shank of the reamer in the bit brace chuck. Then insert the reamer's point far back into the end of the pipe. Turn the axis clockwise with moderate pressure, keeping it parallel to the pipe. The reaming is

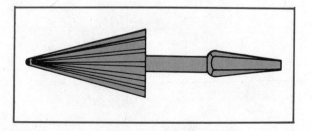

Pipe Reamer

finished when the burr has been removed from the cut pipe's end. If the pipe is to be threaded, the reaming should be done afterwards. *SEE ALSO PLUMBER'S TOOLS & EQUIPMENT.*

Pipe Sizes

Pipe sizes are determined by their diameter. Although most people estimate diameter by the inside of the pipe, correct sizing is determined by the actual outside diameter. Since purchasing is in terms of nominal size, charts list the nominal size as compared to the actual outside diameter. The type of pipe also determines its nominal size. Because different brands of piping

STANDARD CONTINUOUS STEEL PIPE	
Size: Nominal (O.D.)	Outside Diameter
1/8″	.405″
1/4″	.540″
3/8″	.675″
1/2″	.840″
3/4″	1.050″
1″	1.315″
1 1/4″	1.660″
1 1/2″	1.900″
2″	2.375″
2 1/2″	2.875″
3″	3.500″
3 1/2″	4.000″
4″	4.500″

COPPER DRAINAGE TUBE (DWV)	
Nominal Size	Actual Outside Diameter
1 1/4″	1.375″
1 1/2″	1.625″
2 ″	2.125″
3 ″	3.125″
4 ″	4.125″
5 ″	5.125″
6 ″	6.125″

COPPER WATER-SUPPLY TUBE — TYPE L MEDIUM WEIGHT		
NOMINAL DIMENSIONS		
Nominal Size	Outside Diameter	Inside Diameter
1/4″	.375″	.315″
3/8″	.500″	.430″
1/2″	.625″	.545″
5/8″	.750″	.666″
3/4″	.875″	.785″
1″	1.125	1.025″
1 1/4″	1.375″	1.265″
1 1/2″	1.625″	1.505″
2″	2.125″	1.985″

may have variations in the method of sizing, double check that brand's information when size factor is crucial. *SEE ALSO PIPE MEASURING.*

Pipe Threader

A pipe threader is a tool which has a central steel stock on which thread-cutting dies are clamped. Two steel handles extend outwardly. It is used for threading steel and iron pipes.

To operate a pipe threader, the thumb nut holding the cover plate on the stock must first be loosened and the cover plate opened. Put a thread-cutting die, which matches the pipe's size, in the cover plate with the printed side facing the cover. Then tighten the cover plate to hold the die. The opening at the other end of the stock is where the guides that match the pipe diameter's size are set. Slide the proper sized guide onto the pipe end in front of the thread-cutting die. Be sure that the die is straight on the pipe. The tool should be pushed onto the pipe until the end of the die is contacted. Then slowly turn the tool clockwise, pressing firmly on the pipe until there is enough thread to support the tool. At this point, plenty of cutting oil should be applied to the pipe and die. Continue turning the tool half a turn clockwise, then a quarter turn counter-clockwise until the entire thread has been cut. The pipe's end becomes flush with the outside surface once the job is completed.

When working with a pipe threader, be sure to use plenty of cutting oil and a sharp die. The tool may be unscrewed from the pipe by turning it counterclockwise. Clean the metal chips which remain in the die and on the threads of the pipe. *SEE ALSO PLUMBER'S TOOLS & EQUIPMENT.*

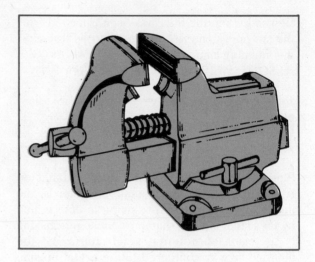

Pipe Vise

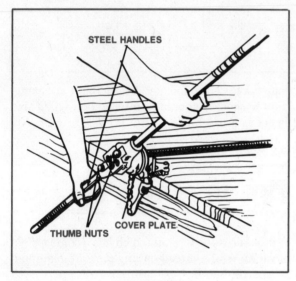

Pipe Threader

Pipe Tools

[SEE PLUMBER'S TOOLS & EQUIPMENT.]

Pipe Vise

A pipe vise or steel vise is a pair of jaws that act as a clamp for pipes. A part of a bench vise, the pipe vise is located under the uppermost portion. Its jagged jaws are in a semi-circular position so that they will firmly grip the pipe. *SEE ALSO HAND TOOLS.*

Piston Pump

A piston pump is a motorized version of an old lift pump, used for shallow wells. The old lift pump is an iron cylinder containing a leather-rimmed piston and a handle for moving the piston up and down. Near the top of the cylinder is a projected spout. A pipe from the bottom of the cylinder goes down into the well water. A foot valve on the lower end of the pipe lets water in and contains it so that the pump doesn't have to be reprimed after filling.

The pump piston is pulled up from the bottom of the cylinder to take water into the pipe. This makes a forced one-way valve in the base of the cylinder. As more water pushes through the foot valve, the water already in the cylinder is lifted up and out of the spout. The water's weight will close the valve at the base of the pump and the foot valve below.

When the pump piston is pushed down again, a one-way valve opens to let water flow upward. When the piston goes all the way to the bottom again, water is let in as it descends. When it starts back up, the valve closes so that the water above the piston is lifted on the upward movement.

The motorized piston pump used today is sealed for pressure build-up in the water tank. Air is contained in the tank to maintain the pressure. It is kept steady by water rising in the tank and compressing the air. The pressure is maintained when the pump is shut off by the pressure switch connected to the pump by a copper tube. Water pressure in the tube increases and pushes a diaphragm in the switch outward until it clicks off. From water usage in the house, the pressure decreases and the diaphragm will flex in the opposite direction until the switch goes on again. *SEE ALSO WELL PUMP SYSTEMS.*

Pitch

Pitch is the degree of incline or slope of roofs, stairs, floors, pipelines or the ground. It may be measured in inches or incline for each foot of run, or by the ratio of the incline to the span.

Pitch of Pipe

The pitch of pipe is the angle at which a pipe is set in a plumbing system. A downward pitch of pipe should be established and maintained in a septic system to help the downflow of sewage. In a water supply system, the sloping pitch of pipe leads to one or more drainage valves. The normal pitch, ranging from 1/8 inch to 1/4 inch, is so small that any little grading variations can disrupt it. For this reason, short pipe sections must be used carefully. *SEE ALSO PLUMBING SYSTEMS.*

Plain-Face Hammer

A plain-face hammer is almost flat, and if not used carefully, will probably leave hammer marks. For this reason, the hammer is preferred for rough work or special kinds of work, such as toenailing in house framing. The flat face of the

Plain-Face Hammer

hammer helps to control the angling of the nail at the beginning. The hammer face also helps to drive the nail up tight easily when striking the last blows near the edge of the nail head. *SEE ALSO HAND TOOLS.*

Plain-Sawed
[SEE LUMBER.]

Plancher

A plancher, also spelled plancier, planch and planche, is the underside of a cornice or eave and usually runs horizontally. *SEE ALSO ROOF CONSTRUCTION.*

Planes

The plane is one of several tools used in smoothing and shaping wood. Smooth and jack planes are considered two of the most standard because of their size and versatility. *SEE ALSO HAND TOOLS.*

Planks

Planks are pieces of sawed timber generally 1¹/₂ to 4¹/₂ inches thick and six or more inches wide. Planks are primarily used in roof construction or as a finish floor, and those used for these purposes will usually be two to four inches wide. Planks should have a tongue-and-groove edge for easy assembling and for providing a strong surface. Be careful in selecting planks where the surfaces will be exposed. Marred faces would make an unattractive floor or ceiling. Plank roofs constructed in cold areas require not only insulation, but a special vapor barrier installed between the insulation and the planks.

Planters

A planter may be the best way for the avid gardener to show off plants. A planter can be placed almost anywhere, inside the house or out. It can edge an sidewalk, patio or driveway. It can also be part of a sun deck or raised patio or hung under a window.

Planters can be as temporary as a window box or as permanent as the planting box that is part of the home frontage. Personal taste and the design of the house will dictate what type of planter to build. Remember that while a planter provides easy access to plants, it also sets up an artificial environment and as a result, plants may suffer more quickly from neglect. Although common topsoil may be right for plants in the garden, it is never adequate in a planter. A planter's soil is limited, it dries quickly and, if watered too much or too often, the nutrients are washed away. Therefore, it must be reinforced with good compost or the equivalent. A good formula is a mixture of grit, such as cinders or sand, leaf mold, peat moss and old, rotted manure added to common top soil. To each bushel of that mixture, add a pint of bone meal, half a pint of 5-10-5 fertilizer and a pint of lime. Try to replace the soil each year. If that is not possible, add the

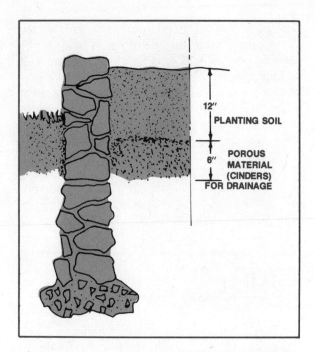

This cross section shows the proper way to plant in a box adjacent to a wall. Notice how the foundation is deep in the ground supporting the heavy natural stone of the planter. Adequate drainage has been provided by the layer of porous material. Cinders are used here to provide the drainage. Be sure to tamp the soil firmly and water well.

last three ingredients to the existing soil before replanting.

Heat can be a problem for planters, especially for the metal ones found in most stores. In the summer, plants can literally bake from the sun and heat reflected off a wall near a window box or off concrete or brick near a patio planter. The trick here is to select heat-resistant plants such as nasturtiums, geraniums, petunias, zinnias or heliotrope. On the other hand, if the planter is in heavy shade, a choice of fushias, begonias, morning glories or wishflowers would be best. Research a little before planting and if direct sun is a problem, turn it into an asset with the right types of flowers.

Winter produces a problem for planters. Since they are not insulated naturally, they have to be protected from freezing temperatures. The best way to avert a hard freeze is to group the movable planters together for the winter and insulate around, between and over with straw. Annuals

Courtesy of the California Redwood Association

A square, tongue and groove planter such as this one has a bit of oriental flavor with the bed of smooth rocks at its base. This planter is designed to hold a small tree as well as smaller plants such as a brilliant cascade of petunias. Designed by Ted Osmundson, ASLA.

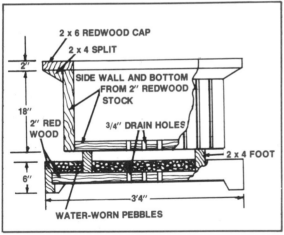

Courtesy of the California Redwood Association

2″ x 6″ clear all heart redwood was used in this planter. The grooves were made with a dado head router three inches apart. Water-smooth pebbles line the bottom for better drainage.

and perennials will usually survive the winter if this is done. After all danger of frost is over, bedding plants such as asters, snapdragons, forget-me-nots and pansies can be planted.

Courtesy of the California Redwood Association

This lovely redwood planter is as serviceable as it is decorative. The sides rise at a 45° angle to regulate drainage and root growth. This would be an interesting project for any homeowner.

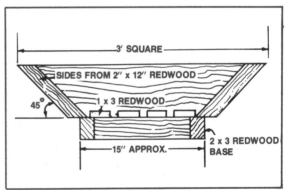

Courtesy of the California Redwood Association

Mitered corners should be the most difficult problem with this design. However, the basic simplicity of design makes this planter designed by William Van Fleet a welcome addition to any patio or entrance-way.

When building a planter, or selecting a prefabricated window box or wooden planter, be sure that adequate drainage has been included. If a planter is being built onto or next to an existing structure, make certain that the footings or foundations are sturdy enough to accommodate the weight of the planter. If it is not adequate, the entire planter may collapse or pull away from the adjoining structure.

Plasterboard

Plasterboard or wallboard is a thin board, framed of plaster and paper layers, used in building walls, ceilings and partitions. Standard plasterboard comes in three thicknesses: $3/8$ inch. $1/2$ inch and $5/8$ inch. The panels come predecorated or ready-to-finish in 4-foot widths and up to 16 feet in length. *SEE ALSO WALL & CEILING CONSTRUCTION.*

Plaster of Paris

Plaster of paris is a white heavy powder which forms a quick-setting paste when mixed with water. The material, which originated in Paris, France, is also known as calcined gypsum. It is used for making casts and molds, for surgical bandages and for building materials such as plasters, tiles, blocks, moldings and stuccowork.

Plaster of paris is one of the least expensive patching materials. It works well for repairing cracks and breaks in plaster walls.

Before mixing plaster of paris for repairs, read the instructions on the powder can carefully to find out how it is best used and the estimated time of its working life. Adding vinegar to the mixing water will extend the working life of plaster of paris.

Judge the amount of material needed for a patch and pour that amount of water in a square pan. Sprinkle powder steadily over the surface until the water has absorbed all it can take. The sprinkling will serve as a gauge to measure the amount of powder needed as it settles. Stir the mixture and scrape it up with a knife. The straight edges of the pan make it easier to scrape. Apply the plaster to the break or crack and smooth over the surface.

Plaster & Plaster Repair

Plaster is made from a combination of cement, sand and lime. Mixed to a consistency of thick paste, it is used to cover walls inside and out. Today plaster is being replaced frequently with large sheets of material called gypsum board. The two materials are similar in appearance.

Plaster is applied like a thin paste over strips of thin wood or sheets of gypsum. It should be allowed to cure for at least two months before it is papered or painted. Longer periods of time for the curing process will be better for the surface.

Cracks may appear on the surface of plaster from time to time. Small ones can be filled with a mixture available at hardware stores called spackling compound. When it dries, it can be sanded down until the surface is smooth. Larger cracks present a different problem. First clean out the crack with a chisel or screwdriver and wipe the surrounding area with a moist cloth to clear away dust and broken particles of plaster.

Fill the crack with casting plaster or plaster of paris. Work quickly or the compound will set up before you have a chance to smooth it into the surface.

If a crack is excessively deep, it must be filled with some material such as newsprint or old scraps of cloth. This reinforcement will readily accept the repair compound and make a tight bond. Remember to clean out every crack and moisten the surrounding area so the compound will adhere to the existing wall.

Plastic Adhesives

Plastics play an important part in many types of adhesives. Polyvinyl acetate is an all-purpose glue designed especially for small jobs involving wood, paper, cardboard, pottery or composition board.

Instead of using nails, butyl rubber phenolic adhesive can be applied to plywood or hardboard wall paneling. This adhesive comes in caulking gun cartridges.

Urea formaldehyde is water-resistant after it has set and is best for wood-to-wood bonding. It is often called *plastic resin,* and in bought as a powder to be mixed with water.

Another plastic adhesive is contact cement, or neoprene phenolic. Its primary use is to secure plastic laminate.

Styrene butadiene adhesive, often called "latex," is best for use on sheet goods, resilient tile or ceramic tile. It can also be used for laying a metal shower door track or installing ceiling tile.

The plastic adhesive recommended for outdoor uses is resorcinol because of its exceptional strength. However, no glue is stonger than epoxy resin adhesive. The components of this glue are mixed together immediately before using. Any combination of porous or non-porous surfaces can be bonded with epoxy resin. *SEE ALSO ADHESIVES.*

Plastic Pipe Fittings

Plastic pipe fittings are available for flexible as well as rigid plastic pipe. A flexible plastic pipe fitting slips on the pipe ends and is then tightened by a joint clamp. A rigid plastic pipe fitting has either threaded fittings or can be solvent welded, a process of coating the pipe end with a plastic cement and fusing the pipe and fitting together by pushing the pipe into the fitting with a slight twisting motion. Among the most common plastic pipe fittings are the tee, coupling, reducer, elbow, steel pipe adapter and a joint clamp.

A tee connects straight run pipe and a branch entering at a right angle. Serving the same purpose of joining straight run pipes, a coupling connects same sized pipe while a reducer joins pipes having different diameters.

The elbow joins two pipes meeting at an angle. The most common elbow for plastic pipe is the 90 degree angle fitting. Joining plastic to steel, the steel pipe adapter is useful when a change in the type of pipe is needed in a plumbing system. Used mainly for flexible plastic pipe, a joint clamp slips on the ends of the pipes and is secured by tightening the clamp. *SEE ALSO PIPE FITTINGS.*

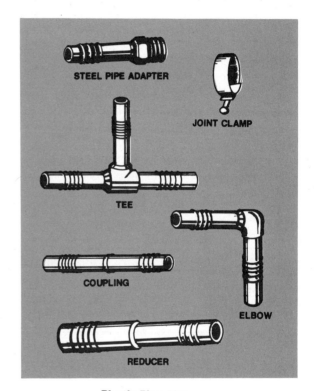

Plastic Pipe Fittings

Plastic Sheet Materials

WORKING WITH ACRYLIC PLASTIC SHEETS

Acrylic plastic sheet is a rigid, resilient material most familiar in its colorless form, but also available in transparent tints, translucent and opaque colors and in a hammered-glass pattern.

Plastic Sheet Materials

The most important properties of acrylic sheet for use in the home and workshop are optical clarity, safety due to its breakage resistance, light weight, chemical resistance, resistance to yellowing, weather and corrosion and ease of cleaning.

Acrylic sheet is made in various formulations including two types of Plexiglas sold in the consumer market, a general purpose material for creative crafts projects and safety glazing, and K, a more economical safety glazing grade. The only significant difference between the two is that the latter type cannot be solvent cemented. Both meet the rigid requirements of the American National Standards Institute, ANSI Z97. 1-1966572 tests for safety glazing materials and are so certified by the Safety Glazing Certification Council. This is important to the homeowner because in states with safety glazing laws or building codes, each pane of glazing installed in hazardous locations such as storm doors, shower and tub enclosures, entrance and exit ways and other areas where glass might be dangerous, must be permanently labeled to show that it meets these tests.

Sizes and Types

It is helpful in planning projects to know in advance what thicknesses and sizes of a material are available. Retailers stock clear Plexiglas K, safety glazing grade in the following sizes and thicknesses:

.080″ Thickness	1/10″ Thickness	1/8″ Thickness	3/16 Thickness
18″ x 24″	18″ x 24″	18″ x 24″	24″ x48″
20″ x 32″	20″ x 32″	24″ x 24″	30″ x 34″
24″ x 48″	24″ x 48″	26″ x 28″	36″ x 48″
26″ x 28″	26″ x 28″	28″ x 30″	
28″ x 30″	28″ x 30″	30″ x 34″	
30″ x 34″	30″ x 34″	36″ x 36″	
30″ x 36″	30″ x 36″	36″ x 38″	
32″ x 40″	32″ x 40″		

The safety glazing and decorative grade, G, is commonly found in 1/8 inch thickness in the same sizes as type K; and in 1/4 inch thickness in 24 x 48 inch, 36 x 36 inch, and 36 x 48 inch sizes. There are more than 40 colors of acrylic sheet available. The material comes in a wide range of transparent, translucent and opaque colors, several solar control tints (smoke tones) and in eight textured-surface patterns. With so many colors made, it is not feasible for a distributor or dealer to stock the complete range of colors as well as various patterns and thicknesses, so it may be necessary to try more than one dealer to obtain a specific combination of color, thickness, size and pattern.

Advantages of Acrylics

Breakage Resistance: A good acrylic-plastic sheet is as much as 17 times more breakage-resistant than glass. Its use reduces the hazard of injury because when it is subjected to blows beyond its resistance it breaks into large, relatively dull-edged pieces which disperse at low velocity due to its light weight.

Transparency: Clear acrylic is as transparent as the finest optical glass. Its total light transmittance is 92 percent.

Weather Resistance: Acrylics withstand exposure to all types of weather. Fifteen-year exposure tests of colorless Plexiglas show negligible loss in light transmission and resistance to discoloration.

Ease of Fabrication: This kind of plastic is a safe and easy material to work with. It can be sawed, drilled and cemented like wood or soft metal. In addition, it can be bent along a straight line by heating with a special tool called a strip heater.

Uses

The following are some home, hobby, shop and general do-it-yourself uses that have been found

for acrylic sheets materials: storm door and window glazing, air conditioner window panels, splash panels, chair rails, push and kick plates for doors, chair mats to protect rugs, lighting diffusers (white translucent), garage door glazing, hanging partitions, cutting boards, table top protectors, room dividers, cabinet sliding doors, cube and other occasional tables, vase and sculpture pedestals, shelves, picture framing, floor protectors for planters, record turntable covers, display cases for art objects and other delicate collectors' items, i.e., model ships, butterflies, etc., cook book stand, game boards, magazine racks, shower doors, floor protectors for kitchens and bathroom, coasters and dining table accessories.

How to Work with Acrylics

Acrylics can be worked much like wood or soft metals following these directions.

Scribing and Breaking (up to $1/4''$ thickness). Using a straight edge as a guide, place the point of the scribing tool at the edge of the material and, applying firm pressure, draw the cutting point the full width of the material five or six times for thicknesses from $1/10''$ to $3/16''$ and seven to ten times for $1/4''$. The scribed line should be positioned face-up over a $3/4''$ diameter wood dowel running the length of the intended break. To break, hold the sheet with one hand and apply downward pressure on the short side of the break with the other. The hands should be kept adjacent to one another and successively repositioned about two inches in back of the break as it progresses along the scribed line. The minimum cut-off width is about $1 1/2''$. Patterned acrylic cannot be scored and broken.

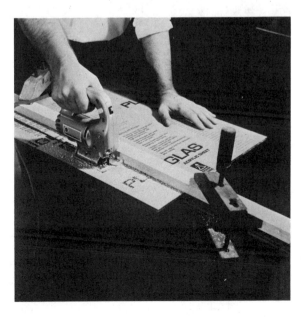

Plastic Sheet Materials

Cutting With Saws. Do *not* remove protective masking paper before cutting. If cutting an unmasked sheet is unavoidable, apply masking tape on both sides of intended cut to reduce friction and gumming behind blade.

With sabre, band and reciprocating jig saws, curved shapes are easily cut. Sabre and reciprocating jigsaws, should have fine-toothed blades (14 teeth per inch for $3/16$ and $1/4$ inch acrylic sheets, and 32 teeth per inch for $1/10$ and $1/8$ inch. Straight cuts can be made with a sabre or hand jigsaw by guiding the tool along a straight edge. Band saws should have at least 10 teeth per inch. Hold plastic down firmly when cutting. Do not force feed. (Follow edge finishing instructions.)

Circular saws are ideal for straight cutting. Use the "Cope RH-600" or "RH-800 Circular Saw Blade for Plexiglas" or a steel cross-cut blade which is recommended for finish cuts on plywood, veneers, laminates, etc. The blade should have at least 6 teeth per inch. All the teeth should be of the same shape, height and point to point distance. Set the blade height just a little above the thickness of the sheet to prevent chipping. Hold the plastic sheet down firmly when cutting. Do not force feed.

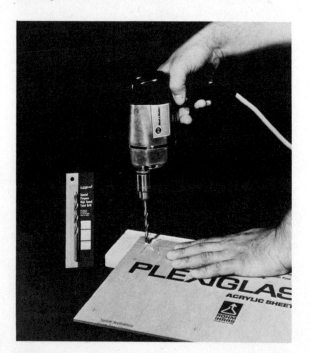

Drilling. When drilling by hand, use standard twist drills commonly used for metals. Back the plastic sheet with wood. Clamp or hold firmly. Use a sharp drill, very slow speed and minimum pressure. If too much speed is used, the plastic sheet will tend to climb the drill. If too much pressure is used, chipping will occur on the back side of the hole. Specially ground drills (Hanson Special Purpose Drills for Plexiglas) are required when using power equipment to drill acrylics. Tighten drill securely in chuck. Back the plastic with soft wood and clamp or hold it firmly and use highest speed available up to 3000 rpm. When drilling holes $3/8$ inch or larger, slower drill speed (1000-2000 rpm) will improve the quality. Do not force feed. Slow feed as the drill point penetrates second surface.

Edge finishing. There are three stages to edge finishing: smooth finish, satin finish and transparent finish. For a smooth finish sawed edges and other tool marks should be removed to insure maximum breakage resistance. Rounding corners and smoothing out uneven cuts can be accomplished by filing with medium- to fine-toothed metal files. File, saw and other tool marks are easily removed by scraping the edge with a sharpened piece of metal such as the *back* of a hacksaw blade or by sanding with medium grit (60-80) production paper.

For a satin finish, to further improve the appearance of the edge and prepare it for cementing, sand it with increasingly finer grits (150-320) of wet-or-dry paper. Take care not to round edge sides as this will result in bubbles in the cemented joint.

For a transparent high gloss edge, continue sanding with finer grits (400-500) of wet-or-dry paper and then buff the edge, using clean muslin wheel dressed with a good grade of fine-grit buffing compound (the Dico buffing kit is recommended).

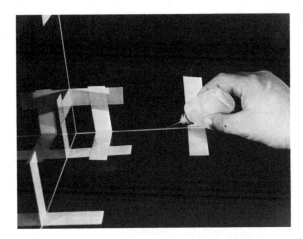

Cementing. Capillary cementing with a solvent is an easy method of joining two pieces of acrylic sheet. The K, or glazing grade, cannot be cemented with these solvents. Finish edges to be cemented to a satin finish stage, and do not polish. Remove the protective masking paper and hold pieces together with strips of masking tape. Apply the solvent to the joint with a solvent applicator keeping the cement joint horizontal. Let joint dry thoroughly.

Caution: Solvents may be toxic if inhaled for extended periods of time or if swallowed; many are also flammable. Use in a well-ventilated area. Keep them away from children.

Thickened solvent cements produce high-strength joints with good outdoor weather-ability on both general purpose and K glazing grade acrylics. Finish the edges to the satin finish stages and do not polish. Remove the protective masking paper and check for good fit of parts. Apply a small bead of cement to joint. Gently join pieces being cemented and clamp or hold firmly until set. Let joint cure thoroughly for about two hours.

Caution: Thickened cements also contain solvents which may be toxic if inhaled for extended periods of time or if swallowed and are flammable. Use in a well-ventilated area, away from children.

Thickened cements are also good for use in mending and filling-in scratches. Several applications may be required to fill a scratch. Allow 24 hours drying time between applications. Sand with very fine wet-or-dry paper and buff to transparency as in edge finishing.

Readily available contact cements and adhesives such as those used to adhere floor tile and counter tops, silicones and some household cements can be used to produce non-transparent joints between acrylic sheets or between acrylics and wood panels. These joints can be covered with decorative, pressure sensitive tapes including cellophane, vinyl, plastic coated cloths and other plastic tapes to provide an eye appealing finish to the final assembly.

Strip heat forming. An acrylic sheet may be formed along a straight line by strip heating. To strip-heat-bend acrylic plastic, remove the protective masking paper. Mark a line on the Plexiglas where you want to bend with a Blaisdell china marker, and place plastic sheet on the heater with the line to be bent centered over the heating element. Allow the material to heat until it softens or wilts in the area to be formed (about 5 or 6 minutes for $1/8$ inch material and 12 to 15 minutes for $1/4$ inch). Bend gently to the desired angle, keeping the heated side of the material on

the *outside* of bend and holding it firmly until cool.

Bending material before it is thoroughly heated will result in stress crazing (small internal fractures) along the bend. Overheating may cause scorching and bubbling; if this occurs, check to be sure that the distance between the heating element and the sheet is approximately 1/8 inch. Practice on scrap material first. Plastic in thicknesses greater than 1/4 inch requires a commercial strip heater for bending.

For safety: Do not leave strip heater unattended. Work in a well-ventilated area. Have a general purpose ABC rated (dry powder) fire extinguisher nearby. Do not heat acrylic plastic with an open flame or in kitchen ovens; such ovens are not equipped with adequate temperature controls and safety devices for this type of work. Heating Plexiglas in an oven produces monomer bleed-off. These gases are combustible, and if ignited, can cause severe explosions. Kitchen ovens and other heating devices, which do not circulate air to prevent accumulation of these gases, and which are not equipped with proper temperature controls and safety devices for this type of work, should not be used.

Decorating. For painting acrylics, you can use lacquers, enamels and oil-based paints, when no outdoor exposure is anticipated. If outdoor use is a factor, acrylic-based lacquers will provide the best adhesion and resistance to weather. Water-based or latex paints have relatively poor adhesion and difficult spreading characteristics when used with acrylic sheet.

Spray painting will provide the most uniform distribution of coating. Brush coating generally tends to produce a fine pattern of brush hair strokes on the finished product. Allow longer drying times than applicable when painting porous surfaces such as wood.

Decorative effects can be obtained by applying papers, cloth, foils, etc., which have pressure-sensitive adhesive backings. These are used to create artistic and decorative effects in partitions, doors and window glazing. Papers, cloth and foils without pressure-sensitive adhesive backings can be applied with either spray-on adhesives applied to both surfaces or with clear lacquer sprayed on the plastic.

Any sharp pointed instrument can be used to scribe designs in the surfaces of acrylics. Working on both surfaces of the transparent plastic produces interesting three-dimensional effects. Acrylic can be grooved on a table saw, textured by a variety of machine tools and sanded by hand or machine to provide selective matte and polished surfaces.

How to Clean Acrylics

Always damp-dust acrylic sheet. For best results, mix a solution of one teaspoon of dishwashing liquid, or other mild soap or detergent and water. Apply this solution with an atomizer or spray bottle and wipe until dry and glossy smooth with a clean cotton flannel jersey cloth.

Wash with a mild soap or detergent and lukewarm water solution. Use a clean soft cloth or sponge and as much solution as possible. Rinse well and dry by blotting with a damp cloth or chamois. Do not use window-cleaning fluids, scouring compounds, gritty cloths, leaded or ethyl gasolines or strong solvents such as alcohol, acetone, carbon tetrachloride on acrylics. To remove tar, grease, or paint, use a good grade of naphtha or kerosene.

Polish acrylic with special polish for Plexiglas, following instructions on package. A periodic waxing with a good grade of automobile paste wax (not a cleaner-wax combination) will protect the surface and maintain its beautiful lustre.

Apply a thin coating of wax with a soft clean cloth. Buff lightly with a clean cotton flannel or jersey cloth. After waxing, wipe with a clean damp cloth to remove static charges which may attract dust particles. Do not use household spray waxes as many of these contain agents harmful to acrylic surfaces.

Like wood or silver, acrylic plastic can be scratched. But unlike the situation with most other materials, a scratch on the surface of an acrylic sheet can be removed. Minor surface scratches can be made to vanish by sanding out with 400-600 grit wet-or-dry sandpaper and buffing with a clean muslin wheel dressed with a good grade of fine-grit buffing compound.

FIBERGLASS REINFORCED PLASTIC

Translucent fiberglass-reinforced plastic panels are now so varied in color and contour, so adaptable to home-improvement tasks, that they are no longer to be thought of, as in the past, as just patio roofing material. Although corrugated types remain the most common, they are now varied with corrugations having squared-off tops and bottoms. There are shapes with ribs and V-crimps in the manner of the corrugated metal they are designed to match. The flat sheets make attractive oriental looking walls, fences and lighting devices.

Translucent FRP (fiberglass-reinforced plastic) has improved greatly in the quarter-century since the first came on the market. Covering patios is, by far, the primary home of the FRP panels, with such similar applications as awnings, porch roofs and carports also included. Other home uses include fences, walls, partitions, dividers, luminous ceilings, skylights and sliding doors (the last few named using flat sheets of FRP rather than the corrugated or shaped variety).

HOW TO STAY COOL WITH FIBERGLASS PLASTIC

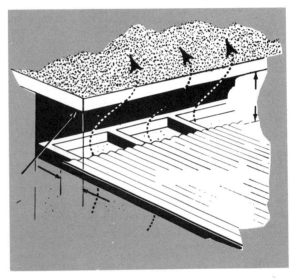

A plastic roof can produce an oven if it's built to catch the sun's heat and trap the air. If height permits, set plastic roof below existing roofline and set the panels to end several inches from the wall.

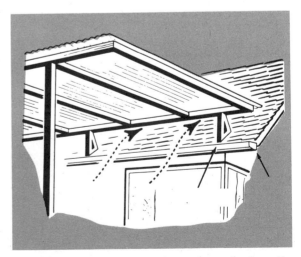

If existing roof is too low to drop your plastic patio roof below it, set it above and leave a ventilating opening.

Courtesy of Filon-Visitron, Corp.

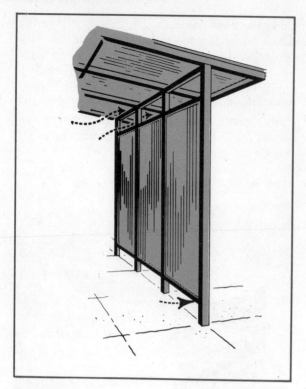

Ventilate vertical walls by providing openings at top and bottom. Top openings along one side and bottom ones along the other are often enough.

Another way to provide heat escape is with plastic roof panels alternated above and below framing. Overlap them 3 or 4 inches to catch rain.

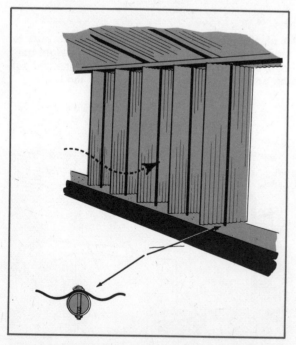

For maximum privacy with minimum interference with breezes, build louvers. They can be fixed or, for flexibility in use, mounted on pipes.

If your design for patio or porch roof or awning calls for side valances, leave ventilating openings like this.

Another major use of FRP panels in the home is in manufactured, translucent garage doors, that come in sections that move up and down on a track. The advantages of FRP in garage doors are both its light-admitting property and its light weight.

Is FRP Right For The Job?

All the various properties of fiberglass-plastic panels enter into the key question facing the do-it-yourselfer: whether to use it for a particular project and, if so, which kind to select from the vast variety shown in manufacturers' catalogs. If built-in color, light transmission and ease of construction and handling are important to the project, or could add something to it that you had not thought about before, then you should consider FRP. However it is better to use wood or metal if seeking a Colonial or rustic style house. Also use metal or regular roofing if you are planning a patio or porch roof in a mountain fire district. Building codes usually require noncombustible materials in such areas. The same holds true if you are planning to fully enclose a patio or porch. Code officials consider that to be an addition to the dwelling area, making the roof subject to the same regulations that apply to the house roof.

Some other factors enter into the FRP panel decision. Because it's rot-proof and virtually vermin-proof, fiberglass-plastic can be installed in the earth, or in constant contact with it, and no preservatives are needed. So an FRP panel fence, for instance, can be both simpler to erect and will not cut off light from plantings on either side, while offering privacy to both sides of the plot line.

Finally, one other aspect to consider, with both advantages and drawbacks, is that in overhead applications (patio roofs, awnings, skylights) the same light-admitting feature that is FRP's greatest attraction also produces a need to keep the panels cleaner than you would with completely opaque materials. Accumulations of dirt, dead leaves, etc., will show up as unsightly shadows below and, even more important, can hasten the day when the panels will need refinishing with a clear acrylic liquid. On the other hand, keeping the panels relatively clean is simply a matter of rinsing with a garden hose a few times a year.

Choosing the Right Panel

Next you will have to decide which kind of panel. You'll have to make choices in three areas: shape, weight and color.

Shape. There are three types: flat sheets, corrugated panels and rib-shaped. Flat sheets of equal weight are as strong as the other two but much more flexible and not as easy to use if your installation must be watertight. They are more suited, therefore, to vertical uses (fences, partitions, dividers or sliding doors) where they are not called upon to span more than 18 to 24 inches in width or height. The choice between the corrugated shape and the crisper, angular ribbed shape is mainly one of personal preference.

While most FRP panel manufacturers offer a large variety of colors, patterns, shapes, weights and special-purpose formulations, most lumberyards and home centers carry only a few variations in stock. However, any dealer can special-order a particular product from a manufacturer's brochure or catalog. If you plan ahead and order material well in advance, it will be available when you want it.

Weight. This is expressed in ounces per square foot of panel. For residential construction, this is usually four or five ounces per square foot, although dealers in heavy snow areas also stock six ounce and eight ounce panels. Very low priced panels that are called four ounce weight may actually be as much as 20 to 25 percent lighter and are not recommended for load bearing applications.

To decide which weight is best consider how you will be using the panels and how much support structure will be necessary. On a typical patio roof, for instance, a five-ounce panel (corrugated or ribbed) needs purlins spaced three feet on center. A six-ounce panel will cost about twenty per cent more, but its purlin requirements are four feet on center for the same load-bearing capacity. In terms of cost, then, it is even. A good compromise is the five-ounce panel, as it is offered in the widest choice of shapes, colors and patterns.

Colors and patterns. You have a selection far more varied than the white, green or yellow you will find in most retail stocks. Most retailers stock or can get the new patterns such as the one called *Filon-Stripes*. This pattern, based on a white background, has bold passes of earth tones or brighter "sun and sky" colors for contrast. In the same ribbed shape as Filon-Stripes is a type called *Sunguard*. As the name implies, the background colors are much deeper, to reduce the transmission of solar energy and the striping is merely accent bars of black. In the traditional curved currugation, there is a choice of sun yellow and orange stripes on white, or parrot green and crystal blue on the same white background.

Besides personal choice, the matter of color is directly related to personal comfort or discomfort under a patio or porch roof made with FRP panels.

The color of the panel will change the color of light coming through and the *density* of pigment will determine the transmission of heat. So, while dark green might be a cool looking color, a panel in that shade can be made with relatively little pigment, meaning that a great deal of solar energy will pass through. This is probably the reason why white is by far the most popular color of FRP panels. It transmits a good deal of light, and the density of pigment required for white panel virtually assures a comfortable level of solar energy transmission.

Sizes. For residential construction, sizes are standardized. Both the corrugated and ribbed shapes are available in 26 inch widths, in lengths of 8, 10 and 12 feet. The standard width allows placement on rafters spaced 24 inches o.c., with a 2 inch overlap. Longer lengths can be special-ordered, up to about 39 feet, but delivery times may be delayed.

How to Build with FRP

Building with FRP panels is relatively simple as it does not require special tools. Any ordinary saw (hand, sabre, circular) will cut the panels, although a fine-tooth blade or an abrasive disc on a power saw is best. Fastening the panels is best accomplished by aluminum screw-type nails in outdoor installations. Manufacturers recommend pre-drilling with a 5/16 inch bit. This helps avoid tiny cracks around the nail hole that could lead to leakage.

Most of the knacks involved in building with FRP panels revolve around the fact that the panels are shaped, rather than flat. Here are some of the main things to bear in mind:

Understructure. The understructure must be planned to accommodate available sizes and the load-bearing capacity of the panels you will be using. Rafters (in overhead installations) or studs (in vertical projects) should be spaced 24 inches o.c. for 26 inch wide corrugated or ribbed panels. While the panels derive their rigidity from the supporting members that run across the corrugations or ribs (purlins or grits), the rafter or stud spacing provides overall structural integrity, while also serving to hide the panel lap-joint. As noted above, spacing of cross-supports depends on the panel weight per square foot, but there is another factor, too: the depth of the panel's shape. In the case of panels sold for residential use, these spacings are recommended for purlins: for economy grades, 24 inches to 28 inches; for true four ounce weights, 30 inches; or five ounce, 36 inches; for six and eight ounce weights, 48 inches. In vertical installations, grit spacing may be increased about 20 to 25 percent.

Fastening. As noted, it is best to pre-drill nail holes and to use the aluminum twist-shank nails sold for use with FRP panels; they will not corrode or leave stains on the panels and they are equipped with neoprene washers under the heads to fill in the nail holes. To avoid water leaks, always fasten in the *crowns* of corrugations or ribs, as valley-fastening produces nail holes in the very channels that carry run-off. It also invites cracking from misdirected hammer blows.

If your framework is metal rather than wood, you can use self-tapping screws with built-in metal and neoprene washers, designed for use with thin materials such as FRP panels. Too, there are expansion-type fasteners available for instances where panels must be fastened together without any understructure to fasten into. These are machine screws with a neoprene sleeve that holds a nut at the end. Drill a hole through the overlapped panels, push the assembly through the hole and, as you tighten the screw (a slotted hex-head), the nut draws the neoprene sleeve up to form a weather tight washer. The sleeve holds the nut, too, making it a one-person operation.

Because the holding area of a nail-head or screw-head is limited, FRP panel manufacturers suggest using a metal-plated neoprene washer under the fastener head, especially in highwind situations. The neoprene keeps the metal part of the washer from cutting into the panel and the metal provides the necessary bearing strength.

Filler Strips. Cost-conscious homeowners often try to get by without these thin redwood strips, sometimes called *wiggle molding* after their corrugated shape. (They are also available in a shape to fit the ribbed panels.) Omitting these accessories may be a mistake, as their chief function is to provide a solid fastening surface, especially needed because nails or screws are driven into the *crown* of the corrugations or ribs. Without the filler strips, you could overdrive the fasteners, distorting the panels, or else not fasten snugly enough, allowing the panels to rattle. Because the filler strips have a slight thickness, they raise the panels that much above the framework. So you will need filler strips atop all your rafters, headers, and purlins. (On purlins and headers, use the corrugated or ribbed strips that match the FRP panel shape.) Use a panel to make sure the strips (available in six foot or eight foot lengths) are properly aligned before tacking them down with finishing nails. Vertical filler strips, half round molding for corrugated panels, square for the ribbed shape, go atop the rafters. These can be cut to fit between the horizontal rows of the shaped moldings. They are also sold in six or eight foot lengths.

Sealing. A good-quality FRP panel will be uniform in both thickness and shape, allowing for a tight overlap between adjoining panels. Because water can creep into even the tightest lap through capillary action, you will need to seal or caulk the joints between panels. The sealant should be non-drying and should remain flexible; otherwise, the normal expansion and contraction of the panels would break the seal. It should be clear, too, since a dark sealant would show up between translucent panels. The butyrate-type sealants sold by FRP panel firms

meet these requirements, as do the more costly silicone sealants. Both are available in standard-size caulking cartridges.

Working Safely

Basic safety considerations to be aware of are use 1 x 12 boards when standing or kneeling on a patio roof while nailing. A panel, when supported as suggested above, will carry about 100 pounds per square foot. A 180 pound man, standing with his feet together, will exert almost double that load. The board will spread the load.

It should be kept in mind that FRP panels will burn at about the same rate as wood of similar thickness. It takes a direct flame to ignite FRP panels (a lighted cigarette or a small ember will not do it) but, once lit, they will burn rapidly. Just as with wood, you should not start a roaring fire in a barbeque if the flames could come near the patio roof or the fence. If you are planning to cut a hole in an FRP panel roof to permit passage of a metal chimney stack, use insulation between the metal and the panels. The stack should, of course, be equipped with a good spark arrester.

Well-known brands conform to standards published by the National Bureau of Standards, but compliance is voluntary, rather than mandatory. A very low price may indicate that the batch of panels being offered has nothing more wrong than visual blemishes that will not affect structural strength, but the panels may have been manufactured with little or no regard for durability. Since a homeowner cannot perform the elaborate tests required to determine panel quality, he should check the following: does each panel carry a label, giving at least the manufacturer's name and address? Does the label state the weight per square foot? Does it note conformance with the government's product standard? Does the dealer have instruction brochures from the same manufacturer?

Refinishing FRP Panels

After several years, FRP panels will begin to lose their characteristic glossiness, a sign that the panels need refinishing right away. At this point, hose down the panels thoroughly, let them dry, then apply a coat of panel refinisher by either brushing or spraying. The refinisher is a clear acrylic liquid, usually available from dealers who sell the panels. It will last for about one to three years, depending on climate.

If the panels are not refinished the exposed surface will start to get fuzzy as the reinforcing glass fibers near the surface become exposed; then they will trap dirt and fungus which cannot be hosed off. You will have to scrape off the exposed fibers and matted dirt with 0-grade steel wool, (using a 1 x 12 board to support your weight). You can fashion a "brush" out of one of the redwood filler strips saved from the construction job; simply staple pads of steel wool to the corrugations or ribs and rub down the panels to cover a lot more area with the same amount of effort. After the dirt and exposed fibers are off, you will find you have just about restored the original color. A coat or two of resurfacing liquid will seal the panel surface, completing the restoration job.

Plastic Tubing

Plastic tubing, designed to make drainage work easier, is light-weight, highly resistant to corrosive elements, low in cost and easy to assemble. Since few types of plastic tubing can stand hot-water temperatures, they are ideal in cold-water systems. Though not used extensively in household systems, plastic tubing is widely used in industry.

There are two types of plastic tubing. Flexible plastic tubing, a polyethylene, is very easy to work with. Because it is light-weight, flexible and available in coils up to 1000 feet, flexible plastic tubing is excellent for use in wells. Flexible plastic tubing joints are formed by slipping a metal joint clamp on the end of the pipe, pushing the pipe as far as it will go on the fitting and tightening the clamp.

Rigid plastic pipe is another type of plastic tube. Sold in lengths, it has been approved by some state and local codes for waste-system plumbing. Rigid plastic tubing joints are made to be used

with threaded fittings or connected by solvent welding systems. The solvent welding system involves applying a special plastic cement to the tubing and pushing this tube into the fitting with a twisting motion. The solvent will fuse the pipe and the fittings. SEE ALSO PLUMBING MATERIALS.

Plastic Wood

Plastic wood is a fast-drying wood filler available in wood grain colors and clear. It shrinks slightly and is not always suitable for shallow holes but can be built up in layers in deep holes letting one layer dry before adding a new one. Plastic wood adheres easily to rough surfaces and can be applied with putty knives, scrapers, chisels or fingers. Plastic wood does not stain easily so it is best to stain the surface first, then use pre-colored plastic wood or plastic wood mixed with stain to fill in the hole and, if needed, stain again.

Plate

A plate is the horizontal member at the top or bottom of a frame wall, A top plate supports rafters; a sole plate joins walls and floors. The top plate is supported by the wall studs. It serves as a link between the wall and the roof

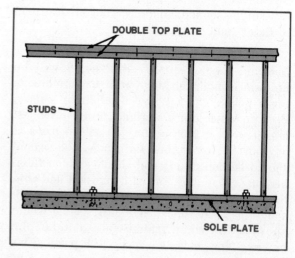

and forms a finish for the wall. The plate is made up of one or two planks that are the same size as the studs. A sole plate is a piece of timber laid horizontally on the floor joists to support the bottom end of the partition wall studs and the outside wall studs. The sole plate is made up of a 2 x 4 plank or a board of the same thickness as the wall. *SEE ALSO WALL & CEILING CONSTRUCTION.*

Platform Framing

Platform framing is a type of floor framing which is generally used in residential construction in both one-story and multi-story houses. The first floor rests like a platform on the foundation walls, and in multi-story structures the other floors, which are framed separately, rest on the lower floor wall sections and partitions, which are built again for each floor. The solid platform automatically provides firestopping, and the fire stops built into the second floor prevent the horizontal spread of fire and act as a bridge to hold the joists plumb. *SEE ALSO WALL & CEILING CONSTRUCTION.*

Playhouse

In about six hours and for a surprisingly low cost, you can build this deluxe, two-story playhouse for your children.

MATERIALS LIST
1 panel $\frac{1}{2}$" x 4' x 8' EXT-DFPA-AA or AB Plywood
4 panels $\frac{1}{2}$" x 4' x 6' EXT-DFPA-AA or AB Plywood
1 piece $\frac{3}{4}$" x 4' x 4' EXT-DFPA-AA or A Plywood
8 pieces 2" x 3" x 8' V.G. Fir
6 pieces 2" x 2" x 8' V.G. Fir
6 linear feet of 1" dowel
$\frac{1}{2}$ pound 8d galvanized Box Nails
$\frac{1}{4}$ pound 4d galvanized Box Nails
60-1$\frac{1}{2}$" wood screws
1$\frac{1}{2}$ gallons of paint
2 pieces of galvanized 24 gauge Flashing

CONSTRUCTION INSTRUCTIONS

1. Following the cutting diagram and parts schedule, lay out plywood parts to size on panels. Make allowance for saw kerfs between adjacent parts.

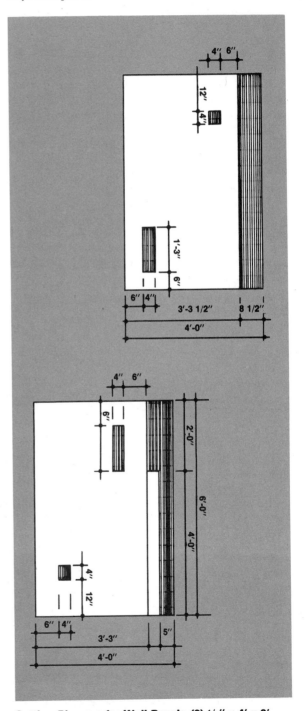

Cutting Diagram for Wall Panels (2) $\frac{1}{2}$" x 4' x 8'

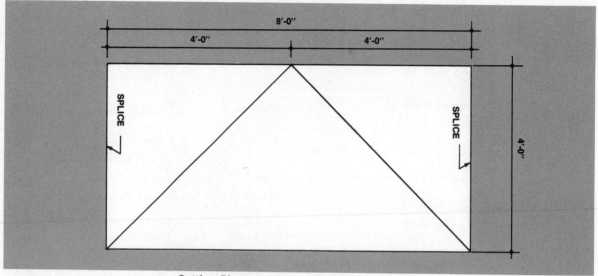

Cutting Diagram for Roof Panels 1/2″ x 4′ x 4′

2. Precut 2-inch by 3-inch studs and predrill tops of vertical members to receive 1-inch round dowel stock.

3. Put dowels in place and secure with waterproof glue.

4. Construct wall frames according to plan.

5. Attach plywood wall panels to frames with 4d nails spaced 4 inches on center.

6. Raise wall panels into position and attach at overlapping corners with 1½-inch wood screws spaced 4 inches on center.

7. Position notched attic floor to bear on horizontal 2-inch by 3-inch middle wall member and secure with 1½-inch wood screws, 6 inches on center.

Plan

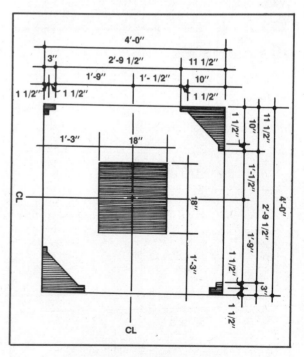

Cutting Diagram for Attic Floor

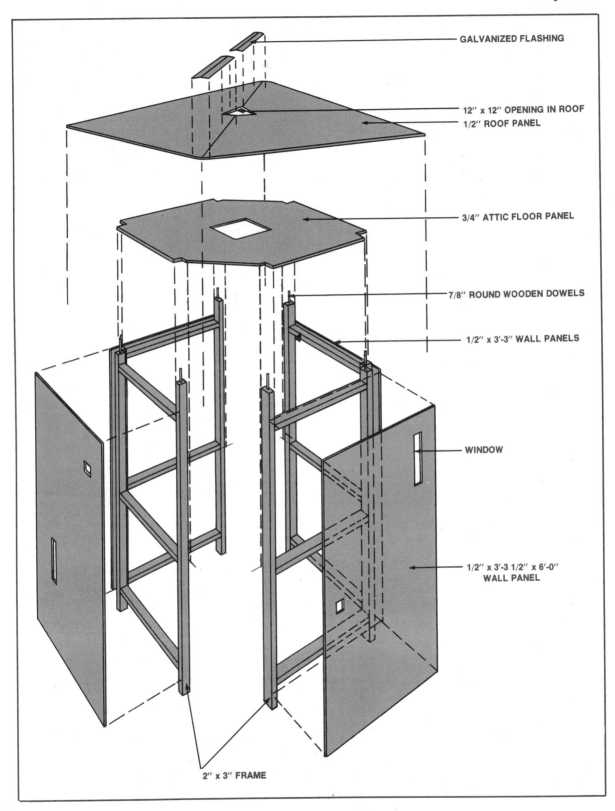

GALVANIZED FLASHING

12" x 12" OPENING IN ROOF
1/2" ROOF PANEL

3/4" ATTIC FLOOR PANEL

7/8" ROUND WOODEN DOWELS

1/2" x 3'-3" WALL PANELS

WINDOW

1/2" x 3'-3 1/2" x 6'-0"
WALL PANEL

2" x 3" FRAME

Exploded Construction View

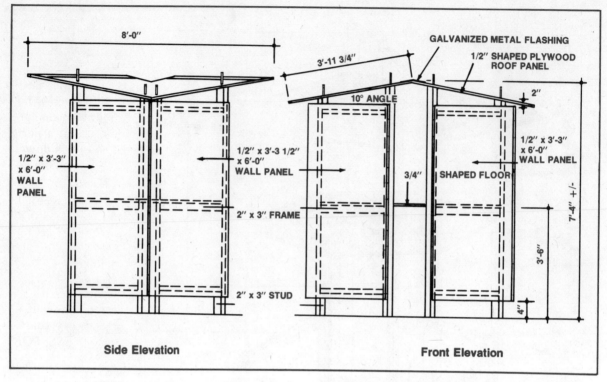

8'-0''

GALVANIZED METAL FLASHING

1/2'' SHAPED PLYWOOD ROOF PANEL

3'-11 3/4''

10° ANGLE

2''

1/2'' x 3'-3'' x 6'-0'' WALL PANEL

1/2'' x 3'-3 1/2'' x 6'-0'' WALL PANEL

1/2'' x 3'-3'' x 6'-0'' WALL PANEL

3/4''

SHAPED FLOOR

2'' x 3'' FRAME

7'-4'' +/-

3'-6''

2'' x 3'' STUD

4''

Side Elevation

Front Elevation

8. Place predrilled roof panel in position.

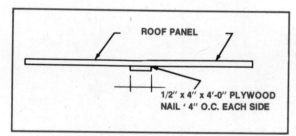

ROOF PANEL

1/2'' x 4'' x 4'-0'' PLYWOOD
NAIL ' 4'' O.C. EACH SIDE

Splice Detail

9. Attach galvanized metal ridge flashing with galvanized roofing nails.

10. Using a rasp, plane and 1-0 sandpaper, round off sharp corners and ease all edges. Fill all exposed plywood edges and nail or screw holes with paste wood filler and sand with 3-0 sandpaper.

11. Then, give your playhouse a coat of exterior house paint undercoat. Follow with at least two coats of quality house paint. For glossy finish, use exterior sash and trim enamel.

Courtesy of Western Wood Products Association.

Pliers & Cutters

Pliers and cutters are used for cutting practically anything from bolts to wire. Needlenose, slip-joint and combination pliers, bolt cutters, nippers and scissors are some used in both wood and metalwork. *SEE ALSO HAND TOOLS.*

Plier Wrench

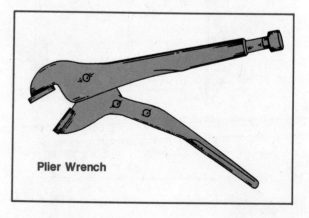

Plier Wrench

A plier wrench is a combination of a plier, a wrench and a vise. Also known as the vise grip or the locking-plier wrench, its main use is loosening rusted nuts and studs that have flat or rounded surfaces. The plier wrench is also used as a clamping tool and vise. With a squeeze, the wrench is locked into position, while a light touch of the finger releases the lock. *SEE ALSO HAND TOOLS.*

Plow Plane

The plow plane, instead of smoothing the surface, cuts a slot or groove. While the depth and path of the cut are controlled by a depth gauge and adjustable fence, the width depends on the width of the cutter used. Usually this type of grooving plane is furnished with seven cutters, ranging in width from 1/8'' to 3/8''. Useful in sash and cabinet work, it can be compared to a very narrow plane that moves in a fixed path along the wood surface. *SEE ALSO HAND TOOLS.*

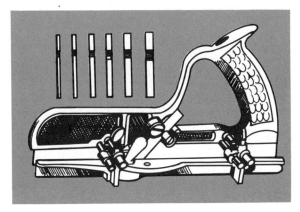

Plow Plane

Plug

A plug is a galvanized steel pipe fitting. Having a threaded end, a plug screws into a turn or pipe end. It can end a length of pipe or unnecessary inlet of a fitting. In addition, this fitting, like a cleanout plug, can allow easy access into a pipe. *SEE ALSO PIPE FITTINGS.*

Plug Cutter

A plug cutter is a tool which cuts small pieces of dowel for plugging in counterbored screw holes or plugging in joints. Wood with the same grain can be used for cutting plugs so that a perfect match is made, instead of purchasing a dowel at a hardware store which may not match the grain as well.

A plug cutter may also be used in a drill press to make dowels. However, this limits the length of the dowel to two inches (which is long enough for dowel joints). Scraps of lumber may be used as stock.

Besides making wooden plugs and dowels, the plug cutter can also make tenons of square or round stock. *SEE ALSO DRILL PRESS; PORTABLE POWER TOOLS.*

Plugs & Cords

PLUGS

Electrical plugs are available in many different styles, depending on their use. Molded plugs are made as an intregal part of the wire from the appliance, and are molded to the cord. Another more conventional type of plug is attached to the cord with terminal screws. Some plugs are designed to facilitate frequent appliance changes at one outlet. Still others are decoratively designed to allow the cord to run out of the plug close to the wall, making both almost invisible in living areas where they may be unsightly.

Replacing Terminal Screw Plugs

Always before replacing a malfunctioning terminal screw plug, first be sure that the terminal screws are tightened. It may be that the wires are not making good contact with the screws, and tightening the screws may improve the flow of electricity through the plug. However, if there is any sign of fissure in the plug itself, replacement is as easy as it is necessary for both the standard two-prong and the three-prong grounded plugs. This type of plug will often have a protective cover which must first be removed. Then, after carefully loosening the wires from the terminal screws and removing the useless plug, pull the wires through the new plug. If an *Underwriters' Knot* is to be used to reduce strain on the wires, be sure to pull enough wire through for it. The Underwriters' Knot prevents wires from slipping off the terminal screws when the cord, rather than the plug, is pulled. Be sure and tie the wires securely. If there is not room for an Underwriters' Knot, a small wrapping of electrical tape will serve the same purpose.

After pulling the wires down into the recess between the prongs, give the fine wires a firm twist before attaching them to the terminal screws in the direction that the screws turn. Tighten the screws securely. Also, snip off any loose strands that might short across the plug, causing dangerous sparks or blowing a fuse. Replace the protective cover, if there is one.

Follow the same removal process for a three-prong grounded plug. With this type of plug, all three wires are looped together for the Underwriters' Knot when plug space allows for it. After looping the wires and tightening the terminal screws, be sure to tighten the outside screws that secure the cord to the plug. Be sure that the protective cover is replaced.

Replacing Molded Plugs

When a two-wire molded plug fails, it must be cut off and replaced with either another molded plug cut from another cord, or a plug with terminal screws. Replacing a molded plug requires baring the wires. When doing this, separate the two wires very carefully with a single-edged razor blade or a trimming knife, taking care not to disturb the individual insulation of the wires in the cord. The penknife is probably safer to use, as a razor blade might cut some of the fine strands of wire. Be sure that the new plug is suited to the receptacle where it will be most used. For instance, if old wiring has been replaced with raceway, the duplex outlets are very close together and would require a slim plug. The slim plug may be the type that requires no

stripping, which makes them one of the easiest for the amateur to use in replacement jobs, and no tools. Simply open the locking lever on the plug and insert the unstripped wires. Then, close the lever firmly so that the prongs in the plug make good contact, and the new plug is ready to use.

Circuit Breaker Plugs

A *circuit-breaker plug* fits in an outlet and accepts plugs from tools or appliance cords. If an overload occurs, a button pops up and the tool or appliance is automatically disconnected. A *circuit-breaker cord plug* can be used to replace an ordinary plug on an appliance cord. It automatically disconnects the appliance or tool in case of an overload, and is reset by a lever. A *polarized circuit-breaker* does the same job as the others, but it is designed for tools and appliances with three-pronged grounded plugs. It is also reset by a lever or button.

Other Plugs & Plug-Ins

Other types of plugs and plug-ins include series-wired and multi-outlet plugs, night light and standard bulb plugs. The series-wired plug adapts an outlet so that two lamp cords draw power from the outlet, using less current. Multi-outlet plugs connect three lamp plugs into one outlet. The bulb adapter plugs allow the use of a bulb wherever there is an outlet.

CORDS

Since cords are such a regular and important part of living with electricity, various types are available for household use in operating appliances, lighting fixtures, etc., and are classified according to how they are used and constructed. The cord that comes attached to appliances is the power supply cord. When the appliance is not close enough to plug it directly into an outlet, an extension cord set may be used to give quick and easy reach to an appliance. Some appliances require cords that are specially insulated to withstand heat, while others that are connected and disconnected frequently require a flexible type.

In all cord, each conductor is made up of many strands of fine wire to provide flexibility. A cotton covering over the twisted strands retains full flexibility by keeping the insulation from bonding directly to the strands. The type of insulation and its thickness varies according to how the cord is to be used. Very old cords and those that have been subjected to considerable heat near radiators and hot-air ducts should be checked frequently for signs of cracking. If cracks are present, flexing may crumble away the insulation, leaving bare sections of wire and a serious hazard. The only remedy is replacement.

In any case, whether replacing or extending a power supply cord, the cord must meet the requirements of the appliance it is to be used with.

Underwriters' Cord Type SPT

The simplest and most common type of cord is lamp cord, which consists of two stranded copper wires covered by rubber or plastic insulation. These are commonly used for lamps, radios and other small appliances and are usually available in brown or ivory-colored insulation. Another type of lamp cord contains the same double wires with cotton or silk braid to match upholstery, rugs or other household furnishings. Type SP is similar, but insulated with rubber instead of plastic. Use it for low-temperature flexibility. Both are commonly available in No. 18 and No. 16.

Underwriters' Type S

Type S cord is of better quality and more expensive than SP or SPT. Type S is round, and each wire is rubber insulated. Paper twine or jute fills out the form of the cord and high-quality rubber covers the outside, so, this cord can take plenty of punishment. Type SJ is another kind of rubber-covered cord, but the outer layer is considerably thinner than that of Type S. Type SJ is mostly used around the home with larger appliances like refrigerators and washing machines. Cords that are covered with neoprene, making them oil-resistant, are designated Type SO-EZC for Type S and SJO-EZC for Type SJ.

Underwriters' Type HPD

When a cord has to tolerate considerable amounts of heat, as with irons, toasters and other heat-producing appliances, "heater cord" should be used. With Type HPD, a layer of asbestos covers each wire completely, and cotton or rayon covers the outside.

Prohibitions Against Flexible Cord

The use of flexible cord is prohibited in its use as a substitute for fixed wiring in a structure where it is run through holes in walls, ceilings or floors, where run through doorways, windows or similar openings, where attached to building surfaces or where concealed behind building walls, ceilings or floors. In other words, no type of cord should ever be used in place of permanent wiring.

Some uses of cords are very specialized. So, when replacing any cord, be sure to duplicate exactly the kind used by the manufacturer. Don't assume that a similar-looking cord will do. When in doubt, take a sample of the old cord to your electrical supply house or hardware store to make a perfect match, in both wire size, insulation and outer covering. Also, be sure to match the length of the cord. A cord that is too short for the job may overload the cord; one that is too long causes too much resistance and affects the performance of the cord.

The same advice applies to extension cords also. Excessive voltage drop may result if the extension cord cannot handle the distance and the load. When an extension cord is needed for an appliance, match it to the cord on the appliance. Never run a cord of any type under a rug, because abrasion will wear away the insulation and create a fire hazard. When adding extension cords, take into consideration the length of the original cord plus the extension, as it is explained in the Cord Selection Chart.

Repairing Damaged Cords

When repairing a damaged cord, never cut the cord without first disconnecting it, as serious damage or injury may result.

To repair a cord in an emergency, cut away the damaged section and separate the wires. Then, cut the two wires so the splices will be staggered. This method makes a smoother, safer joint, as

CORD SELECTION CHART

Types and usage of extension cords

	Type	Wire Size	Use
Ordinary Lamp Cord	SP SPT	No. 16 or 18	In residences for lamps or small appliances.
Heavy-duty—with thicker covering	S or SJ	No. 10, 12, 14 or 16	In shops, and outdoors for larger motors, lawn mowers, outdoor lighting, etc.

Ability of cord to carry current (2 or 3-wire cord)

Wire Size	Type	Normal Load	Capacity Load
No. 18	S, SJ or SP	5.0 Amp. (600W)	7 Amp. (840W)
No. 16	S, SJ or SP	8.3 Amp. (1000W)	10 Amp. (1200W)
No. 14	S	12.5 Amp. (1500W)	15 Amp. (1800W)
No. 12	S	16.6 Amp. (1900W)	20 Amp. (2400W)

Selecting the length of wire

Light Load (to 7 Amps.)	Medium Load (7-10 Amps.)	Heavy Load (10-15 Amps.)
To 15 Ft.—Use No. 18	To 15 Ft.—Use No. 16	To 15 Ft.—Use No. 14
To 25 Ft.—Use No. 16	To 25 Ft.—Use No. 14	To 25 Ft.—Use No. 12
To 35 Ft.—Use No. 14		To 45 Ft.—Use No. 10

NOTE: As a safety precaution be sure to use only cords which are listed by Underwriters' Laboratories.

there is less chance of shorting across the wires in case of an insulation failure or if you run short of insulation tape. Make a pigtail splice in each wire, being sure that you follow the original twist, or the wires will tend to unwind. Tape each splice with plenty of tape. And, at the first opportunity, replace the entire cord for the safety of your home and family. Replacement is always better than repair, in the case of electrical cords. *SEE ALSO ELECTRICAL WIRING.*

Plumb

Plumb is a term which refers to an exactly perpendicular or vertical position or surface, such as on windows.

Plumb Bob

The plumb bob is a tool made of metal, iron, brass or lead and is used for measuring. To use the plumb bob, suspend it from a cord of predetermined length so that the point is downward. Its weight will pull the line in a true vertical position for making accurate layouts and measurements. *SEE ALSO CARPENTER'S TOOLS & EQUIPMENT.*

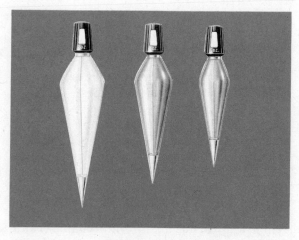

Plumb Bob

Plumber's Putty

Plumber's putty is a pasty cement composed of any number of ingredients. Used to caulk seams and pack joints, plumber's putty is occasionally substituted for similar material such as oakum. The main purpose of plumber's putty is to form a water-tight seal. *SEE ALSO PLUMBING MATERIALS.*

Plumber's Tools & Equipment

Many of the familiar household repair tools are also used for common plumbing repair jobs. Some of these tools may already be in your workshop. Very rarely will any costly tools be needed for plumbing repairs unless a principal section of the plumbing system is being replaced or something is being added to it. A few of the basic plumbing jobs include pipe soldering, minor sink, toilet or faucet repairs and pipe threading and cutting.

When soldering brass or copper pipe fittings, a handy propane gas torch will be needed. For big-

ger tasks which require more heat, such as assembling cast-iron pipes, a blowtorch may be used. Both kinds of torches may be employed in many jobs besides plumbing ones, such as removing paint.

Another way of connecting pipes is by enlarging the end of a pipe so that a second one can be inserted and clamped in place. When soldering techniques are not practical because of pipe material or hazardous flames, a flaring process is used. The flaring or flanging tools, which enlarge the ends of pipes, may be used for this type of pipe connecting.

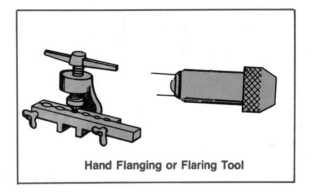

Hand Flanging or Flaring Tool

Getting to hard-to-reach water pipes and faucets behind lavatories and sinks will require a specialized tool known as the basin wrench. This tool is able to grip, turn and remove nuts in difficult places which a standard tool cannot.

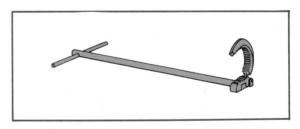

Basin Wrench

A very common household plumbing problem is clogged drains in sinks or toilets, which call for either a force cup or plumber's snake when repairing. First try freeing the clogged material by using a force cup which forces the matter up or washes it down the drain. If the force cup fails to free the clogged matter, try using a plumber's

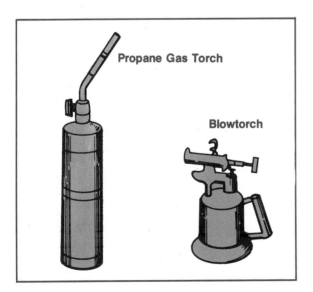

Propane Gas Torch

Blowtorch

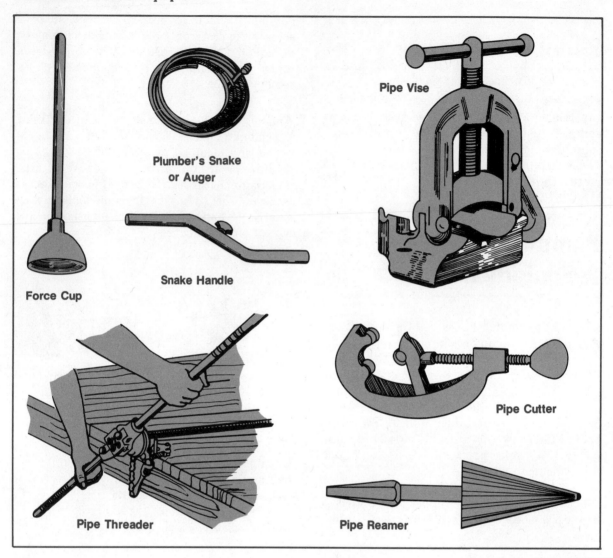

Plumber's Snake or Auger

Pipe Vise

Force Cup

Snake Handle

Pipe Cutter

Pipe Threader

Pipe Reamer

snake or a clean-out auger, which are long, flexible steel tools. They are pushed into the drain opening and on to the pipe to break up the clogged material.

Threading steel and iron pipes involves using a pipe threader, which is a tool with a main steel stock and two steel handles extending outward. To hold the pipe for threading or cutting, a pipe or machinist's vise is needed. Making right angle cuts around pipes, which is done with a pipe cutter, is important for threading and connecting pipes. When a pipe has been cut, the burr or rough edge on the inside of the pipe may be removed by using a pipe reamer. *SEE ALSO HAND TOOLS.*

Plumbing Emergencies

Plumbing emergencies are conditions that need immediate attention. There are five major areas that demand instant service.

The most common emergencies are the clogged drain and toilet. Before beginning work on a clogged toilet, first check the outflow passage to see if a large object is causing bowl stoppage. If there is an obstacle, remove it. When a lodged obstacle is not the problem, bring the water above normal level. In the case of overflowing, bail enough water to prevent further spillage. Insert a force cup at an angle to remove trapped air from beneath the rubber portion of the tool and plunge rhythmically 20 to 30 times. Remove the force cup and repeat the procedure. If this does not remove the clog, use a closet auger, commonly referred to as a snake. After placing the tube in the outflow passage, turn the closet auger handle to crank the steel ribbon through the passage. This should loosen and dislodge the clog. In instances where the stoppage is caused by an article such as a diaper, the closet auger will twist into the article without freeing the flow of water. Periodic removal of the tool will remove such obstacles and help loosen stubborn clogs.

Although unusual, overflowing toilet tanks can happen. Frequently when there is a failure in the tank mechanism, water flows from the tank, to the bowl, through the soil pipe and into the sewer. If there is a leak in the refill tube or the float valve is broken or the overflow pipes become clogged, water will fill the tank and overflow. All of these malfunctions are easily fixed and parts can be quickly replaced.

Unclogging a drain calls for the same procedures as the clogged toilet. When working on a double sink or a basin with an overflow opening, place a

stopper or sponge over the opening and hold it securely when the plunging begins to prevent a stream of dirty water from shooting out. After the clog has been cleared by a force cup or auger, a drain cleaner can be used to eliminate any additional debris in the passage. Do not use a drain cleaner in a clogged drain or while plunging. Always use cold water when flushing.

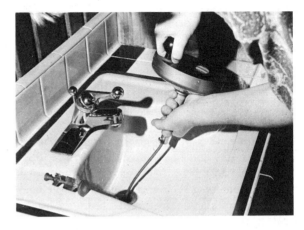

Use a closet auger to remove clogs that a force cup does not.

Since they must be thawed before the pipe begins to split, frozen pipes create an emergency situation. Using an electric iron, heating pad or heating cable will thaw frozen pipes just as efficiently as wrapping heavy cloth around the pipe and pouring boiling water on it. Only if the pipe is free of any flammable materials can a propane torch be used. Do not allow the pipe to become

Place hand, sponge or stopper over the opening in the sink when using a force cup.

Do not heat the pipe to a temperature greater than the hand can tolerate.

any hotter than the hand can tolerate. When using a propane torch, all faucets must be open to release steam pressure. Other than releasing pressure, open faucets allow water pressure to help speed thawing and let the worker know when the water is running freely.

In dealing with frozen pipes, the second step is to prevent freezing from recurring. Wrapping insulation material around pipes or surrounding surfaces helps prevent freezing. Focusing a heat light on the wall where unreachable pipes are located also helps eliminate freezing. To reduce the chance of freezing within the house, open doors to rooms so that warm air can circulate.

Although bothersome, pipe leaks can be taken care of simply and easily. Rusty cold water pipes can be given a coat of rust-inhibiting paint to prevent pinhole leaks. While straight-run pipe leaks are fixed by placing the rubber lining of a pipe leak clamp over the leak and tightening the screws, a drain-pipe leak is fixed by wrapping rubber electrician's tape around the pipe and overlapping the edges of the tape. Cast-iron drainage leaks occur at a leaded joint and are fixed by spreading lead from the joint around the joint itself. Using either a caulking tool or the flattened head of a nail sharpened at the end like a chisel, tap the joint to form small cuts and smooth and chipped lead against the pipe joint surfaces. This process will prevent seepage. *SEE ALSO PLUMBING REPAIRS.*

Plumbing Fixtures

Plumbing fixtures receive or make water available or receive liquid or water-borne waste to send through the home drainage system. Basic plumbing fixtures in bathrooms and kitchens range in size, design and color combinations. Most plumbing fixtures are made from three materials: enameled stamped steel, enameled cast iron and vitreous china.

The kitchen sink is a fixture which functions to supply water for washing dishes and for food preparation. A sink has one or two bowls and comes in cabinet models or wall-hung models.

Garbage disposal units may be attached to any sink. However, the two-bowl sink must have a separate trap-and-waste pipe connection for this unit.

Kitchen sink faucets come in a variety of designs and are made of such materials as chromium and acrylic. The faucet may have one or two handles and may have washers or be washerless. The deck faucet with two handles measuring from four to six to eight inches between stems is a common kitchen fixture. The one-handle washerless faucets are becoming more and more common. These washerless faucets require less repairs and can be attractive design features as well. Sinks may also include a separate spray attachment.

Most faucets today are equipped with an aerator, a small device composed of fine screen discs which produce a vacuum area where air is drawn in to mix with the water stream and reduce splashing.

Bathroom fixtures include a lavatory, bathtub, shower, toilet and sometimes a bidet.

The lavatory supplies water for washing the hands and face, for shaving and for light washing. It is produced from materials such as vitreous china, formed steel or plastic and cast-iron. Vitreous china is the strongest, composed of mineral combinations and clay, with glazing and kiln firing for hardening. A lavatory can be found in any shape — round, oval, rectangular or triangular. It may extend from the wall or be contained in a cabinet over or under counter surface.

Like the kitchen faucet, a lavatory faucet comes in different styles including deck and one-handle washerless. Depending on the bathroom design, handles may be sleek or sculptured, antique or modern and even old-fashioned.

In addition to hot-and-cold water faucets and a drain, many lavatories also contain an overflow drain as an added safety feature.

The bathtub, designed for bathing, is usually enclosed by walls around the sides and back. A shower head may be included above the tub. The bathroom shower is a device used for bathing in which the body is sprayed with fine streams of water in jet-like action from an opening above head level. The shower head attaches to the end of an arm extending from the wall and connected to the water supply system. The shower head is slightly above head level and is usually funnel-shaped. A flange connects the shower head to the arm.

When water flows to the bathtub supply, it may flow through the faucet or the shower head. A handle controls the direction of flow.

A shower light should be vapor proof and is installed in the ceiling or the shower stall. It is a safety device for an otherwise dark bathing area. The connecting switch for a shower light should be out-of-reach of the stall to prevent accidental electric shock.

A bathroom toilet is a bowl-shaped plumbing fixture which is designed to flush out waste. Two valves, to let water in and out of the toilet bowl tank, are the main working mechanisms. These valves are connected by levers and wires to the flush handle on the outside of the tank. When this handle is turned, a valving sequence takes place using from four to ten gallons of water to flush the tank. The water is replaced by pipes leading into the tank from the home's water supply system.

Some toilets attach to the floor while other more modern ones attach to the wall for easier cleaning. Some are built as tank-bowl combinations which are less prone to overflowing.

The three types of toilets include the siphon washdown, reverse trap and siphon jet. The latter is the most modern. The traps which force water into the bowl in flushing, are designed differently in these models.

The siphon washdown has been deleted from some modern manufacturers' lists. With a front trap, it is inexpensive but uses more water, is

slower and louder than other types. Water level is low in the bowl, making cleaning difficult.

The siphon-jet, with its vacuum-like action speeds water through the toilet bowl for quiet, effective flushing.

Becoming more prevalent in bathroom fixtures, the bidet, in conjunction with and close to the toilet in the bath area, is used to cleanse the genito-urinary area. After toilet use, it functions to prevent irritations and infections. The user sits astride it facing the wall and water controls, and activates the rinse-spray attachment. A transfer valve permits water to enter and cleanse the bowl surface after using.

Plumbing Fixture Symbols

Plumbing fixture symbols are used on blueprints to represent placement of plumbing fixtures. Because plans are drawn on a small scale, fixtures cannot be drawn as they actually appear. Therefore, symbols are used to simplify the preparing and reading of plans. *SEE ALSO BLUEPRINTS.*

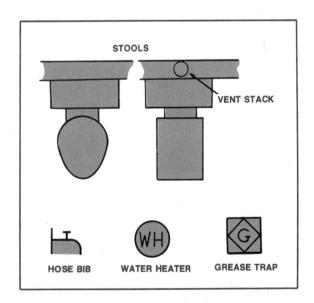

Plumbing Fixture Symbols

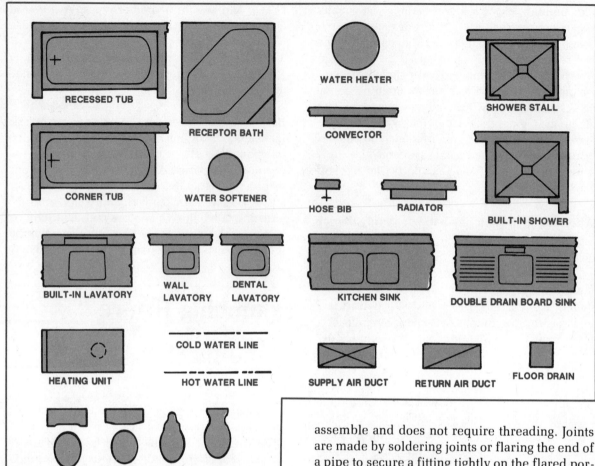

Plumbing Fixture Symbols

Plumbing Joints
[SEE PIPE JOINTS.]

Plumbing Materials

Plumbing materials, considered as the basic necessities for establishing a plumbing system, are pipes, pipe fittings and sealing materials.

PIPES

The first major plumbing materials are types of indoor pipes. Copper pipe and tubing is easy to assemble and does not require threading. Joints are made by soldering joints or flaring the end of a pipe to secure a fitting tightly on the flared portion. Galvanized steel pipe can withstand blows that occur to exposed pipes in areas such as the workshop. Besides durability, it is cheaper and more likely to be available than copper pipe and tubing. Steel pipe is used for drainage systems.

Plastic pipe is light-weight, easy to assemble, resistant to many corrosive elements and inexpensive. Often used in wells, plastic pipe has not been widely accepted for use in household plumbing because it is unable to withstand hot-water temperatures.

Cast iron is probably the most durable of the pipes. To form continuous sections, it has a hub on one end and a spigot on the other. These ends fit into each other. After packing oakum, a sealing material, around the spigot that has been centered in the hub, molten lead is poured over it to form a leakproof joint.

Outdoor plumbing materials include four types

of drainage pipes. Laid end to end with a space between in drain fields, these short pipes allow liquid to flow through them and seep into the earth around the ends of the pipe. Tar or roofing paper should cover the opening between the pipes to prevent soil from clogging the passage.

The most inexpensive drainage pipe is cement or concrete tile. Better grades of the popular fiber pipe are made with a coal-tar formula. The tar fuses the fitting to the pipe by friction created from twisting the fitting on the pipe. Fiber pipe is also available with small, evenly spaced holes on the sides of it to allow seepage of the liquid into the ground. Vitrified tile pipe is dark reddish-brown in color, and has a number of commercial uses. Yellowish or red, clay tile is kiln-hardened.

PIPE FITTINGS

Pipe fittings are divided according to the type of pipe that they are used on.

Copper pipe fittings include a sanitary tee, closet flange, closet bend, drum trap, Y branch, coupling, 1/4-bend, 1/8-bend, steel pipe adapter, cleanout with plug, sanitary tee with side inlet, slip coupling, cast-iron pipe adapter and street elbow.

Copper tube flare type fittings are a regular tee, union, 90° elbow, male adapter and female adapter.

Copper tube sweat type fittings include a regular tee, 90° elbow, 45° elbow, stop-and-waste valve, reducing tee, union, coupling, male copper-to-steel adapter and female copper-to-steel adapter.

The galvanized steel pipe fitting group has a regular tee, 90° elbow, 45° elbow, 90° street elbow, reducing tee, union, reducer, coupling, hose adapter, bushing, plug and cap.

Plastic pipe fittings are tee, coupling, elbow, steel pipe adapter, reducer and joint clamp.

The fiber pipe fitting group incorporates a Y branch, tee, cross, 1/4-bend, cast-iron pipe adapter, 1/8-bend, joining sleeve, coupling and snap coupling.

Steel pipe drainage fittings are a regular elbow, long turn elbow, tee branch, street elbow, 45° elbow, regular Y, long turn Y and p-trap.

The cast-iron soil pipe fittings include a long 1/4-bend, 1/4-bend with inlet, 1/8-bend, long 1/4-bend, sanitary tee, 45° Y branch, sanitary tee with side inlet, vent increaser, test tee, soil p-trap, floor drain, reducer, cleanout ferrule with plug, calking spigot and hub-vent fitting.

SEALING MATERIALS

Plumber's putty is used to form water-tight seals in cracks and joints. One form of a plumber's putty is oakum, a braided hemp saturated with tar. Most putties are flexible but dry to a hard surface.

Plumbing Noises

Plumbing noises, resulting from faulty parts or water pressure, occur frequently in home water systems and connections. Although these noises are annoying, they can often be easily remedied.

Water pipes can react loudly when subjected to heavy water pressure. If a great amount of water moving at a fast speed through the pipes is suddenly shut off, it causes the pipes to bang and vibrate. This noise, called *water hammer,* can be eliminated by the use of air chambers. These chambers are foot-long pipes connected to the regular water pipes close to the faucet. They contain air and are sealed airtight so that fast-moving water compresses into them when it's shut off. These cushioning devices quiet the water stoppage.

If, after water has just been turned on, it must move sharply at right angles, the plumbing may hit against its supports. The sound that results is called *angle bang.* It is not quite as loud or as frequent as water hammer. To prevent this, the angled pipes should be either cushioned at their hangers or blocked in with wooden planks to prevent movement.

Plumbing Noises

In hot-water heating systems, pipes squeak when they expand and contract from the heated water moving through them. As the expansion pushes the pipes through devices hooked onto them, the friction produced causes a squeaking sound. To eliminate this noise, the hangers through which the pipes run should be insulated with a material such as rock wool. This material cushions the pipes and lessens friction.

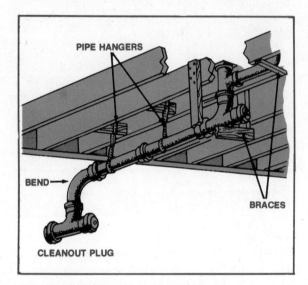

Pipe Supported by Strap Hangers

Pipes may also react to the abrupt opening and closing of the water valves by vibration against their hangers. In this case, the hangers should be tightened and extra ones added.

A *singing toilet* is the result of a toilet tank that does not properly fill after flushing. When the soft rubber valve at the tank bottom does not fit into place properly, it allows water to rush through it. This causes a whistling noise. If jiggling the handle does not set it into the correct position, the valve may need to be replaced or parts connected to it readjusted.

A singing toilet may also occur in a filled tank when the rubber float has become disattached and the valve has failed to cut off the water's flow. If the float does not screw back onto the float arm, it can be replaced.

Faucet stutter is an audible vibration which oc-

curs when a faucet is not opened completely. It is caused by a loose washer on the faucet stem. The washer can be replaced or tightened. This plumbing noise is characteristic of outdoor faucets and utility outlets rather than indoor fixtures. *SEE ALSO PLUMBING REPAIRS.*

Plumbing Repairs

Plumbing repairs can be uncomplicated when the home plumber has the necessary simple tools and replacement parts and a basic idea of how different plumbing systems operate in the home.

There are two main pipe systems in household plumbing lines: a water supply system, carrying water into the home, and a sewage pipe system, carrying waste water and sewage out of the home.

The water supply system is controlled by faucets and shutoffs. The pipes are very small usually, but under heavy pressure. Risers are pipes which extend upward.

Air chambers are installed in water supply pipe systems to prevent water hammer, a loud banging noise which results when faucets are shut off abruptly. Heavy water pressure going through the pipes, when stopped, causes them to shake and resound. These air chambers are small airtight pipes, about a foot in length, which are connected to the regular pipes. The air bubbles they contain act as cushions which are compressed by the water to eliminate noise.

BLOCKED SEWERS

Drainage pipes are the largest pipes in the home plumbing system because of the cubic volume of wastes that must slowly flow through them. Large vertical pipes which carry waste from one or more fixtures are called *soil stacks.* The *main soil stack* carries toilet waste. A smaller pipe or *secondary stack* drains into a stack and does not carry toilet waste. *Branch drains* join fixtures to their stacks. Stacks extend from above-roof vents to connect to the main house drain. The main drainage line or house drain extends as far as ten feet through the foundation until it reaches the house sewer. Sewer lines can become blocked with waste, grease, or tree roots which commonly grow through joints in them. To clear the lines, in such a case, the sewage above the clean-out plug must first be removed. (Indoor fixtures may also be drained.) Loosen the plug and let the liquid drain into a container underneath. When the container fills, tighten the plug. Continue this process until all liquid has been disposed. Take a clean-out tape or plumber's snake and push it through the pipe until it breaks through the obstruction. Remove the snake from the pipe and clean it outdoors. If tree roots have caused the stoppage, they should be killed by flushing the sewer line with a copper sulfate solution.

TOILETS

Bathroom fixtures, such as the toilet, require basic plumbing repairs from time to time. Most toilet tanks work the same way, with two main valves connected by parts which let water in and out in flushing.

The main parts of a toilet include the handle, upper and lower lift wires, guide wire, refill tubes, stopper ball, flush valve, float valve, float, float arm, and flush and valve levers.

Besides having replacement parts for the repair, tools necessary include a wrench, pliers and a screwdriver.

When making repairs inside the tank, always shut off the water at the inlet valve beneath the tank and flush. This process clears the tank and bowl for needed repair work.

One common problem in tanks is the water continuing to run long after flushing. This problem is usually caused by a worn stopper ball at the flush valve outlet and may result in a whistling or hissing noise referred to as *singing toilet.*

A worn stopper ball or flush valve problem may be corrected by unscrewing the stopper and replacing with a new one. Clean the valve seat when making the replacement. If preferred, an entire valve unit may be bought.

Other reasons for continuously running water might be a bent wire in the valve linkage or a guide wire out of place. These wires can be bent into place by hand and the guide wire repositioned by jiggling.

When the tank has filled, but the water continues to run, the float may either be leaking or be too low in the tank. Leaking floats are easily replaced; low floats are repositioned by bending the float arm.

The new flapper flush-valve units prevent many problems. All rubber, they are slipped over the overflow pipe with a chain linking the valve to the flushing arm. Flapper valves may be bought in entire units if they become faulty.

A flange and cylinder attachment also replaces the old flush valve unit in modern toilets. The cylinder takes in water after flushing and drains as water leaves the tank. It settles on the valve seat as the stopper ball in an older unit. It is replaced the same way but rarely becomes worn.

A tank which flushes partially usually needs a wire adjustment because the stopper ball does not go high enough to allow water to rush out. Shortening the lift wire which connects to the stopper valve remedies this.

Tanks which sweat may be insulated with foam sheeting. A tempering unit, which is called a temperator, may be installed to allow warm water from the hot-water lines into the tank. This device keeps the tank walls at a warmer temperature, preventing sweating. Terry cloth covers for the tank are helpful, too.

Cracks or breaks in tanks and bowls may be repaired with silicone tub caulk. This is a sealant which comes packaged with directions for repairing porcelain.

FAUCETS

Leaking, dribbling or stuttering in faucets can be repaired by replacement of worn parts or minor readjustments.

The basic parts of the standard faucet are the handle, handlescrew, bonnet, bonnet packing, bib washer, spindle or stem, faucet washer, faucet screws, slip joint washer and brass friction ring.

A leaky faucet may result from a worn faucet washer, which is located at the base of the stem. A washer is the plastic or rubber ring which forms the seal to stop the flow of water. The washer turns with the handle's turn in less-modern faucets. This movement makes the washer wear away easily.

To replace a worn washer, have either a monkey or crescent wrench and screwdriver plus an assortment of different-sized washers. If the only available washer is too large, it may be sanded down to the correct size.

Turn off the water at the shut-off valve below the faucet. Remove the handle by removing the large handlescrew, then loosen the packing nut. Lift out the spindle and inspect the washer. If badly worn or damaged, replace. Reverse these steps to put the faucet back together.

For antique china faucets, use special care in removing handles since parts of this faucet are delicate. *Hot* and *cold* discs must be removed to unscrew the handles. They contain two six-sided caps inside — the upper one tightens packing and the lower larger one contains the washer unit. Repairs for this are basically like the standard.

Uneven edges in faucet seats may be smoothed with a faucet reamer, an adjustable hand tool, though some valve seats are replaceable.

Washerless faucets, such as the diaphragm type, have metal discs instead of washers. These parts do not wear easily but if so, they may be easily replaced. Diaphragm faucets may be bought in complete units for replacement if badly damaged. Unscrewing the stem of one will lift out the entire assembly

Disc valve faucets have movable plates which turn against stationary ones for water control. They are usually sealed with O-rings instead of packing. All parts take long wear.

The sleeves or sliding ports in modern single-lever faucets, which control water flow and temperature variations, may be replaced also. This can be done by removing the covers and exposing the inner parts.

Leaking around a faucet's stem indicates worn packing under the packing nut or bonnet. This fibrous corded packing may be replaced after removing the handle, examining the bonnet and removing the old material. A leak at the stem may often be stopped by simply tightening the packing cap.

Faucet stutter, due to a loose washer, may be remedied by tightening the screw which holds the washer in place. This problem is usually found only in outdoor faucets and utility fixtures.

RADIATORS

Before each heating season, home radiators should be bled to remove trapped air in their pipes. Bleeding allows more thorough heating and is done by opening vents in relief pipes which attach to the tops of radiators. A small faucet attached to the pipe is opened until water begins to flow. Then it is closed off immediately to prevent losing needed radiator supply water. If there is a large screw in place of a faucet, it is loosened in like manner.

The bleeding process should begin with radiators located at the highest point in the house. *SEE ALSO PLUMBING EMERGENCIES.*

Plumbing Stack

Plumbing stack is a general term used for soil, waste or vent pipes. It is a vertical pipe leading from the top of the roof vent down through the house to the sewer line. All plumbing fixtures, such as toilets and sinks, drain into this stack. Sewage gas exits through the top of the vent which prevents gas build-up in the plumbing system. *SEE ALSO PLUMBING SYSTEMS.*

Plumbing Systems

A home plumbing system consists of all the piping and piping accessories needed to bring water into and through the house, and all the piping and piping accessories needed to carry waste water out of the house. Each plumbing fixture (i.e., lavatory, water closet, bathtub, shower stall, sink, etc.) is connected to a supply of water. Each of these fixtures is also connected to a drain pipe that carries the used water away.

This basic in-out circuit becomes more complex when a fixture requires both hot and cold water (as most fixtures do) and when several fixtures are connected to the same supply and drain pipes. In addition, the drainage system must be vented to the atmosphere through special vent pipes if it is to function correctly, and these vent lines increase the apparent complexity of the overall system.

The actual complexity (and thus the cost) of a plumbing installation depends mainly on the number and locations of the fixtures in the house. Fixtures grouped closely together so they can all be supplied by one branch line and drained by one drain line make the least expensive installation. In planning a plumbing installation, therefore, the homeowner should strive as much as possible to group his fixtures together, and he should also try to reduce the overall length of the piping runs to and from the fixtures as much as possible.

WATER DISTRIBUTION SYSTEM

A *supply main* carries water from its source—whether this be a municipal water main, a well or a reservoir—into the house. The supply main delivers the water to one or more *supply branches* or risers, which are in turn connected to the fixtures, the boiler, the hot-water and other equipment.

The supply main contains a main *shutoff valve,* a *water meter* and, sometimes, an *air chamber.* The main shutoff valve is located in the line just after the supply main enters the house, downstream of the meter. The valve, of course, cuts off the supply of water from the entire house. The air chamber, if installed, will eliminate any pressure surges in the system that could result in harmful water hammering. The chamber is usually made from a pipe six inches in diameter and is about 24 inches long. Shutoff valves and petcocks connected to the water inline and to the chamber itself enable the chamber to be drained of water at periodic intervals (the air in the chamber gradually dissolves into the water).

If the incoming water pressure should be in excess of 50 psi (pounds per square inch), a *pressure* reducing valve should be installed in the supply main upstream of the main shutoff valve to reduce the water pressure to something less than 50 psi. The minimum acceptable water pressure *at the fixture* is 8 psi, or 15 psi if flushometer valves are installed on the water closets instead of tanks. If the pressure at the fixtures is less than 8 or 15 psi, a pump system, or a pump and elevated tank system, of some type will have to be installed in the water distribution system to supply sufficient pressure.

Each riser should also have a valve installed at its base to allow the riser to be worked on, if this should ever become necessary. There should also be a valve at each fixture to allow the fixtures to be worked on without the water supply in the entire riser circuit being shut off. In addition, drip valves should be installed at the base of each riser and at the low points in the system generally to allow each riser or the entire system to be completely drained.

The most suitable type of valve to install as the main shutoff, the riser shutoffs and the fixture shutoffs is a *gate* valve, since this type of valve does not interfere with the flow of water when it is fully open. Thus, it does not reduce the water pressure in the system. *Globe* valves, which do drop the system pressure, should be installed only in normally closed lines where some control over the rate of water flow is desired; on hose bibbs, for example, or on boiler feedwater lines.

Plumbing Systems

PIPE SIZES AND MATERIALS

Experience has shown that the following minimum pipe sizes are satisfactory for the great majority of houses:

Supply Main
  (If Three Bathrooms or More) .... 1 in.
Supply Main
  (If Two Bathrooms or Less)............. $3/4$
Supply Risers and Branches .... $3/4$
To Fixtures:
  Hot-Water Heater, Hot-Water Boiler,
  Clothes Washer, Laundry Trays,
  Hose Bibbs .... $3/4$
Bathtub, Shower Stall, Dishwasher,
Kitchen Sink........................... $1/2$
Lavatories, Water Closets .... $3/8$

Of course, if the house is a considerable distance from its source of water, more than 100 feet, say, the size of the supply main may have to be increased to $1\frac{1}{4}$ inch or more to compensate for the drop in water pressure that occurs because of line friction. The homeowner must also be aware of excessive pressure drops in supply branches or risers when these lines are longer than usual or when they have a great many bends. In a general way, in the design of a plumbing system the size of the supply main should be calculated to provide a velocity of four feet per second or less. For a branch line, the velocity should be six feet per second or less.

Galvanized steel is the traditional material for water piping. Copper tubing, though more expensive per foot, is also widely used since it is usually cheaper to install. Brass or bronze piping is often used in place of galvanized steel when the possibility of corrosion is great, especially in hot-water lines.

Galvanized steel and brass piping is fastened together by threaded fittings, which means the pipes must be accurately cut to length. Copper tubing should be accurately cut to length also, of course, but the flexibility of copper gives the plumber some leeway in working the tubing through openings and around obstructions and in making joints. Galvanized steel and brass piping must be cut accurately to length for another

reason: any force-fitting of the pipe sections to connect them together is likely to result in fatigue cracks after a period of time. One of the greatest advantages to the use of copper tubing is the smoothness of the inner bore, which helps to maintain the water pressure in long runs. The fact that copper fittings are attached by brazing or silver-soldering also helps to maintain the line pressure. In galvanized steel and brass piping, on the other hand, system pressure losses tend to be greater because of the interference offered by the screwed-on fittings.

Plastic pipe is being used more and more for plumbing systems as the plastic materials prove themselves more and more capable of long-term, trouble-free service. For all practical purposes, plastic piping is immune to attack by corrosion and to the chemicals found in water. However, many local plumbing codes still prohibit the use of plastic piping, or ignore its existence, and it is the local code that must be followed. Plastic piping is available in long coils, which reduces the number of fittings to a minimum. Where rigid plastic piping is used, connections are made using a solvent that joins the pipe sections together.

Plastics used for cold-water systems include polyethylene (PE), polyvinyl chloride (PVC) and acrilonitrile-butadiene-styrene (ABS). For hot-water systems, chlorinated polyvinyl chloride (CPVC) has proved satisfactory.

HOT-WATER PLUMBING

Hot-water systems are of two basic types: one in which the hot water is heated instantaneously in a boiler to meet an immediate demand, and the other the hot water is heated and then stored in a tank in anticipation of future demands.

Instantaneous or tankless, heaters require that heating coils be submerged in the hot water generated by a boiler. Therefore, to satisfy the instantaneous demand for hot water, either the boiler must be operated continuously, even during the summer months, or it must be capable of starting up quickly to meet a sudden demand. Instantaneous hot-water systems are not used very often in private houses because of these requirements; there is no point in installing one, in any case, if the house has a warm-air heating system.

Storage-tank water heating systems usually consist of free-standing tanks having a combustion chamber underneath the tank. The tank is usually constructed of galvanized sheet steel, the inner surface of which is lined with vitrified clay; this is called a glass liner. The tank is surrounded by a layer of one inch thick insulation which is in turn covered by a suitably painted sheet metal. The combustion chamber underneath the storage tank may be fired by gas, oil or electricity.

There are also combination hot-water heating systems in which the output of an instantaneous heater is discharged into a storage tank and the supply of hot water is drawn from the tank as needed. This hybrid system requires a separate combustion chamber underneath the storage tank to heat the water during the summer months.

The heater used with the storage tank must be capable of raising the temperature of the cold water by 100°F. That is, if the usual temperature of the incoming cold water is 40°F, the heater must be capable of heating this water to 140°F in the quantities desired.

Domestic hot-water consumption is usually calculated on the following basis:

Lavatory	2 gallons per hr, each
Bathtub	20
Kitchen Sink	10
Dishwasher	15
Clothes Washer	75
Laundry Tub	20 gal per hr, each
Shower Stall	30

The actual consumption will depend, of course, not on the number of fixtures installed, but on the number of occupants in the house, their overall rate of water consumption and on their living habits.

It is generally considered that a cold-water system should supply about 50 gallons of cold water per day per occupant, though this figure

may vary anywhere between 20 and 80 gallons, depending on the particular family. Hot-water demand is usually estimated to be one-third of the cold-water demand, whatever this demand may be.

Storage-tank size, therefore, is based on the estimated maximum hourly demand for hot water. If, for example, a family of four has a total cold-water consumption per day of 50 gallons each, or a total of 200 gallons per day, it is reasonable to assume that the hot-water demand will be one-third this, or approximately 63 gallons per day. To arrive at the maximum hourly demand, the total daily consumption is divided by 10, which in this case would result in 6.3 gallons.

Each manufacturer of hot-water supply tanks has his own method of calculating the storage capacity of tanks for families of different sizes and/or different hot-water demands. They all publish tables similar to the table below that a family can use to judge the size of tank required for its own needs.

Occupants	Max. Hr. H.W. Demand	Average H.W. Demand	BTU Rating	Nominal Size in Gals.
2	6.7	2.8	16,000	15
3	10.05	4.2	20,000	20
4	13.40	5.6	25,000	30
5	16.75	7.0	30,000	40
6	20.10	8.4	40,000	50

There are two basic types of piping system used to carry the hot water to the fixtures. In one type, the hot water is supplied from a hot-water main to individual branch circuits and risers just as the cold water is supplied. In this system, if there has not been a demand for hot water recently, the water will have cooled in the lines and the faucet must be left open for some time before hot water emerges.

In the second type of piping system, the hot water circulates continuously through a closed loop, and the risers and branches are connected to this loop. Thus, the hot water is quickly available upon demand.

The hot-water piping should be insulated to conserve the hot water. The pipes can be covered with a 1/2 inch layer of glass fiber or mineral wool, which is in turn wrapped in aluminum foil or a similar heat-reflecting material.

ROUGHING-IN AND TESTING

The actual construction of the plumbing system is called *roughing-in*. Roughing-in refers to the installation of the piping that will later be buried within the walls and under the flooring of the house. The roughing-in must be done, therefore, while the framework of the house is still exposed. The fixtures are usually installed after the remainder of the house construction has been completed, at which time the actual connections between the fixtures and the piping are made.

However, the piping system must be tested for leaks after the roughing-in work has been completed and the pipes are still exposed to view. The testing is usually accomplished under the supervision of a local buildings department official, who will approve the plumbing as being watertight at the conclusion of the test.

The plumbing may be tested in sections or as a complete entity, depending on what is most convenient.

Assuming the system is being tested as a whole, all of the pipe openings are plugged shut except for the highest opening, which is usually the vent opening on the roof. The entire system, except for this opening, must be subjected to a 10-foot pressure head. The entire system is completely filled with water, and the water is allowed to stand for at least 15 minutes. The system is then checked for leaks, usually by observing the water level at the highest opening and noting whether the water level has dropped.

Large leaks can be found by inspection. Small leaks may be more difficult to find, in which case the entire system may be air-tested. All the openings are again plugged shut, including the uppermost opening, and an air pump is connected to the system. Air is pumped into the system until a pressure of 5 psi is attained. The system must

maintain this pressure for at least 15 minutes if it is to be considered air-tight. If the pressure falls off, soapy water is brushed around suspect pipe connections. Bubbles will indicate a leaking connection.

Plumb Line

The plumb line is a piece of string weighted at one end, generally used to mark a vertical line for wall panels or in making door frames. To mark a wall with a plumb line, coat the line with chalk, attach the plumb bob to one end and leave the other suspended from a position above. When the plumb line stops swinging, hold it tightly against the wall with one hand, pull the string out with the thumb and forefinger of the other hand, then let it snap back. The chalk on the plumb line will make an accurate mark on the wall. *SEE ALSO CARPENTER'S TOOLS & EQUIPMENT.*

Ply

A ply is one of the veneer sheets that forms plywood. Plywood is made up of these thin sheets with the grain of each ply running at a right angle to the next one. A ply is also one of the layers of building paper, felt and some types of insulation.

Plywood

Plywood is wood that has been sliced into thin veneers and then glued back together with the veneer grain running in different directions. It is an engineered product that retains many of the qualities of the wood while adding new ones of its own, probably the most important being freedom from splitting. Plywood usually comes in 4 x 8 foot sheets, although longer panels, and occasionally wider ones, are available.

Up close where you could see the stony texture of the walls of this half-timbered-style Indianapolis home, the last word you'd think of is plywood. But it is built of panels of aggregate-coated plywood.

To make maximum use of the valuable qualities of plywood you must know how to work with it, and you must make an informed choice of the plywood to use. At least eight characteristics — type, grade, thickness, etc. — determine its suitability for your intended project.

Consider what kind of wood you want. Douglas fir is the most popular plywood, especially in building construction. Just about every known kind of tree is made into plywood on occasion, however, and there is a wide variety of choices. Along with the other softwoods, California redwood and Western cedar are popular plywood materials. Used primarily for their appearance, both are suitable for interior paneling and exterior siding, as well as non-construction uses. Philippine mahogany plywood has come into wide use in recent years because it offers an attractive hardwood surface at a bargain price. Although other hardwood plywoods are more expensive, they still offer an economical way to buy and use costly kinds of lumber.

Thickness is a basic decision, too. Plywood is available in thicknesses running from about $1/8$ inch to $1 1/8$ inches. Anything thinner than $1/4$ inch you will ordinarily see only as a prefinished wall panel meant primarily to be used over a solid surface. For paneling to go directly onto wall studs or furring strips, you will need material at least $1/4$ inch thick. Even when applied directly to studs, without sheathing, plywood for outside walls of houses is often as thin as $3/8$ inch, though some tastes and some conditions will call for $5/8$ inch. Use of plywood in which the pattern is created by deep grooves will also make the thicker material necessary since the grooving has weakened it appreciably — as is not the case with shallow grooving.

Whether you will require $1/2$, $5/8$, or $3/4$ inch plywood for a subfloor or a roof deck will depend upon the distance spanned between supports. Plywood panels designed for structural uses commonly bear markings that indicate the permissible span.

Plywood

Plywood 1¹/₈ inches thick, usually with tongue-and-groove edges, is sold under the designation 2.4.1, the meaning of which is "two for one" or two uses for a single sheet, which serves as both subfloor and underlayment. It is often glued as well as nailed to joists to increase stiffness and reduce squeaks.

Your third consideration in choosing plywood for your purpose may be quality of veneers. Quality in certain respects determines whether the panel is graded Exterior or Interior, Exterior Glue. Frequently more important is the kind of veneer used for outer plies, which may be graded anything from A to D.

Exterior type plywood is the only thing to use outdoors, for boats or for any situation where there will be exposure to water. So your fourth decision will be whether to use exterior type, interior type or the kind that will not meet extreme exposure requirements but is made with the same waterproof glue used for exterior type.

In respect to surface, plywood may be either rough or sanded. You can sometimes save by buying a rough, or sheathing, grade, and you will get the advantage of greater thickness since sanding removes an appreciable amount of thickness. For some purposes, the unsanded will work just as well as the sanded and for a few others it will work even better, since the rough texture can be pleasing to the eye. Irregularities can be filled and sanded to make inexpensive rough or reject plywood suitable for painting where smoothness is wanted or where some surfacing material like linoleum or plastic laminate is to be applied.

Pattern, most often in the form of grooves, has become the usual thing in plywood intended for wall use, either as interior paneling or exterior siding. Most patterns are V-grooves or square channels, sometimes of saw-kerf width, cut into the surface of the panel at regular or random intervals. Even the patterns that appear to be random, however, will usually have grooves at 16-inch intervals at the points where they will fall over the studs in a typical wall.

Finish is not ordinarily a part of softwood or hardwood plywood as it comes from the mill. It

Courtesy of American Plywood Association

Appearance of etched-surface plywood, useful for interior paneling though more often seen as siding, depends very much on the nature of the grain of the wood species selected. Western cedar gives variations like this.

Courtesy of American Plywood Association

Reverse-board-and-batten style plywood is a ⁵/₈ inch thick panel in which very wide grooves have been cut at the mill. Stained in a light shade, it contrasts effectively here with dark trim.

Quite different effect is produced by essentially similar panels when grooves are spaced alternately 4 inches and 12 inches apart. This is "all heart" redwood, having and needing no finish.

is applied by the user with the big exception of much of the plywood intended for inside and outside walls. Prefinished plywood is now the rule for inside walls. Much of the plywood sold for siding use, especially the patterned varieties, will have been factory treated with a preservative sealer, making on-job staining optional if added color is wanted. Siding may also be bought already stained. Generally the textured or patterned sidings should be used as they come or treated with stain (preferably of a heavy-bodied type) rather than painted.

Almost all kinds of plywood manufactured can be obtained in the familiar 4 x 8 foot sheets. When longer sheets are needed, most often because of height of wall, the availability of 4 x 9 or 4 x 10 sheets may become a factor in choosing a kind of plywood. Choice becomes especially limited when making a table-tennis table, since oversize material is required.

Much of the information that follows has been adapted and condensed by permission of the American Plywood Association. This trade organization represents most of the nation's producers of softwood plywood, doing research, inspection, testing and promotion.

An example of innovative development in plywood, of interest to builders of houses or cabins in regions where basements are used (and elsewhere, in cases of split-level and hillside construction) is a plywood basement wall. It takes the place of the traditional poured-concrete or block construction for a waterproof below-grade wall.

To be both water-tight and decay-resistant, any such wall must be built right, and the accompanying drawing shows the details of construction. Naturally, all wood and plywood used are treated against decay. Complete information about using this system can be obtained from the American Plywood Association, 1119 A Street, Tacoma, Washington 98401.

GRADES OF PLYWOOD

A-A Interior: A sanded panel grade described by grades of face (A) and back (A) veneers, with minimum D quality inner plies, bonded with interior or exterior glue. Commonly used in cabinet doors, built-ins and furniture where both sides will show, A-A interior plywood can be painted or stained.

A-A Exterior: A sanded panel grade described by grades of face (A) and back (A) veneers, with minimum C quality inner plies, bonded with exterior glue meeting all the performance requirements of exterior type plywood. It can be used for fences, built-ins, signs and boats where both sides will show.

A-B Interior: A sanded panel grade described by grades of face (A) and back (B) veneers, with minimum D quality inner plies, bonded with interior or exterior glue. It is commonly used as an alternate for A-A interior where the appearance of one side is less important.

A-B Exterior: A sanded panel grade described by grades of face (A) and back (B) veneers, with

1253

minimum C quality inner plies, bonded with exterior glue. A-B exterior can be used as an alternate for A-A exterior where the appearance of one side is less important.

A-C: A sanded exterior panel grade described by grades of face (A) and back (C) veneers with minimum C quality inner plies, bonded with exterior glue meeting all the requirements of exterior type plywood. Used in siding, soffits and fences, it can be painted or stained. The face is finish grade.

A-D: A sanded interior panel grade described by grades of face (A) and back (D) veneers, with minimum D quality inner plies, bonded with interior or exterior glue with a finish-grade face for paneling, built-ins and backing. A-D plywood can be painted or stained.

B-B Exterior: A sanded panel grade described by face (B) and back (B) veneers, with minimum C quality inner plies and bonded with exterior glue meeting all the performance requirements of exterior type plywood. It is an outdoor utility panel with solid paintable faces.

B-B Interior: A sanded panel grade described by face (B) and back (B) veneers; with minimum D quality inner plies bonded with interior or exterior glue. It permits circular plugs and is paintable.

B-B Plyform: A sanded panel grade described by face (B) and back (B) veneers, with minimum C quality inner plies and bonded with exterior glue meeting all the performance requirements of exterior type plywood. A concrete form grade with a high re-use factor, the edges are sealed and the surface is mill-oiled unless otherwise specified.

B-C: An exterior panel grade described by grades of face (B) and back (C) veneers, with minimum C quality inner plies bonded with exterior glue meeting all the requirements of exterior type plywood. It is used for utility uses such as farm building and some kinds of fences.

B-D: An interior panel grade described by grades of face (B) and back (D) veneers with

minimum D quality inner plies and bonded with interior or exterior glue. This is a utility grade with one paintable side. B-D plywood is used for backing, cabinet sides, etc.

C-C: Exterior unsanded panel grade described by grade and face (C) and back (C) veneers with minimum C quality inner plies bonded with exterior glue meeting all the requirements of exterior plywood. The lowest grade of exterior plywood, it is used for rough construction that is exposed to weather.

C-C Plugged: An exterior panel described by grade of face (C-Plugged) and back (C) veneers, with minimum C inner plies bonded with exterior glue meeting the requirements of Exterior type plywood. The face is plugged with open defects not larger than $1/4 \times 1/2$ inch. Used as underlayment, pallet bins, boxcar and truck floors, and linings, sanded or tough sanded panels may be specified.

C-D: An interior unsanded panel grade described by grade of face (C) and back (D) veneers, with minimum D quality inner plies bonded with interior or exterior glue. Use for sheathing and for structural uses such as subflooring.

CDX: Trade usage only. This in NOT an exterior panel.

Clear Face: Plywood panel with face ply free of knots, knotholes, patches or resin fills. In some cases a few small, well-matched repairs are permitted. Clear face definition varies from mill to mill.

Structure I & II: Unsanded construction grades of plywood with limitations on species, veneer, grade and workmanship. Recommended for heavy load applications where plywood's strength properties are of maximum importance, as for truss gussets. These grades are all bonded with exterior glue.

Texture 1-11: American Plywood Association trade name for a $5/8$ inch exterior siding panel with $3/8$ inch wide vertical grooving spaced 2, 4 or 8 inches on center. Panels have shiplapped edges to maintain pattern continuity when installed.

Veneer Grades: Standard grades of veneer used in plywood manufacture. The six grades are described as follows:

N Special order *natural finish* veneer. Select all heartwood or all sapwood. Free of open defects. Allows some repairs.

A Smooth and paintable. Neatly made repairs permissible. Also used for natural finish in less demanding applications.

B Solid surface veneer. Circular repair plugs and tight knots permitted.

C Knotholes to 1″. Occasional knotholes $1/2″$ larger permitted providing total width of all knots and knotholes within a specified section does not exceed certain limits. Limited splits permitted. Minimum veneer permitted in exterior type plywood.

C Improved C veneer, splits limited to $1/8″$, knotholes limited to $1/4″$ by $1/2″$.

D Permits knots and knotholes to 2 $1/2″$ width, and $1/2″$ larger under certain specified limits. Limited splits permitted.

HOW TO WORK WITH PLYWOOD

Sawing

In *hand sawing* plywood, use a 10 to 15 point (teeth per inch) crosscut saw. Support the panel firmly, face up. Hold saw nearly flat to the panel face to score the surface with forward strokes only, then cut through with saw held at normal angle. For inside cuts start hole with drill, then use coping or keyhole saw. For *power sawing*, a plywood blade gives best results, but a combination blade may be used. Place the panel face down for *hand power sawing*; panel face up for *table power sawing*. With the first cuts reduce the panel to pieces small enough for easy handling. Use a piece of scrap lumber underneath panel, clamped or tacked securely in place to prevent splintering on back side. Plan to cut

Courtesy of American Plywood Association

When hand-sawing, place plywood with the good side up. Use a saw having 10 to 15 points (teeth) to the inch, and support the panel firmly so it won't sag. Reduce splitting by putting a scrap of lumber under the plywood and sawing it at the same time. Keep saw at a low angle.

Courtesy of American Plywood Association

Power sawing on a radial or table saw should be done with good side of plywood up—except when pushing the panel through a radial saw set for ripping. Use a sharp combination blade or a fine-tooth one with little set. Let the blade protrude just the height of the teeth.

Plywood

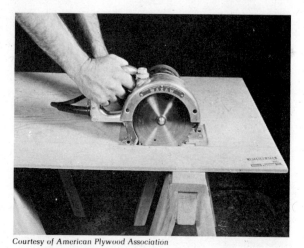

Courtesy of American Plywood Association

Put good face of plywood down when cutting with a portable circular saw or an electric sabre saw, to minimize splitting out of face ply. Tack a strip of lumber to the top of each saw horse and you'll be able to saw right through its surface without damaging the horse.

matching parts with same saw setting. Use a fine tooth coping saw for curves. If available, you may use a jigsaw, sabre saw or bandsaw for curved parts; just be sure blade enters face of panel. When planning the project always allow for material lost in saw kerfs.

Planing

Courtesy of American Plywood Association

Sanding before sealer or prime coat is applied should be confined to edges. Too much sanding of the surface will merely remove soft grain. After sealing, sand in direction of grain only. A sanding block, one type of which is shown, will prevent gouging.

Planing plywood edges with a plane or jointer is often unnecessary, if the saw cut has been made with a sharp saw blade. If planing is necessary, work from both ends toward the center to avoid tearing out plies at the end of the cut. For best results use a hollow ground blade and make very shallow cuts.

CONCRETE WORK.

Plywood is used for concrete form work because it is tough, durable, easy to handle, split resistant and lightweight. Plywood can be bent for curved forms and liners, and the natural insulating properties help level out temperature variations to provide more consistent curing conditions. Plywood used for concrete form work is called plyform and is available in two grades: Class 1 and Class II. Strength and stiffness are greater in Class I. The choice is determined by loads, framing costs and nature of a job. Both classes of plyform are also available with High Density Overlay (HDO) and a variety of special-purpose, mill-applied coatings. All plywood for concrete form work is sanded on two sides, edge sealed and (unless otherwise specified) mill oiled.

DRILLING:

In drilling plywood with brace and bit, the trick is to use the tool properly. *For large diameter holes* (up to 3 inches), it is important to protect the plywood from splintering. Do this by backing the panel with a scrap of wood clamped behind the area being drilled. This prevents splintering when the bit pierces the panel. Another technique is to bore from one side until the spur (point) of the bit comes through on the opposite side. Then, drill from the opposite side to complete the hole.

Using an expansion bit, you will get better leverage making partial turns with the brace ratchet. Otherwise, the resistance of the side cutter tends to tear the wood.

For small diameter holes, such as where fastening must be very close to a plywood edge, either a hand drill or a push drill is preferable. Best results are obtained by holding the drill steady and turning the operating crank evenly, at the same time keeping pressure on the handle. A

Courtesy of American Plywood Association

Pre-drilling is called for a careful work where nails must be very close to an edge. As indicated here, drill bit should be slightly smaller in diameter than the nail to be used.

drill bit slightly smaller than the fastener diameter should be used.

FINISHING

Exterior Finishing

All edges of plywood to be painted should be sealed with heavy applications of exterior oil-base house paint primer or a similar sealer. If the plywood is not to be painted (pre-stained textured siding, for example), edge-seal with a water-repellent preservative. The easiest time to seal the edges of plywood is while it is stacked.

The most important part of painting, the prime coat, should be applied as soon as possible after the panels are cut to size or installed. Primer provides the all-important bond between the wood and the finish coats. The best results are given by normal-drying, high-grade exterior primers, thoroughly brushed. Primers containing mildewcide are available and should be used in areas of continuous warm, damp conditions where there is a danger that mildew might discolor the paint finish. Primers for wood should be free of zinc oxide, even if a zinc-containing

Courtesy of American Plywood Association

Rough surfaces of Douglas fir panels take color stains well, give an economical siding material. Reverse-batten pattern gives the effect of siding made with boards nailed over battens applied previously.

paint is used for the finish coat. Brush application is best since it allows working the paint thoroughly into the wood. Spray application is acceptable only if care is taken to avoid pinholes and thin spots. Application with a long-napped roller is better than spray but not as good as brushing. With paint, two topcoats are better than one. With rough or textured sidings, stains are best; they will give better performance if applied by brush. Do not use clear finishes on plywood exposed outdoors.

Interior finishing

Preparation for interior finish is minimal. Overlaid (MDO and HDO) and textured plywood need no preparation: sanded grades require only touch sanding to smooth filler or spackle applied to fill any openings in the panel face or to remove blemishes. Always sand with the grain, using fine sandpaper. Do not paint over dust or spots of oil or glue. All knots, pitch streaks, or sap spots in sanded or textured plywood should be touched up with sealer or shellac before panels are painted.

Flat finish oil-base paints are rolled, brushed or sprayed on where washability and durability are

Plywood

most important. Generally, these are alkyd resin base enamels, characterized by good hiding properties. Some are self-priming on wood. Flat finish water-base paints (often called latex) have some degree of washability. They are easily applied with brush, roller or spray. When using these paints, prime plywood surface with an oil-base or recommended primer. Gloss and semi-gloss enamels are extremely durable, washable finishes. Brush, roll or spray over recommended primer.

Plywood for natural finishes should be carefully selected for pattern and appearance. For the most natural effect, use two coats of clear sealer. Plywood's repairs and grain irregularities can be pleasantly subdued with either color toning or light stain.

Color toning requires companion stains and non-penetrating sealers. These are combined and applied by brush or spray. After drying and light sanding, a coat of clear finish gives luster and

Exterior Applications

TYPE OF FINISH	RECOMMENDED FOR	APPLICATION	ESTIMATED LIFE
PAINT Acrylic Latex	Medium Density Overlaid, striated, or regular plywood panel, or lap siding. Also Texture 1-11 and rough sawn	Apply recommended primer plus two finish coats.	6 years or more (Mfg. claim) on overlaid. Up to 5 years on other.
Oil-Alkyd	Medium Density Overlaid	Apply with zinc-free primer, using two or three coats (including primer).	6 years or more.
STAIN Opaque or highly pigmented stain	Unsanded plywood (rough sawn and Texture 1-11)	One or two-coat systems as recommended by the manufacturer.	Up to 3 years.
Semitransparent or penetrating stain	Unsanded plywood (rough sawn and Texture 1-11)	One or two-coat systems as recommended by the manufacturer.	Up to 5 years.

Interior Applications.

TYPE OF FINISH	RECOMMENDED FOR	APPLICATIONS
PAINT		
Oil-flat paint, semigloss or gloss enamel	Medium Density Overlaid, regular plywood, striated, embossed.	Apply over primer or may be self-priming.
Latex emulsion	Regular and textured plywood, Medium Density Overlaid.	Apply with oil or stain-resistant primer.
Texture, multicolor, spatter	Regular plywood, Medium Density Overlaid, Texture 1-11.	Use oil base or stain-resistant primer.
STAINS, SEALERS	Regular plywood, textured	Apply stains with companion sealer or over sealer separately applied. Where sealer alone is desired, use two coats.

Narrow-V-grooved, or saw-kerfed patterns in textured plywood give much of the massive effect possible with ungrooved panels. But they offer the advan- **tage that joints between panels almost disappear as the beveled edges butt together and form similar V-joints, especially important for interior use.**

durability. Tones of light gray, brown or tan go well with wood colors and provide best grain masking.

With light stain, the panel is first whitened with pigmented resin sealer or thinned interior white undercoat, then wiped to show grain. Clear resin sealer is applied, allowed to dry and sanded lightly. Color is added (tinted undercoat, thin enamel, pigmented resin sealer or light stain) and wiped to the proper color depth. A final coat of satin varnish or brushing lacquer provides luster and durability.

For special effects, stipple texture paints can be applied, usually over taping to high panel joints, after oil-base priming coat. Multicolor spatter finish (usually lacquer) achieves a distinctive effect when sprayed over colored or primed panels.

For an attractive natural finish, textured plywood (rough sawn, patterned surfaces, Texture 1-11, etc.) should be protected against soiling with two coats of a clear sealer or pigmented stain. If desired, the few repairs and grain irregularities can be subdued by color toning or light stains.

Refinishing

Application of new surface treatment (stain, paint or sealer) can renew the appearance and prolong the life of the plywood.

For previously stained plywood remove surface dust and finish chalk using a mild detergent solution followed by thorough rinsing. (If surface fibers are loose, remove with light bristle brushing before cleaning.) If opaque stain was original finish, remove loosened film using a water blaster (available from equipment rental

1259

agencies). *For previously painted surfaces,* remove all loose paint, surface dirt and chalk. On textured plywood, use a stiff brush or power tools. Feather the edges of remaining paint by sanding. Wash and rinse off surface dirt and allow to dry. If plywood has checked, fill checks with a pliable patching compound before re-painting. *For mildewed surfaces,* scrub lightly with mild detergent, rinse with household bleach, rinse with clear water and dry.

MECHANICAL PROPERTIES

The strength and stiffness characteristics of plywood affecting its structural behavior in use are its mechanical properties. These include the following: *Resistance to impact loads* due to its cross-laminated construction. Grain running crosswise in alternate layers distributes impact forces down the length and width of the panel. *Resistance to racking,* the ability to resist forces that would pull a plywood panel from its rectangular shape. Tests prove 1/4 inch plywood wall sheathing on a standard stud wall has twice the strength and rigidity of 1 x 8 diagonal board sheathing. *Stiffness,* strongest and stiffest when panels are installed with the face grain across supports. For best results lay panels over 3 or more supports. *Strength in bending,* large panel size with high bending strength makes plywood an excellent material for bulkheads, retaining walls and grain bin lining. *Tension and Compression,* plywood splice plates are used to transfer tension (pulling loads) and compression (pushing loads) between skins of stressed-skin panels.

PHYSICAL PROPERTIES

The physical properties are the characteristics of plywood as a material other than those relating to strength. *Thermal conductivity:* Under normal room temperature and humidity conditions, plywood is a natural insulator. *Electrical conductivity:* At low moisture content, plywood is normally classified as an electrical insulator; however, its resistance to passage of current decreases as moisture content increases. *Reaction to chemical exposure:* plywood behaves much like solid wood with good resistance to chemicals. *Vapor transmission:* plywood has good resistance to moisture passing through it;

however, for best construction install with a vapor barrier such as polyethylene film. *Acoustics:* thicker plywood panels are better sound insulators than thin panels.

STORAGE

Reasonable care should be used in handling plywood to avoid damaging edges and corners. Damage of this nature will not ordinarily affect the structural capabilities of the panel, but it can add unnecessary in-place repair costs.

If plywood must be kept a long time, store it inside. General rules for storing plywood are as follows:

Never store plywood in direct contact with the ground. It should rest on stringers of 2 x 4's or other supports. They should be level and there should be at least three in the 8 foot length of the panels, one centered and the other two approximately 12 to 16 inches from the ends.

Store plywood covered. Even though the elements will not affect the structural integrity of exterior bonds, plywood should be covered when stored outside to keep it clean and to prevent accumulations of moisture which might result in warping or twisting, especially of the top panels. If plastic sheets or tarps are used, keep them open and away from sides and bottom of piles for good air circulation around the panels.

Pocket Chisel

The pocket chisel is a popular sized chisel having flat blades which are parallel on each side.

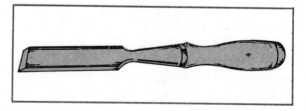

Pocket Chisel

This chisel's handy size makes it good for general use and shop work. The blade's length ranges from 4'' to 5'' with the overall length ranging from 9'' to 10¹/₂''. Because of the short blades, more accurate work is possible. *SEE ALSO HAND TOOLS.*

Polishers, Floor
[SEE FLOOR POLISHER REPAIR.]

Polyurethane

Polyurethane is a durable, water-resistant finish. It is especially suited for bars and table tops.

Before applying polyurethane, any staining must be thoroughly dry. The finish may be brushed, sprayed or rolled on. If a second coat is desired, the surface should be sanded lightly before applying.

Colored transparent polyurethane finishes are like the clear finishes, but offer a variety of color possibilities. Each successive coat will darken the color. If the color desired is reached before the desired luster, apply a coat of clear polyurethane finish.

Pool Care & Maintenance
[SEE SWIMMING POOLS.]

Pool Construction
[SEE SWIMMING POOLS.]

Popcorn Popper Repair

Popcorn poppers are one of the simplest home appliances to repair. They usually consist of an open-coil nichrome wire supported by porcelain insulators. Often a thermostatic disc is used to turn off the heat when the corn has reached the popping temperature. This helps to prevent overheating and subsequent burning of the corn after it is done.

Spills and drops are the major source of problems in popcorn poppers. The hot grease can insulate the terminals and prevent good contact. Most popcorn poppers don't have switches; they simply plug into an outlet to allow them to operate. Like other heating appliances, it shouldn't be used when other small heating appliances such as toasters or waffle makers are being operated on the same circuits at the same time.

If the popcorn popper fails to operate, check the receptacle first with a table lamp. If this proves okay, unplug the popper and look at the plug area and the terminal on the popcorn popper. Most such poppers have removable cords. Some have switches at the popper base attaching receptacle. If this is the case and the element appears to be okay, open the switch and check the switch contacts and the points where the wiring connects to the female terminals with the switch.

To gain access to the thermostat and the heating element of the popcorn popper, you'll often have to remove the cover plate. This is held in place

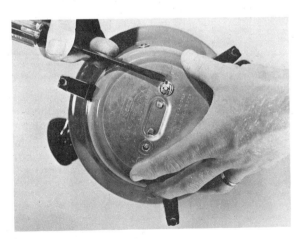

Popcorn poppers are disassembled by removing clips or screws at base of unit. Some poppers may have exposed element in base. Others have cover plate.

with a screw connected to the base of the unit. The method of disassembling should be obvious.

Any break in the heating element should be visible. Look carefully around the point where it connects to the terminals and to the thermostat. These should be clean and tight. If they are burned and corroded, loosen the nut that attaches the element to the terminals and clean this portion until it is bright and shiny. Then tighten the nut on the terminal, being sure that it is snug and that the element is making contact.

With cover plate removed, nichrome heating element is visible resting upon porcelain supports. Bimetal thermostat in unit above is not found on all models.

The operating portion of the thermostat is not visible — usually a disc-type bimetal is used in this application. To check it you will need a VOM or a continuity tester. The thermostat should be closed when it is cool and should open when heated with a match. This doesn't tell you the exact temperature at opening, simply whether or not it is opening.

If a popcorn popper becomes too hot and burns the corn, there are several things that could be at fault. One is the moisture content of the corn itself. Before condemning the popper, try another batch from a different container.

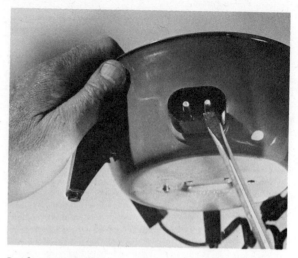

Look around the area where terminals fasten for signs of corroded or loose connections. Be sure they are clean and shiny before retightening.

If the popper shocks the user, it is usually due to a sagging heating element. Check the element carefully. The problems may be due simply to a coil support that has fallen out of place. In some cases a sagging element can be tightened up, but if it is necessary to stretch the element to any large extent it should be replaced. Even a small amount of element that is cut away from the remainder will cause the resistance to decrease and it will begin to operate at a hotter temperature than it was designed to.

Inspect the corn popper carefully and check the appliance for grounds with a VOM on the highest resistance scale before putting it back into use after repairs. *SEE ALSO APPLIANCE REPAIR, SMALL.*

Poplar Wood

Poplar wood is a moderately soft, porous, even textured hardwood. It has a minimum grain and is resistant to warping. Its heartwood is olive-brown and the sapwood is greyish-white. Poplar wood is quite versatile and, when treated, may resemble mahogany or walnut. It holds paint and stain better than the majority of woods. Because of this feature, poplar wood is preferred over pine when painting is required on furniture and trim.

Poplar wood is used for core stock for plywood, exterior portions of inexpensive furniture and interior portions of more expensive furniture, especially Early American, as a cross band for veneers, pattern stock, hat blocks, trunks, cabinets and toys. Poplar wood comes from the yellow poplar also known as a tulip tree. *SEE ALSO WOOD IDENTIFICATION.*

Porch & Bay Framing

A porch and bay window project from the exterior wall of a house and consideration of these projections must be made when constructing the floor, wall and roof frames. The addition of a porch or a bay window adds considerable floor space and windows.

Porch or bay window framing presents special design features that the architect usually details in the original house plans. In some cases, however, the details are sketchy and an experienced carpenter must develop the construction details. *SEE ALSO BAY WINDOW; PORCH CONVERSION & CONSTRUCTION.*

Porch Conversion & Construction

Many homeowners choose to eliminate the front porch as part of an exterior remodeling project. Often, this gives the house a more crisp, modern appearance, especially if the old porch has begun to sag, a common situation with porches that were built on foundations of untreated lumber. Since the porch is usually an appendage rather than an integral part of the house structure, it is relatively simple to remove.

Other homeowners look to the porch for added living space. If it is structurally sound, it can easily be enclosed to become another room for the house. With the floor and the roof already in place, all that is needed is to build the walls. These may be partial or total window walls, making a year-round sun room or normal stud walls can be built and the room used as a family room, den, or extra bedroom.

ENCLOSING A PORCH

Most porches have crawl spaces underneath. If this area is especially damp, cover the earth with heavy tarpaper overlapping the piece at least 3 inches. Coat the seams and edges with asphalt compound to seal out the dampness. Staple insulation between the joists (you may prefer to leave this job until after electrical wiring and heating pipes or ducts are installed).

Porches generally have pitched floors to allow for rain run-off. You can leave the old floor exposed in your new room or if you plan to put down a new floor, tile or carpet, for example, it can be leveled at the same time. Most porch floors are slightly lower than the floors of the house, usually a few inches. Place 1 x 2 "sleepers" over the porch floor on 16 inch centers, then shim where necessary to make them level. Nail plywood subflooring over the sleepers.

If the porch has a railing, this must be removed. For a sunroom, the only framing that is necessary is to fit the windows and door. If the

Courtesy of the Window Shade Manufacturers Association

Enclosing the porch with window walls makes it a delightful sun room for entertaining or relaxing.

The old front porch, with its magnificent valley view, was preserved and improved when this 1880's farmhouse in rural Michigan was renovated

In the rear of the venerable house, a new porch was built, fully enclosed by windows and sliding glass doors, to take advantage of another great view.

window units are floor-to-ceiling, simply fit them in place and apply trim. Hang the door and your room is enclosed. All that is left are the finishing touches.

The job is more complicated if you are building a stud wall. In most cases, the posts that support the roof will have to be removed along with the railing. To provide a temporary roof support, set a 2 x 4 plate on the ground in front of the porch and secure it to stakes driven deep into the ground. Cut 2 x 4s to fit tightly between the plate and the edge of the roof and wedge them in place at 6 foot intervals. Now it is safe to remove the posts.

Erect the stud walls, leaving openings for a door and windows. When these are in place, the temporary bracing can be removed. Install windows and hang the door, then apply sheathing and siding to match the rest of the house.

Once you have enclosed the room, finish the inside. Remove the siding from the house wall

Complete enclosure turns an old back porch into a new "mother-in-law" apartment, complete with picture window. The roof deck, which opens off the master bedroom, was part of the original structure.

(which is now the inside wall of the new room). The old sheathing can remain in place as a base for the new wall covering material. Remove the inside wall and nail stud framing inside these holes. Remove the door from the inside wall, unless it is to remain as part of your planned use of the new room. (Note: If the windows and door are to be used in the new wall, they will obviously have to be switched at an earlier stage. The only consideration here is to select a day on which you are unlikely to encounter any weather problems during the transition phase.)

Before finishing the inside walls, install wiring for electrical switches and outlets. Since the new room is likely to see a good deal of use, plan on enough outlets to provide sufficient lighting throughout. If your present furnace is adequate to heat the new room, this is also the time to extend the pipes or ductwork to convectors or baseboard registers on the former porch. If your furnace is already working at full capacity, the new room can be heated with individual electric baseboard units. Install wiring for these now; the units themselves are put in after the wall covering is in place.

If the porch has a ceiling that is in good condition, this can serve as the ceiling in the new

The trend may be away from porches, but this family felt the need for a bright, sunny, multi-purpose room. So they built this addition. Note the concrete block foundation under construction. The large, wood-sash windows slide open at a touch to provide ventilation as well as light.

room, or as a base for new ceiling of tile or gypsum board. If there is no ceiling at present, you can either install a ceiling to the existing rafters or nail up 2 x 4 or 2 x 6 joists and install the ceiling to them. First staple insulation between the rafters or joists, then apply finish wall and floor materials.

BUILDING A NEW PORCH

While the trend seems to be away from porches toward less formal patios and decks, there are cases where a porch may be preferred for an outdoor living area. A wood deck looks very much out of place on certain styles of houses.

Courtesy of California Redwood Association

Facelifting makes a world of difference. "Before," this house looked as undistinguished as the beat-up car parked in its driveway.

As with any addition to your home, check the local building department before you start. There may be restrictions on the type of structure you are allowed to build. If the porch will be built near the lot line, there is probably a minimum setback that must be observed. You may have to supply plans (usually, simple ones that you can even draw up yourself) and file for a building permit.

With legal technicalities taken care of, you can start to work. For the home handyman, a concrete block foundation wall is a good choice. The easy-to-handle units go up quickly. Generally, the porch floor should be a few inches below the level of the interior floor. If the porch is being built where there is already an entry to the house, the existing stairs will have to be re-

Courtesy of California Redwood Association

Narrow urban home was dramatically updated by the addition of porches, sliding doors and new windows that open it up for indoor-outdoor living.

moved before the porch is built; these will be rebuilt later at the edge of the porch. Floor joists are set on sills bolted to the foundation walls. A joist should be pitched slightly away from the house to provide for drainage. Tongue-and-groove floor boards are nailed across the joists.

The porch roof is supported by post-and-beam construction. Make sure that the posts are perfectly plumb and the beams level and that the entire support structure is securely tied together and to the house. The roof is of conventional construction. The roof line should match that of the house, or be set at a complementary angle. Roof shingles should match those of the existing roof as closely as possible.

Install ceiling joists of 2 x 4 or 2 x 6 lumber, depending on the span they cover. If there is any possibility that you might completely enclose the porch in the future, install insulation batts between the joists. For a finished ceiling, nail tongue-and-groove boards to the ceiling joists, or use ¼ inch plywood, with two inch batten strips nailed over the joints to conceal them.

The porch railing can be simple or elaborate. On the simple side, balusters and a bottom rail of 2 x 2s, spaced about three inches apart and topped by a 2 x 3 rail, will do the job. A more elaborate rail can be made with turned spindles purchased from a millwork shop. Nail spindles between a 2 x 3 bottom rail and a 2 x 6 top rail, beveling the top rail in one or both directions. Mount the rail between posts.

You may wish to screen the porch. You can purchase stock fixed-frame screens and build short stud walls to fit them. Then you would have to build a door frame on the porch and hang a screen door. If there is no entry to the house where the porch is built, this, of course, will have to be provided also. The easiest way is to remove an existing window and enlarge the opening for a door. If no window is convenient for this purpose, you will have to break through the wall to install the door. In this case, make sure you provide support overhead. A header of doubled 2 x 6s is adequate for most conventional-width doorways.

Courtesy of Robbins & Myers, Inc.

Fully screened porch has an old-fashioned ceiling fan to keep the breezes moving. Note plywood ceiling, with batten strips covering the joints.

The staircase that you removed earlier may be salvaged to provide access to the porch. If it is damaged or otherwise unusable, build new steps of wood or concrete.

Apply at least two coats of porch-and-deck enamel to the porch floor. Paint the posts, rails and other exposed wood to match the main body of the house.

Porches

A porch is a covered entrance to a building which projects from the wall and is covered by a separate roof. The porch is also an open or enclosed gallery or a room on the outside of a building.

A comfortable addition to any home, the porch may be the family's most popular accomodation in fair weather. On many homes, the porch is just a squared appendage connected to the front door. A porch such as this can be extended to create a patio porch which becomes a vantage point for viewing the lawn, and for lounging and sunbathing. Patio porches with planter walls, modern lighting and surrounding shrubbery are assets to a house structure.

Porches

Adding a porch roof can utilize wasted space above a porch or garage. Modifications range from a simple sun deck to an additional room. To eliminate direct sunlight on a deck, place a canvas canopy on it, supported by a 1" pipe framework. The framework should be made so it can be taken apart for storage.

Another variation for a sun deck is making it into a play area for children. The porch railing for the play area is fenced in higher than average railing. If the deck is large enough, a small play house can be placed on it.

An enclosed porch as a permanent improvement, increases the size and value of the home. Windows may be installed around the length of the enclosure and be screened for summer. A more elaborate deck improvement would be converting it into a spare bedroom. Even in small designs, there is usually adequate space for beds along the longest wall. Owners of vacation homes benefit from the extra-room porch. Installation of screens on a regular-deck porch make it feasible for sleeping quarters in this type of home. An open porch on a vacation home which contains hammocks, chairs, card tables and dining furniture may likely be its most frequently occupied annex.

Open porch floors are exposed to rain and for this reason they should be pitched slightly to drain away from the house. Floor joists running parallel to the house wall should be pitched 1 inch for every 6 feet. Joists running at right angles to the house wall need a lower outer sill for desired pitch. Plain-edged floorboards with ⅛ inch gaps are used for porch floors in areas where it rains frequently. For a more close-fitted floor, use tongue-and-groove redwood or cypress flooring.

Portable Electric Generators

With the advent of the energy crisis, many families are interested in buying a portable electric generator. The price of a generator may seem prohibitive until one considers the damage that a brownout can do to your appliances, if they are running. Home appliances are designed to run at a steady speed. When the power company is forced to reduce voltage, because more power is being used than can be produced, lights dim and motors slow down. It will not hurt the lights, but the motors heat up. If too much heat is generated, the windings will burn out. To avoid burnout, motorized appliances must be turned off or be provided with alternate power.

If you have ever needed power to saw, drill, or paint-spray in the corner of your yard or planned a wilderness vacation, it would have been much easier if you had owned a portable electric plant. A private power source can go anywhere, practically, to run anything up to its maximum capacity.

Power anywhere is the promise of having your own portable electric plant. Among the good ones are (l. to r.): 1600-watt Pincor 160H, 1750-watt Onan, Kohler 1500-watt, 1500-watt McCulloch, and 1250-watt Majol.

All portable generators consist of four-stroke cycle, air-cooled gasoline engines which are directly coupled to generating units of different manufactures. The generating unit may be either an alternating-current generator or an alternator. Sometimes called motor-generator set, or just MG set, each comes with a self-governor to maintain near-constant 3600-rpm engine speed. This produces 120-volt 60-cycle A.C. just like you have at home. Plug-in receptacles are includ-

Five portable MG sets in the bed of pickup represent a total of 7.5 kilowatts of go-anywhere electric power. (Top) 1600-watt Pincor 1600H enclosed camper model, 1750-watt Onan, (middle) 1500-watt McCulloch, 1250-watt Majol, (bottom) 1500-watt Kohler.

A wide stance is desirable in a portable electric plant to keep it from tipping over when you haul it around in your Carryall or in the trunk of your car. Majol, shown here, has it.

ed, as well as a recoil rope starting, cushioned feet and a carry-handle. A self-containing fuel tank, gravity or suction feed, is part of the package, too.

Some manufacturers offer accessories to tailor the unit to your needs, even run it on another fuel, but then, it is no longer portable.

Most portable electric plants weigh well over 60 pounds. While you will have no trouble carrying your portable MG set from the garage to the house or house to car, much more than that would be uncomfortable. To carry the heavier units more than a few steps, two people are required.

SIZE

Size of electric plants goes by generating capacity in watts. The portable range from 500 watts (will light five 100-watt bulbs at one time) to about 1800 watts (18 100-watt bulbs). Generally, the more watts of output, the heavier the unit.

What size of portable you need depends on the maximum load at one time. A 1500-watt unit will

handle a sump pump, or the refrigerator and furnace blower. It will also run a freezer. Decide what the minimum power you need is, then get a plant to match it. Remember that motorized appliances must be started, and that starting takes more power than running. If you plug them in separately while the unit is running, the generator will have the most chance of handling the separate starting loads. The unit should have a larger wattage capacity than all the running wattages combined, so that some power is left for starting the last motor.

PORTABLE ELECTRIC GENERATORS

APPLIANCE	POWER (watts)
Sump Pump, 1/4 hp	300
Fuel-fired furnace	600
Water Pump, 1/2 hp	700
Refrigerator	250
Food freezer	400
Television, B&W	300
Television, Color	700
Lights	(as labeled)

TRANSFER SWITCH

Unless you plug lights and appliances in-dividually into the generator's power outlets, you will need what is called a transfer switch. This switches off high-line power before hitting the wires with your home-grown power. Your utility company will require a transfer to protect power line workers from reverse flow of your volts into what should be a "dead" line.

FEATURES

The features a portable electric plant should have depends on how it will be used. The camper generators have spark-arrester screens. You'll be required to have this feature if you camp with a generator in a national forest or park campground. Most camper units also offer 12 volt D.C. generating capacity, and a set of plug-in 12 volt leads is provided. This is for charging 12 volt batteries in your car, travel trailer or pickup-camper. The better camper units contain oversized, quiet mufflers while some feature totally enclosed design to further quiet the engine. Other convenient features are an on-off switch, operating indicator light, and overload trip-out protector.

Most portable MG sets use alternators rather than generators because they are less expensive to make. An alternator has no costly commutator.

This is one of a few units that feature overload trip-out protection with indicator light. This acts automatically like a circuit breaker to cut power under a continuous overload that could otherwise damage the generator or the appliance connected to it.

It is generally lighter than a generator of the same output. Surge capacity is the ability to generate more than rated wattage for a brief period, such as when starting an electric motor. Some units have a larger surge capacity than others. The surge capacity of most portable MG sets is 25 percent more than their rated output. If

For camping you get an electric plant that is totally enclosed. Its advantages are a clear TV reception and quiet running, a Forest-Service-approved muffler with a 12-volt battery-charging capability.

Large-diameter rotor and special design gives the McCulloch H-1500 tremendous surge power. Though tough test of starting a ¾-hp DeWalt radial saw slowed its 3-hp Briggs engine almost to stalling speed, the saw started and ran well.

you are in doubt, ask your dealer about the capacity of his unit.

TELEVISION RECEPTION

Not every MG set is capable of producing a good television picture on a TV plugged into it. The problem is three-fold: synchronization, voltage variation, and interference. By far the worst is interference and a few units have shielded ignition systems to help solve that problem. A shielded system is easy to spot as its spark plug is encased in a metal can or around the entire unit, as in the totally enclosed camper units. Shielding doesn't solve the whole problem as interference can come from the generating unit itself. However, some unshielded portables produce acceptable TV pictures.

Voltage variation problems can come from uneven loading on the generating unit and from uneven engine speed. A lowering voltage causes the TV picture to shrink, sometimes perceptibly. To hold engine speed as nearly constant as possible and control voltage variations from that source, a good MG set's engine should have a mechanical governor as air-vane governors are not as reliable. Fortunately, nearly all portable MG sets now have mechanical governors. If an arm comes out of the side of the engine crankcase and a control rod connects it to the carburetor throttle arm, the unit has a mechanical governor. Some units control voltage variations still further by means of solid-state circuitry or else externally mounted reactors that look much like transformers.

Because your electric plant cannot possibly run in exact phase with commercial power used by television broadcasters you can expect to see a slight "swimming" of the picture when watching on portable power. It's most noticeable when a still picture is being transmitted, as during a station break. Otherwise, the swimming movement can be masked by the usual action across the tube.

All of the camper units have USFS-approval mufflers and 12-volt capability should give good TV reception, since this is one of the major uses for them.

QUALITY

The length of service you get from a generating unit will depend on its quality and on the care you give it. Most of the small motor-generator sets are built with what are basically lawn-mower engines. On your lawnmower these engines get used about 17 hours a year on the average. Therefore, they last for years. When they are run at 3600 rpm hour after hour a whole year's use can get thrown at an engine in a single day of emergency power duty. Add the emergencies to nights of camping and weekends of sanding and drilling on a vacation house, and the electric plant will soon wear out as these units are intended for intermittent use. For continuous duty an 1800-rpm nonportable unit is required.

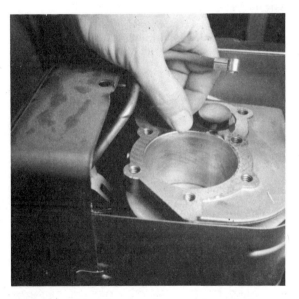

Most portable electric plant engine blocks are aluminum. The Onan's is too. However, it has a cast-iron cylinder sleeve that increases engine life by reducing wear. Because of the many hours MG sets pile up, long engine life is important.

With instruction-manual care, you can expect about a month of solid 24-hour-a-day duty from an average engine, but that is all. Then it will need a new short block (cylinder-crankshaft-piston-valve assembly). This will last for another month and by then, the generating unit itself is worn out. However, in intermittent use this is the equivalent of six hours use a month for about 10 years before the original engine wears out. One

Kohler fuel shutoff is located at one end of the gas tank where it's easy to reach. Large-size wingnut was eay to turn. Other engines had hard-to-reach, hard-to-work fuel shutoffs.

exception is built for industrial duty, and should outlast the less expensive units by about two to one.

Not all of the units will be correctly regulated to the 3600-rpm speed when you get them. To adjust one, load the generator to about half its output by plugging in a single-slice toaster, and then plug in an electric clock. The speed can be adjusted with the external governor speed nut to make the clock's second hand do a complete revolution in exactly one minute.

Econo-Throttle on the Kohler automatically idles the engine until power is needed. When drill trigger was squeezed, a solenoid control (beneath the large indicator light) cycled a solenoid which opened the throttle and ran the drill.

To learn more about specific models and where to buy them, contact the manufacturers: American Honda, Box 50, Gardena, Calif. 90247; Generac Corp., Box 8, Waukesha, Wisc. 53186; Hol-Gar Mfg. Corp. (Zeus), 500 Mildred Ave., Primos, Pa. 19018; Homelite Div., Riverdale & Nelson Sts., Port Chester, N.Y. 10573; Kohler Co., Kohler, Wisc. 53044; Majol Power Systems, 6 Orchard St., Nanuet, N.Y. 10954; McCulloch Corp., 6101 Century Blvd., Los Angeles, Calif. 90045; Montgomery Ward, Chicago, Ill. 60607; Onan, 1400 73rd Ave., N.E., Minneapolis, Minn. 55432, Pincor, 5841 W. Dickens Ave., Chicago, Ill. 60639; and Sears, Chicago, Ill. 60607.

SMALL PORTABLE ELECTRIC PLANTS (115-volt AC, 60-cycle, single-phase, 3600-rpm)						
MAKE, MODEL	WATTS OUTPUT	DRY WEIGHT	USFS-APR. MUFFLER	12-VOLT CHARGER	GEN. OR ALT.	FEATURES, ACCESSORIES AVAILABLE
Majol C-125	1250	78 lbs.	No	No	Gen.	Overload trip-out protector with indicator light. Options include cast iron engine, electric-start, dual voltage, lo-noise muffler, wheel kit, LPG-natural gas carb., remote-start control, transfer switch, elec. fuel pump.
McCulloch H-1500	1500	68 lbs.	No	No	Alt.	Lightweight, compact. Takes fantastic 54-amp dead short, ball bearing engine crankshaft, extended oil filler.

SMALL PORTABLE ELECTRIC PLANTS (115-volt AC, 60-cycle, single-phase, 3600-rpm)

MAKE, MODEL	WATTS OUTPUT	DRY WEIGHT	USFS-APR. MUFFLER	12-VOLT CHARGER	GEN. OR ALT.	FEATURES, ACCESSORIES AVAILABLE
Kohler 1.5MM25	1500	96 lbs.	No	No	Gen.	Designed for industrial use. Cast iron, ball-bearing engine. Quiet-running. All-Kohler throughout. Econo-throttle idles engine when power not being used. Options include pushbutton start, exhaust silencer, LPG or nat. gas carb.
Onan 1.7PC-1P	1750	86 lbs.	No	No	Alt.	Trouble-free rectifier excitation, steel-sleeve engine.
Pincor RF 10 AC/DC	1000	68 lbs.	Yes	Yes	Alt.	Solid-state exciter system, high surge capacity, shielded ignition.
Pincor RF1600 H	1600	105 lbs.	Yes	Yes	Alt.	Same as above, plus enclosed design with twin carry-handles.
Pincor RF1000 H	1000	68 lbs.	No	No	Alt.	Same as RF 10.
Pincor RF1500 H	1500	75 lbs.	No	No	Alt.	Same as RF 10.
Generac 5630 "Camper Special"	1500	74 lbs.	Yes	Yes	Alt.	Solid-state voltage regulation.
Zeus Z-1000	1000	60 lbs.	No	No	Alt.	No brushes or slip rings, visual fuel and oil gauges, overload protection. Available in gasoline, LP-gas or natural gas. Options include automatic idler, dolly, quiet muffler, exhaust extension, large fuel tank, voltmeter, LPG conversion kit.
Zeus Z-1250	1250	76 lbs.	No	No	Alt.	Same as above.
Zeus ZA-1250	1250	78 lbs.	No	No	Alt.	Same as above but built for heavier service.
Zeus Z-1500	1500	105 lbs.	No	No	Alt.	Same as above.
Niagara 1000	1000	64 lbs.	No	No	Alt.	Static-free for radio, TV. Optional quiet muffler.
Niagara 1500	1500	70 lbs.	No	No	Alt.	Same as above.
Honda ER400	300	41 lbs.	No	Yes	Alt.	Enclosed design.
Honda ER900A	800	86 lbs.	No	Yes	Alt.	Enclosed design.

SMALL PORTABLE ELECTRIC PLANTS (115-volt AC, 60-cycle, single-phase, 3600-rpm)						
MAKE, MODEL	WATTS OUTPUT	DRY WEIGHT	USFS-APR. MUFFLER	12-VOLT CHARGER	GEN. OR ALT.	FEATURES, ACCESSORIES AVAILABLE
Honda ER1500A	1250	117 lbs.	No	Yes	Alt.	Enclosed design.
Homelite 128 A10-1	1000	52 lbs.	No	No	Alt.	Low-cost model. Better models available in 1000- and 1500-watt.
Sears 32004N	1400	87 lbs.	Yes	Yes	Alt.	Enclosed design, quiet-running, on-off power switch, overload protection with warning light, permanent magnetic core, twin carrying handles.
Sears 32005N	1100	60 lbs.	Yes	Yes	Alt.	Built-in overload protection, permanent magnetic core.
Sears 32008N	1250	61 lbs.	No	Yes	Alt.	Oversize muffler, permanent magnetic core, voltage control.
Sears 32042N	1500	75 lbs.	No	Yes	Alt.	Oversize muffler, permanent magnetic core, voltage control, twin carry handles.
Sears 32041N	1100	65 lbs.	No	No	Alt.	Oversize muffler, permanent magnetic core.
Wards 27331R	1100	67 lbs.	Yes	Yes	Alt.	Designed as camper unit.
Wards 27332R	1800	112 lbs.	Yes	Yes	Alt.	Operating indicator light, overload protection, on-off switch, enclosed design, quiet-running, twin carry handles.
Wards 27334R	1100	67 lbs.	No	No	Alt.	Lo-tone muffler, shielded ignition cap, heavy stator windings for cooler running, longer life.
Wards 27340R	1250	71 lbs.	No	No	Alt.	Same as above.

Portable Electric Heater Repair

Portable electric heaters are often classified as a heating appliance, although many of them also use a small blower motor to force more warm air out of the housing. Most of these heaters are made to take advantage of both convected and radiated heat. Behind the heating element there is a large reflective panel of highly polished metal. This is shaped and contoured to direct the heat into the room area. If a blower is used, it forces air behind the panel and out vents that surround it, adding to the efficiency of the unit.

It's important to vacuum away the dust, lint and hair that collects on the outer grill of these heaters. The frequency of cleaning depends on

Front panel of heater can be removed by removing screws or retaining clips.

the amount of usage. Under heavy usage conditions, once a week is not too often. If lint is allowed to accumulate on the grill, it blocks the air flow. This interferes with the workings of the heating element, can destroy motor bearings and sometimes causes thermostat or control failure. It can also be a fire hazard.

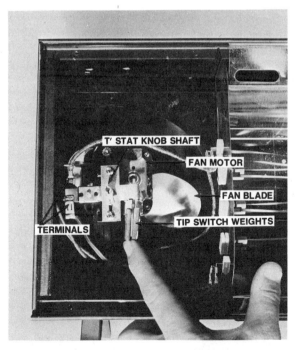

Fan and thermostat (which includes tip switch assembly) is located behind the control panel. Vacuum away any lint, and lubricate fan motor yearly if required.

The heating element can be made of coil nichrome wrapped around a porcelain insulator, ribbon nichrome suspended by porcelain insulators or the enclosed type element. The ribbon-element insulators can be replaced. Often spring tension is used on the porcelain supports to maintain tension on the element during expansion periods when it's heating. The coil type elements can often be replaced by unscrewing a porcelain block which is fitted with a lamp base. These are used on many radiation type heaters without blowers. If an enclosed element fails, an exact replacement will have to be obtained. It will have a mounting flange to hold it in place.

On most heaters a thermostat is used to control the amount of heat output. It is connected in series with the heating element and is usually of the bimetal type. If the unit has a blower, the thermostat is placed so that it senses the temperature of the air entering the grill to be circulated behind the radiant heater. When the incoming air temperature is at the proper level determined by the dial setting, the thermostat turns off both the heating element and the blower.

In addition to the thermostat, two safety devices are also used on most modern heaters. One is a bimetallic safety thermostat that senses the temperature of the element. If for any reason the blower should stop or the air flow become obstructed by lint, hair or dust, the safety thermostat will turn the heating element off. The other device is known as a tip switch. It is a weighted arm that will open the thermostat contacts if the heater is knocked over for any reason. Of course, those models with a tip switch must be in an upright or relatively level position to operate.

If the heater doesn't operate properly or doesn't operate at all, check the receptacle with a table lamp to see if it burns. If voltage reaches the receptacle, unplug the heater and check the plug of the appliance and the point where it enters the cabinet.

If it is necessary to disassemble the appliance, you can begin by removing the screws that hold the front panel in place. On this appliance they are usually obvious. Before removing the panel, first remove any knobs that protrude from the inside. With the panels off, you have easy access to the blower, thermostat, safety switches and the heating element. Examine the thermostat contacts closely. If they are burned or pitted, they should be cleaned with an automotive point file. Then they can be burnished with a hardwood stick or the striking surface from a book of paper matches.

The tip switch is often a part of thermostat itself and opens the same contacts. The bimetal limit switch is a safety device and will normally be closed. It's usually an enclosed wafer-type switch and you'll need to make a continuity test to see if the circuit is complete through the switch.

If open type heating elements are used, any break will usually be obvious. Don't attempt to splice one of these elements — at best it's a short lived repair. If an element fails, always replace it with a new one. If the element is the coil-type nichrome, you can purchase it by length from an appliance parts distributor. He'll cut off a length based upon the wattage found on the model number plate of your heater. You'll have to stretch this coil to the exact length, but it's not a hard job. Fasten it securely at one end, preferably in a vise, then grip the other end with a pair of pliers. Pull it toward you until the exact length is reached. Don't stand directly behind the coil.

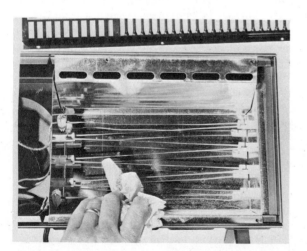

Reflective panel should be cleaned thoroughly when it becomes tarnished or dirty. Elements are ribbon type, held in place by porcelain insulators.

If the opposite end should slip free, it can snap back at you like a door spring.

If the radiant panel has become tarnished, clean it with a damp cloth and mild detergent. Be sure and vacuum away all lint and dust from inside the heater.

The symptoms tell you a lot about the ailment of the heater. For instance, if the blower operates, but the heating element doesn't, you can be sure that power is reaching the appliance and the problem is internal. This should warn you to check the element side of the circuit. On the other hand, if the element operates and the blower does not, the problem is likely a blower motor which has stuck bearings or an inoperable motor.

If lint should clog the motor bearings, it causes them to bind. Clear away all the lint with a stiff brush (such as an old toothbrush), then apply one drop of oil to the rotor at each end of the bearing. Spin it by hand a few times, and in most cases, the motor will become free.

When you are reassembling a portable electric heater, be sure and check for grounds with a volt-ohm-meter before putting it back into operation. *SEE ALSO APPLIANCE REPAIR, SMALL.*

Portable Humidifier Repair

Portable humidifiers are used frequently in homes during the winter months to add warmth and comfort. They raise room humidity, enabling people within to feel warmer, even when the temperature is reduced. This is because moisture in the skin tends to evaporate more slowly when a humidifier is used to raise relative humidity.

Most portable humidifiers operate by forcing room air through a sponge-like belt saturated with water. The belt material, or media, is kept wet by a motor drive which continuously rotates it through a reservoir in the bottom of the

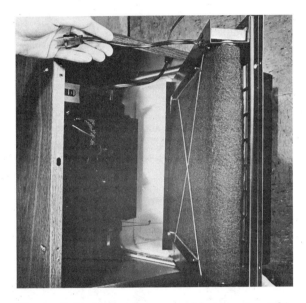

Front grille and panel can be removed for servicing after first unplugging humidifier. Reservoir is seen at bottom photograph.

humidifier. As the air passes through the saturated belt, it picks up moisture.

The water in the reservoir is replenished by filling it manually from a container or, in some models, by connecting it permanently to a water line. The low energy consumption of the humidifier is more than offset by the gain in comfort and reduced heating temperatures possible in the home.

You can help your humidifier do its job better by using only the most mineral-free water available. If you live in a hard water area, perhaps your best bet is to collect some rain water during periods of rain fall. Filter it through a cloth before adding it to the humidifier. Also, cleaning the humidifier thoroughly during the season will help keep it free from mineral buildup, one of the primary causes of problems within this appliance.

You can usually see if the media belt is turning and if the fan motor is operating without removing the panels. If the unit does not operate at all check to be sure that power is reaching the receptacle by plugging in a table lamp.

To disassemble the humidifier, unplug it first. Remove both front and rear covers. Proceed to

the area where your observation indicates that the problem lies.

If the media belt fails to turn, it may be due to a mineral build up in the mechanism itself or within the pan. This is usually apparent. Remove the belt and remove the part involved. Scrape and clean as necessary to remove all traces of minerals. After the heavy deposits are removed, the remainder of the film can be cleaned away by using the cleaner recommended by the manufacturer or in a solution of white vinegar. Soaking the media belt will help loosen any minerals from its pores.

The media belt is easily removed for cleaning. This entire assembly can be unplugged, allowing it to be pulled completely out of the humidifier.

If a belt becomes brittle and dry it should be replaced. These belts are available from the dealer or the distributor for the manufacturer that built the humidifier. The belt is an expendable part and may have to be replaced every couple of years, even when cleaning has been carried out regularly.

If the fan motor seems to be at fault, check to be sure that bearings are lubricated and free. Do this by simply spinning the fan blade. It should move smoothly within the motor. Be sure that no lint or dust is around the shaft where it enters the motor housing. A drop of oil at each shaft

Portable Electric Humidifier Repair

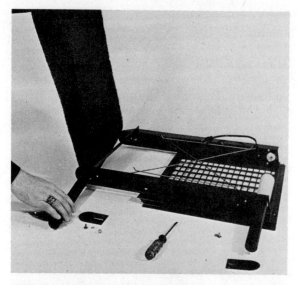

With the belt assembly removed, it's easy to remove rollers and lift belt away for cleaning. Media belt can be cleaned in 50% solution of white vinegar and water or a manufacturer's solution.

end will help to lubricate it. If oil ports are provided, use a couple of drops of SAE-20 non-detergent oil or that recommended by the manufacturer for the humidifier.

Fan motor is accessible from rear on this humidifier model.

Many humidifiers have a float-type indicator which will tell you how much water is left in the reservoir. Some of these have a switch attachment which will stop operation of the humidifier in case the reservoir runs out of water. If the switch is actuating prematurely, it can shut the humidifier down. You can check this by raising or lowering the float rod extending into the reservoir and listening for the click of the switch. It should turn off just before the float is at the bottom of the reservoir.

A humidistat is used on many humidifiers to turn the unit off when the surrounding area has reached a certain level of humidity. A humidistat works very much like a thermostat except that it senses moisture in the air rather than the temperature of the air. A stretched sensing element which is capable of absorbing moisture (often made of human hair) controls the switch section of the humidistat. Calibration of this control is accomplished by setting the unit outside for several hours, then checking with the local weather bureau to find the prevailing relative humidity. That indicated on the knob of the humidistat should be within ten per cent of the relative humidity for the day. If not, a calibration screw is often provided on the humidistat to allow you to adjust it to closer tolerances — or you may choose to compensate by simply turning the knob to a higher or lower setting.

Some humidifiers also have a heater built into the humidifier to raise the air temperatures somewhat above that in the room. This "reheat" feature prevents cooling effect of the moving moist air directly in front of the humidifier. This element can be cycled in and out and controlled by a switch. The element is usually of the open type, and any breaks or poor connections should be visible.

Leaks within the water storage compartment can usually be remedied. In case of a leaking reservoir, epoxy will form a permanent, hard seal. Be sure to clean the adjacent area well before applying the epoxy to the affected area. Clean and remove all water before storing at the end of the season. Check the humidifier for grounds with the VOM on the highest resistance scale before putting it back into use after servicing. *SEE ALSO APPLIANCE REPAIR, SMALL.*

Portable Power Drill
[SEE PORTABLE POWER TOOLS.]

Some Commonly Used Portable Power Tools.

PORTABLE DRILL

ROUTER

PORTABLE DRILL

FLEX SHAFT

SABRE SAW

SANDER

DISC SANDER

CIRCULAR SAW

Portable Power Tools

CIRCULAR SAWS

Today there are dozens of portable circular saws available made by many different manufacturers. It's common to hear such names as "cutoff saw," "utility saw" and "builder's saw." All these descriptive titles fit, but it's an error to limit this saw's applications to just the one type of work implied by each of these names.

The portable circular saw was developed originally as an aid to construction men so house framing timbers could be sized right on the job without the time and effort previously required by the handsaw. Just the time saved is impressive. It might take as much as a minute to cut through a 2 x 4 with a handsaw. The powered tool will do it in seconds.

With some know-how and a few jigs, you can broaden a portable circular saw's applications until it comes close to matching the performance of a table saw or radial arm saw. You can use it to cut rabbets or dadoes, bevels and miters, as well as to size identical pieces. It will not replace the stationary tools, but in some areas it has advantages over them. Its greatest advantage is its portability; you can carry the tool in your hand and apply it to the work whether you are doing preliminary cuts on a large plywood panel in the shop or trimming roof or deck boards at the actual work site.

Saw size is indicated by the diameter of the blade. This is important but should not be the sole factor in choosing a portable circular saw. Also consider the depth of cut—the thickness of material the blade can get through on both straight cuts and on 45° bevels. If all you plan to use it on is $3/4''$ stock, then there really is no problem. But it's more realistic to think in terms of material up to 2″ thick. Even here, consider the difference between *dressed* lumber and *rough* lumber. There can be a $3/8''$ difference in thickness between the two. So, if you plan to use much rough lumber, you may need more depth of cut than the person who works on dressed stock only.

Since saw sharpenings reduce the diameter of the blade, getting a blade that is just big enough for the piece of work when the blade is new may not be wise. Also, a blade that is constantly buried in the cut will not function as efficiently as it should. All of this seems to indicate that it's better to overestimate when judging the tool's capacity.

Models that are most available to homecraftsmen range from about $6^1/2''$ up to $7^1/2''$. Most of these will pass the basic depth-of-cut test. Generally, the larger the size, the more powerful, heavier and more expensive the tool will be. Getting the biggest size just because you can afford it isn't good practice. You might be better off choosing a smaller size as long as the tool performs as you demand, simply because it may be more comfortable to handle.

Blade speed is measured in rpm's when the blade is running free. This number indicates the cutting speed only when the tool is sufficiently powered to stay close to the same number of rpm's when you are cutting. This means that a fast turning saw that slows down considerably when cutting isn't really going to be faster than a slower tool that does not bog down.

If you can possibly arrange it, it's a good idea to actually test a sample of the tool you are in-

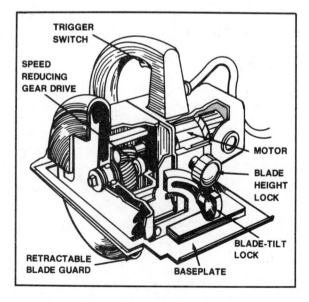

Parts of a typical portable circular saw.

terested in or have the salesman do it for you with a demonstrator model. Be sure to "heft" it yourself. When all other factors are satisfactory, how the tool feels in your hands can logically determine which saw you choose from a variety of units. Weight and ease of handling can also be important safety factors. A tool that is too heavy for you or that feels awkward when you grip it can be hazardous.

General Characteristics

Once you have purchased a portable circular saw, you should spend more than a few minutes in your workshop becoming familiar with the tool and how it handles. Make test cuts on some $3/4''$ plywood clamped securely to a bench and on a length of 2 x 4 supported on sawhorses or some other platform. Set the blade projection so it is about $1/4''$ more than the thickness of the material you are working on. A greater projection is actually more efficient, but for safety's sake keep it to a minimum. Place your right hand on the handle with a finger on the trigger and your left

For good work position, weight of the saw should be on the bulk of the work, not the cutoff portion. The tool should be gripped firmly, with both hands when possible.

hand on the knob. Position yourself so you are out of the line cut. Work so the weight of the saw is supported by the bulk of the stock, not the cutoff portion.

The upper portion of the saw blade is guarded by a fixed housing. The lower portion is covered by a guard that should automatically telescope into the top housing as you move the tool forward to make the cut. Be aware, therefore, that the portion of the saw blade in the cut and the amount of the saw blade that extends below the stock are not covered by the guard as you are cutting. At the end of the cut, the lower guard will swing down to encase the saw blade.

When you face the blade, it is turning in a counterclockwise direction. This means it is cutting on the "up" stroke and suggests that the good face of the stock should be "down" when you cut. This factor is critical only when the material you are cutting deserves such consideration.

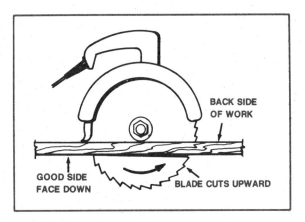

BACK SIDE OF WORK

GOOD SIDE FACE DOWN

BLADE CUTS UPWARD

Saw blades turn in a counterclockwise direction which means they cut on the "up" stroke. Therefore, the good face of the work should be down since most splintering will occur when the teeth leave the cut.

Feed speed should be judged by how the saw is cutting. The thickness of the stock, whether you are cutting with or across the grain, and the hardness of the material are factors that should help you determine how fast you can cut. Most important is to keep the blade cutting steady without undue strain on the motor and keep the blade cutting on a straight line. Portable circular saws will kick back easily if you bind the blade by going off the line. Binding can also happen on green wood when the kerf closes. When your first cut indicates that this is likely to happen on subsequent cuts, it's wise to be cautious by tapping a shim in the kerf to keep it open. Do this only when the cut is long enough to permit doing it and only after the saw blade has stopped turning.

Some saws are equipped with a "riving" knife. This accessory is the equivalent of a splitter on the table saw, and it doesn't hurt to keep the knife on the circular saw for general use. It can interfere with plunge cuts but at such times can easily be removed.

Many tools are equipped with a "slip clutch." Its job is to allow the saw blade to slip when the blade is confronted with an adverse situation, such as a knot in the wood, even though the motor continues to turn. Such a device is a tricky mechanism simply because its efficiency depends on how it is adjusted. The instructions you get with your tool will tell you how to properly adjust it.

In most cases it's simply a question of tightening the retaining nut on the arbor. However, if you tighten this nut too much, the clutch won't work. If you loosen it too much, you may get slippage to the point where the saw loses efficiency. When the situation is optimum, the slip clutch will protect the motor and help avoid kickback. If you have a slip clutch, it can improve the safe operation of your circular saw but remember that the most dependable safety devices are a sharp blade and a feed speed that lets you cut through the wood quickly and smoothly.

Another safety factor in some portable circular saws is an electronic brake. No extra buttons to push or procedures are required to operate this brake. When you release the trigger, the brake automatically works; the blade says "whoosh" and stops — just like that!

Cutting Techniques

Straight Cuts

Crosscutting is a job frequently done with the portable circular saw. Whenever possible, whether you are working in the shop or on location, it makes sense to clamp a guide strip to the work to keep the tool on a straight line. You should establish the distance from the edge of the baseplate to the cut line by test cuts. Thus, you will always know how far from the cut the guide strip should be clamped. This dimension can vary depending on the style of saw blade you are using, so you must check it each time you change blades. As a matter of fact, it should also be checked after you have a blade sharpened.

On narrow cuts, it's often more convenient to use a guide that you can hold to the work by hand. For example, you can use a common shop square as a guide or you can make a guide with more capacity merely by nailing two pieces of wood together in an "L" shape. The short leg should bear against the edge of the work, and the long leg should act as a guide for the saw.

"Riving" knife (where arrow points) attaches to upper housing and sits in the kerf to act as a splitter which helps to keep the kerf from closing and thus binding the blade.

Of course, you can do such work freehand by relying on yourself to keep the blade on the cut line. In any case, to start the operation, place the front edge of the baseplate on the work so the guide notch is in line with the cut mark. Start the saw; after the blade has revved up to full speed, move the tool forward to start the actual cutting. Remember that the saw kerf has width, so the actual cut must be made on the waste side.

When you approach the end of the cut, the guide-notch area of the baseplate will be off the work, so you'll have to watch the blade itself. This is more pertinent on freehand cutting than when you are working against a guide. In the latter case you shouldn't have to watch the cut line at all. Just be sure to keep the baseplate snug against the guide strip thoughout the pass.

One-hand operation is safe if the other hand, presumably holding the work, is well away from the cut area. Keep your body to the left of the cut line.

Working with both hands on the saw is a good idea but not always possible. You may need one hand to hold a guide, support the work, or even brace yourself.

The last should be avoided if possible. Just be aware that both you and the tool should be in stable positions. When in doubt, step back and reconsider. It is always important to be aware of the situation and what it demands of you.

Try to keep the saw on the bulk of the work. This isn't always possible, especially on out-of-the-shop jobs, but many times you can make a choice. For example, let's assume that you are trimming off the end of a long 2 x 4. Whether the

saw will rest on the waste portion of the 2 x 4 or on the body of the work depends on which side of the 2 x 4 you stand. Apply this thinking also if the cutoff portion is the part you need. The only extra thinking you have to do is determining which side of the cut mark you want the kerf to be on.

Get through extra-thick stock by making matching cuts from opposite sides. Good layout and accurate placement of the saw for each cut are important.

Cutting thick stock beyond the maximum depth of cut of the saw can be accomplished by making matching cuts from opposite sides. In such a case, layout and correct positioning of the saw are of primary importance if the two cuts are to meet exactly. When you have many such cuts to do on similar materials, it will pay to make a special U-shaped guide that can be clamped to the work so the two saw cuts will mate. Another way is to make a setup so the work can be flipped in correct position for the second cut after the first one has been accomplished.

Butt Cuts

The following little trick will help when you must trim the ends of boards to make a matching joint. Just overlap the board ends and cut through both of them at the same time. Thus, even a slight error in cutting will not affect how the two ends join together. This method works whether you are making a straight, angular, long or short cut in ripping or cross-cutting.

Cutting to Length

In using a portable saw to cut similar pieces, whether you are working in the shop or on the job, usually the easiest technique is to nail down a backup board and then cut a guide block that will determine the length of the pieces you will produce. The guide block is the length of the part you want less the distance from baseplate edge to saw blade. The work and the guide are butted against the backup, and the saw is moved along the guide to make the cut. In this example, the guide and work are hand held for the cut.

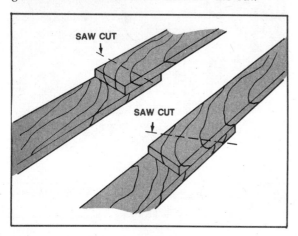

Straight or angular butt cuts can be done by overlapping the pieces and cutting through both of them at the same time to assure a perfect joint between the cut edges.

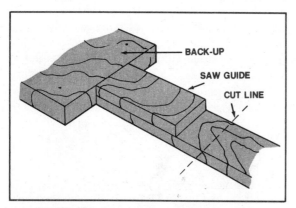

One way to cut many pieces of similar length. The saw guide equals the length of the workpiece less the distance from the edge of the saw's baseplate to the cut line.

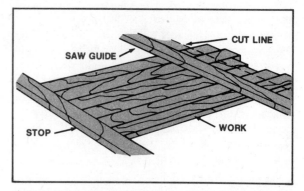

One pass trimming of multiple pieces can be done as shown. Nail the saw guide to the first and last workpieces.

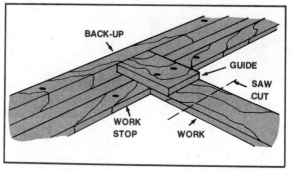

To cut many pieces of similar length when the pieces needed are short, use method shown. Guide, work stop and backup should be clamped or nailed securely to the work platform.

A second example involves a work stop in addition to the backup and the guide. Since all three of these items are nailed down, you can be concerned with just holding the work and making the cut.

Another possibility, when you need to trim many pieces to the same length, is to butt the pieces edge-to-edge and cut across all of them at the same time. Many professionals do this kind of thing freehand, but accuracy is easier if you use a stop against which you can butt the ends of the pieces, plus a saw guide. It isn't necessary to do more than tack-nail the guide to the first and the last piece in the set you are cutting.

It's also possible to make a bed jig so you can do accurate cutting of any material that fits between the bed sides, whether it's a piece of plywood or a set of individual pieces. The depth of the bed

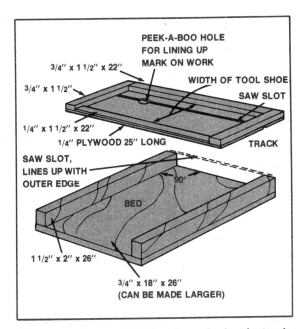

PEEK-A-BOO HOLE
FOR LINING UP
MARK ON WORK

3/4" x 1 1/2" x 22"

3/4" x 1 1/2"

WIDTH OF TOOL SHOE

SAW SLOT

1/4" x 1 1/2" x 22"

1/4" PLYWOOD 25" LONG

TRACK

SAW SLOT,
LINES UP WITH
OUTER EDGE

90°

BED

1 1/2" x 2" x 26"

3/4" x 18" x 26"
(CAN BE MADE LARGER)

Jig setup for crosscutting involves a bed and a track. Work is positioned in the bed; the tool rides the track above to make the cut.

determines the thickness of the material you can so handle. A bed jig is good for anything up to dressed 2x stock. The saw blade rides the slot cut in the platform; the saw-blade edge of the baseplate rides against the outboard frame member of the platform. This kind of jig can be made small or large, depending on the kind of work you plan to do. It can even be large enough to handle a 4' x 8' plywood panel.

Ripping

A good deal of what has been said so far applies to rip cuts as well as crosscuts. The primary distinction — whether you are cutting with the grain or across it — doesn't seem nearly as important as the length of the cut. Even the importance of choosing the right saw blade is minimized, since in so much portable saw work the supersmoothness of the cut edge is not so critical.

As in crosscutting, use a clamped-on guide or an edge guide to help produce a straight cut. A commercial edge guide is fine to use when the width of the cut permits. Remember, however, that it's not as easy to be accurate with such an edge guide as you can be with a wood strip simply

because it does not prevent you from being wobbly with the saw.

Most saws are designed so the guide may be used on either side of the blade. To choose which side to place the guide, just consider which position involves the least extension of the guide and which provides the most saw support. Sometimes your decision has to be based on which end of the board you are going to start from, especially if the board is part of a fixed assembly and you don't have much choice in determining operator position.

A guide strip is nothing more than a straight piece of wood. It can be clamped in some mid-way area or . . .

close to an edge. Be sure to maintain full contact between baseplate edge and the guide strip throughout pass.

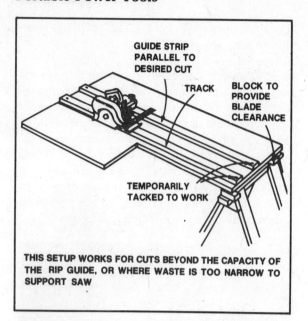

GUIDE STRIP
PARALLEL TO
DESIRED CUT

TRACK

BLOCK TO
PROVIDE
BLADE
CLEARANCE

TEMPORARILY
TACKED TO WORK

THIS SETUP WORKS FOR CUTS BEYOND THE CAPACITY OF
THE RIP GUIDE, OR WHERE WASTE IS TOO NARROW TO
SUPPORT SAW

Rip cuts beyond reach of the standard guide can be accurately made if the shoe rides against a fence tacked or clamped to the face of the stock. If the saw's shoe doesn't project outside the blade, and its motor housing is too low to clear a fence, use the setup shown.

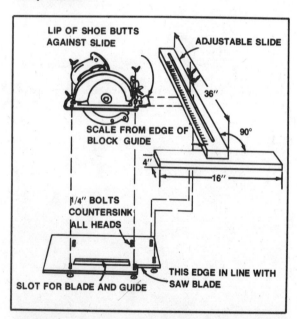

LIP OF SHOE BUTTS
AGAINST SLIDE

ADJUSTABLE SLIDE

36"

SCALE FROM EDGE OF
BLOCK GUIDE

90°

4"

16"

1/4" BOLTS
COUNTERSINK
ALL HEADS

THIS EDGE IN LINE WITH
SAW BLADE

SLOT FOR BLADE AND GUIDE

Jig shown is designed so the guide and the saw move together in making extra-wide rip cuts. The position of the saw on the guide arm determines the width of the cut.

With some edge guides you can create a setup by using both a clamped-on strip and the guide.

This combination can be useful when you need to cut a number of long pieces of equal width. In this situation, the edge guide rides against the clamped-on strip, and you adjust the guide after each cut you make, using the calibrations on the edge-guide bar if they are provided. Similarity in width will depend on how accurately you adjust the edge guide after each of the cuts.

When material thickness allows and you must cut the same amount from a number of pieces, you can do the job by stacking the parts and cutting through them all at the same time. This method is very feasible, regardless of the maximum depth of cut of your tool, when you are working with $1/8''$ and up to $1/4''$ paneling. Of course, the thicker the material, the fewer the number of pieces you can stack for cutting.

Grooves and Notches

You can form dadoes and grooves by setting the blade projection to the depth of cut you require and then making a series of overlapping cuts. Your best bet is to use a guide strip for the outline cuts. Then you can work freehand to remove

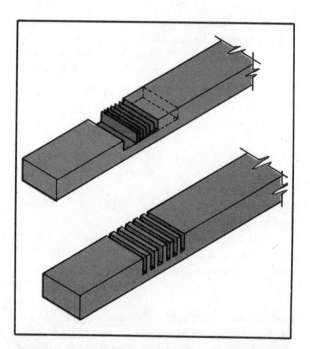

Cut dadoes by making a series of overlapping, parallel cuts to remove waste stock completely (top), or space the cuts and remove the remaining wood between the cuts with a chisel (bottom).

the waste material between them. It's also possible to make a series of parallel cuts that do not overlap and then rely on a hand chisel and mallet to remove the waste. This technique might be more applicable to short dadoes and notches than to long grooves.

To cut notches, such as the ones you need in a stairway stringer, make two cuts that meet at the base of the angle. In order to clean out the corner, you must make the cuts a bit longer than is needed to form the notch. To minimize this extra cutting, use maximum blade projection. If this is not acceptable for appearance, cut just to the line and then finish up with a handsaw or a sabre saw.

Angular Cuts

To do cross or rip bevels, tilt the circular saw to the angle you require. Most machines have tilt scales, but when the accuracy of the cut is critical, it's best to use the scale setting as a guide only. Check the test cut with a protractor before you proceed with the job. Also, check to see if the cut-line edge on the base plate is a good indicator for bevel cuts, as well as for square cuts. Be sure the tilt lock is firm and the leading edge of the base plate is seated firmly on the wood before you make contact with the blade.

The general rules for tool handling and feeding apply in making angular cuts. You'll do better if

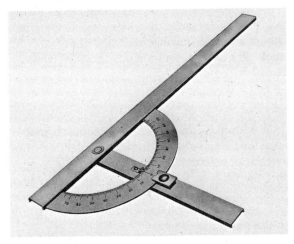

A protractor is the most important accessory you should have. With it, you can set up quickly to guide the saw for square or angular cuts.

you work against a clamped-on guide strip or with an edge guide. It makes sense to check the real distance from the cut to the side of the base plate on any angle setting that you use frequently. Do this by actually making a short cut in a board and then measuring from the cut to the edge of the plate. Thereafter you will know, whether for one cut or many, just where to clamp the guide strip.

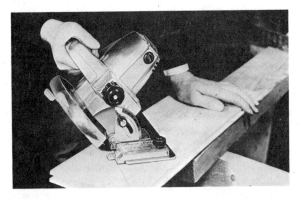

Circular saws will tilt to 45°. When the tool is tilted and a miter cut is made, the result is a compound angle. Depth of cut at 45° should be enough to get through 2x stock.

Handle a simple miter much as you would a crosscut by guiding the saw freehand along a line or by using a guide. Accuracy will depend on how careful you are when doing the layout. Since miter cuts are made most often across narrow widths, you can use an adjustable protractor as a guide. Protractors are available as accessories, or you can make one yourself.

Miter cuts can be done freehand, but accuracy is easier to achieve when you take the time to clamp on or tack-nail a guide strip.

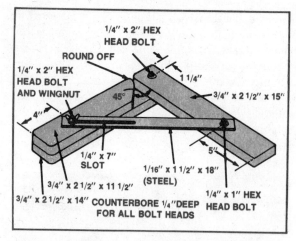

1/4" x 2" HEX HEAD BOLT
ROUND OFF
1/4" x 2" HEX HEAD BOLT AND WINGNUT
45°
4"
1 1/4"
3/4" x 2 1/2" x 15"
5"
1/4" x 7" SLOT
1/16" x 1 1/2" x 18" (STEEL)
3/4" x 2 1/2" x 11 1/2"
3/4" x 2 1/2" x 14"
1/4" x 1" HEX HEAD BOLT
COUNTERBORE 1/4" DEEP FOR ALL BOLT HEADS

This is an adjustable version of a crosscut jig so it can be set for angular cuts. Size the length of the slot so its extremes will be stop-points for 90° and 45° settings.

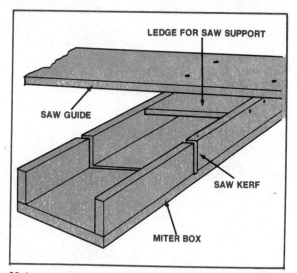

LEDGE FOR SAW SUPPORT
SAW GUIDE
SAW KERF
MITER BOX

Make a special miter box for use with a portable circular saw. Make guides and saw-support ledges for both left-hand and right-hand miter cuts.

To cut many pieces of molding or very narrow pieces, you can work with a kind of miter box ordinarily used with a handsaw. The basic design, a U-shaped trough with cuts across it, is the same, but for the portable saw you add a saw guide and a ledge for saw support. The box you make for a portable saw also has to be longer than one designed for a handsaw. Provide for left- and right-hand miter cuts with a saw guide and support ledge for each. The depth of the box can't be greater than the maximum blade projec-

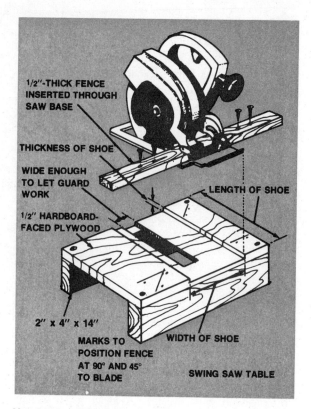

1/2"-THICK FENCE INSERTED THROUGH SAW BASE
THICKNESS OF SHOE
WIDE ENOUGH TO LET GUARD WORK
LENGTH OF SHOE
1/2" HARDBOARD-FACED PLYWOOD
2" x 4" x 14"
MARKS TO POSITION FENCE AT 90° AND 45° TO BLADE
WIDTH OF SHOE
SWING SAW TABLE

Here's a special mitering setup to make yourself. It will work only with saw designs that provide a pivot action to achieve depth of cut.

tion on your saw. It will pay to nail the box to a solid surface. Keep your hands well away from the cut area.

Special mitering setups are available commercially. Some provide for swiveling tracks so the saw can be set on either side of a center line. Others are made strictly for molding and narrow stock. The saw is mounted on a pivot so it can be swung up or down.

Plunge Cuts

Cuts within a panel are easily made no matter what the design of the portable circular saw. The basic approach to making plunge cuts is to support the saw on the work with the blade clear and the guard retracted. Then, with the blade turning, lower the tool slowly until it seats firmly on the base plate.

If the blade projection on your saw is handled by pivot action, it's best to hold the saw so it is tilted

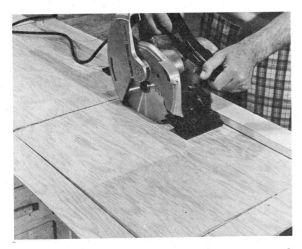

To do plunge cutting, mark the cutout on the work and situate the saw blade to cut on a line. Initially, the blade is above the work. Cutting starts as the blade is lowered to make contact.

When the tool is seated solidly on the baseplate, feed it forward to the next line. The guard will have to be held in a retracted position as you start each plunge cut.

on the front edge of the baseplate. Then turn the saw on and slowly bring it level to the piece of work. If you have an elevator-type depth adjustment, line the retracted blade up with the layout mark and then sink it into the work while the blade is turning.

In order to clean out corners, you must saw a bit beyond the line. Maximum blade projection will minimize this. If you wish to avoid overcutting entirely, saw just to the line from both directions and then clean out the corners with a handsaw or sabre saw.

On the third or fourth cut, clamp or tack-nail a support strip across the waste to keep it from twisting and possibly binding the blade.

It's sometimes advisable, after you have made two or three of the cuts, to nail or clamp a support across the pocket. Securing a support will keep the waste from binding the blade as well as prevent the waste from falling out when the cuts are complete.

Rabbet Cutting

Cutting rabbets is mostly a question of setting up the work so the saw may be positioned for the related cuts. When you make overlapping, parallel cuts, the job is done with repeat passes.

First cut of a two-pass rabbet. Cut shown is the shoulder cut, guided by a strip that is tack-nailed to the work. Saw projection equals the depth of the rabbet.

Portable Power Tools

Your best bet is to use a clamped-on guide for the shoulder cut. Then you can make a series of freehand passes to remove the waste.

For a two-pass rabbet, proceed with the clamped-on guide to do the shoulder cut. Then stand the stock on edge for the second cut. This takes a little more organization since stock edges are rarely wide enough to provide good support for the saw.

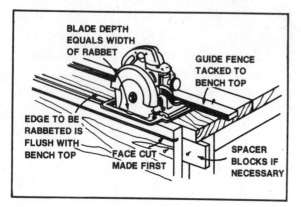

How to set up for the second cut on a two-pass rabbet operation. Note that you can operate in this way on the edge of your workbench.

When you need just one rabbet, use the repeat pass procedure. When you need the same job on many pieces, it will probably pay to set up the two-pass technique.

For example, let's assume that you need 6 or 8 pieces of plywood 1' wide and 4' long with a rabbet cut along the ends. A good way to do this is to cut the rabbets on a full sheet of plywood and then slice up the sheet into 1'-wide pieces.

Circular Cuts

The portable circular saw really isn't designed for such work, but you can cut circles by using a pivot-guiding system and being very patient about getting through the stock. The radius gauge is a strip of wood or metal fastened in the rip-guide slot and pivoting on a nail. The kerf you cut will really be a cove, so feed very slowly and don't attempt very small circles.

The cut has to be made in stages. The first stage of the cut should be just enough to break the sur-

face of the wood. Thereafter, increase depth of cut about $1/16''$ for each pass. Feed the saw slowly and stay on the motor side. These steps are more applicable when you're working on thin panels, but be sure that you supply good support for any piece of work in which you're making a circular cut.

SABRE AND RECIPROCATING SAWS

Not too many years ago, the sabre saw made as big a splash on the power tool market as the portable cutoff saw did when it first appeared. The enthusiasm hasn't waned, and it is completely justifiable because with a sabre saw you can do many on-location jobs that you do on the band saw or the jigsaw in the shop. Even with stationary tools on hand, work size often makes it more convenient to do a chore with a tool that you apply to the work.

The sabre saw does not make stationary tools obsolete. In the case of the band saw, the sabre saw can't compete in cut speed, nor can it rival the

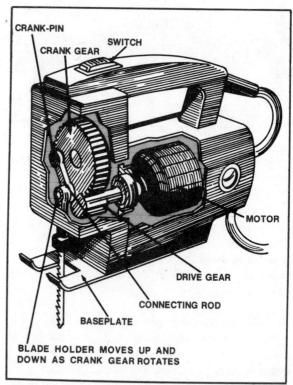

Parts of a typical sabre saw.

big tool in jobs like resawing, pad cutting, or making compound cuts. The concept of the sabre saw demands a stiff, relatively wide blade, so it's not about to challenge the jigsaw in terms of fine, tight-radius fretwork. Its greatest advantage lies in its small, palm-grip size, and in its portability.

It can do piercing without the need of a starting hole. Since the blade is chucked at one end only, it's possible to so angle the tool by resting it on the front edge of the base plate that the blade teeth begin to cut as you bring the tool to a vertical position. This permits cutting into the material's surface and, finally, as you approach normal operating position, to penetrate through the stock.

What makes the tool even more exciting today is the great variety of blades available and the fact that modern versions provide different speeds, even variable speeds. Thus, you can choose a good combination of blade and speed for cutting anything from leather to steel. With the right

blade, you can do heavy-duty work like notching studs or stringers and merely by changing to another blade design (and maybe another speed), go immediately to inside work on cabinets and paneling.

You'll find that stroke length, the up-and-down action of the blade, and available speed or speeds will vary from model to model. Of course, the more you pay for a unit, the more you get. Stroke length, power, speeds, and versatility increase with price. For not much more than $10.00, you can buy a $1/6$ HP model with a $1/2''$ stroke and one speed of 3,200 spm. Even in this price range, the tool may have a tilting base as well as a built-in sawdust blower. The "middle" price range may get you a $1/4$ HP machine with a $3/4''$ stroke and a special switch that lets you select between two speeds, for example, 3,400 spm or 2,700 spm. Get into the top price range, and you can have a full $1''$ stroke and a hearty $1/2''$ HP with a selection of speeds that runs from about 1,300 spm up to 3,200 spm.

The smaller, short-stroke units do not have tremendous cut speed, but many of them have good capacity. There aren't any that won't cut at least $1\,1/2''$ softwood. It's a good idea to check the capacity factor in terms of the work you plan. Usually this is listed as so many inches in hardwood and so many inches in softwood. Many times you will even be told the capacity in aluminum and in steel.

Some units provide a straight up-and-down blade action while others have a canted blade or one that moves in a small orbit. The last two back the blade away on the downstroke and move it forward on the up or cutting stroke. The idea is to reduce power-wasting drag on the downstroke and to free the kerf of waste. This can reduce friction and heat and prolong blade life.

To get the most from a sabre saw, you should be able to tilt it from zero to 45°. This tilting allows you to make bevels, cross-bevels and even compound cuts. Check this feature when you view an "economy" unit. Some models provide special inserts. These attach to the base plate and minimize the opening around the blade to

A great asset of the sabre saw is being able to make plunge cuts, permitting you to cut through stock without a blade insertion hole.

eliminate or at least lessen the amount of chipping that occurs as the blade teeth leave the stock.

Importance of Blades

A close study of the blades that are available for the sabre saw is almost a course in the use of the tool. In most cases, one blade is supplied with the tool when it is purchased. It will be a general-purpose blade, like a combination blade generally supplied with a table saw. To use this single blade for all jobs, however, will impose limitations and restrictions that will reduce the quality of your output and even increase your shop chores.

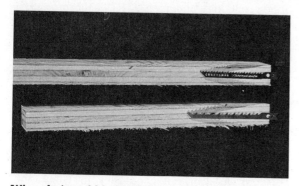

Wise choice of blades can make a big difference in the quality of the cut. Cut on the bottom piece was made with a coarse, few-teeth-per-inch blade. A small-toothed, taper-back blade made the cut on the top piece.

For example, by using a special blade that is designed to cut plywood, you can reduce considerably, and sometimes even eliminate, the follow-through sanding needed to get a good edge. By using a blade with wave-set teeth, like those you find on a common hacksaw blade, you can use the sabre saw like a power hacksaw. For jobs in leather, rubber, cardboard and the like, there is a toothless blade that fits the tool like any other blade but cuts like a knife.

If you are involved in remodeling work, there are blades that can slice through an occasional nail without damage and others that are shaped so that it's possible to cut through moldings and baseboards flush up against a wall. Sabre saw blades are not so expensive that you can't have an all-inclusive assortment to be prepared to cut

anything from a sheet of paper to $1/2''$ steel. Such an assortment can prove the most economical in the long run since you will be less likely to abuse blades on jobs those blades were never meant to do.

Two or three dollars will buy blades to set you up for most wood cutting; another dollar or two will start you on metal cutting. These same blades can also be used on other materials such as hardboard, wallboard, insulation sheeting and floor tiles.

Normally, you should choose a wide blade ($3/8''$ or $1/2''$) for straight cuts and a narrow one ($1/4''$) for doing curves. The thickness of the material should also influence your choice in blade length. Blade lengths can be short (from $2 1/2''$ to $3''$) or long (from $4''$ to $6''$). Lengths can vary according to tool brand, but most manufacturers do supply both long and short blades.

Always choose the shortest blade that will do the job. The big $6''$ varieties are not usually recommended for tools that have less than a full $1''$ stroke.

Of two similar blades, the one that is taper-ground or hollow-ground will produce the smoothest cut, just as a hollow-ground circular saw cuts smoother than a combination blade. A very important point to remember is that a wide

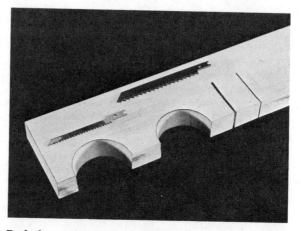

Both the narrow blade and the wide blade made the tight turns. Fewer and heavier-set teeth of the latter cut a wider kerf and thus provide more room for the blade to turn.

blade with few, heavy-set teeth per inch will often turn as tight a radius as a narrow blade with many teeth per inch and little set. It's even possible that the heavy blade might make a tighter turn than the other because the big blade forms a wider kerf and thus the body of the blade has more room to turn.

Bear in mind when the chart recommends a blade for scrollwork that the narrowest, finest-toothed blade you can buy for a sabre saw can't begin to match the fretwork designs you can cut on a jigsaw when it is fitted with a fine jeweler's blade.

Some manufacturers make blades that are intended to fit only their saws. When you are in doubt about which blade to buy for your tool, take the old blade with you and be sure to match the shank end. Though the trend is toward standardization, there is some discrepancy in the combinations of teeth per inch, set, lengths and widths the makers offer. Be sure to study the owner's manual that comes with the tool you buy for any specifics concerning the tool-blade relationship.

All blades, stiff as they are, can still bend, twist or arc in the cut. The main cause of such problems is forcing the cut, trying to get the teeth to chew out more material than they were designed to handle. You can easily tell when you are doing this by sound and feel. If the cut isn't progressing steadily without excessive feed pressure, the blade is being overworked, it's dull or you may be using the wrong one.

Do not use woodworking blades to cut any metal except do-it-yourself materials, such as aluminum, that can be worked with ordinary woodworking tools. In a pinch, however, you can use metal-cutting blades to cut wood, hardboards and similar materials.

As far as speeds are concerned, use low speeds for tough jobs and high speeds for the easy ones, but always remember that choosing the right blade for the job you are doing is your best assurance of good work quality and long blade life. An advantage of speed control, regardless of the blade, is that you can alter speed in the mid-

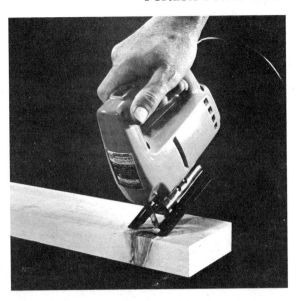

Rocking the saw will often make it easier to get through a knotty area. Combine the technique with a slower speed.

dle of a job. For example, slow down a bit when you hit a particularly dense grain area or a knot in a piece of wood.

Consider Teflon-coated blades, even though they are more expensive, if you plan to do much work with green, damp or pitchy lumber. When doing such work, select a blade with few teeth per inch and lots of set. When you are working on heavy stock but want a nice finish, it's all right to go to a smoother-cutting blade, but you must work much slower than you would with the recommended blade.

"Toothless" Blades

These are new tungsten-carbide blades, first introduced for industry but now available to home workshoppers. These blades cut almost anything and have a very long life. While a circular blade has teeth, these new sabre saw blades do not. Instead, the cutting edges consist of hundreds of particles of tungsten-carbide granules fused to the blade material.

Cutting speed is not a strong point of the new blades. A group of teeth will chew out more material than a line of grit and generally do it faster. Judged under home workshop conditions,

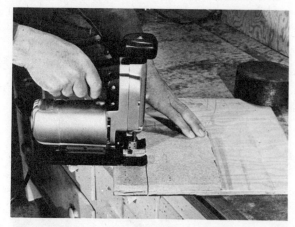

With a toothless, tungsten-carbide blade, you can easily cut materials like ceramic tile. The work must be firmly supported to avoid cracking the material.

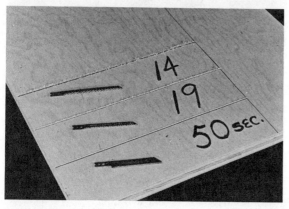

Even though toothless blades cut on both the "up" and the "down" stroke, they are not speed demons. It took 50 seconds for one to make a cut in this wood while regular toothed blades did it in 14 and 19 seconds. However, note obvious difference in splintering at the surface.

this suggests that the toothless blades do not — and probably aren't meant to — replace comparable toothed ones. But they do provide a valuable supplement, since no conventional blade can cut easily through ceramic tile or slate or through unsandwiched sheet metal without excessive burring and edge lifting.

The blades will work on wood, and they leave an impressive, almost sanded edge with minimal splintering and feathering. But they do not cut as fast as conventional blades.

Under test conditions, a medium-grit tungsten sabre-saw blade took about 50 seconds to make a

10″ cut through ³/₄″ DF plywood. A 10-tooth-per-inch, taper-back blade made it in about 19 seconds. A 7-tooth-per-inch blade with set teeth ran the 10″ in about 14 seconds. There was, however, a big difference in the cut quality. Although the taper-back blade (designed for the purpose) left a respectable edge, the tungsten blade came out on top.

Tungsten-carbide blades are also a good choice when cutting hard metals. Testing again showed that it took about 92 seconds to go through a 1¼″ OD, heavy-walled steel tube with a 32-tooth, wave-set sabre-saw blade. With a coarse-grit tungsten blade, it took about 80 seconds. This is not a great difference in time, but the results were startling as far as durability was concerned. The conventional blade was obviously tired after the job, while the toothless blade was ready to repeat the chore many times over.

The durability factor applies to the toothless blades generally. There is no question that they will outlast conventional blades by a most impressive margin.

In some cases in the home workshop, there is no basis for comparison with conventional blades. The toothless ones will cut ceramic tile, slate, asbestos cement, clay pipe, brick, stainless steel, countertop material and many other similar problem materials.

All of the grit types cut comparatively smooth edges with little feathering and chipping. The fine grit works best in thin, hard materials when cut quality is important and when chipping or delamination might be a problem. Medium-grit blades can be used if you wish the job to go faster or if you find that the material you are cutting is packing between the tungsten-carbide particles.

Coarse-grit blades cut the fastest and, since they form a wider kerf, will make smaller radius cuts than blades with finer grits. This feature is comparable to being able to make a tighter turn with a wide, heavy-set blade than a no-set, narrow blade. There is simply more room to maneuver.

Tool speed can be a factor in working most efficiently with the toothless blades. Slower speeds work best on such materials as stainless steel and countertop laminates. In all cases, tests indicate that it's wise to start at slow speeds and build up spm to the point where the blade is cutting most efficiently. Do this, at least for the first time, on each new material you tackle.

The Plunge Cut

With a sabre saw, you can do internal cutting without a lead-in cut from an edge of the stock, and you can get started without even having to drill a blade insertion hole.

Angle the tool so it rests on the forward edge of the baseplate. This angle must be such that you are presenting the teeth of the blade to the surface of the stock. A snug grip and a firm contact between the work and the baseplate are in order. Turn on the motor and very slowly tilt the machine back to make contact. You must avoid causing the initial contact to be between the point of the blade and the work. If you don't, the tool will do nothing but bounce up and down.

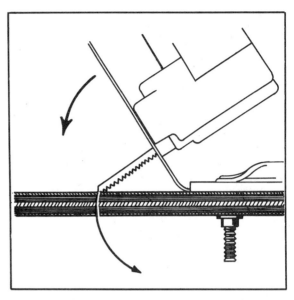

Another method of protecting the surface is to clamp a piece of wood to the work and brace the toe of the baseplate against the edge of the clamped-down piece.

The initial cut is a groove. As you continue to tilt the tool back, the groove lengthens and deepens and finally penetrates. Keep the contact between the baseplate and the work very firm. If you allow the tool to move back, you'll bounce off the back end of the groove. Also, letting the tool jiggle as you penetrate can mar the surface of the stock. To minimize this possibility, place a thin piece of scrap between the baseplate and the work — even heavy cardboard will do. Another way to provide firm support until penetration occurs is to clamp a piece of scrap to the work. Then you can brace the toe of the baseplate against the edge of the scrap.

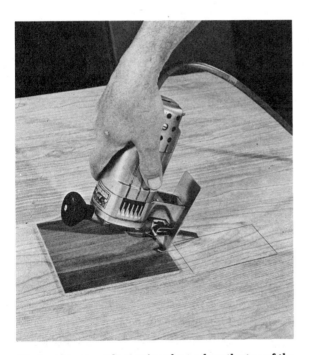

Start a plunge cut by resting the tool on the toe of the baseplate. Angle must be such that the teeth, not the point of the blade, are presented to the surface of the work. As a precaution against marring fancy-surfaced materials like hardwood paneling, rest the toe of the baseplate on a small piece of scrap stock.

When you try the plunge cut for the first time, do it in a waste area. After some practice you'll be able to accomplish it directly on a cut line. Before feeding to cut further, be sure you have penetrated sufficiently to seat the tool solidly in its normal, fully flat baseplate position. If the cutout is circular, then you just proceed in one direction to complete the operation. When square corners are involved, slant toward a line and then to a corner. Back out and then slant to an adjacent line so you can make a second cut at right angles to the first one. This will have to be repeated for each corner. If the corners are rounded, then, of

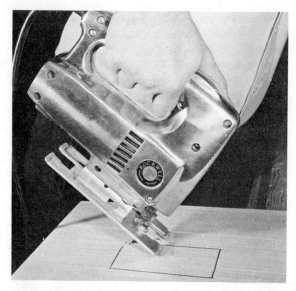

Slowly tilt the tool back so the teeth start to cut a groove. The more you tilt, the deeper the groove gets until you finally penetrate.

The amount of relief material that must be removed to do corners will depend on the width of the blade and, to some extent, the thickness of the stock. Sharp corners must be approached from two directions.

course, you can just make a turn. In such situations, it often pays to drill holes at the corners. This provides the shape you want and also eliminates the need for plunging. Incidentally, the plunging process can be overdone. It's nice to know you can do it when necessary, but if you are doing some complicated piercing work that would call for many plunge cuts or if you are in-

volved with some delicate material and it is possible to do blade insertion holes, be safer and do that instead.

Many of the ideas given in the jigsaw entry in relation to piercing, backtracking, etc. can also apply to sabre-saw work.

Freehand Cutting

The one thing you should avoid is vibration either in the tool or the work. Therefore, work that is not large enough to sit solidly on its own should be clamped or weighted down. To keep the tool still, apply firm pressure both down and forward. Avoid sideways pressure on the blade. Remember that the blade is chucked at one end only; lateral force can cause problems, damage to the blade and substandard cut quality being the most obvious.

Be sure that the baseplate is in firm contact with the work at all times. The only exception to this rule might occur when you hit a knot in the wood. Here, rocking the tool might help the blade get through more easily. The idea is to pivot up on the toe and thus decrease the contact area between the blade and the work. Coming back down does the same thing. In effect, you are concentrating the cutting power.

Sabre-saw blades cut on the "up" stroke so splintering and feathering will occur on the sur-

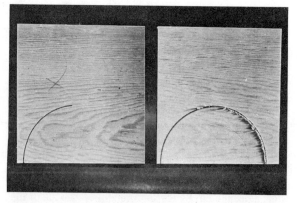

Remember that the blade cuts on the "up" stroke. Bottom and top views of a cut made with the same blade are shown. Clean cut on the left (bottom of work) suggests that all materials should be cut with the good side down.

In many cases, you can get around a difficult arc by first making the kind of radial cuts shown here. Waste that falls off as you proceed with the cut gives the blade more room to swing outward as it goes around.

Some tools come equipped with a rip guide. If yours doesn't, you can buy one as an accessory.

face of the work that is in contact with the baseplate. This suggests that anytime the finish cut is important, you work with the good side of the stock down. This is not always possible. You may, for example, need a hole through installed wall paneling. In such cases, work with a blade designed to produce a smooth cut even though cut speed might be reduced. A little trick that may come in handy is to place a strip of transparent tape over the cut line before you saw. This does the job of holding the wood fibers still regardless of the blade action. Another solution, if your saw is so equipped, is to use the special insert mentioned earlier.

Visualize the cut before you start working. Sometimes preliminary incuts will save you considerable backtracking. Don't force blades around turns they are obviously struggling to make. In some cases, radial cuts can be used with the sabre saw. For example, if you need to cut a small half circle in the edge of a piece of stock, you could facilitate things by making a series of cuts from the board edge to the line before you start to saw the arc. This would cause pieces of stock to fall away as you cut and provide more room for the blade to maneuver.

Guided Cuts

While it isn't difficult to do freehand straight cuts, you can relieve yourself of some of the strain by using a guide to gain better accuracy. The most common guide is a rip guide. This is very similar to those supplied for portable circular saws. Sometimes, one is supplied with the tool when you buy it. If not, you can buy one as an accessory. The guide is inserted through slots (or some similar arrangement) in the baseplate and is secured with screws. To use it, you measure from the fence on the guide to a tooth that is set in the guide's direction. As you cut, the fence rides the edge of the stock and maintains a uniform cut width. The guide may be used with almost any blade, but you will be most successful, especially on heavy stock, if you work with a wide blade. Although the accessory is called a rip guide, there is no reason why you can't use it on crosscuts as well.

When the cut you are making is too far from the stock edge to use the rip guide (or maybe it's at an angle to the edge), you can use a straight piece of wood in its place. Tack-nail or clamp the "straightedge" to the work. Position it away from the line of cut a distance that will be equal to the measurement from the edge of the baseplate in constant contact with the guide.

Most rip guides are designed so they can be used for pivot-cutting circles. For jobs beyond a guide's capacity, substitute a straight piece of wood, feed, and let the pivot do the guiding.

In most cases, the rip guide will serve to do pivot cutting of circles. Adjust the guide so the distance from the pivot point to a tooth set in its direction is equal to the radius of the circle you require. Follow that rule if the disc you are cutting out is the part you want. If the circle in the work is what you want, then measure from a tooth on the opposite side of the blade. Your best bet is to make a plunge cut before you set the pivot point. Then, holding the pivot point firmly, feed the tool slowly; let the pivot device do the guiding.

When the circle you require is beyond the capacity of the rip guide, you can substitute a straight piece of wood that is sized to fit the baseplate slots. A nail driven through the strip of wood serves as the pivot.

A good guide for crosscutting, when work width permits, can be an ordinary adjustable square or, for larger work, a carpenter's square. Hand hold these guides firmly as you move the tool along the blade. Any of the guides mentioned for use with a portable cutoff saw, including some of the homemade ones, can be used with a sabre saw as well.

You can also shape guides for doing curve cuts, although the technique is most applicable when the curve is not too extreme. Using such guides is a good way to cut delicate curved pieces. The important thing is to maintain a constant tangent contact between the guide and the edge of the baseplate.

Cutting Metal

With the right metal-cutting blade and a suitable speed, you can cut any metal that can be touched with a hacksaw blade. You can also do it faster and with much less effort. Actually, you increase capacity since you are not hindered by the yoke shape on the conventional hacksaw.

Regardless of the material, be sure at least two teeth are in contact with the edge of the stock. Thin material can sit between the teeth of a coarse blade, and this can result in stripping the teeth or bending and maybe breaking the blade. Of course, this does not apply to tungsten-carbide toothless blades.

As the material gets thicker, you can use coarser blades. In fact, it often pays to do this since very small teeth can clog quickly.

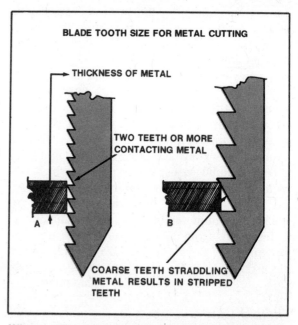

When cutting thin materials, be sure that at least two teeth of the blade contact the edge. Coarse teeth that straddle the material can be stripped.

Galvanized material like gutters and downspouts can be cut pretty cleanly with a fine-tooth, wave-set blade or a tungsten-carbide, toothless blade.

On thin sheets of metal, a better cut will result if the work is taped to a backup sheet of scrap wood.

All work must be firmly supported. When possible, if it is small, grip the workpiece in a vise. Other items can be clamped to or weighted down on a bench top. Very heavy sheet metals do not require any special consideration other than wise blade and speed choice. Thin sheet metals should either be supported on the underside with scrap wood or sandwiched between covers of thin plywood or hardboard. Set up in this way, even intricate shapes can be cut from thin sheets, and the parts will have smooth edges and little burr.

When working with heavy nonferrous metals, it pays to apply a grease stick lubricant to the blade

as you work. This will help keep the teeth from becoming clogged with waste metal.

Reciprocating Saws

It's difficult to select a name for this tool. They are called "reciprocating" saws, "bayonet" saws and "all-purpose" saws.

What emerges from the names, descriptive titles and uses is a heavy-duty, all-purpose sawing tool that works something like a sabre saw but is far from being one. Reciprocating saws drive a blade to-and-fro on a horizontal plane as opposed to the vertical action of the sabre saw.

Reciprocating saws are often described as the "you name it, they'll cut it" tool. From 12" diameter logs to steel pipe and bar stock, woods and plastics and other materials, this saw will do things you should not attempt with other, portable sawing tools.

Reciprocating saws can drive blades as long as 12", although 6" is more commonly used, and stroke length may be well over an inch. Most of

Because the reciprocating saw is so rugged, it is a fine unit to have for remodeling jobs. Always use the shortest blade that is adequate for the job.

them will supply more than one speed, while some have a built-in variable speed control mechanism. Because the saw is designed for a multitude of uses on various materials, being able to select a speed for the job and a blade to go with it is almost a necessity.

Most of these saws permit adjustment so you can cut close to walls and into corners. Prices start at about $40.00 and go up to considerably more depending on whether the tool is designed for commercial use or for home use. It's hard to find one tool in the category that is delicate in any way. The big ones can pull as many as 8.0 amps; few if any, pull less than 4.0.

If a plumber, electrician, carpenter, installation man or remodeler had to choose between a sabre saw and a reciprocating saw, chances are he would choose the latter. And this is a good clue to the tool's capabilities.

For average in-shop and on-location chores, the homecraftsman will be quite content with a good sabre saw. For those times when you might be building a carport or deck, cutting up firewood, building a fence, making a retaining wall, doing a major house remodeling job, cutting through a wall to install a new window or door or doing other jobs of that nature, the reciprocating saw can be a fine tool to have. *SEE ALSO BAND SAW; BENCH GRINDER; DRILL PRESS; JIGSAW; JOINTER; LATHE; RADIAL ARM SAW; SHAPER; STATIONARY BELT & DISC SANDER; TABLE SAW.*

DRILLS

Statistics indicate, as far as sales are concerned, that portable drills are the most popular power tools. The reason is simple: the portable drill is an excellent, basic tool-kit accessory even if the owner's involvement in do-it-yourself activities is limited to an occasional cut with a handsaw. Also, the modern drill, especially in the light-duty, small capacity range, has become more and more inexpensive while, at the same time, it has been improved to offer additional, practical features.

On the other hand, you can view the electric drill as a power source to drive a wide variety of ac-

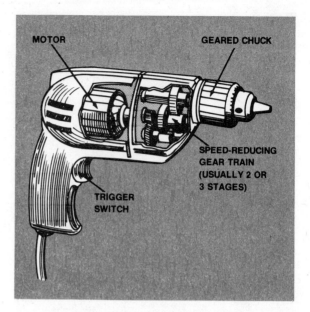

Parts of a typical electric drill.

cessories with activity ranges from polishing shoes to sawing wood. Therefore, the power drill can become the basis of a fairly efficient power tool shop. Ironically, the total cost of the attachments will usually far outweigh the original cost of the drill!

If you plan to use a power drill only occasionally, you would be wise to select a low-cost, light-duty unit. So equipped, you can do a variety of jobs, such as drilling holes for screws or drilling through a wall and into a stud, or drilling holes in masonry. However, it would not be reasonable to expect a less than ten dollar, $1/4''$ tool to do everything a house builder requires very many times. The final choice of a drill must be based on what you need it for. Price can't be the sole factor.

Sizes

Common sizes of electric drills are $1/4''$, $3/8''$, and $1/2''$. The size indicates the maximum shank diameter that can be gripped in the chuck — not the drilling capacity. Many cutting tools, like spade bits that go up to $1 1/2''$, have shanks turned down to $1/4''$. Circle cutters, fly cutters and the like form holes well over $1/4''$, but many of them have $1/4''$ shanks and can be gripped in a small capacity drill. However, complete freedom to do this is another matter. The drill may not have the power for the job, especially over an extended period of time.

Generally, the user can quickly judge if he is overtaxing the tool. It will get warm quickly, it will stall, or the speed may decrease to the point where the bit won't cut. Heed such warning signs and avoid abuse.

Your expectations of any drill must, first of all, be based on the size of the drill. Larger drills, of course, have more power. Secondly, judge a drill on how the manufacturer lists the tool. You'll find different "ratings" even in a given same-size category. If the maker lists one for "commercial duty" and another for "light duty," you can expect to find differences in the two that go beyond price. In addition, terms like "good," "better" and "best" that are used in the manufacturer's literature about the tool are clear indicators of the drill's quality. Another signal to look for is the length of the guarantee. In the manufacturer's catalog, one $1/4''$ drill might be guaranteed for 90 days, another for a full year.

Speeds

There was a time when you did not have a choice concerning the speed of the drill. In essence, you bought a drill for its power or its chuck capacity, and you got one compatible speed. The combination of size, power and speed made the unit ideal for a particular category of work. You can still do this, and it might even be a wise basis for selection if you wanted exceptional performance in a limited area. However, the tool would be a compromise if you checked it out for general-purpose applications.

The major drill feature today is built-in variable speed, and you get it in any drill size. An interesting factor here, which points up the logic of lower speeds being more compatible with greater capacities, is that even with variable speeds the range decreases as the drill size increases. A $1/4''$ drill may·go from zero to 2,000 rpm's or more, a $3/8''$ drill may have a top speed of 1,000 rpm's, and a big $1/2''$ tool may be limited to a maximum of 700 rpm's.

In the final analysis, no one drill will be ideal for every application you can think of. This point is

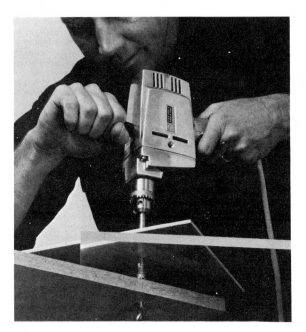

A great advantage of the variable speed drill, regardless of its size, is the fact that you can choose a good speed for the material you are working on and the size of the hole being formed. Bigger drill sizes often take lower speeds.

made because portable drills are the most abused of power tools. The best choice for anyone must be in line with how the tool will be used.

Variable speed will make any drill more flexible, but it doesn't change some basic concepts. A $1/4''$ drill, even at the right speed, isn't likely to hold up too long forming oversize holes in masonry or steel. A $1/2''$ unit might be awkward to handle on small drilling jobs. When you think in terms of some accessories, you'll find that light-duty units may have a nice speed range for broad application but lack power for the more demanding chores.

Features to Look For

The prices of portable drills are not so far out of line that a fellow can't think in terms of having more than one. A $3/8''$ unit with variable speed might be the best first choice simply because it can accomplish more than a $1/4''$ model but also do the jobs of smaller units.

An adjustable speed control knob is a good feature. It is set to provide a predetermined

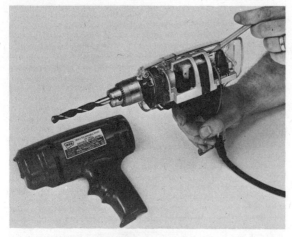

The purpose of double insulation is to provide a safety barrier between possible electric leaks and your hand. Disassembling such tools yourself is not recommended.

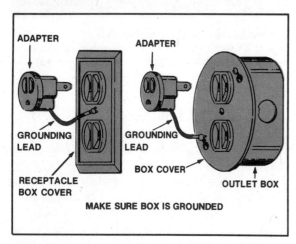

ADAPTER

ADAPTER

GROUNDING LEAD

GROUNDING LEAD

BOX COVER

RECEPTACLE BOX COVER

OUTLET BOX

MAKE SURE BOX IS GROUNDED

Most tools that are not double insulated come with an adapter plug so you can work with two-hole outlets. Be sure to follow instructions for attaching grounding lead that is part of the adapter.

speed. Thus, you can do any number of similar operations that require a particular rpm without reliance on finger control.

Double insulation is a good feature to look for simply because it eliminates the need to follow through on the 3-wire system that is a part of conventional units. In essence, double insulation provides safety barriers between a possible electric leak and your hand.

A reversing switch is recommendable since it will permit you to loosen things as well as

tighten them. Also, you can do a better job with such accessories as sanding drums, wire brushes and buffing wheels when you can change from one direction of rotation to another. It will also help these accessories last longer.

How the tool "feels" in your hand can be important. Some handles are placed centrally; others are more like a pistol grip. Centered handles might provide better balance. Most of the drills of interest to the do-it-yourselfer start at about 2 lbs. and run close to 5 lbs. The more power the tool has, the greater its capacity and the more it will weigh. Assuming all other critical factors among an assortment of tools are similar, then it's sound to base your choice on how the tool feels in your hand.

Operating Techniques

Since drill handling and scope of application relate more to what you grip in the chuck than to the tool itself, a minimum of text is used to point out general operating techniques.

The more powerful the drill, the more torque there will be at the cutting end. Heavy, $1/2''$ drills are strong enough so that, should the cutter jam in the hole, the drill will spin and take you with it. To a lesser extent, this is also true of small units. To avoid such problems, always maintain a firm grip. You can do this with one hand or with two. Often, when the work is small and the drilling is light, you can hold the work in one hand, the drill in the other if hand pressure is sufficient to keep the work firmly down on a workbench or sawhorse. Holding the job in midair and then applying the drill is not good practice. When necessary, secure the work to a bench with clamps or in a vise.

Many jobs call for drilling on a well fastened item. You might be forming access holes through studs for wiring or plumbing or maybe cutting into masonry. In such cases, grip the drill with both hands, using any auxiliary handle that may be provided with the drill.

Be sure to use the chuck key at all times and be certain you have removed it before pressing the switch. Otherwise, it might fly out. Before you

When you are drilling into or through a wall, be aware of what you might hit. Spaces between studs often contain electric wiring, plumbing or insulation.

work, also check to be sure the shank of the tool is centered in the chuck. It is possible to grip it off-center.

When working with a single speed model, it's a good idea to make a dent with a center punch at the point the bit should enter. This method will keep the bit from "walking." Using a center punch is very important on hard materials but a good precaution on soft materials as well.

If you wish, you can do without the center-punch chore when working with a variable speed model. Just place the tip of the bit where you wish to drill and start at minimum speed. Apply pressure and stay at slow speed until you have formed a pilot cut; then you will not have to worry about the bit moving off. Gradually increase the speed until the bit is cutting efficiently.

Many tables could be made of optimal speeds for every bit size and for every material that can be drilled. Such tabulations might be essential in industry but difficult to compile at home using a portable drill. First of all, while you might be able to control speed, there is no gauge to pinpoint all the speeds throughout the range. Sec-

ondly, the free-running speed of the drill is not the load speed. Lastly, it isn't critical that you use the optimal speed for all jobs. Getting close enough to it to do a good job without damage either to the work or to the tool is not all that difficult.

Use this general rule as a guide: high speeds for small holes, low speeds for big holes. This rule does not apply to spade bits where speeds between 1,000 and 2,000 rpm's should be used. In fact, you don't have to worry about speeds at all if you remember that the correct combination of feed pressure and speed will keep the tool cutting constantly and without stalling. If you are not making chips or dust, you are just burnishing.

When drilling holes, use a piece of scrap, as a backup to minimize splintering on breakthrough. This also applies to sheet metals to eliminate buckling that can occur under drill pressure. When using twist drills, especially in metal, it's a good idea to drill "up" to the size you want. This method applies to any hole size above $^1/_8$" and simply means that you start with a small pilot hole and enlarge it by stages. Here too, remember that as the hole gets larger, the speed should be reduced gradually.

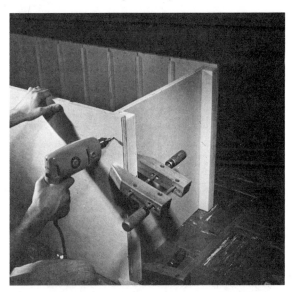

When drilling holes that go completely through the material and the appearance of the rear side counts, use backup blocks. These will minimize or eliminate the splintering that occurs on breakthrough.

You can do an occasional hole in masonry even with a small-size drill, but you must be careful to avoid damage to the tool or the bit.

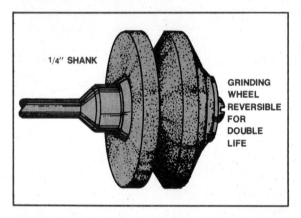

1/4" SHANK

GRINDING WHEEL REVERSIBLE FOR DOUBLE LIFE

Special grinding wheel accessories sharpen such items as lawn mower blades, knives and scissors.

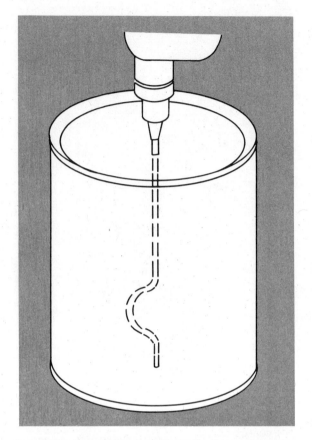

For mixing paint, you can bend a rod yourself to insert in your portable drill or buy a commercial accessory made for the purpose.

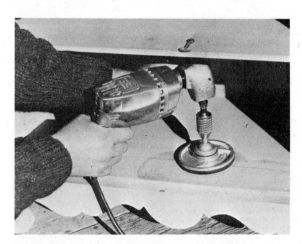

Most useful disc sander is a flexible rubber backup disc faced with an abrasive sheet that is secured with a center screw. One shown is a swivel type being driven with a right-angle drive.

Variable speed drill is very handy to drive screws. If drill has a reversing switch, you can also remove screws. Bit should fit the screw-head slot, and a slow speed should be used.

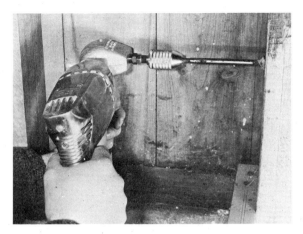

A right angle drive that chucks in the drill like any other cutter makes it possible to work in confined places.

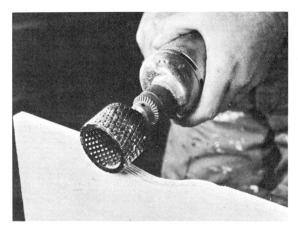

"Surform" drum (Stanley) works like a drum sander but removes material more quickly. In general, it should be the tool to use before you go to a conventional drum sander.

Types of hole saws shown provide different "saw blades" for various size holes. They also include a slug-ejector, a spring-loaded device that pushes out the cut disc. In addition, they can cut different hole depths as well as different diameters.

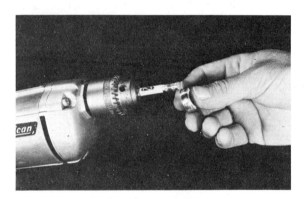

An ordinary pencil eraser makes a fairly good tool for polishing small pieces of jewelry. The average pencil is easily gripped in the chuck jaws of a 1/4" drill.

Some drills are designed so that a stop rod may be used to limit penetration.

This type of stand lets you use a portable drill in stationary drill-press fashion. The designs are not universal enough to permit the use of any drill in any stand. Check to see if the manufacturer of your drill also provides a stand for it.

DRILL BIT SIZES				
Screw No.	Shank Diam.	Lengths Available	Lead Holes	
			Hardwood	Softwood
0	.060"	1/4"-3/8"	70(1/32)	75(1/64)
1	.073"	1/4"-1/2"	66(1/32)	71(1/32)
2	.086"	1/4"-3/4"	56(3/64)	65(1/32)
3	.099"	1/4"-1"	54(1/16)	58(3/64)
4	.112"	1/4"-1 1/2"	52(1/16)	55(3/64)
5	.125"	3/8"-1 1/2"	49(5/64)	53(1/16)
6	.138"	3/8"-2 1/2"	47(5/64)	52(1/16)
7	.151"	3/8"-2 1/2"	44(3/32)	51(1/16)
8	.164"	3/8"-3"	40(3/32)	48(5/64)
9	.177"	1/2"-3"	37(7/64)	45(5/64)
10	.190"	1/2"-3 1/2"	33(7/64)	43(3/32)
11	.203"	5/8"-3 1/2"	29(1/8)	40(3/32)
12	.216"	5/8"-4"	25(1/8)	38(7/64)
14	.242"	3/4"-5"	14(3/16)	32(7/64)
16	.268"	1"-5"	10(3/16)	29(9/64)
18	.294"	1 1/4"-5"	6(13/64)	26(9/64)
20	.320"	1 1/2"-5"	3(7/32)	19(11/64)
24	.372"	3"-5"	1(1/4)	15(3/16)

When working with materials such as glass, slate and ceramics, the drilling should be done at slow speeds and, generally, with special carbide-tipped tools. These are specially made for such drilling and do a fine job. You'll get nowhere with conventional bits. Start the drill at minimum speed while exerting a firm, steady pressure. Once you have formed a pilot cut, apply some water or a special coolant that has been compounded for the purpose. At this point, you can pick up on speed until you get steady results.

Most accessories designed to be powered by an electric drill come with literature that tells you a good operating speed. In many cases, the best speed must be a compromise. For example, consider shaping accessories for power drills. Shaping is best done at high speeds — as high as 30,000 rpm's. However, you can't even approach this rate with a portable drill. Even so, you can do an acceptable job. The best procedure is to slow up on feed while you use the highest speed available. Slow feed lets more teeth pass over a given area of the work and this is approximately equal to the combination of fast speed and normal feed.

There are also safety considerations in judging the speed to use. For example, some cutting discs might be dangerous if turned at higher speeds than they were designed for. Buy yourself a pair of safety goggles for general shop use as well as portable drill applications. These goggles are essential for any job that throws off chips, dust or splinters.

Most drill accessories are available in large hardware stores, home handyman supply centers and large department stores.

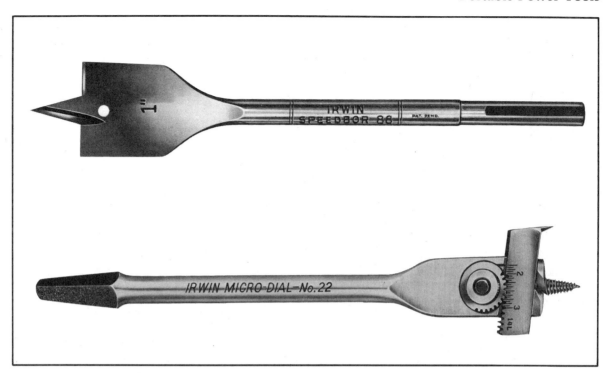

Avoid using tools that have screw tips. These are best handled in a bit-and-brace setup.
Spur bits form exceptionally clean holes because the spurs cut even before waste
removal begins. Spade bits are very fine, all-around, wood-drilling tools.

For vertical cuts, be sure the tool is perpendicular
before you turn it on. If accuracy is critical, use a
square as a guide.

Tile is brittle and you must exercise care, especially
when starting the hole. Use minimum speed until a
pilot cut is formed. Dab on some water and increase
the speed a little.

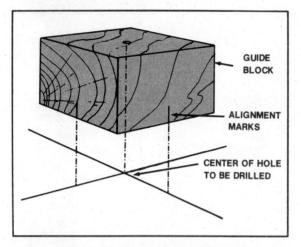

Guide block to keep drill vertical. Alignment marks on the block can be set on intersecting lines on work that determine the hole location. Keep the hole in the guide block small. Use a hardwood for the guide block.

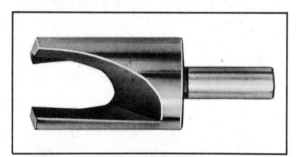

Plugs are cut with plug cutters which come in different sizes and form plugs up to about ¾" long. Since they can be used across the grain, it is easy to match the grain pattern of the plug and the work.

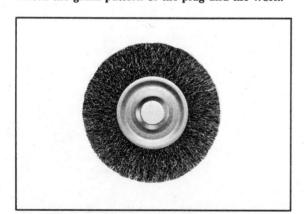

There are many types of wire brushes available. Most are shanked for gripping in a chuck. Others require an arbor. Use them (with goggles) for cleaning chores, for brushing wood, for putting a satin finish on soft metals, etc.

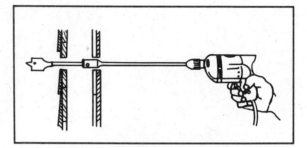

Extensions are available for use with spade bits and other drilling tools. Combining extensions can give you a good reach but pose the problem of whip. Be sure the bit point is firmly seated before starting the motor.

Rotary files (and rasps) are good for carving surfaces and edges into various shapes. They work best at high speeds.

ROUTERS

If you associate a sabre saw with a jigsaw or band saw, a portable drill with a drill press, a cutoff saw with a table saw or radial arm machine, then the router must correspond to the shaper. With a router, you can form fancy edges on workpieces, but the uses of the router are broader than its purely decorative applications.

For example, with one accessory, the beginner can produce dovetail joints that look professionally done. It's also a fine tool for making dadoes, grooves and rabbets, and it can't be beat for trimming laminated countertops. With special template guides installed in the base, it will follow almost any pattern you care to design with speed and precision. It can incise or pierce, and if the model is really powered, it can cut through plies of material to produce duplicate pieces.

The router is basically a simple tool. Most models consist of a motor with a gripping device at one end and an encasing sleeve affair that has an attached base on which the whole unit rides. Speeds are high, anywhere between 18,000 and 35,000 rpm's, and this feature is partially responsible for producing cuts smooth enough to require little further attention.

Router prices vary considerably. Generally speaking, the more you pay, the more power you get. This factor, however, shouldn't discourage anyone who is on a limited budget. All of the models offered by manufacturers can be considered either light-duty ($1/3$ HP to $1/2$ HP) or heavy-duty ($3/4$ HP and above). The difference in the two types is not in the scope of their applications but in the speed with which a job can be accomplished. A job done in one pass with a big machine may require two, or even three, passes

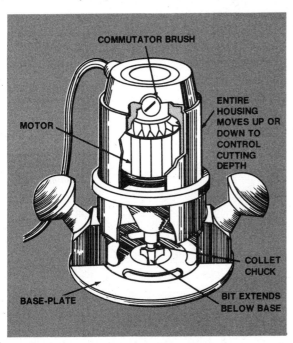

Parts of a typical router

COMMUTATOR BRUSH

MOTOR

ENTIRE HOUSING MOVES UP OR DOWN TO CONTROL CUTTING DEPTH

BASE-PLATE

COLLET CHUCK

BIT EXTENDS BELOW BASE

with a lighter model, but the end result will be the same.

The router is an uncomplicated machine, but this fact shouldn't cause you to be casual when using it; it does turn bits that can slice through hardwoods. So respect for this tool is as necessary as with any power tool. Use only those accessories specifically designed for operation in a high speed tool. Be sure the accessories you buy are mountable in the machine you own. Check and recheck for bit security before you turn on the motor. When you flick the switch, be sure the cutter is not in contact with the work. Keep a firm grip on the router since it has considerable starting torque. Obey all the safety procedures that are printed in the literature that comes with the tool and, as always, do not wear loose clothing that can be snagged by revolving bits and cutters.

Cutters

Cutters are mounted in a gripping device that is on the free end of the motor shaft. How a cutter is securely attached relates to the particular tool's design. Some models require one wrench, some two to lock the cutter in place, but whichever is the case, the cutting tool must be locked firmly. It's never a good idea to minimize the amount of tool shank gripped in the chuck in order to achieve more depth of cut. A $1/2''$ insertion is minimal, $3/4''$ even better. Some routers have a button device to secure the shaft as you lock on the bit. Others have flats on the shaft so you use one wrench there and a second one to tighten the chuck.

A good deal of router versatility is due to the vast assortment of cutters and bits that can be mounted in its gripping device. Shank sizes can run from $1/4''$ up to $1/2''$, but you'll find the greatest variety in the $1/4''$ size simply because any router on the market is designed to grip that diameter. Even the big units that can grip $1/2''$ shanks are usually designed to take interchangeable chucks so that they can also accommodate the smaller bits.

Cutters can be one-piece units or screw-on types. With the latter, you can employ one shaft

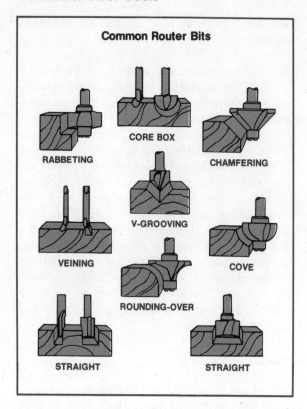

Common Router Bits

RABBETING

CORE BOX

CHAMFERING

V-GROOVING

VEINING

COVE

ROUNDING-OVER

STRAIGHT

STRAIGHT

to mount various profiles. Many designs are pilot-tipped: the area below the profile is a smooth shank, and this rides against the work edge as a guide for the cut. There isn't much control in this situation for the width of the cut, but the depth of cut relates to how much the bit extends below the baseplate. It's important that the pilot has substantial bearing surface against the work edge. Also, it is important for the pilot area to be as smooth as possible. It rotates at router speed as it rides the work edge. Therefore, maximum performance can be achieved only if the area is free of dirt and gummy deposits that can accumulate.

Piloted cutters can be used in a freehand manner. Other types, like the dovetail, sash cope or even straight bits, can be more easily controlled when the router is guided by mechanical means. These guides are special accessories that you can buy or make. For example, the dovetail cutter — when used for multiple, mating cuts — is best guided by a dovetail jig. This jig provides for precise fitting of "male" and "female" forms and, in most cases, the two can be accomplished in one operation. At the other extreme concerning guides is the simple, clamped strip of wood

that lets you accurately cut a dado, a rabbet, a groove or whatever. In addition, a pivot arrangement allows you to rout a perfect circle or arc.

Buying anything less than bits of high speed steel is a waste of money since they won't hold up. For special applications or particular jobs that you will repeat very often, purchasing long-wearing, carbide-tipped cutters makes a lot of sense. If you are going to do a great deal of router work on laminates, plastics or plywood, seriously consider buying the carbides. Laminated material has a lot of abrasives in it and so contributes more to dulling than solid wood materials.

Operating the Router

If you take a bird's eye view of the router, you will see that the motor rotation, and thus the direction of cut, is in a clockwise direction. The router should be used, whenever possible, so that the cutter tends to pull itself into the work. If, for example, you are using a clamped strip as a guide to cut a groove, you should feed from left to right. Working from the other direction gives the router freedom to run along the edge of the wood, and the whole operation will require more control in order to produce the smooth cut you want.

There are times, however, when this rule must be broken or when it's more convenient to use several feed directions. You'll encounter the

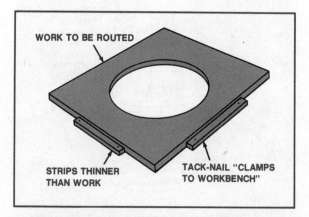

WORK TO BE ROUTED

STRIPS THINNER THAN WORK

TACK-NAIL "CLAMPS TO WORKBENCH"

It's important to secure all work by clamping or by using weights. On small jobs, use thin strips as shown to frame the work and thus hold it steady for the cuts.

necessity for this type of approach quite a bit in freehand routing. Most importantly, grip the router firmly at all times so that you have control. A firm grip is necessary for guided cuts as well as freehand work.

Feed speed and depth of cut go hand in hand, even though it's not farfetched to say that the slower the feed, the smoother the cut will be regardless of the cut depth. But you must keep the cutter working. Generally, the more wood you are cutting away, the slower the feed should be. If you feed too fast, you will reduce the efficiency of the motor. This will be apparent from the sound of the motor, if nothing else. If you feed too slowly, you will accomplish nothing worthwhile, and you may hold contact between the bit and a part of the wood long enough to generate excessive heat. This will definitely burn the wood and may even draw the temper from the cutting tool. At the correct "load," (which has to be a combination of feed and cut), the tool will operate at constant speed without overheating, the cut will be smooth and there will be no burning. Be sure, after turning on the switch, that you allow the tool to reach full speed before coming in to make contact with the work.

The more powerful the tool you own, the faster you can feed and the deeper you can cut. Final judgments have to be made by the individual in line with the equipment he is working with. If it's obvious that the tool is struggling to make a particular cut, decrease the depth of cut for the first pass and then make a second one after adjusting the bit to get the full cut you want.

Simple Cutting

The most common method of guiding the router for straight cuts is to work along the edge of a board that is clamped to the work. The guide board must have a smooth edge and should be fairly stiff, especially if the cut is a long one.

Direction of feed is from left to right, and you may either push or pull the tool — a decision based mostly on operational convenience. Whichever you do, it pays to exert some lateral force as well. The object is to keep the router base snug against the board as you are feeding for the cut.

When possible, work with a cutter that matches the dado width you need. When this isn't practical, accomplish the job by making several passes. On extra wide cuts, it's a good idea to use two guide boards. Place the two boards in such a manner that the router will be guided for the outline cuts. The waste between the initial cuts can be removed freehand.

When this kind of setup is wise and you need many similar cuts, join the two guide boards with a nailed-on crosspiece at each end. These crosspieces will hold the distance between the two boards no matter where you use them on the project.

The edge guide that comes with the tool or that you buy as an accessory is very useful for straight cuts, especially when the cuts are close

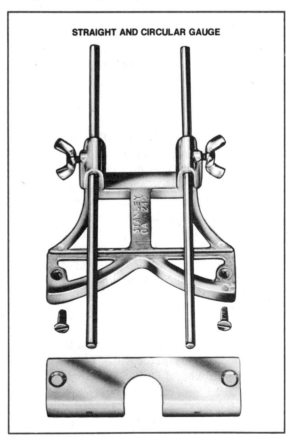

STRAIGHT AND CIRCULAR GAUGE

The router edge guide is a very practical accessory. With it you can maintain edge distance on straight and, sometimes, circular cuts. Some tools come equipped with this item;

to an edge. An edge guide is also good to use when the router itself must be placed on the edge of the stock. If the edge is narrow, which means very little support for the tool, clamp pieces of wood against both sides of the stock. The purpose is to expand the work edge to gain a better bearing surface for the tool.

Decorative trim cuts on edges may also be guided by clamped-on boards, or you can work with pilot-tipped cutters. There are times when a guide board or a commercial edge guide is good to use even when the cutter has a pilot. You may find the use of a guide board or edge guide especially practical on hardwoods, allowing you to minimize the pressure you must exert to keep the pilot in contact with the work edge and thereby reducing the possibility of burning the workpiece.

Remember, when using profile cutters, that it is often possible to vary the results you can get from one cutter simply by experimenting with the depth-of-cut setting.

Circles and Curves

Cutting circles or curves with the router is primarily a matter of good layout followed by techniques that enable you to accurately guide the tool along the lines. Anyone with a compass and a straightedge can quickly make a variety of frivolous designs, but it seems more sensible to use these tools so they produce practical solutions to workshop problems. Such a problem might involve no more than the need to round off the corner of a board or sheet of plywood — a problem that might be solved merely by tracing around a handy paint can.

There is nothing wrong with that method if the paint can happens to be close to the desired diameter. But what if you want to rout a decorative matching groove inside the curved edge? The same paint can won't do. Since you are forming arcs of concentric circles, the second radius must be just so. The "points of tangency" (where the curve blends into the straight line or edge) can't be haphazard. And it isn't likely that you will have a second paint can that has just the right dimensions for the job.

Curved grooves can be formed by using a pattern. The guide is clamped or tack-nailed to the work and the router is fed around it for the cut. It's all right to rotate the router body, but you'll spoil the cut if you pivot at point of contact between the base and the pattern.

A tangent is a straight line that touches the circumference of a circle at one fixed point. The transition from curve to straight line is perfect at that point. To locate it, construct a radius that is square to the line at that point. This important layout trick remains constant no matter what scale you work in.

When you construct four tangents that are square to each other, you automatically have a perfect square. Divide that square into four equal squares, and you come up with two perpendicular diameters of the circle. The points where the diameters meet the sides of the square are points of tangency.

Tangency also occurs where two circumferences touch. For a design involving reverse (S) curves, one arc should move away from the other at the exact point where the curves touch — even if the circles are of different size.

The circle is the "womb" within which any multi-sided shape can be formed. The simplest example is the square you construct by connecting the tangency points of perpendicular diameters. The five-pointed star, or an octagon,

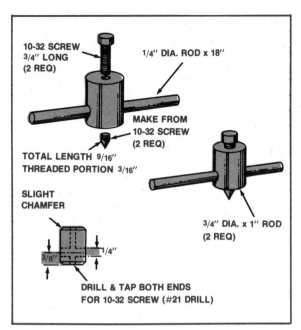

Construction details of a trammel tool can be made for layout work and for use as a router pivot guide. For layout work, the trammel tool needs two heads. As a pivot guide for the router, it needs only one head.

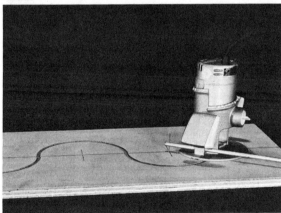

A good way to form uniform reverse curves while using the pivot system is to locate the new pivot point after each half-circle cut. Keep the router bit in the end of the cut already formed and tap down the pivot pin in its new location.

are easy to create when you construct them inside a circle.

All the constructions discussed here are based on geometrical facts. If you strike the arcs and make the connections as indicated, the results will be perfect whatever the size of the project.

Carelessness in layout will destroy the whole pattern. It's quite easy to be precise enough so that your construction of a perpendicular can be used to check the accuracy of a carpenter's square. If the square doesn't fit the 90° corner of the perpendicular you construct, the tool is wrong!

Any line you draw with a compass can be duplicated with the router, but you can't guide the router by eye and expect accurate results. Instead use a length of steel rod or a dowel with a hole near one end for a nail pivot to accurately guide the router through arcs or full circles. The diameter of the rod must fit the holes in the router base that are there for the edge guide.

Template Work

To do template routing, you incorporate special guides in the router base. The guide provides what is essentially a sleeve through which the cutter passes. You use the router in a normal manner, making certain that the sleeve is in constant contact with the pattern or "template" that you have made. Since the sleeve on the guide has thickness, the cutter will be held away from the pattern by that amount. On some jobs this may not be at all critical. When it is, you simply compensate by making your pattern just that much larger for inside cuts or that much smaller for outside cuts. For example, the pattern for an in-

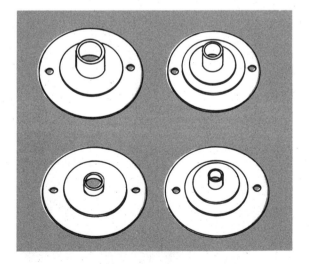

Various size template guides are available. Size difference is in the ID of the sleeve. Most common sizes are for router bits that range from 1/8" to 3/8".

side circle would be the radius of the circle you need plus the thickness of the sleeve wall.

The pattern you make can be a full duplicate of what you wish to rout into the work, or it can be just a detail that you wish to repeat in various places. Quite often a simple pattern can be used in a repeat, overlapping fashion to create a very complicated design. Either way, be sure the pattern is attached firmly to the work by clamping or by tack-nailing.

Joint Ideas

The router is the most impressive when it is used to turn out dovetail joints. This type of very fine craftsmanship would be much too discouraging to accomplish by hand, but with a router you'll have no excuse for not using them on all your high quality furniture projects.

Making dovetail joints in fine style isn't just a question of skill but more a question of acquiring a special jig and template that you use with the router and a dovetail bit. Once you are familiar with the jig, it shouldn't take much more than a minute to do each corner of an average-size drawer. The jig provides for holding two pieces of wood (for example, the front and the side of a drawer) in correct position. Since the shapes are cut simultaneously in both members, they fit exactly.

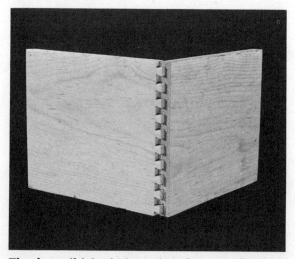

The dovetail joint in its various forms used to be a sign of supercraftsmanship. Today, with a router, they can be turned out like any production-line item.

Dovetail accessory is used with a router and a dovetail bit. Pieces to be joined are held by the fixture, and the mating cuts are formed at the same time.

The dovetail jigs are very common. Most manufacturers who make routers list the jigs as accessories. Just be sure that you read the instructions that come with the jig very carefully and that you follow them to the letter. Go through the procedures on a couple of scrap pieces before you tackle an actual project.

You can also use the dovetail cutter in the router without the special jig to form single dovetails. These can be accomplished in stock edges or on surfaces to make permanent joints or interlocking, sliding parts. When you are making such a cut in the stock surface, it's a good idea to employ two guide strips. These form a track in which the router can fit snugly and thus assure a straight-line cut.

When doing the job on the edge of a board, secure the work in a vise or some other fastening device and clamp support pieces on each side of it to create a surface on which the router can rest solidly. Then you can work with the router edge guide to be sure the cut will be down the center of the workpiece. To do the tongue part, you follow the same procedure, but you must make two passes, one along each edge of the stock. It doesn't matter that you might also be cutting into the edge of the clamped-on support blocks. Here, you must work very carefully when setting the router guide to be sure the tongue fits the slot. Making the tongue just a fraction narrower than

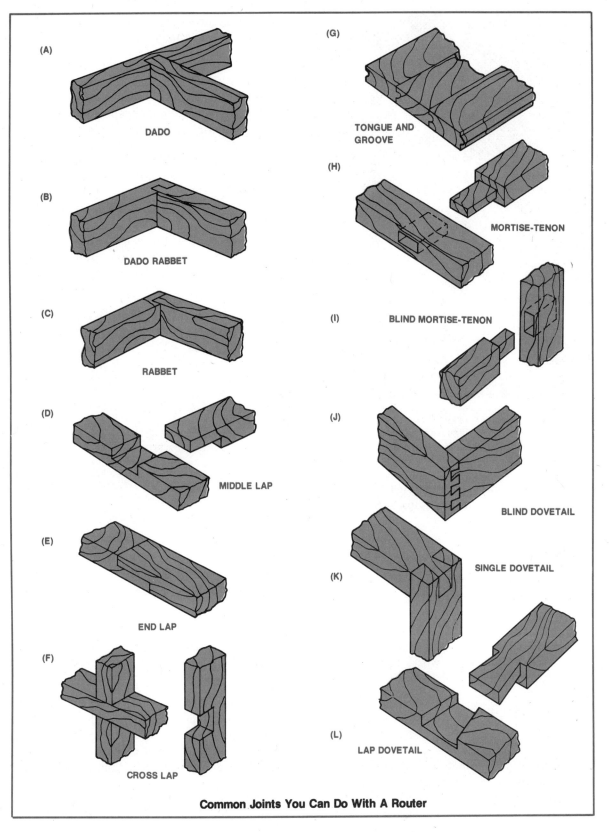

(A) DADO

(B) DADO RABBET

(C) RABBET

(D) MIDDLE LAP

(E) END LAP

(F) CROSS LAP

(G) TONGUE AND GROOVE

(H) MORTISE-TENON

(I) BLIND MORTISE-TENON

(J) BLIND DOVETAIL

SINGLE DOVETAIL

(K)

(L) LAP DOVETAIL

Common Joints You Can Do With A Router

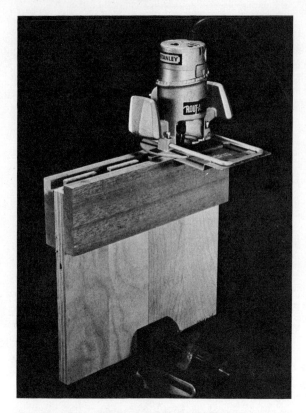

Use the edge guide to do rabbet cuts as long as there is enough bearing surface for the flange on the guide. Special rabbeting bits are available, but these are best used in a high-powered router.

the slot is good practice. If you must hammer the two parts together, you are trying to be too precise.

A similar setup can be employed with straight bits to form mortises. These will have round ends so you must either square them with a chisel after the router work is done or use them as is and round off the edges of the tenon to match. When the mortise must be right in the center of an edge, set the edge guide so you can cut from both sides of the work. Thus, you will assure that the distance between the cavity and the work edge is the same on both sides. Always cut the mortises first; then size the tenons to fit.

Laminate Trimming

Trimming plastic laminate materials is a major use of the router; even special routerlike tools are made for that one specific purpose. However, these tools are commercial items, and

you can do the same job in your own home by using a standard router and a special attachment.

In most cases, you replace the regular router base with a special veneer trim kit. In essence, these kits are assemblies that have a bearing or a pilot of some sort that is independent of the cutter. The bearing rides against the edge of the work, and this controls the amount of material that will be removed by the cutter. The arm that is part of the bearing is adjustable; therefore, you have very fine control over cut depth.

Different types of bits are available with the trimmer kits. Most times these bits are either solid carbide or carbide-tipped which is necessary to cut material that is so hard and abrasive.

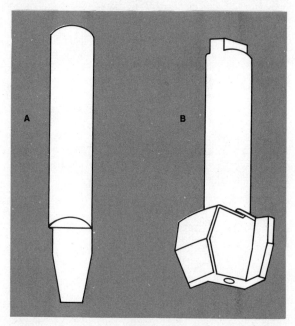

Typical bits to use with the laminate trimmer accessory. "A" is solid carbide; "B" is carbide tipped. They can be used to make either bevel or flush cuts, depending on the depth at which they are set.

It's also possible to get trimming bits that can be used without a special guide. These are designed so that just a small section of the bit actually does the cutting. The remainder of the bit is smooth and serves as a guide against the work edge.

Getting a good job done is more a question of being careful when setting the cutter than anything else. It is critical, of course, to hold the router in correct position throughout the pass. Any accidental tilting can cause the cutter to dig into the work. Effective slow passes are possible, but you shouldn't be so cautious that you end up doing more burnishing than cutting.

Hinge Mortising

Professionals who do quite a bit of hinge mortising employ a special jamb and door butt template that is especially designed to do the job. These are completely adjustable so you can organize them for any size door, whether two or three hinges are involved. If you had a dozen doors to do, it might pay you to rent one of these, but for an occasional job you can get by in good fashion by making a pattern and working with a template guide. Door hinges are fairly standard in size, so once you have made the template, you can store it for future use.

Many hinges have square corners, and for these you must do some chisel work after recessing with the router. You can, on the other hand, buy hinges that are rounded off. The entire job of installing such hinges can be done with a router. Depth of cut is important, but there is a little trick you can use to assure precision. Set the cutter so its end is flush with the bottom of the router baseplate. Then use the hinge itself as a gauge to determine the cutter projection. When you are working with a template, use the template plus the hinge to establish cutter projection.

Inlay Work

The router is a fine tool to use to create the recess into which you glue ready-made inlay. When the inlay is a strip, choose a straight cutter that matches its width and work with a clamped guide or the router edge guide to form a very shallow groove. The groove, or any other recess, must never be deeper than the thickness of the inlay, but it can be a bit less because the final sanding will bring the inlay flush to the adjacent surfaces.

With round, rectangular or odd-shaped inlays, it's best to position the inlay and mark around it with a sharp knife. Then use the router freehand to remove the waste. If you are confident

Easy way to set an inlay is to scribe around the inlay itself with a sharp knife. Then use the router freehand to remove the waste. Depth of cut should be a fraction less than the thickness of the inlay.

enough, you can work right up to the knife line. Otherwise, remove the bulk of the waste and finish off with a sharp chisel.

It's possible to work with a template and template guide. In this case, use the inlay itself to mark the cutout you need in the template and then increase the cutout size by the thickness of the wall of the template sleeve. This method is especially effective when you have many similar inlays to do.

A special recess and insert guide with a ring is available. This guide enables you to use one template to cut the inlay itself and then to rout out the recess into which it will be placed. What you do is rout out the recess with the special ring attached to the guide. Then you remove the ring and, using the same template, cut the inlay.

As a Shaper

The router can provide you with some of the advantages of a stationary shaper providing you either make or buy a special table for mounting it. Quite often, the router edge guide is clamped to the router in an inverted position. In effect, this position makes the edge guide a fixed shaper fence and can be quite practical for straight-line cuts that do not remove the entire edge of the stock.

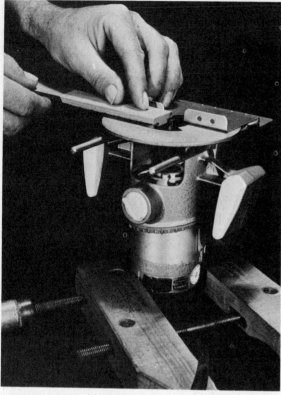

When the router is held securely, the edge guide can be utilized as a "shaper fence." This setup limits what can be accomplished, but is practical when the work size permits.

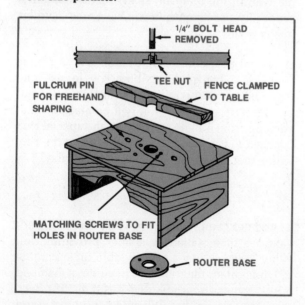

1/4" BOLT HEAD REMOVED

TEE NUT

FULCRUM PIN FOR FREEHAND SHAPING

FENCE CLAMPED TO TABLE

MATCHING SCREWS TO FIT HOLES IN ROUTER BASE

ROUTER BASE

This simple table will permit the router to be mounted so it can be used as a stationary shaper. If the fulcrum pins are included, freehand shaping can be done on pieces that can't be fed by a fence.

Many manufacturers list "shaper" tables in their catalogs as accessories for the router. Whether you make such a table or buy it, it is a handy item to have for jobs where bringing the work to the tool is better than applying the tool to the work.

With a table, you can work with a fence or with fulcrum pins, or you can employ pilot-tipped cutters as you would in a normal manner. That is, the pilot rides the edge of the work to control the cut.

Freehand Routing

Freehand routing can be a lot of fun, but since you don't have a mechanical guide, the results depend on how you handle the tool. You can sketch any design on a board and follow the lines with a router bit or you can recess between them.

Freehand routing can be done on any wood — even non-wood materials — but you'll find it easiest to do on woods that have a minimum of grain. For example, the router will be easier to control on basswood than on fir because hard grain areas will tend to lead the bit.

Control of the router for such applications is mostly a matter of practice. Clamping a couple of pieces of wood (preferably different types) to your workbench and "carving" them with freehand application of the router is good training in this area.

Start with very light cuts since these will provide the least resistance to changes in feed direction. A firm grip is essential whether you are cutting with the grain, against the grain or across it.

V-bits and veining bits are commonly used for feedhand work involving letters. Core-box bits are very good for recessing. Even a pilot-tipped profile bit can be used to shape the edges of a recess you have formed with straight bits.

Tapered Flutes

If you cut a slot in a board that is shaped like a ramp, you can use it as a guide to form tapered cuts in another board. It is best to use a template guide in the base of the router and to form the

To get tapered flutes, use a template that causes the router to move up (or down) a ramp. This, in effect, gradually changes the cut depth of the tool.

slot in the board so its width matches the outside diameter of the sleeve on the guide.

The procedure to follow is simply to make straight cuts that are guided by the ramped slot. As you go down the ramp, the depth of cut of the bit gradually increases. This is done quite often in circular or half-circle fashion, but don't make a template that has a series of radial slots. Instead, make a template with a single slot and drive a nail through one end to serve as a simple central pivot. The degree of taper is determined by the slope of the ramp on the template. The length of the cuts is unlimited: you can make the ramp template six feet long if you wish to.

As a Lathe Tool

Using the fast spinning cutter of a router instead of a wood-turning chisel opens up a whole new world of possibilities for turned-wood projects. The jig required is very simple, and once you have made it, you can use your router on the lathe to make any number of identical spindles or to "turn" sections that might be too slender and limber to do with a conventional chisel. True cylinders or cones can be done almost automatically, and you'll be able to do uniformly shaped and spaced flutes or facets.

Make the jig from 3/4″ plywood with the parallel top rails about 4″ wide and spaced about 3″ apart. The top surfaces should be about 1½″

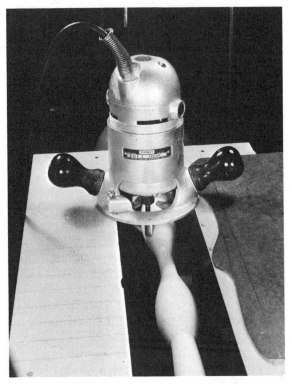

Shaping spindles with a router works best when the cutting tool contacts the work about 45° forward of the vertical center line. Cut the material away in easy stages until you can make one final, light sweep with the router base held in full contact with the template.

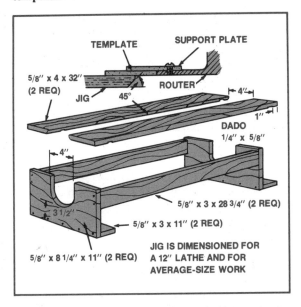

Construction details of jig to be used with router for turned-wood projects. Check the dimensions against your own equipment before cutting parts.

above the lathe centers for most work. A core-box router bit will work best for most jobs, but ordinary countersinks and rotary-file burrs can also be used if they are especially right for the job you are doing. Straight router cutters should be used for turning straight cylinders and for fluting and grooving.

Be sure to clamp the jig firmly to the lathe bed. Adjust for depth of cut on the router so that the cutter will touch the stock about midway between the horizontal and vertical center line when the router base is resting on the top rails of the jig. This position seems to be best for good cutting action, but if experimentation with a particular cutter proves otherwise, don't hesitate to change a bit one way or the other.

With the lathe turning at about 1,000 rpm's, move the router slowly from left to right, removing no more than $1/8''$ of stock at a pass.

To mass produce duplicate spindles, cut a template from tempered hardboard. You can mount a sample between centers and then clamp a strip of hardwood to the jig's rear platform. Then use the router itself as a marking gauge by moving it along the spindle with the cutter held in contact with the work while you trace the contour on the hardboard with a pencil. Do this with neither the lathe nor the router turning! After the contour is marked on the hardboard, remove it from the jig and saw it to shape. Sand the profile edge smooth and then replace the template on the jig's platform.

Now, for as many pieces as you care to make, the template will guide the router and assure accurate duplication.

Fluting cuts are done with the work in a locked position and with only the router working. For peripheral cuts, both the lathe and the router must be turning.

BELT AND PAD SANDERS

Whether you are finishing a newly assembled item or refinishing an old item, a powered sander is necessary to properly sand the raw wood before applying the finish or to remove the existing finish. For best results, the use of this power tool is also essential between and after applications of the finish, whether it is stain, varnish or enamel.

The two basic home workshop portable electric sanders are the belt sander and the pad sander. Despite the fact that there can be considerable overlap in function, neither tool is an acceptable substitute for what the other does best. The belt sander is a real workhorse. With a wise selection of abrasive material and grit size, you can quickly smooth down unplaned lumber, remove old finishes, polish metal, reduce stock thickness, even re-edge garden tools like shovels and hoes. In some homecraft areas, like boatbuilding, the belt sander is almost indispensable. It will also be extremely useful on such jobs as reducing a door's width or length to get a good fit, putting a bevel on a door's edge, working on slate or marble and getting an even surface on 2 x 4's that you have laminated for a bench top.

The pad sander is also capable of some heavy-duty work, but it is essentially a tool for finer, lighter work. It is useful on fine furniture — coated or uncoated — where a belt or a disc might gouge dangerously. With a pad sander, you can also smooth down taped joints on sheetrock before sealing and painting, work on lacquer after it has dried to get a mirrorlike gleam, do smoothing between applications of shellac or varnish and produce satin-smooth finishes on metals and plastics as well as wood.

The Belt Sander

Today's portable belt sanders are to older models what new, compact cars are to military tanks. But there is an important exception: the compact, modern sander can do the same job as the old giant sanders. An old unit was heavy and cumbersome and could gouge up a board before the new owner mastered its use.

Units that are now available to the homecraftsman are smaller, lighter, easier-to-handle packages. Most of them have greater power, and many offer a larger, more effective abrasive surface than old models without necessarily an

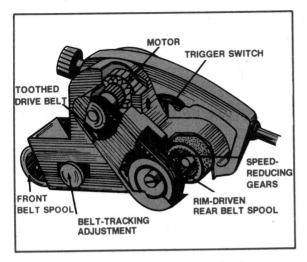

The Working Parts of a Belt Sander

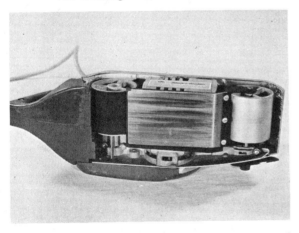

The platen is the plate on the underside of the tool that determines how much abrasive surface will contact the work. The "endless" belt rides the two drums.

increase in belt size; this may be achieved with a larger shoe, the platen that describes the area that makes contact with the work.

For example, compare a 4″ belt moving over a 4″ x 4″ shoe with a 3″ belt moving over a 3″ x 5″ shoe. Actual abrasive contact with the work is much the same so power requirements should be similar. The 4″ machine has to be bigger to enclose the wider belt, but even so, the weight increase is less than startling. For example, one manufacturer's 4″ sander is $3\frac{1}{2}$ pounds heavier than their 3″ sander. In two other cases, the weight difference between 4″ models and 3″ models is only 2 pounds.

However, even such minimal increases in weight should be evaluated if you are going to do a lot of jobs that require extensive sanding on vertical or overhead surfaces. In such cases, the extra weight will seem to increase in proportion to the length of the work time.

Speeds

Available speeds (called out in surface feet per minute) range from about 750 to about 1,500. Higher speeds generally correspond to increases in power and price. You'll get a better sander at a higher price, but generally you'll be buying it for more productive sanding, not better sanding. A low speed sander can do the same job as a high speed sander, but it will take longer. A slow feed with a low speed sander will permit as much abrasive action over a given area of the work as a fast feed with a high speed tool.

Models that supply different speeds are available. The difference between a "high" and a "low" setting can be as little as 200 SFPM. That is not a startling difference but not to be discounted. There will be many times when you wish to move the tool faster without decreasing the amount of sanding done. Also, a coarse-grit belt moving at high speed will remove stock the fastest. With a very fine grit belt, a slower speed will minimize the possibility of burning the work and clogging the abrasive. The slow speed is also better for many types of polishing jobs.

Sizes

The size of the belt sander is called out in terms of belt width. The most common sizes are 3″ and 4″ with a belt length of 21″ or 24″. An increase in length does not always mean an increase in width. There are 4″ x 24″ and 4″ x 21″ sizes as well as 3″ x 24″ and 3″ x 21″ sizes. Wider belts do make it easier to keep the tool flat and also help prevent wavy surfaces and gouging.

Other Features

On many jobs it will be convenient if you can work up against a vertical surface. For example, you might be sanding a floor or smoothing a shelf and wish to work flush to the wall. Most models are designed to provide for this kind of flush sanding. If this operation is important to you, then check for protrusions on the open side that might prevent such use.

Dust collectors are built into some units or may be purchased as accessories. They are efficient enough to make them worth considering, especially for in-the-house chores. The tools make a lot of dust quickly so when you have a collector mounted, be sure to empty it fre-

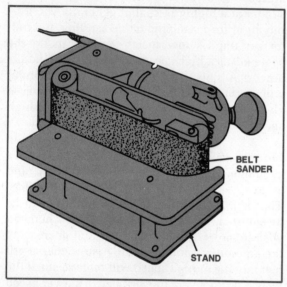

This accessory stand places the belt sander on its side. Be sure, if you are interested in obtaining this kind of stand, that the unit will fit the sander you own.

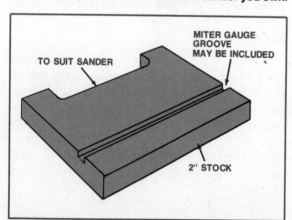

Make an accessory stand that places the belt sander on its side simply by cutting a piece of heavy stock to fit the machine. Shims and clamps will have to be used to keep the sander in position.

quently. A stuffed bag will reduce sander efficiency. When you change from wood sanding to metal work, clean the bag. Metal sparks can cause fires in wood dust.

Many manufacturers list stands as accessories. These hold the belt sander so it can be used like a stationary tool. The stand may position it for horizontal and vertical use just like a stationary belt sander, or it may provide for the sander to be used flat.

Adjustments

The belt sander uses a continuous belt of coated abrasive running over two drums, one at each end of the machine. The rear drum is powered by the motor, the front drum is an idler that is adjustable for both belt tension and tracking. All belts are marked with an arrow on the uncoated side to indicate correct direction of rotation, which is in a clockwise direction. When you mount the belt, be sure the arrow conforms correctly.

To mount a belt, you must decrease the distance between the drums. In most cases, this is accomplished by standing the tool on its front drum and pushing down firmly until the front drum is locked in a retracted position. Then the belt is slipped over the drums and a lever (or a similar device) is pressed to release the front drum. This mechanism is spring powered to provide the needed tension.

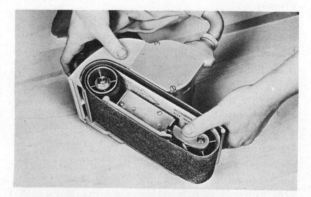

Belt changing is accomplished by decreasing the distance between the two drums. Usually, the front drum locks in a retracted position. After mounting the belt, press a lever to cause the front drum to spring forward to provide correct belt tension.

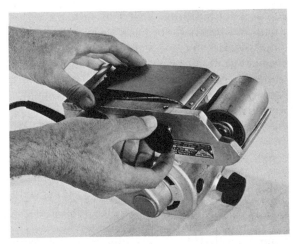

Tracking is done by turning a knob on the side of the tool. This alters the angle of the front drum to cause the belt to move laterally and adjust for good in-line rotation.

Tracking is done by aligning the belt perfectly so that it runs in a straight line over the two drums. No lateral motion can be allowed since that can cause the belt to move off the drums or move the other way to rub against the machine casing. A knob on the side of the tool is turned to alter the angle of the front drum. After the belt is mounted and tensioned, use the tracking knob until the front drum appears correct. Then, quickly turn the machine on and off and observe the results. If necessary, make a slight adjustment and then turn on the tool. Make the final adjustment as the belt is running. When it is tracking correctly, the outboard edge of the belt should run approximately along the outboard edge of the drums. Don't worry if the tracking isn't exactly correct after you have used the sander. This usually happens and simply requires an additional touch with the adjustment knob.

On the other hand, if you must constantly make adjustments to keep the belt in proper alignment, then you should have the sander checked professionally.

Some tools have a belt guide or "traction block" mounted to the frame at the left and rear of the idler drum. This guide is to protect the frame of the machine against abrasive action due to poor tracking. The belt should run evenly across this block. The belt can very lightly touch the guide, but it must not rub against it. Such guides are usually replaceable; therefore, if it becomes worn and uneven, get a new one.

Operating Techniques

If you set down a belt sander and then flip the switch, it will travel like a tractor on treads and will not do any sanding. So the first rule to learn is to start the tool before you make contact with the work. Then keep it moving. Holding it in one spot will create depressions that are difficult to smooth out.

Generally you should work in strokes that parallel the grain, going to and fro and adding a very short lateral motion so you will be overlapping the main strokes. If you feed laterally instead of using an in-line action, you will, in effect, be doing cross-grain sanding. The end result will not be acceptable and will show, especially after a stain application.

The major feature of the belt sander is that it has a straight-line action that permits you to sand parallel to the wood grain. This action always produces best finishing results. When you go against the grain with a belt sander, you can raise considerable nap which does not produce the smoothest surfaces. However, going against the grain can be used for faster stock removal.

Keep the platen flat on the work at all times and don't bear down on the tool more than you need

Start the sander before making contact with the work. Keep a firm grip but do not attempt to weigh down the machine with your body.

to keep the sandpaper cutting. Many times the weight of the sander itself will provide adequate pressure. Turn the sander off after you have broken contact with the work and don't set it down on a bench or whatever until the belt has stopped running.

When you come off the end of the work, keep the sander on the same plane. Allowing it to tilt will round off the end of the workpiece.

Just as the belt sander can travel like a tractor and take off on its own unless you hold and

Keep the tool level when coming off a stroke. Letting it tilt, as shown, will cause the end of the work to be rounded. Turn the machine off after you have broken contact with the surface of the work.

Whenever possible, especially on small pieces, use a backup strip to brace the work. The strip must be narrower than the stock thickness. It may be tacknailed or clamped.

guide it with firmness, it can grip pieces of wood and throw them back toward the operator. Anytime you are sanding material that is not heavy enough to sit on its own and is not attached to something solid, secure the job to a bench top or across sawhorses by using clamps, weights or even tack-nails in waste areas. When the part is small, brace it against a backup strip that is clamped or tack-nailed to the bench top. This, of course, should be thinner than the stock thickness. Don't try to hand hold small pieces while you control the sander with the other hand. You could lose a fingernail.

Remember that the belt sander, especially with coarser grit papers, removes material quickly. When you are sanding plywoods or veneers, be careful. It isn't difficult to sand right through the surface layer.

Do cross-grain sanding when you wish to remove material quickly. Going directly cross-grain removes material fastest, but you can also use an angular feed. These methods are best for jobs such as smoothing down stock that you have laminated for a bench top or for a table slab, removing the roughness from a tree slab that you might wish to use as a bench or coffee table or eliminating the roughness from unplaned lumber. In all cases, the cross-grain work is an initial step. Follow with straight-line passes using finer grits of paper.

You can sand edges with a belt sander, but you must be very careful to keep the platen flat on the work. The narrower the work, the more

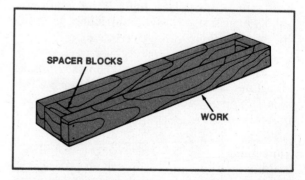

When you need one piece, add a support strip and clamp the two together with a spacer block between. Total width must not be greater than the belt width.

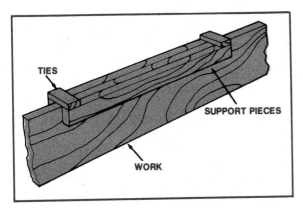

It is easier to sand edges square when you add support pieces to broaden the work surface. Clamp these in place or, as shown, use ties.

difficult this is to do. You can add narrow strips of wood that you clamp to the work in order to broaden the edge you must work on. When you have two pieces to do, you can clamp them together with a spacer block between. With this setup the total width should not be more than the width of the tool's platen.

When you have many pieces to do, you can clamp them together as a pad. Then all the pieces may be done as if the assembly were a solid block of wood. This method is also applicable for curves. If, for example, you wish to sand the curved ends of fence pickets, clamp a dozen or so into a pad and sand them all at the same time.

Removing Old Finishes

Make the first passes with an open-coat abrasive. Choose a grit in relation to the thickness of the finish. The thinner the coating, the less coarseness you need. Remember, however, that thick coatings of paint, some of which can soften under the belt action, will quickly clog even tough, open-coat abrasive belts. In such situations, you can save considerable effort and some money by removing the bulk of the finish with a solvent that is made for the purpose or with a scraper. Then you can use the belt sander.

Generally, it's best to work so you are pulling the sander toward you. Start the strokes from the end of the project that is farthest from you

so you will be moving the sander from abraded areas back into painted ones. In effect, you will be sanding with the rear of the machine. In most cases, you will discover that this helps to prevent belt clogging. Nevertheless, examine the belt frequently. Use a stiff brush on it to help keep it clean as you go.

Metals

For smoothing and removing blemishes, the techniques to use do not differ from those for woodworking except that you select an abrasive that does a better job on hard materials. For final finishing, try to work with special belts and materials that are made for the purpose. With all such materials, the manufacturer supplies detailed instructions for use so be sure to read the literature that comes in the package.

Quite often, you can polish or get a satin finish on metal simply by working with a very fine-grit paper. Another trick is to make a lubricant by mixing 3 parts of kerosene to 1 part of heavy oil. Stir the two materials and then apply the mixture to the work surface. Mount a fine belt (about 3/0 or 4/0) and work as if you were doing a sanding job. Be careful when working with such flammable mixtures. Provide good ventilation and clean the sander thoroughly after the job is done.

The Pad Sander

Many times pad sanders are called "finishing sanders," a good clue to the tool's application. The tool isn't built for heavy stock removal, but it can do some heavy work. However, its major use is for fine smoothing and for putting an elegant, mirrorlike gleam on lacquer, varnish and even shellac. You can use it with a wider variety of abrasives than is feasible with other power sanders, but for the most part it actually does its best work with comparatively fine grits.

It's a mistake to assume that the pad sander is just a substitute for "elbow grease," even though fine finishes can be produced by hand. The broad, flat pad on the powered sander makes it possible to maintain an even, level,

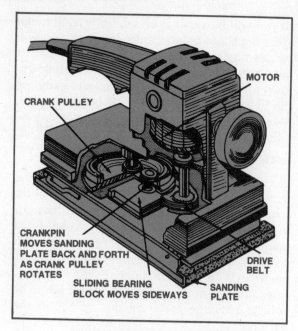

Working Parts of a Pad Sander

CRANK PULLEY

MOTOR

CRANKPIN MOVES SANDING PLATE BACK AND FORTH AS CRANK PULLEY ROTATES

SLIDING BEARING BLOCK MOVES SIDEWAYS

DRIVE BELT

SANDING PLATE

abrasive-to-work contact that is difficult to imitate with fingers.

Directions of Movement

The pad sander comes with straight-line action, orbital action or both. On the straight-line design, the pad moves to and fro. The orbital action is circular. Some tools are available so you can change from one action to the other. Many homecraftsmen prefer a minimal orbit, high speed machine. It does fast work and leaves "swirl" marks you'd need a microscope to find. The orbital action does cross-grain work, but obvious scratches will occur only with coarse papers or slow speeds.

Mounting Paper

The design of the machine must provide for pulling and keeping the abrasive sheet taut across the pad. If the paper is loose so that it doesn't move as a unit with the pad, sanding efficiency will be impaired. Be sure to study carefully the literature that comes with the tool you buy so you will be able to achieve and maintain paper tightness across the pad.

Incidentally, most pads are sized so you can cut three sheets for the sander from a standard

A regular pad can be replaced with a hard pad secured by using projecting brads.

sheet of sandpaper. Special packs of precut sheets — some of one single type, some containing assortments — are also available. In either case, you have a broad selection of types and grits.

The Pad

All sanders come with a soft felt pad that provides the right flexibility for average work. On some materials, like fir with its hard-and-soft-grain pattern, a hard shoe will provide a more efficient backing for the paper. You can create a hard shoe by using a sheet of thin hardboard between the regular pad and the paper.

Conversely, a softer shoe than that provided may be an advantage when smoothing down an existing finish or when working between applications of a finishing material. To improvise, you can use a section cut from an old rug or a piece of thin sponge or foam rubber. It's good to test the use of the extrasoft paper backing when you are working on convex or concave surfaces or on some molding designs, columns or spheres.

Using the Tool

Many pad sanders are equipped with an extra knob that permits two-hand operation. This

Most tools provide for two-hand use to guide the tool more accurately, not to apply more pressure.

feature is mostly for guiding the machine, not a means of applying extra pressure. In some situations, like sanding vertical surfaces, the extra knob provides handling convenience. In most cases, when you are doing routine work on flat, horizontal surfaces, the weight of the tool is about all you need to provide sufficient abrasive bite. Too much pressure can actually produce scratches that you would then have to remove.

When working against obstructions, you'll find that the open side of the tool creates less chatter. There is no abrasive or metal on the open side to bang against the wood.

No matter what the action of the sander is, it's usually best to work in strokes that parallel the grain, using some slight lateral motion so that the main strokes are overlapped as much as 75%. Because of the variety of work that you will encounter, it's not always possible to work this way. When you must use a feed that is cross-grain, go slowly, let the abrasive work on given areas of the wood.

With a pad sander, it's possible to feed directly into a corner or flush to a vertical surface. This is true whether you are working horizontally or vertically. It's usually the "open" side of the sander that you should bring to bear against an obstruction. You'll know when you are wrong because contact between the tool and the obstruction will cause very obvious vibration.

Edge Sanding

With edge sanding, a two-hand grip is a help in keeping the tool level so that you won't round off the edge. Edge sanding is not too bad a job to do freehand, but when squareness is critical, clamp pieces together into a pad so you can sand them as if they were a solid block. When you have one or two to do, use the extra support pieces described for use with the belt sander. The whole idea is to provide enough work surface so it becomes easy to keep the sander on a level plane. If you don't have enough pieces to make a pad, add extra support pieces so that you accomplish the same thing.

Changing the Pad

In most cases, the original pad is held down with screws that secure it to a baseplate. When you wish to change to a softer or harder pad, use the original one as a pattern for the new one and attach in basic fashion. Another way to change a pad — and this works best with a hard pad — is to drive some small brads through the new pad and the pad that is on the machine. This is usually sufficient for the new pad to function efficiently.

Typical uses for a hard pad include sanding woods that have a very prominent hard-and-soft-grain pattern and using the sander as a honing tool.

Pad sanders are excellent tools for smoothing down between finishing coats and for a final touch on the last coat.

Sanding Finish Coats

With a pad sander, you can sand a finish coat of lacquer, enamel, shellac, varnish or whatever. How you work on the top coat will depend on the material involved and how much gloss you want. A basic procedure is to use a ready-made rubbing compound, which is a standard item that you can buy in hardware and auto-supply stores.

The compound is applied to the work surface and then gone over with the sander using a piece of carpeting in place of the regular pad and paper. You can also work with burlap, and often it's possible to agitate the burlap simply by gripping it tightly about the base of the machine with one hand as you do the feeding with the other hand.

For a smooth furniture finish, you can do wet sanding with a silicon-carbide, very fine-grit, waterproof paper mounted on the sander. There are many lubricants you can use for wet sanding, but many people still prefer the clean water and soap combination. This is done by rubbing the abrasive with ordinary hand soap and wetting down the work surface with a sponge. Always wear rubber gloves as well as insulated shop shoes.

There are also other techniques you can use. Various grades of pumice and rottenstone may be mixed with light or heavy oils. Sometimes just a light oil and a very fine emery paper will produce the finish you want.

You can also do wax finishes. Apply the wax to the work by hand, Then make a pad of cheesecloth or some similar material and place the sander in the center of it. Apply just enough pressure on the sander so that the sander pad will move the cloth pad.

DISC SANDERS AND POLISHERS

Sander-polishers is a category of portable power tools that can be misunderstood and unappreciated. All too often sander-polishers are confused with pad sanders or even belt sanders.

Both the pad sander and the belt sander may be used for some amount of polishing work, but it's incorrect to refer to them as sander-polishers. Inserting the word *disc* into the name lessens the confusion between a disc sander and a pad sander or a belt sander. This applies

Disc sander-polisher kits are available. This kit includes a yoke and handle so the machine can be set up for doing floors.

whether the disc sander is purchased as an individual tool or as one half of a combination tool that is also used as a polisher.

You can buy a separate disc sander, an individual polisher or a unit designed to do both jobs. Assuming all other factors are similar, the only difference between a portable disc sander and a portable polisher is speed. The disc sander works best at speeds that are too high for optimum results when polishing. Therefore, the combination sander-polisher should offer an adequate sander speed (between approximately 3,400 and 5,000 rpm's) and an adequate polisher speed (between 1,800 and 2,500 rpm's). Some single-speed units provide for doing both disc sanding and polishing at an "in-between" speed.

Some units are designed to take such accessories as drill chucks, wire wheels, and even grinding wheels; others require adapters in order that they can be so equipped. It is wise to consider such flexibility if you envision multipurpose application.

Another tool in this general area is often called a "sander-grinder." Speeds are generally high, running about 5,000 or 6,000 rpm's; better than 1 HP is not unusual. Quite a few of them are industrially rated; all of them are heavy-duty tools. Accessories for such units may include grinding wheels and discs, even cup grinding wheels and wire cup brushes. This is the kind of tool you will find in welding shops, autobody repair and remodeling garages and any place where heavy-duty sanding is the rule of the day.

Offset and In-Line Designs

The in-line design looks like a portable drill. The weight of the motor is directly over the pressure area; the control handles are in positions that will be familiar to you if you have done any portable drill work.

A right-angle bend is the major feature of the offset design. Since such tools have a longer body, your hands will be more widely separated. They can provide a greater reach and are

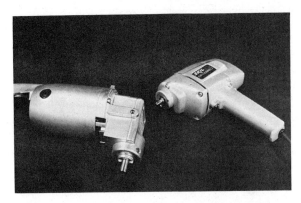

In-line design (right) has the same appearance as a portable drill. Offset version (left) has a right-angle bend and a much longer body.

often handier for getting into tight places. For example, it's easier to reach the center line of an automobile roof with an offset polisher.

Considering the job these tools are designed specifically to do, the offset is often preferred, even though for average jobs the in-line design will probably feel more natural for most people. It seems easier to let the weight of the tool supply pressure to the pad. With an offset, most of the tool weight is between your right hand and the working end of the machine. This dictates that your left hand supply any pressure you need above what is there simply by resting the tool on the work. Controlling the offset isn't really difficult; you simply have to learn a new handling technique before you become at ease with the tool.

Sizes of these tools are listed in terms of disc diameter, the average being 7".

Using the Disc Sander

In many situations, the portable disc sander will remove more stock faster than a belt sander. It will never do a final sanding as smoothly, but it just isn't designed for that purpose. It should be used for fast, preliminary smoothing of rough stock, for "taking down" and feathering fiberglass work and filled dents on automobile bodies, refinishing of metal surfaces, removing old paint and varnish and even, with the correct abrasive, smoothing down stone or concrete.

HOLD AT SLIGHT
ANGLE FOR
SMOOTH CUT

To use properly, tilt the machine to make contact with about 1/4 to 1/3 of the abrasive surface.

If you wish to get to fine finishing on rough stock, use the disc before you take over with a belt or a pad sander. Often, by working through progressively finer grits of paper, you can go directly from the disc sanding operation to pad sanding. Less critical surface preparation like exterior paint jobs may require nothing beyond the disc, especially if you use one of the new foam backup pads with a fine paper. Always remember that the disc has a rotary action which is essentially crossgrain sanding.

A particular handling technique is necessary for successful portable disc sanding. Never place the disc flat on the work. If you did so and

While in operation, resting the tool flat on the work will result in swirl marks, scored circles and quickly clogged paper. Tilt the machine at a slight angle.

kept the tool in one spot, you would do nothing but cut circular grooves. You would also clog the abrasive very quickly.

The first rule is to tilt the machine and apply just enough pressure to bend the rubber backup pad. Quite often the weight of the tool itself is sufficient to do the job. Apply additional pressure only if the job requires it but never so much pressure that the rpm's are drastically reduced.

The tilt of the machine should be such that about 1/4 to 1/3 of the abrasive surface comes in contact with the work.

Too much tilt is as bad as none since you will be using only the edge of the disc which can result in grooving the work. It certainly doesn't take maximum advantage of the abrasive disc.

The second rule is to turn on the motor before you make contact with the work and then to keep the tool moving constantly. A haphazard feed pattern is incorrect. Instead, use sweeping, straight-line, overlapping strokes. Even with the disc sander, try to work in line with the grain when you are doing the final strokes.

Open-coat paper is recommended for most sanding operations; it's essential when you are removing an existing finish. Coarser grades of paper will rough out material quickly. Finer grades won't cut as fast, but they will produce smoother finishes. Generally, coarser grades should be used on hardwoods, at least to start, while finer grades may be used on softwoods.

Replace the abrasive disc when it is dull or has become glazed, especially with paint. You can try to clean glazed discs, but if you are unsuccessful, throw them away. You can, however, get more use out of dull discs by limiting their use to curved surfaces. Also, a dull disc will actually produce a finer finish than you can get by using a new disc of the same grit number.

Work surfaces should be cleaned with a brush or a vacuum cleaner to remove loose grit, paint particles and other loose material. This will lengthen the life of the abrasive and will pre-

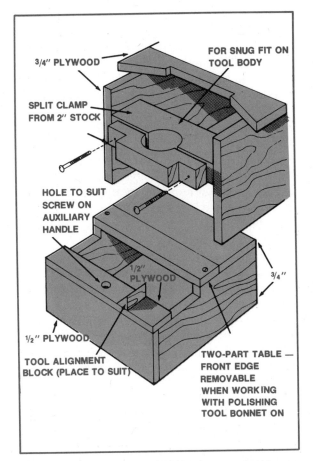

3/4" PLYWOOD

FOR SNUG FIT ON TOOL BODY

SPLIT CLAMP FROM 2" STOCK

HOLE TO SUIT SCREW ON AUXILIARY HANDLE

1/2" PLYWOOD

3/4"

1/2" PLYWOOD

TOOL ALIGNMENT BLOCK (PLACE TO SUIT)

TWO-PART TABLE — FRONT EDGE REMOVABLE WHEN WORKING WITH POLISHING TOOL BONNET ON

Here are designs that will let you organize for an offset tool (top) or an in-line tool (bottom). Use plywood for all parts except the split clamp. Make split clamp from 2" solid stock, sizing it according to your machine.

vent scratches caused by foreign material being stuck between abrasive grains.

When sanding existing finishes, you may find that the high sanding speed will soften paint and cause the disc to clog quickly. When this happens, switch to the lower polishing speed to reduce the heat that is softening the paint and keep the tool moving fast over the work.

Stationary Mounting

Some manufacturers supply a special stand as an accessory so the tool can be locked down for stationary use. If not, you may wish to save some money by making your own. A table setup can be provided whether the tool you own is an offset or in-line design. The table sur-

face is made in two pieces so that you can remove the forward section when you need more room for items like polishing bonnets.

Polishing

As a polisher, the disc sander-polisher can be useful to either husband or wife. With proper instruction and an accessory or two, the lady of the house will use it as often as you do. Both of you will achieve glossy surfaces on your car, your furniture, your walls and your floors that you couldn't get any other way.

Tool handling when polishing doesn't differ much from disc sanding except that when you begin a polishing job, you can rest the bonnet flat on the work surface. Then you can finish by tilting the tool and using a section of the bonnet in a sweeping motion as described for disc sanding. If you have a two-speed tool, be sure to switch to the low polishing speed.

Hold the tool firmly but operate with an easy, free motion. Don't force the tool by applying unnecessary pressure. When you are doing a flat surface, the weight of the tool alone is usually enough to exert sufficient pressure for a good polishing job.

Keep the tool moving. Use long sweeping motions in a back-and-forth action that advances along the surface being polished. Don't work in a circular or spiral pattern because this will only create swirls in the finish.

Be sure to read the instructions that are printed on the container of wax or polish that you buy. Some materials must be buffed while in a damp state; others must be allowed to dry. Use polishes or compounds that are designed for machine work. Some that are intended for hand application will mat a powered polishing pad and can burn or smear the finish.

Do initial work with the bonnet resting flat on the surface. After most of the wax film or the polish has been removed, you can tilt the machine as described for disc sanding operations. The tilting enables you to bring a cleaner section of the bonnet into play.

Portable Power Tools

When working on a vertical surface, start at the top and work down. This will keep dust and film from being deposited on completed sections. On flat surfaces, start at the point farthest away from you so that as you work, you won't be dragging the tool's power cord over finished areas.

Pads and buffs that you use on a machine polisher can become clogged or gummed up after they have been used a while. When this happens, wash them in soap and warm water and then rinse thoroughly. Shake off as much of the water as possible and then mount on the tool to "spin dry." A lamb's wool bonnet can be treated in similar fashion and left to dry completely while still on the rubber backup pad. This will minimize shrinkage of the bonnet.

Since disc sanding and machine polishing chores do spew out particles of waste and grit, it's wise to wear safety goggles when operating the tools.

Tips on Car Polishing

Work in an area that is out of the sun or choose an overcast day. Do a good wash job first to remove all dirt and grease. Very light deposits of road tar and oil can be removed with cleaners and polishes, but stubborn accumulations should be worked on with special solvents that are sold for the purpose. Do this by hand with a clean cloth.

A liquid, combination cleaner-polish will do a good job but check to be sure that it does not contain abrasives; it must be a type that can be used with a power tool. Read the instructions on the container and apply the liquid as recommended. Heavy-duty polishes are available for use on old cars or cars that have badly dulled or oxidized surfaces.

Apply the liquid from the top of the car down and let dry. Remember that drying will occur more slowly in cold weather. The liquids will often form a white film when they are dry.

Start with a pile fabric pad which is available as an accessory that you attach directly to the standard rubber backup pad. Begin at the top of the car and work down, using long slow strokes and allowing the weight of the tool to supply pressure. It is not important to remove all of the cleaner in this operation. What you miss in corners or around edges will be eliminated by the last buffing.

Replace the fabric pad with a lamb's wool bonnet. Be sure to center the bonnet on the pad and to tie it as tightly as possible. A taut buff is essential for smooth operation and good balance. After tying, tuck in the ends of the lacing so they will not fly out when you are working.

Go over the entire car again to buff the finish to a high luster. If your car has not had this kind of attention, you may have to repeat the entire procedure in order to get a new-car sheen. After that, occasional touches with the bonnet will keep the finish looking good until another full job is in order. When you use the bonnet between complete jobs, be sure that the car is free of dust.

After you are through with the machine operation, you may notice a slight haze and some swirl marks. A few swipes by hand with a clean cloth will remove them quickly and leave a high luster.

HAND GRINDERS AND FLEX SHAFTS

From the homecraftsman to the diemaker, from the dentist to the podiatrist, the handful of speed and power known as the hand grinder can be a most helpful power tool. Quite often, it's true talents are unappreciated, probably because its small size creates an image of delicate precision and very light-duty applications. Paradoxically, these qualities in themselves are enough justification for rating the hand grinder as an important shop tool. It can get into places that other tools can't reach. A touch with a hand grinder will often add a crafted look to an otherwise routinely finished project.

But the hand grinder is not a toy; it is not a hobby tool. Modern versions are much improved in

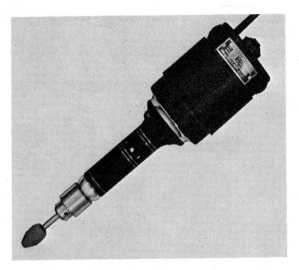

The modern palm-size hand grinder has considerably more power and durability than older models. They may be used freehand, or in stands.

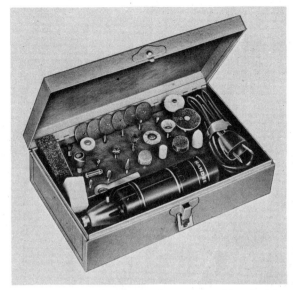

Hand grinders can often be bought in kits that include a good storage case, plus an assortment of sanding discs, wire brushes, steel cutters, and buffs. Usually, extra collets are also included.

terms of power and durability. There is a wide range of designs available. Not all of them are palm size; those that are recommended for tool and die rooms and for tool post grinding are comparatively husky. Weights of the small ones are listed in ounces, while the big ones are called out in pounds.

In application, the tools should be visualized as high-speed shaping equipment that will drive an endless assortment of abrasive wheels, brushes, buffs, drums, bits, saws and discs. They will do machining jobs on most any material, as well as drill, cut, smooth and polish. They can be used to shape or sand wood or metal. They can be used on plastics and will mark steel or glass. Often, they enter areas of sharpening, engraving and routing. You can drill holes with them that would be hard to do with a conventional drill. Therefore, the term "grinder" does not describe the tool fully. What you can accomplish with the tool depends on what you lock in the chuck.

The secret of the tool's fast, smooth performance is speed. Speeds can range from 17,000 rpm's to over 30,000 rpm's, and such revolutions are available no matter what you pay for the tool. Prices can range from under $20.00 to over $50.00; generally, the more you pay, the more weight and power you will get. Heavier models will handle larger cutting tools; their collets or

chucks will take shank sizes up to $1/4''$. The smaller units will take shank sizes up to about $1/8''$.

Weight is an important factor in choosing a hand grinder. The big units do heavier jobs than you should attempt with palm-size versions, but they may also be used for delicate touch work.

Because of the variety of accessory holders that are available commercially or that you can make yourself, the grinder does not have to be limited to hand-held use. With some stands, it can often be used in combination with other tools. Team it with a lathe or a drill press, for instance, and you can use it as a precision milling, grinding or routing accessory that can do many jobs normally possible only with much costlier machines.

There are many stands — even drill-press versions — available so the hand grinder can be used as a stationary tool. It may be held vertically, horizontally, tipped at an angle or inverted for use as a miniature shaper. By clamping the tool in a rigid position, you can apply the work to the cutter as you would with any stationary tool, and this often guarantees precision that is difficult to duplicate when working freehand.

Portable Power Tools

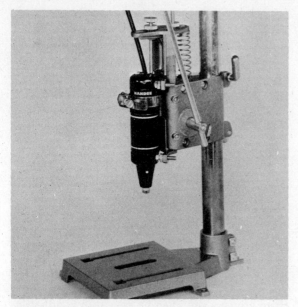

Many types of stands are available, such as this design that works much like a conventional drill press. The main adjustment to the work is done by situating the head; feeding is done by using the lever.

Cutting Tools

The word "cutters" is used in a general sense to encompass all items that you can lock in the chuck of the tool. Generally, any cutter that has a larger than $1/8''$ shank is meant for bigger, heavier grinders, whereas any cutter that has a $1/8''$ shank or smaller is meant for light-duty grinders

Cutters come either mounted or unmounted. The mounted ones have the cutter permanently attached to the shaft. When the cutter is worn, you throw the whole unit away. Incidentally, dentists accept minimum use of their cutters in order to save you discomfort. These partially used cutters can still be used on wood and metal in a home shop; therefore, you might ask your family dentist to save you his discards.

Unmounted cutters are locked on a special fixture that is called a *mandrel*. This is a shaft with a device at one end for gripping the cutter. The lock-on arrangement may resemble a small nut and bolt, a straight or tapered thread or a flathead screw that you turn into a threaded hole in the end of the shaft. Typical accessories for mounting on mandrels are felt wheels for polish-

CUTTERS FOR CARVING, ROUTING, MILLING, AND ENGRAVING

STEEL AND BRISTLE BRUSHES

GRINDING WHEELS FOR SHAPING AND SHARPENING

SANDING, POLISHING, AND SAW DISCS

DRUM SANDER   MINIATURE DRILL BITS

Typical categories of accessory bits show wide variety of jobs that can be done with the hand grinder.

ing, small buffs, rubber polishers and small steel saws.

In most cases, brushes are permanently mounted and are available in various types. Steel wire, brass wire, nylon and bristle are very common. Use the soft brushes for cleaning operations on soft materials and the hard one on tougher materials or when you wish to produce a decorative brushed effect on metal surfaces. Mild abrasive compounds such as ordinary cleansers may be used with the brushes.

Use steel saws to cut wood, very soft metals and plastics. Abrasive discs (also called "saws") are good for cutting or slotting nonferrous and ferrous metals and for many applications on stones used in lapidary work.

Mounted abrasive wheels come in an endless variety and numerous grades and grains. Since they are adequately described and pictured in major manufacturers' accessory catalogs, interested readers can write to companies and ask for detailed listings.

Most small-size grinders use collets to grip the shank of the cutting tool, and it is important to use the correct collet. If you don't, you will not grip the cutting tool securely. For example, a $1/8''$ collet will grip shank sizes from $3/32''$ up to $1/8''$. A $3/32''$ collet will grip shank sizes from $1/16''$ up to $3/32''$. A $1/16''$ collet will grip shank sizes from $1/64''$ up to $1/16''$. There are also adapter chucks for use with collets for gripping very tiny (60/80) drills.

Make a Storage Chest

The hand grinder (or a machine specifically designed to drive a flex shaft) can be considered a small workshop in itself. Because the numerous cutting tools and other accessories that go along with grinder use are usually small and easy to damage or lose, it pays to make a special case to house the equipment.

A case interior can easily be organized to accommodate just a hand grinder or both types of tools. The important thing is to lay out all the equipment you have and to design the case specifically for each piece, plus other items you plan to add later. Making the case as a closed box and then slicing off the lid on a table saw is a good way to assure an accurate fit.

The cutters are stored on shelves that are drilled to receive the tool shanks. This system works very well for mounted cutters. For unmounted

Construction details of the tote-about case. Dimensions can easily be altered to suit your needs.

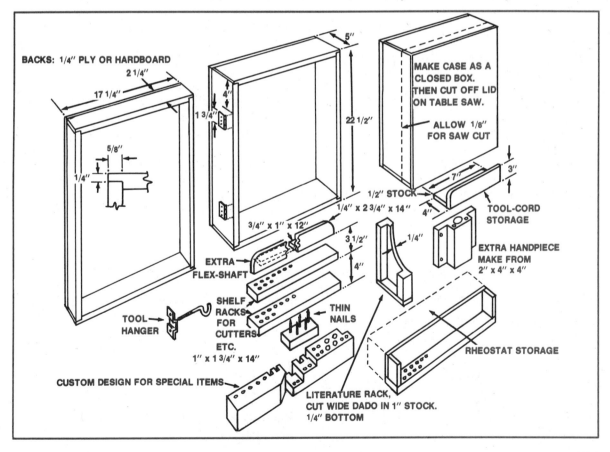

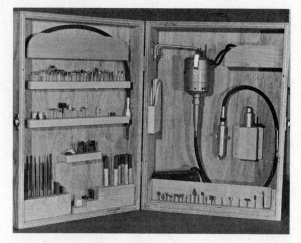

A tote-about chest is a good way to house your hand-grinder workshop. This one is arranged for a motor-flex shaft combination, but you can change the interior design to suit your own equipment.

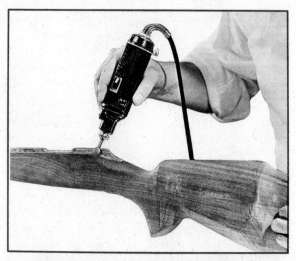

In using a hand grinder, keep the cutter moving. Grip the work and the tool to keep vibration at a minimum level.

ones, drive slim nails up through the bottom of the shelf. Be sure to dull the points on the nails.

The overall size of the case is about $7^1/_2''$ x $17^1/_2''$ x $22^1/_2''$. These dimensions can be increased a few inches without making the case unwieldy. Install a handle at the top and a latch to keep it closed; then you can carry it to any work you must do outside the shop.

Operational Hints

Always rely on the speed of the tool to do the work. For example, a tool that is running at 24,000 rpm's and is driving a cutter that has 16 flutes is actually making 384,000 cuts every minute. That kind of cutting speed seldom requires excessive pressure to get the job done. Too many beginners apply too much pressure which almost stalls the tool. Then they lessen the pressure and allow the rpm's to build up again and, unfortunately, go about doing the same thing over again. This is very bad practice as far as work quality is concerned, and it can do considerable harm to the tool. If the tool gets hot or if there is an obvious decrease in speed, it's almost certain that you are trying to force the cut. Choose the right style of cutter and the right cutter shape for the job you must do, use a touch that is just light enough to keep the cutter working and you will get maximum efficiency and work quality.

Work that is large enough to sit on its own or that can be gripped securely in one hand may be worked on in a freehand manner. Grip the work in one hand, the tool in the other. Establish one rule: avoid pointing the cutter toward your gripping hand. Then if you should slip, you won't cut more than the work.

Small work is best gripped in a vise or clamped to a bench top. A handscrew clamp, with cardboard used when necessary between the work and the clamp jaws, makes a good "vise" for holding pieces.

There is no law that says you must not grip the grinder in two hands. Often, you can work more accurately if you grip the cutting end of the tool between thumb and fingers of the left hand and "palm" the other end of the tool in your right hand.

When working with wood, do the final passes so you are cutting with the grain. You'll find that a minimum of sanding with a fine-grit paper will finish the job quickly. If you wish to get a sculptured effect on small pieces, work with a rotary brush to remove wood from between hard grain areas.

Tips on Plastics

Plastics are either *thermosetting* or *thermoplastic*. Once the first type has set, it will not become pliable again. The second type becomes pliable when correct heat is applied.

Thermoplastics will soften if you generate enough heat with the cutter. The gummy result can quickly clog the tool and even cause a drill to be cemented in the hole you are trying to drill. The answer is to work with light touches and frequent retractions to minimize heat buildup. Use coarser fluted cutters than you would use on wood or metal. Check the cutter frequently for signs of gumming and when it occurs, stop working long enough for things to cool down. Clean the cutters with a small brush. Often, plastic chips that have cooled on the cutter can be flicked off with a fingernail.

As a Sharpener

Most any tool in the shop or in the house can be ground or honed by using a hand grinder as long as you fit it with the correct abrasive. Mostly, the hand grinder serves best as a touchup tool or as a honer. The removal of a lot of material, necessary when you are forming a new edge, is best done on a bench grinder.

Many times the success of a sharpening job depends entirely on wheel choice. This is true, for example, when you are cleaning out the gullets of a circular saw blade or redoing the teeth of a chain saw. Wise choice of cutter automatically produces the shape you need. All you do is apply the tool at the correct angle.

Don't use a small hand grinder in place of a bench grinder. Instead, use it, as shown here, to do final touches after you have renewed the edge of a tool on a bench grinder.

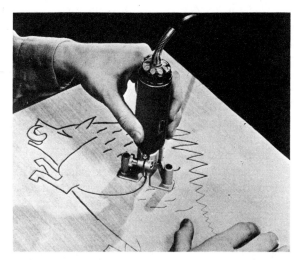

A "shaping table" attached to the cutting end of the tool and combined with a bench stand can be used as shown here to provide accurate control for freehand routing. The table is adjustable for depth of cut.

As a Router

The small hand grinder is not about to rival the big jobs you can do with a regular portable router, but on a small-job basis it can match the regular one almost function for function. In fact, for many techniques, particularly in light-cut applications such as inlay or marquetry work, the palm-size tool can be more convenient to use while still doing an exemplary job.

With some of the hand grinders, accessories are available that are specially designed so the tool can function as a miniature router-shaper that will do some surprising things in a woodworking shop.

Such accessories are light and neat, easy to attach and handle and are used pretty much like larger, conventional portable router bases. Adjustments are provided for depth of cut, and the accessory may include an edge-guide fence so you can do straight cuts parallel to an edge.

Adjustment of the fence in terms of distance from the cutter runs from zero to about $3\frac{1}{4}''$ — not a startling capacity but when it proves limiting, you can remove the edge guide and work against a clamped guide strip as you would with a conventional router. It's also possible to substitute longer rods than those provided with the guide. An extra piece of rod, which you can buy in any hardware store, will come in handy as a pivot for guiding the tool through perfect circular cuts.

The palm-size tool does have limitations. Don't expect to form full-size bead-and-cove or drop-leaf table edges on 1″ stock. It will be possible to do such functions on ¼″ or maybe even ½″ stock. Much, beyond the full profile shape of the cutter itself, can be accomplished simply by making repeat passes to deepen the shape achieved with the cutter or by using different cutters on the same edge to create your own form.

Other practical applications for the tool include mortising for hinges and strikes, raising or carving figures for nameplates or house numbers, inletting for escutcheons and forming decorative or joint-type grooves.

How fast you can feed depends on the hardness of the material. Feed must never be so fast or so heavy that you stall the tool or allow the cutter and the work to get too hot.

Make a Shaper Table

This simple table you can make in minutes. It provides an upside-down anchor for the grinder

A shaper table will broaden the use of the tool. This simple version can be made in minutes. It provides for an upside-down anchor arrangement for the grinder. A straight piece of wood clamped to the table serves as a fence.

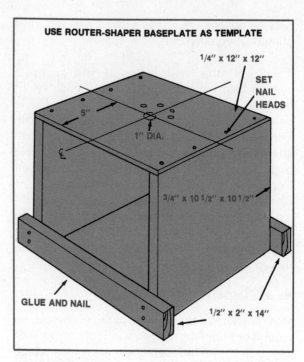

USE ROUTER-SHAPER BASEPLATE AS TEMPLATE

1/4″ x 12″ x 12″

SET NAIL HEADS

5″

1″ DIA.

3/4″ x 10 1/2″ x 10 1/2″

GLUE AND NAIL

1/2″ x 2″ x 14″

Construction details of the shaper table. The grinder is secured with screws that normally hold the baseplate.

which is secured with screws normally used to hold the baseplate. Depth-of-cut adjustments are handled as they are for normal use; a clamped block will serve as a fence. Remember that the table is designed for use with a router-base accessory on the grinder.

Make a Swivel Jig

With this unusual fixture you can cut many decorative patterns. Since it is designed so the whole bit can be applied to the work, there are no limitations on where you can use it. Cuts can be made on parts before assembly, or you can work on a completed project.

The jig permits the grinder to rotate as well as swivel so you can cut a wide variety of geometric designs. While the jig is not difficult to make, it does require careful work to avoid extra play in either of the actions. The hole in the stand can be formed accurately on a drill press. The indexer disc can be formed in similar fashion but be sure its OD fits well in the stand hole. Actually, it's best to cut the indexer a fraction oversize and then sand it for a perfect fit. The swivel collar is best done on a lathe with the work mounted on a screwcenter.

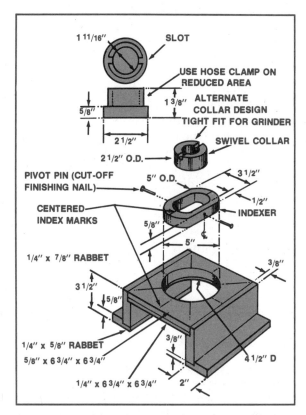

Construction details of the swivel jig. Use hard maple for all parts. Do construction work carefully. You want to avoid play between the collar and the indexer as well as between the indexer and the hole in the platform.

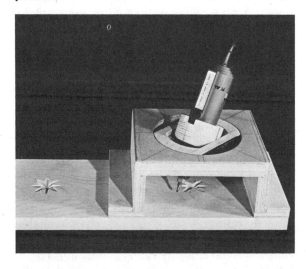

You can make a swivel jig for almost any type of hand grinder. Tool rests and pivots in swivel collar.

Since the grinder rotates as well as swivels, the jig will let you cut an endless variety of geometric designs such as those shown. Note that the tool can be swung through a full arc so that all cuts have a central intersection point, or the cuts can be stopped.

Flex Shafts

With a flexible shaft, you can grip any cutter that is operable in a hand grinder, but you can work as if your fingers were a drill chuck powered by a motor in your shoulder! That is not too unrealistic a picture of what a flexible shaft is. The torque and the rpm of whatever power source you choose to nestle in the palm of your hand, and the dexterity of your fingers, wrist and elbow directs the power exactly where you want it.

Using a flex shaft allows you to be no longer hampered by the rigidity of a solid, straight-line

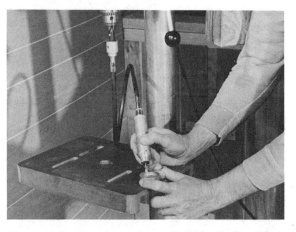

Be careful when powering a flexible shaft with a drill press or a lathe or even a portable drill. Many times, such tools have more torque than the flex shaft was designed to take.

shaft as you are when using cutters in, for example, a drill press, a portable drill or even a hand grinder.

You can use a flex shaft with the delicacy of a surgeon or the muscle of a steel worker; but to do either efficiently, you must make a wise choice of shaft and motor. The power source for small flex shafts can be existing shop tools such as a drill press, lathe or portable drill. However, many of these tools have a lot more torque than small shafts are designed for.

The Right Core Size

Jobs of delicate precision are accomplished more with speed than with power. On the other hand, heavy sanding or weld grinding require husky torque more than they do speed. In general, small-core shafts are made for high speed (as high as 35,000 rpm's) and a light touch; large-core units are designed for jobs that are done with heavy feed pressure.

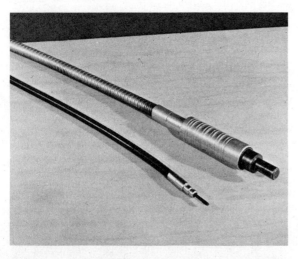

Range of flex-shaft sizes is indicated by typical light-duty and heavy-duty shafts. The small one relies on light touch and high speed. The big flex shaft will do well under heavy power and heavy feed pressure.

The core size is the diameter of the shaft itself, not the casing; however, it's reasonable to assume that the larger the casing, the larger the core.

A large core can run from about $5/16''$ up to $1/2''$. Small-core units can start as fine as $1/16''$. Make

$3/16''$ the maximum core for jobs that require flexibility and control more than power. A $1/4''$ or $5/16''$ shaft is fine for light-duty jobs such as polishing, buffing and grinding. For jobs such as heavy sanding and grinding, a core that is at least $3/8''$ in diameter is needed.

All flex shafts include a core, which turns, and a casing, which doesn't. The casing can be a hoselike affair or a spirally wound steel tube that resembles the type of armored cable often used in electrical work. In good units, the core (no matter whether it is large or small) is made up of spirally wound, directionally alternating layers of steel wire. The "pitch" of the final layer of wire indicates the direction of rotation.

The most common pitch lets you use most motors and shop tools as power sources. But since shaft cores are sometimes made with unusual pitches, check this feature before you equip yourself.

The Rotation Rule

Literature that comes with the tool — and usually an arrow marked on the casing — will tell you the correct direction of rotation. Failure to comply can result in unwinding the core wires, especially under heavy-torque conditions. It's possible to ignore the rule, but to do it safely requires a technical decision that must be based on loading the unit to no more than half its power rating. Such information may not be available to you and even if it were, the limits would be difficult to establish in a home shop. Therefore, adhere to the one-direction-of-rotation rule.

Shaft Ends

The coupling end of larger units is usually designed for locking directly to a motor shaft, but the size of the coupling is not always a good indication of the power requirements. For example, a $72'' \times 1/2''$ core shaft, which is available, will fit $1/2''$ or $5/8''$ motor shafts and has a 1 HP capacity rating. A $50'' \times 3/8''$ core shaft available at the same place will also fit $1/2''$ or $5/8''$ motor shafts, but the capacity rating is only a $1/2$ HP. A full load from the larger motor applied to the smaller shaft, even though it fits on the motor spindle, can damage the unit. Therefore, make it a special point to check the capacity of the shaft in terms of HP it can handle.

In Use

The major rule is not to overload. Remember this especially when you drive a small shaft with drill-press or lathe power. The available torque may be far beyond the capacity of the shaft. In other words, let the shaft decide the capacity, not the power source.

The tool-mounting end of many large shafts is a straight, threaded spindle fitted with flanges and a locking nut. This spindle lets you mount any accessory that has a center hole. You can also buy conventional chucks that screw onto the threaded spindle so you can mount shafted tools such as drills and drum sanders.

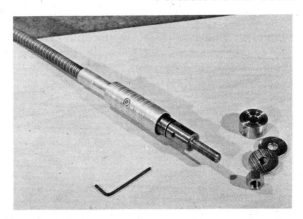

The ends of some flex shafts have arbors for mounting various accessories such as buffs, wire brushes, and grinding wheels. Others have ends designed to accept an adapter so that you can secure items that have a center hole.

Many shafts will permit a chuck mounting. The chuck may be locked with a set screw as shown here or it may be designed to screw on.

Use care with grinding wheels, and be sure to protect yourself by adding accessory wheel guards. These safety devices cover most of the wheel and have a handle that lets you grip with firmness. Safety goggles should be worn.

Although a 6″ grinding wheel can be driven by a 1/2″ core shaft, it's better to stay with 4″ wheels on any of the heavy-duty shafts. When you work

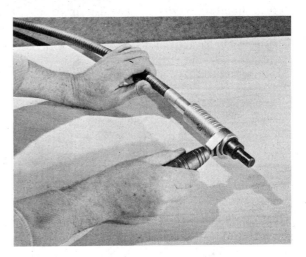

An auxiliary handle to permit two-hand control is excellent to use with a heavy-duty shaft.

with small shafts (for example, a 1/8″ core), the wheel diameter should not exceed 1″. Acceptable speeds are determined by efficiency and safety. A safe speed for a 6″ wheel can range from about 4,000 rpm's to 4,500 rpm's, but this type of determination is not something you need judge for yourself. Maximum rpm's are printed on the flanges of the wheel. Read the instructions and obey them.

Very Small Shafts

While many of the smaller flexible shafts are actually variable-speed tools, they'll be most valuable when used on a universal-type motor with a speed range up to 15,000 to 20,000 rpm's. This is true even though there are applications where less speed is more efficient. To give any of these tools a full range of use, you can always work with a rheostat, which is sold as an accessory, for speed control.

Where high speed and a light touch are needed for the job at hand, you may be disappointed if you are running the shaft off a drill press or similar power source. It would be better to buy a complete assembly that includes the shaft and the motor. Some craftsmen even use a motor salvaged from a sewing machine, or some other high-speed universal motor.

Another solution, when you want more speed than the power source can provide, is to buy a special handpiece with a planetary drive which automatically increases the speed at the handpiece to $2^1/_2$ times the input speed. Thus, for example, if you are driving a shaft at 5,000 rpm's, you'll get 12,500 rpm's at the handpiece.

With small flex-shaft machines, projects such as carving delicate features, engraving plastics and drilling hair-size holes can be accomplished.

How to Equip Yourself

Your interests will, of course, dictate what equipment you choose. For example, if you want to do welding, clean up dents in auto bodies or apply a satin finish to metals or a sculptured texture to large wood panels, then you want a big, heavy-duty shaft, preferably one driven by its own motor and mounted on a roll-around pedestal.

If you are interested in jobs such as carving in various materials, engraving, gunsmithing, model building, jewelery making or polishing, then you should consider a small hand grinder and/or a flex shaft setup, which could be a special power source and flexible shaft tool.

Portable Timers

A portable timer is designed to automatically activate sprinkler systems, lights and other electrical devices. The basic model has a 24-hour dial and can be plugged into any outlet. Then the device to be activated is plugged into the timer.

After the timer has been set, it will work independently day after day. There is a switch for manual control, however. There are different types of timers with varying capacities. The more expensive ones can handle even an electric heater.

One of the most popular uses for timers is as a safety device. Lights can be turned on and off automatically in an empty house to ward off possible intruders. Timers have many other uses, such as starting a coffee pot percolating in the mornings or an air conditioner cooling a home an hour before the family returns from a vacation. *SEE ALSO AUTOMATION.*

Portico

A portico is a porch or covered walk consisting of a roof supported by columns. A portico is also the covered entrance to a building, an open or enclosed gallery or a room on the outside of a building.

Portland Cement

Portland cement is the main ingredient of cement, mortar and concrete and consists of clay, chalk, limestone and other natural elements that are pulverized and then bagged. Each bag usually contains one cubic foot and is sold by hardware stores, lumber yards and building suppliers.

Cement is a mixture of portland cement and sand added to water. Concrete is a mixture of portland cement, sand, and gravel (added for strength and bulk) plus water. Mortar is portland cement, sand, water and ten percent hydrated lime. The lime keeps the mix in liquid form longer and also makes the mix harder when dry. *SEE ALSO CONCRETE.*

Post

A post is a piece of lumber or metal which is fixed securely in an upright position, such as a stay or support, pillar or column. It may also refer to the corner section on furniture, such as a corner post of a bed. Posts can be found mainly in floor construction, house foundations and fences.

FLOOR CONSTRUCTION

In floor construction, the posts have to be strong enough to support the weight and large enough for a full bearing surface for the ends of the beams. Usually the nominal size of the post should not be less than 4 x 4 inches. Some posts are made of solid stock while other posts are made from two inch sections which are fastened together firmly. Where the ends of the beams are connected over a post, the bearing surface should have bearing blocks to increase the area.

Posts extending upward without lateral bracing need a very large cross-sectional area to prevent buckling. The local building codes should list the requirements in a slenderness or 1/d ratio, the 1 representing the length in inches and the d representing the smallest cross-sectional dimension.

Since the basic design of the structure determines the amount of spacing for the posts, its engineering must be done carefully. Normally the posts are spaced evenly along the length of the building and in the areas where free span of the floor or roof planks are permitted.

FOUNDATION CONSTRUCTION

In house foundations, there are posts which support girders, porches and other parts of the house. When setting a post in soil, a concrete form should be used around the base. This helps prevent rotting of the wood as long as a protective coating is kept over the exposed section.

If the wood of a post in the soil becomes rotten, replace the complete post and concrete base. Spread asphalt on the under-section part of the post, and then add a mixture of one part cement, two parts sand and four parts gravel with a little water making it flow slowly and pour around the base.

When the outside edges of a post become rotten on a wood floor porch, cut a rabbet in the post with a saw and remove the extra wood with a chisel. The middle section should be at least half the thickness of the post. Several coated nails should be driven into the middle base and into the bottom side of the exposed area of the post. In the cutout part of the floor, set several large screws. Make a plywood form with $1/2$ inch plywood that will fit around the four sides of the post and coat it inside with grease. The size of the form should be at least two inches wider and longer than the post size. The post base should be coated with asphalt and the same concrete mixture as above should be poured into the form. The upper edge of the cement mix should be beveled toward the post. Allow the cement to harden and then remove the form.

If most of the base has rotted, then cut the post about two inches above the deteriorated part. Firmly hold the post when sawing so that the upper part is not disturbed. In this case the post base can be made of several pieces of wood stacked on top of each other which are beveled to shed water easily. These pieces should be nailed together with aluminum or coated nails which are rust proof. Put the base between the floor and the bottom of the post and nail it in place with the coated nails. Put a caulking compound or asphalt around the base of the post to make it water resistant.

When a wooden post in a concrete porch is rotted at the base, cut the rotted part off with a saw to make two rabbets for the base. Horizontally drive several nails halfway into the lower rabbeted part of the post. They will hold the post firmly in the cement that will be poured into the form. Coat the bottom part with asphalt and pour the cement mixture and a bonding agent into the form. To shed rain easily, the top of the cement should be beveled.

Cylindrical concrete columns with steel rods in the center are used for some house foundations.

Some houses or cabins are completely supported by this type of column. This kind of column is used where there is a very irregular or sharp-sloping terrain.

FENCE CONSTRUCTION

Setting fence posts begins by digging a hole which is about one-third as long as the post at an end position. After positioning the post, be sure it is plumb and then fill the base area with gravel or soil. Then pack the soil or gravel around the post; a 2 x 4 may be used for tamping the soil. After the end post has been set, the first line post may be installed. Make sure that the distance between posts is the same as the plans. Since the first line post determines the position of the other holes, an inaccurate setting of this post will cause the following posts to be set incorrectly.

For the best and more permanent results in sandy ground, set the posts in concrete. Pack or tamp gravel in the hole and form a two inch base. Then pack gravel around the post to support it. Brace the post with nailing braces and then pour the concrete in the hole. When the concrete has dried completely, the braces may be removed. Trowel the concrete to a slope around the top of the hole so that it will shed water.

If a fence has back rails which are exposed, such as stockade, grape stake or vertical boards, the top of the post should be level with the top of the back rail. A fence which is framed without back rails, such as basketweave or townhouse, should have the posts flush with the top of the fence. Sometimes the posts may be slightly higher than the fence.

Post & Beam Construction

Post and beam construction is a type of framing which spaces the usually larger framing members (the posts) much farther apart than conventional framing. It is being used today in residential buildings because of its great versatility of form. Contemporary styles conform well to this type of framing.

Post and beam construction consists of posts, beams and planks. The planks can be applied to either the walls or to the roof. In some instances, it can be applied to sub-flooring.

This type of construction has several major advantages over regular framing. The main one is cost. Since less material is used, it is less expensive. Labor costs are also cut because the pieces are larger and fewer and construction takes less time.

The best structural advantage concerns windows and doors. Since most of the weight is carried by the posts, large openings can be framed without using headers. With the weight off the walls, an entire section can be made of glass. This is being used repeatedly in modern buildings. By moving the weight to the beams and posts, overhangs and extended ceilings can be easily constructed.

There is a definite safety feature in post and beam construction. This method of framing is more heat resistant than regular metal beams. Under intense heat, metal beams tend to buckle and collapse once heat is transmitted through them. Not only are wooden posts less likely to conduct heat, but they prove stronger under intense heat than their metal counterparts.

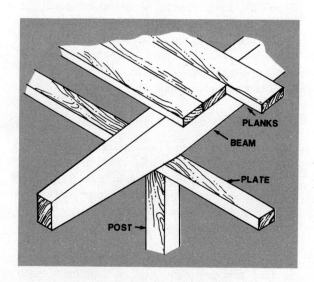

Correct position of beam over post.

There are also disadvantages to post and beam construction. The main one is weight loads. A post and beam constructed floor needs to be reinforced where great weight is concentrated. For example, it should be coupled with regular framing where it must support heavy items such as bathtubs, refrigerators and waterbeds. The posts must rise out of a proper foundation and be strong enough to support the beams. Beams must rest directly on top of the posts or valuable support is lost.

A post should be made from at least 4 x 4 stock. Two by four's can be fastened together to form a post. When the ends of a beam are joined on a post, bearing blocks should be used.

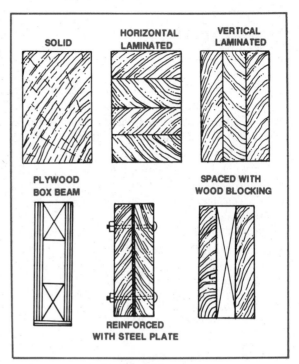

Types of Beams

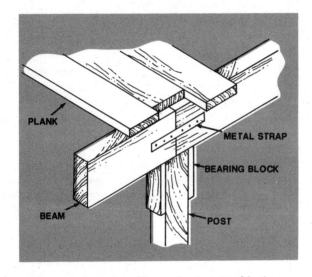

Beam and post position using bearing blocks.

Posts should be spaced apart at the same intervals. The best way to plan the concept of a structure is to space in increments of 16, 24 and 48 inches.

When using this framing design for floors, the beams may be fastened together in a variety of ways. If solid stock is not used, a beam may be built up of a number of strips bonded together. The type of beam is not important since it is concealed in the flooring. The importance here is strength.

It is best to use solid timbers for beams when aiming for a rustic, exposed beam appearance.

However, if the beams are not going to be seen and support is the necessary goal, laminated beams are best. If a combination of strength and rustic appearance is sought, a cased beam is the answer.

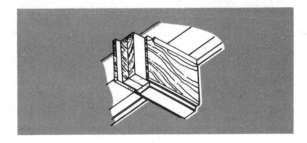

Cased Beam

Beam sizes are based on the distance between the studs and the amount of weight they must carry. There are two types of beams used in this type of construction: transverse and purlin. Transverse beams are used to produce a rustic exposed effect. Purlin beams run parallel to the supporting wall and top ridge beam. Either type of beam should be adequately supported to insure the safety and long life of the structure. *SEE ALSO FRAMING.*

Pouring Wool

Pouring wool is a process by which a home-owner may insulate the walls of an existing structure that was not insulated when the building was first constructed. This process involves drilling a hole in the structure's sideing and *pouring* loose insulation material between the wall and sub-wall. Actually, the entire process is done with air pressure making the job much more expensive than it would have been had the building been insulated originally. *SEE ALSO WALL & CEILING INSULATION.*

Power Drill
[SEE PORTABLE POWER TOOLS.]

Power Sanders
[SEE PORTABLE POWER TOOLS; STATIONARY BELT & DISC SANDER.]

Power Saws
[SEE BAND SAW; CIRCULAR SAW; JIGSAW; PORTABLE POWER TOOLS; RADIAL ARM SAW; TABLE SAW.]

Power Tools
[SEE BAND SAW; BENCH GRINDER; DRILL PRESS; JIGSAW; JOINTER; LATHE; PORTABLE POWER TOOLS; SHARPER; STATIONARY BELT & DISC SANDER; TABLE SAW.]

Prehung Doors

A prehung door is a unit consisting of a door that is factory-installed in a door frame. Usually the holes for the hardware have been cut and the door is prefinished. Prehung doors are available in a variety of frame designs with split jamb being one of the simplest to install. The split jamb style is adjustable to practically any wall thickness which increases the installation speed. The directions for setting up a prehung door vary depending on the style of the frame, so follow the manufacturer's directions closely or have an expert do the job.

Preservatives

Preservatives are substances which prevent the growth and action of wood-decaying fungi and insects. Creosote is probably the most widely known wood preservative. Despite its strong odor and dark color, which is not easily painted over, it is still thought of as the main wood preservative. Over the past few years, other preservatives containing pentachlorophenal (penta) or zinc napthenate have become more popular.

Penta preservatives are usually purchased in the form of an oil base solution that may be applied by soaking, dipping, brushing or spraying. When soaking or dipping a post, stand it in a can full of preservative or lay them in a sheet metal or wood trough that is lined with plastic. Soak the wood for at least one day, preferably more than two. If it is not possible to soak or dip the wood, spray or brush the liquid directly on it. Flood all areas, especially exposed end grain and crevices. When spraying, work in a well-ventilated area and wear a respirator mask.

Wood preservatives containing zinc napthenate are generally in the form of a clear solution and used much the same way as those containing penta. Because some of these preservatives are very clear, they may act as a wood sealer and be applied under varnishes.

Preservatives may also be used on existing wood pieces to protect them. Gutters, shutters, garage doors, fence rails, window frames, ladders and lawn and garden furniture will benefit from an application of preservatives. If an area is already decayed the preservative will not heal the rotted area, but will prevent it from spreading.

Press Screw

A press screw is a simple clamp mechanism used to hold or join together flat wood pieces. Controlled pressure is applied toward the center from opposite ends by the use of screw mechanisms. Press screws contain handles located on the end of the screws for hand turning. The screws are turned simultaneously. *SEE ALSO FASTENERS.*

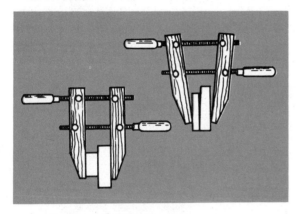

Press Screw

Primary Coil

An induction coil has two sets of windings: the primary coil and the secondary coil. The primary coil begins the induction process by allowing alternating current to pass through its windings. In a step-down transformer, the voltage is reduced when the electricity leaves the primary coil and enters the secondary coil. For example, a primary coil is wound around an iron core ten times and a secondary coil is wound around the same iron core 100 times. If ten volts of electricity passes through the transformer, it will increase to 100 volts of electricity. *SEE ALSO ELECTRIC MOTORS.*

Primer

A primer is the base coat for the finish coat of paint. It helps control corrosion and blisters and provides adhesion to the bare wood. This adhesion helps to protect against moisture.

Several house paints have primers already in them, but most are bought separately in latex or alkyd form. It is recommended that a latex primer be used with a latex flat finish coat and that the alkyd paints be used together, but it is not absolutely necessary.

A coat of priming paint increases the durability of the finish coat and seals soluble pigments in certain woods. Priming helps wood hold paint better, even if it does not usually retain paint well. It should especially be used on a dark surface to be painted with a light colored paint, on trim that has a varnish finish and on new surfaces.

An excellent primer is aluminum house paint. Aluminum paints designed for other purposes should not be used. Other good primers are those that have no zinc oxide content. *SEE ALSO PAINTS & PAINTING.*

Projects

[SEE BARBEQUE CART; BASS BOAT; BIRD FEEDERS, HOUSES & PROTECTION; CATCH-ALL SHELF UNIT; COLONIAL BOOKCASE; GUN & ROD CABINET; MOBILE HOME CONSTRUCTION; MULTI-PURPOSE BENCH; PATIO TABLE & BENCHES; PLAYHOUSE; SAILING PRAM; SANDBOX; STUDENT'S STUDY CENTER; TOY STORAGE CHEST; TREE HOUSE; WALL-HANGING DESK.]

Propane Gas Torch

The propane gas torch is a versatile one-hand tool used in electrical work, craft work and home repair jobs. Soldering copper pipe joints, removing paint, defrosting pipes as well as ice patches on steps, starting blazes in fireplaces, burning ant beds and making leak-proof pipe connections are some of the propane torch's many uses. However, before removing paint from a house, seriously consider the fire hazard involved. The bend and size of the torch burner make it easy for aiming and handling. Different accessories, such as the flame spreader tip, soldering tip and the pencil burner unit, make this tool good for various jobs.

Since the operation of different models of propane gas torches may vary, the instructions supplied by the manufacturer should be read before attempting to use one. The normal procedure begins by tightly screwing the torch burner to the cylinder fitting. The control valve is then opened just enough to let a small amount of gas escape. Immediately light the torch, allowing the burner to become fully heated before opening the valve to a larger flame size.

As a preventive measure, disconnect the burner and gas cylinder of the torch when not in use. In addition, do not use the living area of the house for its storage. *SEE ALSO PLUMBER'S TOOLS & EQUIPMENT.*

Propeller, Boat
[SEE RECREATIONAL BOATS & BOATING.]

Pruning Saws

Pruning saws are designed for trimming vines and trees and usually have coarse enough teeth for cutting green wood. There are two main types of pruning saws: one has straight teeth set into a straight blade which tapers on both sides toward the blade tip; the other saw has teeth that slant toward the tip of a curved blade, which is helpful for pruning in difficult areas. The handle on the straight-blade pruning saw is extended slightly at each end so that one of these extensions may be inserted into a hollow pole for pruning upper branches of trees. The curved-blade pruning saw has either a handle with one extension at its lower end, or a narrow handle that fits easily into a hollow extension rod.

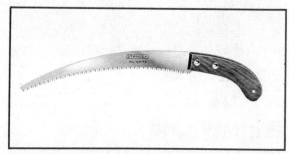
Courtesy of The Stanley Works

Curved-Blade Pruning Saw

FLAME SPREADER
SOLDERING TIP
UTILITY BURNER
SPARK LIGHTER

Courtesy of BernzOmatic Corportation

Propane Gas Torch and Accessories

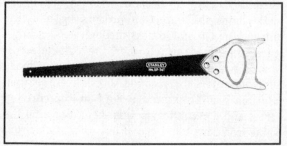
Courtesy of The Stanley Works

Straight-Blade Pruning Saw

Pruning Shears
[SEE LAWNS & GARDENS.]

Prybars & Ripping Bars

Prybars and ripping bars are designed for prying or ripping material apart. Three of the most familiar are the crowbar, wrecking bar and gooseneck ripping bar. *SEE ALSO HAND TOOLS.*

P-Trap

A p-trap is used on any of the different types of pipe. Designed to eliminate pipe odors, the U-shaped portion of a p-trap is filled with water. It is this trap of water that inhibits any backward passage of air. *SEE ALSO PIPE FITTINGS.*

Pull Chain Switch

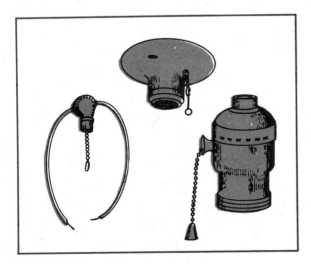

Pull Chain Switches

A pull chain switch has a chain which controls the switch circuit, much the same way a lever controls a wall switch. Pull chain switches are mounted in lamp sockets, porcelain socket fixtures, fluorescent lights or are available separately for attachment to these and other fixtures. *SEE ALSO SWITCHES & OUTLETS.*

Pulley

The pulley is a wheel with a curved rim that either drives or is driven for the purpose of increasing power. Pulleys are used often when converting electrical energy of electric motors to the mechanical energy of electrical appliances. Sometimes the pulley may be a sprocket that turns another sprocket in a chain of cause and effect, like in watches and clocks, or other times pulleys are driven by a belt, as in an automobile system.

Pumps

A pump is a machine that raises or transfers fluids by pressure, suction or both. There are six different types of pumps: deep well, lift, shallow well, submersible, suction and jet.

TYPES

When water is located several hundred feet beneath the surface, only a deep well pump will be effective. Jet, submersible or piston driven, this pump can push water as high as 500 feet.

A lift pump forces water through a valve in the piston to catch water above it. As the piston rises, the water is forced up and out of the pipe. As it falls, the valve in the piston opens and water flows through it again to repeat the procedure.

A shallow well pump is a motorized version of the lift pump. Located between 15 to 30 feet below ground level, the shallow well pump maintains a constant water pressure by an automatic pressure device. When the pressure device is off even though the pump is on, the rising water compresses the air above it to supply a steady water pressure.

A centrifugal pump located at the end of a pipe in a well is called a submersible pump. It delivers more water, more trouble-free service and is more quiet than the other types of pumps. Capable of being used in either a shallow or deep well, submersible pumps are not recommended if the water is sandy since the sand will wear out the pump in a short time.

Suction pumps rely on atmospheric pressure to push water up the pipe. By lowering the pressure in the pipe by means of a cylinder creating a vacuum that forces water out of the aquifer, the atmospheric pressure exerting force on the surrounding liquid forces water up the pipe.

Jet pumps are effective to depths of 250 feet or more. Water is pumped down one pipe, around a hairpin curve and up a second pipe which is the supply pipe for water coming from the well. At the hairpin curve, the inside pipe diameter is narrowed so that a Venturi tube is formed. A Venturi tube forces liquid to flow through a narrow passage much faster than normal to create a low pressure area in the supply pipe. Since the surrounding well water is under normal pressure, it is sucked into the fast moving stream. Since more water is delivered than sent, the excess liquid is diverted into a water-supply tank.

A sump pump is used to drain water from areas located below a sewer line. When the water rises to a predetermined level, a float activates a switch. When the switch turns the pump on, a pipe connected to the discharge outlet of the pump directs the water into a drain, sewer, seepage pit or to the outside. After the pump has drained the water below the set level, the float descends and shuts off the pump. The inlet of a sump pump has a strainer to collect debris that might clog the pump.

SELECTION

Selection of the appropriate pump is based on the existing conditions. Depth of water level needed and water supply in gallons per minute are important factors. If quiet is desired, then types of pumps producing less noise should be considered. When the well depth is much beyond 20 feet, a deep well pump should be substituted for a shallow well pump. Avoid purchasing a pump that will suck a well dry. This information can be obtained from the well driller at the time of installation. Submersible pumps are not recommended for areas with sandy water since the grit will wear out the pump.

Noise level can be lowered in several ways. As mentioned before, a submersible pump is virtually noise free. If silence is important, the pump can be located outside the house. If for some reason this is not possible, the pump can be bolted to the floor using rubber washers above and below the bolt. A rubber ferrule placed around a slightly smaller than usual bolt also lessens the noise level. Use a metal washer above the upper rubber washers to secure the pump. If a piece of flexible plastic pipe approximately two to three feet in length is connected from the supply pipe to the supply tank, noise will not be transmitted through the pipes.

INSTALLATION

When installing the pump in an area where condensation dripping from the pump might cause problems, a drip pan with hose leading to a drain can be placed under the pump, or a fiberglass insulated pump tank can be used to prevent the collection of condensation. It is best to select a pump that can be used with plastic pipe since plastic pipe is easy to assemble, flexible, lightweight and inexpensive. Use only the specified pipe fittings and check to see that the appropriate end of the fitting is used on the correct end of the pipe.

If a jet or submersible pump is being inserted in a well, allow as much of a bending radius as possible for inserting the pump into the well and try not to scrape the pump on any rough edges in the well. After the pump is installed, prime it. It may take a while for the pipe to fill, but when the pipe and tank are full, most pumps operate without further problems for years.

TROUBLESHOOTING

When a pump starts and stops at short intervals, this indicates that the tank is *waterlogged,* not having an air cushion at the top of the tank. Check for a faulty regulator. A part might be stuck so tap the regulator with a pair of pliers to jolt it free. A loose fitting or plug could also be the problem.

If the pump starts at long intervals even when no water is being used, a pinhole leak may be the cause. This can be spotted with a flashlight by removing the sanitary well cap and peering down the well. If it is a leaky foot valve, waiting a few days may allow the valve to seal itself after more use.

If the water pressure is weak on winter mornings, the small tube to the pressure switch may be frozen. To thaw it, simply take a pocket lighter and hold the flame under the copper tube for a minute or two. When the tube thaws, the pump will begin working.

Punches

Punches are used primarily for making pilot holes for screws, brads and nails. The self-centering and center punch are two of the most common types of punches. *SEE ALSO HAND TOOLS.*

Purchasing A Home

Most home buyers have no idea what they really want. They are not sure of how many rooms they need, whether they want a house on one or more levels, or how much house they can afford. They concentrate on such features as the color of the carpeting in the living room, and whether or not the draperies are to be sold with the house, rather than examining the foundations of the house.

Looking for a house calls for some know-how, and since a house is probably the largest purchase you'll ever make in your life, it is well worth your while to take a good look at your family life, how it lives, how your present home satisfies or dissatisfies, and how you would like to improve it. You will also need to take a close look at your financial situation. You'll probably need to talk with your banker or some other financial adviser such as an accountant to see whether you can really afford to buy a house and if so, how much can you afford.

Because you are paying a certain sum for rent, does not mean you can buy a house for exactly that sum in house payments.

In addition to monthly payments on a home, you will have taxes, insurance, upkeep, and some investment in improvements and furnishings, especially when you first move in. There are also closing costs and hidden fees which need to be covered with cash.

You need to consider your future. What will you want in the way of a house five years from now, twenty years from now? A just-married couple planning a family of two children turn out to be a boy and girl who would want their own rooms. Or if they are planning no family, they might still need room for guests, or a place for an aged relative. A real-estate agent could tell them that should they decide to sell, it's far easier to sell a three-bedroom house than a smaller place.

A LOOK AT THE HOUSE YOU ARE LIVING IN

When a housing agent polled families to find why they were dissastisfied with their present homes here is what it tabulated:

Storage space inadequate.

Rooms too small and poorly arranged.

Laundry facilities inconvenient.

Bedrooms not large enough.

No place to eat in the kitchen.

Insufficient kitchen work space.

This list should serve as a guide when you consider the purchase of another house. In addition, here are other features you should include:

Do you need more garage space?

Would you like a workshop or hobby room, a family room?

Is the neighborhood deteriorating? Why?

Are there convenient sources of public transportation? Gasoline shortages are likely to occur in the future. If your present home requires that you drive for every need, you may want to buy a house where you can walk or, at least, get to a bus for essential shopping.

WHERE DO YOU FIND THE RIGHT HOUSE?

Start by making a thorough study of the classifieds in local newspapers. You will have an idea of what is being offered, price range, descriptions of houses now on the market, names and addresses of real-estate brokers, and sometimes photographs of houses. If you see the words "principals only" in a classified, it means the owner wishes to deal directly with a buyer, not through a broker. He hopes to save the broker's commission by selling the house himself. By so doing he may be able to offer his house at a lower price, or more likely, he hopes to make more profit.

Whatever his reason, you stand to profit, too, because there may be a chance to bargain on price.

Owners and real-estate brokers open many of their houses to the public, especially on week ends. An open house ad will tell you how to find the place (sometimes there is a map) and the hours it is open. It is a good way of seeing houses which are above or below your price range to get an idea of how much money will be necessary for your requirements.

Most people have neither the time nor the desire to do house buying research. A real-estate broker has many listings, and also has access to listings of other agencies in the same area. Many of these will not be advertised. Choose a broker you feel you can trust. Give him your house requirements and price range. He can then go over his listings and show you all the homes which seem suitable. If you find a house you want to buy he can handle financial arrangements between you and the owner, see that the deal is transacted legally, may be able to help you arrange a mortgage and can take care of the details of getting you moved in. In some cases he can handle the sale of your own house or a trade-in deal.

There are many advantages in getting the help of a real-estate broker. He wants to make a sale so he will try to get the price down as far as possible. He is also a good judge of house values within the area. He can be held liable (true if the owner sells directly, too) legally if he does not inform you of a serious defect or of some legal problem you might encounter after you buy the house.

Another source of information on home sales is through a housing bureau in a large company, a military base, or university area where personnel changes and transfers occur frequently. A list of houses on the market is available for new personnel, or for anyone else who inquires.

Sources of housing you may never have thought of include the obituary column, as well as news stories announcing industrial closedowns. Following a death there may be an estate sale or auction. Announcement of a will and the name of the executor can lead you to a house sale. If there is a vacant house which interests you, go to the city hall with a description of the house location. You will be given the name and address of the tax payer, since this is public information. You can then write a note to the owner, asking if the place is for sale.

HOUSE LOCATION

Whether you're buying a new house, an older one, or planning to build, any real-estate expert will tell you location is the most important aspect to consider — before anything else. No matter how desirable the appearance or how good a buy the house seems to be, its value will be determined by where it is located.

These are the location features most families want when they buy a house. An area zoned to keep out industry, high-rise buildings, and commercial housing such as motels and hotels, apartment houses. A location where most houses are owned rather than rented. Good schools with bus service or in walking range. A safe street, dead end or cul-de-sac which reduces noise and traffic danger. Existing improvements — city sewer, pavement, city water supply, garbage collection, underground utility wires. Nearby and frequent public transportation service. Street lights, readily available police and fire protection and a community hospital nearby. A shopping center with a variety of stores within a short driving distance, preferably one with medical offices.

Who Built the House?

Check out the builder's reputation. Your bank or your lawyer are two sources of information. Talk to people who are living in houses he's built. Lumber dealers and building suppliers are other sources of information. If the builder puts up groups of houses, or large subdivisions, find out if you can inspect a model house. Remember, however, that a model is a sample of his best work.

If the builder is a small operator, one who puts up only a house or two at a time, there are both advantages and disadvantages. He's probably a local builder, and it will be easy to check his reputation. There will be no model house, but he may arrange for you to visit a house he has built and sold. He frequently will offer a house for sale while it's still in the building stage — an advantage to you, since you can then have a choice of paint color, carpet color, and specify minor changes. Most "one house at a time" builders supervise the work carefully, often do some of it themselves, and take pride in their workmanship.

OUTSIDE OF THE HOUSE

Look at the position of the house on its lot, closeness to neighboring yards, effectiveness of land-scaping. Check the condition of outside of the house. Is there excessive chalking, fading blisters, peeling, cracks?

Notice what kind of driveway and how difficult it is to negotiate. See if there is a turn around or if you must back into traffic. Also is the driveway sound and of a material thick enough to withstand the weight of a moving van or delivery truck without cracking? Does house sag at any point?

Look at the materials which have been used on the exterior and see if it has been recently recovered. If it has find out why and check to see how good a job was done. Be sure of the roof condition. If it is of fireproof or fire-resistant material. Look for signs of leaking on the ceiling floor or carpet. And if possible check the roof out on a rainy day.

How many cars will the garage hold? If yours is a large car, will the doors close after the car is in?

Notice the kind of garage doors and check to see if they are automatic, if not, how easily do they open and close? Is the garage attached to the house with inside entry to kitchen or hall?

Entryway

Is the front door attractive, solid, wide enough to permit furniture to be moved in and out easily? Look for a good lock and burglar-prevention devices. A well-lighted entrance which is sheltered from wind and rain is a welcome convenience. Is the entrance arranged to provide privacy for other living areas of the house? The floor should be made of a material impervious to water and stains. A coat closet should be provided. There would be easy access to kitchen or bedrooms, without crossing the living room.

THE INTERIOR
Kitchen

The kitchen should be accessible from other parts of the house and near the garage or other doors through which supplies are brought in. Plenty of counter space with surfaces of several materials should be available. Is it convenient to dining and outdoor eating areas? It must be well lighted and provide adequate space for two people (minimum) to work and move about freely.

There should be a variety of storage spaces and possibly compartments, a separate pantry, cleaning supply closet is also advantages. Are there any built-ins? Is there an exhaust fan ventilating system? Notice how it is ducted; to the outdoors is best. Is there an eating area in the kitchen such as a bar, slide-out counter or built-in nook. Room for expansion should be available should you want to add another appliance, add dining space, or change a unit of one size for a larger one.

Living Room

The living room should not be a pathway from other rooms but a private restful room. If there is a fireplace check to see if it smokes, (surface above the opening may show smoke stain if it does; if the surface is immaculate this could be an indication that the fireplace has never been used or tried). A re-circulating fireplace can help hold heating costs down by sending heat back into the room. There should be space for wood storage near it also. The hearth must be wide enough to keep sparks from flying onto combustible materials in the room.

Take note of available natural light and the kinds of windows. Small panes can be difficult to clean.

Be aware of the type of floor covering. If the floor is carpeted, check to see if there is hardwood floor beneath it. Hardwood is beautiful, requires more maintenance, may require that you purchase rugs for best effect. Notice if there are permanent lighting fixtures or if you must furnish lamps. Then check on the placement of outlets.

Dining Room

First decide if you prefer an area separate from living area. Some families prefer that it be closed off from kitchen while others want an open-plan dining room. Be sure it is large enough to hold your present furniture. Count the number of people you can entertain at a sit-down meal and

the steps to the kitchen. Look for such as a buffet counter, china cabinet, or shelves. Finally consider if the floor covering is appropriate for your needs.

Bedrooms

Most couples prefer a master bedroom suite with a private bath, one should be suitable as guest bedroom. Bring along measurements of your bedroom furniture to see if it will fit in. Adequately soundproofing is important as well as privacy from the living areas of the house. Cross-ventilation is most desirable. Windows and sliding doors which open should also be equipped with a means of locking them when they are in the open position, as a precaution against an intruder who could open them far enough to slip through. Adequate lighting such as a reading light over the bed, closet lights, desk and dressing table lights are most convenient. There should be more than one exit. In case of emergency there should be at least one door or window with access to the outside. The window should be adequately large to permit the average person to crawl through.

Bathrooms

First the number is important. Many new homes today provide a bath for each bedroom, plus a powder room for guests. Many bathrooms can mean more plumbing problems and much cleaning, however. White or light-colored fixtures are easiest to keep attractive. Dark colors show lint and the residue of cleanser. A soaking tub or deep Roman-style tub are handsome, but may not be used often enough to justify the space and the amount of hot water they use. Bathrooms should be situated in a way which provides no view of the occupants, or of the toilet, when the doors are open. Notice the brands of the plumbing fixtures. An absence of brand name indicates economy fixtures which may give plumbing troubles or need replacement soon. A flexible nozzle with a selfcleaning head is very convenient. Is shower a part of the tub, or a separate enclosure? If the shower compartment is separate, notice the wall material. Tile is the most durable. Fiberglass requires careful cleaning procedure or it loses its glossy surface and attracts soil or water residue, which may be impossible to remove. Again notice the material the tub is made of. Enameled cast-iron is the most durable, and the most comfortable to sit in.

Heat lamps and a supplementary electric heater make for comfort at hours when central heat is not in operation.

Is the medicine cabinet large enough to hold tall bottles? Is there an extra cabinet (lockable) to hold prescription and dangerous products?

Does hot water arrive instantly? Turn it on. A lot of water will be wasted if it must run a minute or longer to reach a comfortable temperature.

The bathroom should have a ventilating system which is ducted to the outdoors. Some types operate automatically when toilet area is in use. A window which opens helps in ventilation.

Washbasins need to be large enough for hair-washing and personal laundry jobs. There should also be a place to dry quick laundry. Is there a linen closet?

The floor covering should be durable, water resistant and easy to clean. Try the faucets, stoppers, shower nozzle and flush the toilet to be sure all the fixtures work well. Emergency water shut-offs need to be easily available.

Storage Areas, Closets

To decide how much storage space is adequate, measure the available space in your present living quarters as a guide to probable need in a new home. Walk-in and large closets are not as useful as medium-sized closets fitted out with shelves, storage drawers, and poles for both long and short garments. Closet depth should be a minimum of 24''. There needs to be a closet for storage of out-of-season garments and bedding and a cedar closet is very convenient. Most families require an attic, small storage room, or storage areas in garage where suitcases, out-of-use items, and sporting equipment can be stored. Check to see if there are any possibilities for expanding the existing closet and storage space.

Utility Areas

The laundry is most convenient when it is close to bedrooms, kitchen, bathrooms rather than in a distant basement or garage area. The area should be wired to take a 240-volt electric dryer or have access for a gas dryer. The dryer also needs to be supplied with an outdoor vent. An exhaust ventilating fan ducted to the outside also helps. Provision should be made to drain off the water, if the washer should overflow.

Will the appliances you now own fit new utility area? Bring measurements of your own appliances, or fact sheets on appliances you plan to buy, in order to check this out. Good lighting in the utility area is a must. Luminous ceilings and skylights are features.

Hallways, Staircases

Make sure the stair treads are safe. They should be at least ten inches deep, and eight inches high. The stair area needs to be well lighted, have safety rails which are smooth to the touch, a comfortable height, and protected with spacers close enough together to keep a small child from becoming wedged or falling through. Two persons should be able to pass each other easily, in a hallway.

In addition to checking off and looking for obvious features in the house there will be many important items which are more difficult to judge. You can test the water flow by turning on faucets. Push up the thermostat to see if the heating system starts up quickly, runs without excessive noise. Also check the insulation. If there's an attic or crawl space you can get a look at it. Four to six inches of mineral wool insulation is excellent.

If the house has central air-conditioning, turn it on to test the noise level. Ask to see figures on utility costs such as records or cancelled checks of previous year's utility bills.

You cannot see the electrical wiring, but you can look at the wiring entrance box. Is it a modern circuit breaker which does not use fuses? Are circuits marked to show you which circuit levers control which rooms? One test you can use: turn several appliances and lights on at the same time. If there is any dimming or flickering, the wiring system may not be adequate.

If there is a basement, look at floors and walls for evidence of moisture. Dark brown streaks running along posts and beams, or small piles of sawdust on ledges or floors may be a sign of termites. A termite inspection, paid for normally by the seller, should be a part of a selling agreement. The company doing the inspection provides a written report describing extent of termite damage and an estimate of the cost to destroy the termites if any, and restore the house to sound condition.

OLD HOUSES, ANTIQUE HOUSES

Old houses, like old furniture, have come out of the bargain and junk class. When you see one advertised for sale, it will probably be described as a "fixer-upper" or "antique." Especially desirable to many buyers are the Victorian houses built in the late 1800's by highly talented craftsmen who produced hand-carved woodwork and stained glass that can't be duplicated today. Remodeling an old house can be more expensive than building a new one, so the best way to come out ahead restoring one of these older homes, is to do the work yourself, especially removing equipment and parts which need replacing, or doing the less skilled jobs such as papering, painting, laying new flooring, and refinishing woodwork and cabinets.

Be Realistic

A fine old barn, an old winery, a gate house on an old estate, old schools and churches have been purchased and made into good homes. Not all buildings age well, and if the price is low enough to tempt you, get some professional advice before you buy. Realistic estimates from contractors, an architect, and suppliers — even if you plan to do much of the work yourself — are a good start. If you cannot finance it yourself, can you find a bank or lending institution which will? When restorations are a part of an urban renewal plan, financial help may be available

through the government or the city itself. The city of Oakland bore the cost of renewing the streets and putting power lines underground in one area where 200 fine old houses were restored.

You will not only have to bring a remodeling job up to your own standards, but in order to get a permit to go ahead with the work, you will be required to comply with zoning laws and building codes. It is unlikely, for example, that the old wiring and plumbing will be adequate or permitted. Tearing the old out and putting new in is usually more costly than starting from scratch.

Guidelines Before Buying

Look to see if old houses in the area have been restored. Paint and surface refurnishing don't count as remodeling.

Make sure the house you are considering is not the only one of its type in the area and that it will not become an orphan surrounded by industry and small business.

Older houses are normally remnants in the heart of an old city. Remember that small industry contributes, not only noise, but hazards to children, if you are planning your restoration to be a family home.

If there are neighbors living in similar houses which have been restored, the owner or occupants may be able to help you with their experiences.

Realize that crime rate tends to be high in older crowded areas. Also if the entire area is under renewal, you may be assessed for renewal of street lighting, curbs, landscaping, or new schools.

Be aware of the current tax on the property and that remodeling inevitable results in reassessment and much higher taxes.

You may be able to cut costs by living in the house while you remodel. Restoration can be a slow process — years if it's a do-it-yourself pro-

Courtesy of American Plywood Association

ject and supporting two houses can quickly become very expensive.

If you plan a conversion to more than one family unit check the zoning laws to be sure you are not limited to single-family occupancy.

Old homes were not a part of the automobile age. You may have to park on a busy street if the lot is not large enough to add a garage. Even if it is, be sure the building code will permit it.

Know the location of the schools. New and attractive schools are usually in the suburbs. If you have children they may have a long trip each day, or you may have to drive them to school.

You will also need to know where the shopping centers and the supermarkets are.

Landscaping costs are a part of a remodeling job. A large old home may have extensive lawns and gardens overgrown and neglected. Will you have to hire landscaping help? Yardwork can be formidable on a place once kept up by several gardeners.

CONDOMINIUMS AND COOPERATIVES

Condominiums and cooperatives are forms of housing which are a blend of private and mutual ownership. The *cooperative* is an older form of joint housing ownership, one in which you and a group of people own an apartment house together, with each of you sharing maintenance costs, taxes, payments and controlling the leasing of the units. When you move into a cooperative housing situation you are actually buying a share in a cooperation. It is like purchasing a

Courtesy of American Plywood Association

share of a business. A cooperative is operated for a profit in which you share, or at a loss which you also have to share. In addition to living in the cooperative, you will be obligated for a monthly fee which covers taxes and maintenance. You will be one of the bosses in that you will have a vote on how the place should be operated, maintained, and what should be done with the profits, if any. If your cooperative is wisely operated by you and your co-owners, the value of the property will increase and the value of your shares in the business will increase.

What are the disadvantages, then of owning a part of a cooperative? You cannot sell, buy or make any drastic changes in your apartment without the approval of all the other owners.

If your building happens to be in a part of town where values are declining, your investment may be a bad one and you might even find yourself in a building where other owners fail to make their tax and maintenance fees and your business verges on bankruptcy.

Condominiums have some, but not all, of the advantages and disadvantages of the cooperative. When you buy a condominium, you make an outright purchase just as you do if you were buying a house. You are not in business with other people who live in the same condominium arrangement. You have your own tax bill and pay on your own mortgage. Jointly with your neighbors, you do own the land.

Each condominium owner pays a monthly fee covering maintenance costs. If however, one of your neighbors fails to meet his monthly fee, you are not legally responsible for his debt.

Since the condominium is, and probably will continue to be, one of the most important forms of new housing (some experts predict that rising land costs will do away with ownership of individual homes for all but the rich), here are the main facts you should know before you decide on a condominium living.

The purchase of a condominium, in an area of high land cost, permits you to own a reasonably

Courtesy of American Plywood Association

priced living unit on land where you could never afford to build an individual home unit. You make your own financial arrangements, seeking out the best possible interest rate and suitable repayment schedule. Or you can buy your condominium for cash and if you need cash in future years, you can refinance.

You are free to sell, sublet, or will your unit to your children or to anyone else for that matter. Your unit is assessed individually and you pay your own property tax. Tax breaks from the IRS are the same as for any home owner. You can deduct mortgage interest, the real estate tax, capital gain if you sell, and you are entitled to the special tax exemption when you reach 65.

If the condominium you are considering is under construction, or still in the planning stage, check the financial responsibility of the builder. Find out if there is a model unit, and how your unit will compare. If a down payment is required before your unit is built, what will happen to it if he defaults? Will you get your down payment back?

Make sure the recreational facilities are adequate. Will the pool or tennis courts be enlarged should they prove inadequate, once all condominiums are sold and fully occupied?

What is the monthly maintenance fee and what does it cover? If other owners refuse to pay their maintenance charges, or get behind on them, check to see if your own fee will be increased to cover the cost necessary to keep the condominium operating properly.

You will want to know if children are permitted. Condominium living means close living and many children mean more noise, bicycles, toys and wear on recreational facilities.

Are animals allowed? Barking dogs and meowing cats, plus the cleanliness problems which they bring, are a source of contention in some condominiums.

Is there a security system such as guards, gate, or alarms. If so, you can leave your unit and know that it will receive better protection than would an individual house.

Condominium ownership frees you from maintenance chores, but it does not free you from a possible increase in the cost of that maintenance. Should you go on a year's vacation around the world or move out and sublet your unit, you will still be responsible for the maintenance fee, unless, of course, you can pass it along to a tenant using or subletting the place from you. If you no longer use the recreational facilities you will still have to keep up these facilities with your share of the upkeep payment.

Condominiums are the wave of the future — at least as long as building costs go up. Most condominiums are new. Once there is a change of tenants or the recreational facilities wear out, and other problems develop from deterioration or mere old age, only those condominiums which have been well built and well managed from the start will be happy places to buy into and live in. Owners who have lived in their units long enough to encounter a few of the problems say that good neighbors are the essence of satisfaction with condominium living, just as they are in any neighborhood, except that in a condominium they are closer to you, where small differences of habit and opinion can make for tension.

SHOPPING FOR A MORTGAGE

In spite of what you may think, the biggest purchase you will ever make is not your new home, but the mortgage that goes along with it. It is a sobering fact when you realize that interest on a typical mortgage more than doubles the price you pay for the house. A 30-year loan at $7^1/2\%$ interest (an optimistic figure these days) will require you to put out $250 for each $100 of the selling price. In other words, everytime you pay back $1 on the principal you pay an additional $1.50 interest. And that $1.50 jumps to $2.00 when interest rates pass $9^1/4\%$.

After making a down payment on a house you will then need a mortgage arrangement called a conventional home loan. Usually you get one at a bank, savings-and loan, mortgage or insurance company, or sometimes from a private lender which pays off the seller. The loan runs as long as 25 years, sometimes more, and is paid off in

Courtesy of Western Wood Products Association.

equal monthly installments. As time goes by the mortgage grows smaller, the interest less, but even after some years of payments you will still find that you owe almost as much as you have paid off.

Distressing though this is, the truth is that during the first years each payment covers far more interest than it does principal. These sobering financial facts are an excellent reason for arranging the best home loan you can find.

At some periods loan organizations compete actively to try and get your mortgage business. When this is true, you may be able to find an arrangement which exactly fits your needs at the lowest possible interest rate. At times when money is extremely hard to find, it will be difficult indeed and require more shrewdness to get a mortgage at all.

What Kind of Loan

The two usual types of loan are: Conventional and government sponsored. Some states have a subsidized loan for veterans. Still another type is the one usually called a GI (or Veterans Administration) loan guaranteed by the government up to $12,500 (or 65 percent if that's lower). One of the big advantages to this type of loan is that it gives the buyer a chance to buy with a very low, or sometimes no down payment, provided the appraiser finds that the house is worth what it's selling for.

Next best is an FHA loan (Federal Housing Administration) which is insured (insurance costs the lender an extra $1/2$ percent), but not subsidized by the government. The government is not a loan company. You will still get such a loan through the usual lending agency such as a bank.

Purchasing a Home

Recent liberalization of old housing legislation may make it easier for you to get an FHA loan. Under the old law, the mortgage ceiling for a one-family home was $33,000, an unrealistic figure in many areas where most homes sell far above that price. If you wanted an expensive house, you had to supply a very large down payment. The ceiling has now been raised to $45,000. On a two or three-family house the old mortgage ceiling was $35,750; it's now $48,750. On a fourplex you can now get a $56,000 FHA mortgage, up from $41,250. FHA has also cut its required down payments to over 70 percent on high-priced houses and by 50 percent on less expensive houses. Similar drastic cuts have been made on the down payment requirements for multiple-family dwellings, a good reason to try to get an FHA loan, especially when a huge downpayment can make the difference between buying a home or not buying one.

Most home loans in some areas are conventional, in other words neither subsidized nor guaranteed. If you are looking for one of the conventional type loans you may be surprised to find how great a variation exists in terms — interest rates charged, size of loan available, personal credit requirements — from one lending institution to another.

One other well-known large institution might be what you need. It's called a private mortgage-insurance company. Best known are Mortgage Guarantee Insurance Corporation (MGIC), Continental Mortgage Insurance, Inc. and American Mortgage Insurance Corporation. Here is what could happen. You find a house which is exactly what you want, but you can't come up with a large enough down payment to qualify for a conventional or FHA loan. A savings and loan will give you the needed loan provided an insurance company will take most of the risk should you default. Through the savings and loan insurance is obtained. You, however, will be charged an appraisal fee plus a first-year cost of $1/2$ of 1 percent of the amount of the mortgage. The insurance company guarantees the top 20 percent of the loan, a deal which is pretty safe for the savings and loan. You will be paying a loan-insurance premium each year along with your mortgage payments. However, sometimes a lender will permit you to drop the insurance after you have been paying promptly for a number of years and your credit with him is excellent.

Can You Get a Large Enough Loan?

Without insurance on the loan, a bank will have a top limit, sometimes 75 percent or less of the appraised value of the property. Other lending institutions have a more liberal lending policy, and until the recent tight-money situation, were financing up to 95 percent of the appraised value of a property.

Banks are conservative in other ways too. They may not lend at all on some types of property, and their rules for determining your capacity and reliability to repay vary. Until lately other lending institutions discriminated against women by refusing to include the working wife's paycheck when calculating how much a working couple could borrow to finance a home purchase. Now a new housing law says a lender must include *all* the wife's pay when calculating repayment ability. When you go shopping for a loan, be sure the lender does not evade this law.

Other factors which enter in: you must show that your income is dependable. Extra income from part time work or from hobby work you engage in during spare hours may bring important funds to you, but a lender will not count this money as reliable. If you have several children approaching college age, parents who are dependent upon you, or a record of slow payment on regular monthly bills, these factors might work against you. You might have to come up with your monthly budget, showing where and how you spend your salary. If you are just barely paying your bills, with no emergency savings backlog, a lender might consider you a poor risk. Illness or unemployment could lead to a mortgage default.

If you carry a lot of life insurance and have adequate sound health insurance policies, these could be plus factors. Age is also important. If you are a couple under 25 or over 55, you will not find it easy to get a mortgage. Couples in the 30 to

Courtesy of American Plywood Association

40 age group are considered safest from the lender's viewpoint.

What's The Interest Rate?

Interest rates go up and down — mostly up during the last few years. But they still vary from one lending agency to another. Fees and costs for making a loan vary greatly also, something to consider if you're considering loans from two lenders with the same interest rates.

One buyer saved a tidy sum on a home loan by learning that although his own bank had upped its interest on home loans to 7¹/₄ percent, another bank which he dealt with occasionally was still lending at 7 percent. The 7 percent loan was ar-ranged and completed only a few days before that bank, too, upped its rate to 7¹/₄ percent. Now he is quite a bit ahead financially because he made his deal at the right bank at just the right moment.

A jump from 8 percent, say, to 9 percent at first does not sound so terrible. On a typical home loan each raise will add $6 to $7 to each monthly installment for each 10,000 of the mortgage loan. If through bad luck (buying a month earlier or later) or failure to shop around carefully, you find you have a 9 percent loan when you could have had one at 8 percent, it will take you five extra years to pay off the same loan at the same monthly rate. The higher rate will have added $10,200 to the payoff cost of a mere $20,000 loan.

Is It a Variable-Rate Mortgage?

This is the trend in mortgages — almost surely one which will spread in our day of high and fluctuating interest rates. It sounds good on the face of it, but it can be very much a financial minus rather than a financial plus to you, the borrower.

As you may already know, it is a mortgage where the interest rate, and your monthly payments with it, increase or decrease with changes in the prevailing rate of interest. The up or down change might be limited to a fraction of a percentage over any period of time, say at five year intervals.

If you feel that interest rates will drop in the future, you will be glad to get a variable-rate mortgage. If you think interest rates are likely to go up even higher than when you get your mortgage, you will avoid such a arrangement. But note that you have nothing to lose in accepting a special kind of variable that surfaced as mortgage rates passed 9 percent in 1973. If at any time within three years the going rate should drop, you could ask to have your rate adjusted to that level, but only once.

Here is how a variable might work for you. Suppose you obtain a 3-year, 8 percent mortgage today for $25,000. Your payments would be about $183 a month. If 5 years from now, say, the rate had risen to 8½% your payments would increase to $198. If, on the other hand, the rate should drop to 7½% your payments would decrease to $176. If interest rates continued to drop, say to 7 percent your payments would then be $169 monthly.

Because no one can look into the future you will do well to avoid the variable feature. When interest jumps, this feature hurts you. When rates go down, you suffer, but only a little. When rates drop rapidly, you already have protection in the form of refinancing.

Points

Point is merely a short way of saying percentage point. It is an extra fee which you may have to pay. It is a one time only charge whereby the lender makes a bigger profit on the loan. It works this way: the lender says he can give you a $22,000 mortgage but you will have to pay two points. This means he is charging you two percent of the entire loan, or another $400, in addition to such charges as closing costs. An FHA borrower is protected by law from this practice. The seller, however, may pay points and when he does this charge is often hidden in the selling price of the house.

Points are basically a way of raising the interest rate to bring it into line with the current value of mortgage money. It may or may not make much difference to you as a borrower. If you should pay off the mortgage after a year — two points will have cost you an additional two percent. Your nine percent mortgage will have cost you about 11 percent. If you go on paying on that mortgage for the next 20 years the 2 points will have cost you only a fraction of 1% each year.

How to Figure a Point

If you keep the mortgage until 20-year maturity, each point is the equivalent of ⅛ of a percentage pointed added to the stated rate of interest. If yours is a 20 year mortgage at 8½ percent plus four points all the way to maturity, its cost is approximately the same as for a nine percent loan with no points.

Prepayment Penalty

A lender who has made a profitable loan does not want it paid off early, thereby depriving him of the interest. Also, since he has to keep your loan in force at a stated interest rate no matter how the business world fluctuates, he does not want you to borrow somewhere else and pay him off should you be able to borrow elsewhere at a lower rate if interest drops. To avoid this he may require that you pay a penalty if you pay the loan off ahead of time. FHA discontinued prepayment penalties back in 1972. If yours is a conventional loan, try to avoid the penalty clause.

Open End Loans

This can be a handy source of money, one that lets you reborrow the money you have already

Courtesy of American Plywood Association

paid in, preferably at the same rate of interest. It is a good way to save money, but also a temptation to spend on less desirable things than a home.

Caution — Is There a Balloon?

This is one huge final payment, sometimes as much as several thousand dollars. It is a way of keeping monthly payments low on a short term mortgage. A balloon payment is often included in a type of house sale financed by a conditional sales agreement.

Closing Costs

These can be an unpleasant surprise if you are a home buyer who has just barely been able to come through with a substantial down payment. You should figure on several hundred (sometimes up to $1,000) for such costs as: appraisal fee, credit report, survey, title insurance, preparation of legal documents, recording fees, escrow fees. About all you can do is try to find

out before you close the deal is what the closing costs will be. This bill may, in fact, influence your choice of lender, should you have more than one possibility. When interest rates are the same, closing costs might differ by hundreds of dollars. Much will depend upon where you live and how expensive a home you are buying.

An Existing Mortgage

If there is an existing mortgage, you may be able to take it over from the mortgagee. The chief advantage is that an older mortgage may have a low interest rate, six to seven percent, when the lowest available rate on a loan is eight to ten percent.

The chief drawback to taking over an existing mortgage is that it might not be as large as you need and would have to be paid off rather quickly. Here's an example: the Jensens, an auto salesman and his wife, came upon a 10-year-old house they wanted very much. The price arrived at after some dickering was $49,200. The existing mortgage, initially $36,000 for 20 years, had been paid down to about $26,400. At a modest seven percent compared to the going rate of nine percent, it sounded like a good deal. However, when Jensen subtracted $26,400 from $49,200, he discovered he'd have to make a $22,800 down payment instead of the $9,840 he'd hoped to arrange. Fortunately the Jensens were able to come up with more cash. If they hadn't the seller might have been willing to take a second mortgage for the extra cash needed. Even if this second were written at a rate somewhat higher than the nine percent current for first mortgages, the combination would still have been a bargain for the Jensens if they could handle the relatively high total monthly payments. Their reward — an early mortgage payoff.

A Second Mortgage

A second mortgage is usually associated with high interest rates and a situation where you, the buyer, could get in over your head. Look carefully at your capacity to pay the combined monthly payments. Play it safe and think of them as one house payment.

Purchase Money

The more usual form of second mortgage may be called purchase money, whereby the seller accepts his down payment partly in cash and partly in a second mortgage to help make it possible for you to buy his house. He feels it is a safe investment because he has confidence in the security behind the arrangement — the house he is selling.

Contract Of Sale

Still another type of financing, becoming more usual when money is tight and conventional loans are available only at very high interest rates, is called a contract of sale. There is no mortgage; the contract takes the place of it. Under this arrangement you, as buyer, would make a down payment and pay off the remainder of the sale price to the seller just as though a lending institution were holding the mortgage. When the entire amount is paid, you will get a clear title, just as you would if you paid off a conventional mortgage.

The arrangement is sometimes called a *conditional sales contract* (sometimes a land contract). In many ways it resembles the contract you sign when you buy a car or a refrigerator. Before buying a house on a contract of sale rather than a mortgage, hire a real estate lawyer to check it over, just to be sure there are no dangers or gimmicks that might give you difficulty should you be unable to keep up the payments. Make sure that the terms of the contract are no more severe than you would encounter under a conventional mortgage agreement.

If you buy on a sales contract, make sure you are not paying a higher rate of interest than you would pay by some other arrangement available to you. A purchase of a home on a contract of sale can have such advantages as: no fixed limitation on size of down payment, free negotiation of size of payments, no heavy closing costs, postponement of recording fees, and probably lower taxes. Property taxes are often adjusted upward when there is a change of ownership. With the contract of sale purchase, recording of the sale could be delayed for many years — until the final payment is made.

Inherent danger in a contract of sale going unrecorded is that the seller might dishonestly sell the same property again, vanish, or go bankrupt. Only if you can trust the seller's honesty and financial soundness should you leave the sale unrecorded. Rules about contract sales are so variable in different states that a buyer will do well to protect his interests by investing in the services of a competent real estate lawyer.

How Much A Month?

Mortgage payments alone are not the whole financial story when buying a house. You must also figure in property taxes, insurance and maintenance. If you're acquiring an older home, it may need extensive repairs or remodeling. A home owner who is handy can cut such costs tremendously in this day of high labor costs.

The older the house the more likely you will have regular breakdowns or a need for replacements of such essentials as hot water heater, furnace, and built-in mechanical devices such as dishwasher, range, oven.

Another item which many families fail to include when moving from one house to another is the cost of transportation. If the new home is farther from family employment than the old home, transportation costs can jump many dollars a month. Or if the new home is isolated from easy shopping and nearby schools, it may be necessary to buy a second car.

MANAGING A MORTGAGE

A mortgage, like your family budget, should occasionally be re-examined to see if it suits your financial needs. Perhaps the payments are too large. Or you would like to pay it off more quickly. Rates may have dropped appreciably since you took it out, if you did so during one of the high-interest periods of recent years.

You might be able to save considerably by refinancing at a lower interest rate, with correspondingly lower monthly payments. Or you may want to switch to a plan which would pay the mortgage off much more quickly now that you're earning more money. Refinancing is particularly feasible once you have considerable equity in your home. This can be arranged, especially if you've paid off a large enough sum to make the property itself adequate security for the balance. Perhaps you have added home improvements, or new and expensive homes have been built in your neighborhood. Both are features which increase home values. As a result of such changes in your home ownership picture you may be able to get a new loan at a lower rate. As noted, small changes in interest rates are far more significant than they seem. Over the life of a 30 year $25,000 mortgage reducing the rate from 9$\frac{1}{2}$ percent to 8$\frac{1}{2}$ percent means a difference of $5,397. It also cuts monthly payments about $18.

In checking the possibilities, you should deduct from the possible savings any costs involved in making the change. These include such possible expenses as appraisal and loan fees, title-insurance costs and any penalty that may be provided for in your present mortgage. Your bank or lending source can help you decide whether the

changeover is beneficial, or whether it may be in the future. If a change is desirable, you can take the profit by reducing your monthly payments and still pay off the mortgage on the original date; or you may be able to pay off the mortgage far sooner than you expected with no extra cost to yourself.

Following may help you decide on mortgage strategy: Payments on a mortgage, taken out nine years ago, runs $227 a month. Maintenance work is expensive and the house is getting shabby. You need to get the payments lowered so you can use the extra money for improvements. By reamortizing you let your present mortgage run for a longer time with lower payments. Lenders do not usually like such an arrangement, but, as the money will go for improvements which will keep up the value of the property, the lender may agree. If your existing mortgage carries an interest rate which is lower than the current rate, it might not be easy to reamortize. If your rate is higher than today's rate, you might be able to get a completely new mortgage. Reamortizing is simpler than getting a new mortgage, since you won't have to pay a new loan fee and for title insurance again. You will be paying more interest, but only to the extent that the mortgage period is extended.

Due to heavier expenses it is difficult for you to meet your mortgage payments. By refinancing and getting a new mortgage from the same lender who holds your present mortgage a new lender if he will give you a better price, you can lower your payments.

If your mortgage carries a 9$\frac{1}{2}$% interest rate, and the lending rate has dropped to 8$\frac{1}{2}$%, it may save money to refinance and get the better rate.

The difference of 1 percentage point between the two mortgages provided the changeover does not involve a large amount for closing costs. Find out what they will be before you go ahead with the changeover.

To be sure refinancing is worthwhile, add up the additional closing costs plus any prepayment penalty in your existing mortgage. Add these figures to the amount you still owe. Next find out what the new payments will be at the lower-interest rate running to the same date as the one you now have.

If you find that by refinancing at a lower rate of interest even with extra closing costs, the monthly payments will be lower, you may be able to cut monthly payments even further by extending the life of the mortgage. You may also be able to get an open-end provision, a way of getting more money later on for improvements. Of course, if you decide to sell, you may be the loser unless you convince the buyer that the lower rate makes it worth the added price — which it is if he happens to want your mortgage.

If you find you can't save enough by refinancing to a lower interest rate, you can still save by pre-payment beyond the monthly amount required by the lender. This is the same as investing the money at $9^1/_4\%$. You will have more equity in your home and you will pay off the mortgage sooner.

If you plan to make prepayments, read your mortgage carefully and talk to the lender. Perhaps you can only pay ahead on the principal. You may be required to give written notice that you are going to pay ahead. If you prepay principal only, a lender may be willing to credit the amount to principal later on should you get in a bind and be unable to make regular payments.

RENT OR BUY?

It is cheaper to rent if your family is required to move every year or so because of frequent employment changes. Some people rent because they do not like the responsibilities of home ownership. However, a family which rents one house and goes right on living in the same place for many years is a loser.

Home ownership is not for everyone. Before you decide to buy, consider your preferences. If you agree with all, or most, of the statements which follow you will probably be happier as a renter, even though it will cost you more in cash outlay and reduced savings.

You must move frequently because of job transfers.

You do not want to be burdened by a lot of possessions.

You plan on extensive travel.

Lawn mowing and gardening do not interest you.

You spend your recreation hours at a golf course or tennis court.

You like to go out in the evenings.

You enjoy eating in restaurants.

You have no pets.

You rarely entertain guests.

You hire someone to do small repair jobs.

You have more than one job.

A buyer would feel exactly the opposite about most of the above statements. Condominium living can solve some of the conflict for many families. There you can own your unit and at the same time avoid maintenance chores.

A compromise, and a good one for some families, in an area where desirable rentals are hard to find is the lease-option. With interest rates high and down-payments increasing, many families cannot obtain a mortgage or save enough for a down payment in a short length of time. A builder with a new house, or an owner who wants to sell an older house, may not be able to sell. After a few months of vacancy the house may be put up for rental to a buyer who would like the house but does not have enough financing or is not sure he is ready to obligate himself to home ownership. The renter has first chance to buy. There is a risk that a serious buyer may come along, in which case the renter may have to move on a month's notice, as a part of the lease arrangement.

One big advantage of the lease-option for the occupants is the opportunity to live in a house which normally would not be for rent. New houses are not built as rentals in these days of difficult finance.

Rental Strategy

Renting is about the only choice if yours is a family whose job situation requires a move every year or two. Wise rental techniques can not only save you money but get you some fascinating and unusual places to live.

First, sign a lease only if you have to. A standard lease form protects the landlord more than it does the renter. You will probably be required to pay the first and last month's rent. If you move out before the year is up you lose that last month's rent, and you may get sued for the rest of the year's rent.

You will probably have to put up a deposit ($100 or more). Get in writing what the fee is for, whether it is a damage fee, a cleaning fee, or both. Go with the landlord on a tour of the place before you move in. Make written notation of existing damage or soil, include the condition of carpets or draperies. Have him initial the statement, and keep it with your lease. You will have some evidence to back up your claim for a refund when you move out. If the deposit is a cleaning fee, you still may have trouble collecting the whole sum.

The lowest rent may not be cheapest. If it is close to public transportation, your job, shops, and recreation it could save you the price of a car.

Find out if the rent includes utilities and how much they normally are. The landlord may include water and garbage collection, if you insist. A place heated by electricity might cost you twice as much for fuel as one heated by gas or oil. Be sure you know who must maintain the yard. Your lease may require you to do it; if you haven't the time, it will cost you a fair sum each month for a yard man.

Get the details on repair arrangements in writing. Are you responsible for repairs? If the landlord makes repairs himself, he may be very slow about coming to fix the leaking faucet or the non-operating garbage grinder. If you have it repaired, will you be reimbursed?

The landlord's insurance covers only his own liability and protection against theft and fire on his own possessions and the building. Make sure that your belongings are insured.

If there are appliances (dish-washer, garbage grinder, self-cleaning mechanism on the oven) ask for booklets showing how to use these sometimes baffling machines.

Find out where water, gas, and electrical service can be cut off quickly. Failure to shut off water when a washing machine hose breaks could ruin floors and furniture. You, not the landlord, are liable for all damages caused by negligence or carelessness.

Some people get free rent. If you have the time you might be able to substitute maintenance services for cash. In an apartment complex, for example, a landlord may offer a free apartment to a couple who do the fix-up jobs and collect rents. A woman who remains at home with small children can handle a good part of the routine work (show vacant apartments, take complaints) and a man can handle the repair jobs on week ends, even though he is fully employed elsewhere.

Free, or reduced rent, is sometimes offered by people who want their houses occupied when they are traveling. They may have pets, plants, and yardwork which need regular care, and they want their homes protected from vandalism. House sitting jobs turn up in the classifieds, or you could advertise your services. Once you've gotten a reputation for honesty and expert house care, your best jobs will come through references and referrals from your previous employers. House sitting, however, requires that you have few possessions of your own and that you do not mind moving frequently.

If you are not too rigid, you will find other rental possibilities than a house. Rentals may be available in a mobile home park, a sublet in a condominium, a gatehouse on a large estate, an apartment above a large garage even a houseboat or a loft in a business building.

HOW TO SELL YOUR HOME

Selling a house — can be both an educational and painful experience. It can also be most profitable, because home values have skyrocketed in recent years. If you decide to sell the house yourself and succeed, you will also earn the considerable commission (usually about 6% of the price) which a real-estate broker would get doing the job for you.

If you're in a hurry to sell, you will do better turning it over to a real-estate broker. It can take months or years, sometimes, to sell a house, especially if it is large and expensive, or during times when houses sell slowly because of tight mortgage money.

Whether you sell your house yourself or turn it over to a real estate agency here are some guidelines to make the results better:

Setting the price. You, the owner, decide on the price. However, it is important that the price be realistic, one reasonably comparable to those on other houses of the same general size and quality. In other words, be aware of current prices. The price you paid for the house will not reflect its current value. Hire an appraiser (professional appraisers are listed in the yellow pages of the phone book). The final figure will be considerably higher than the appraisal, however, if it includes a real-estate commission and an extra thousand or more to allow room for bargaining.

If you turn your house over to a broker to sell, you and he can sit down and come to an agreement on price. He will want it to be low enough so he can sell it more easily, and you will want as high a price as possible. If your house goes on multiple listing (several agencies working together to sell it) a number of real-estate salesmen will look at the house together. Each will propose a selling price, and from these figures you can arrive at an average price.

An owner who does not wish to offer a firm selling price may set a relatively high figure, indicating to potential buyers that he is open to bargaining. This sometimes encourages buyers.

Be firm, however, about quoting the same price to people who look at your house. Potential buyers who tour the same houses, often talk them over with each other. If you quote one price

to one person and another price to someone else, your indecision may lead buyers to lose confidence. Lowering the price occurs when a buyer becomes serious and is in the process of settling a deal. If a real-estate agent handles the sale he will have to consult you before he changes the price.

Multiple listing. If you turn the selling over to professionals, it is quite likely that the first agent you consult will advise that the house be listed with several companies. In that way more potential buyers will see the house. However, an agent who gets an exclusive on your house is more likely to work harder to sell it, since he will not have to share the commission with other real-estate agencies.

Getting the house ready for sale. Make the house look its best. Sweep, dust, clean, paint. Correct dripping faucets, a noise-making toilet, be sure all light fixtures are working properly, and have the carpets cleaned. Although most of these jobs have little or nothing to do with the value of the house, they help give a favorable impression that the house has been well cared for.

Remodel only if it is necessary to make the place saleable. Peeling wallpaper, for example, should be replaced. But papering and re-painting an entire house could be a waste of effort if a potential buyer does not agree with your taste and is afraid the price includes the redecorating costs. Major remodeling such as adding a swimming pool or putting in a recreation room could be detrimental to a sale.

Not so many years ago many people put bomb shelters in or under their homes. Today real estate agents advise sellers not to mention the shelters. A buyer who feels it unnecessary will not want the cost of a bomb shelter added to the house price.

Concentrate the showing times. The best way of doing this is to have open house, usually Saturday and Sunday afternoon. You get a lot of people who are just looking, but you will also get serious buyers who only have weekends for house shopping. You will not need to have your house neat every day of the week. If a real-estate firm is handling the house sale, take your own family away during the open house.

Offers — good and bad. Few serious buyers will agree to pay your exact asking price. Some offers may be so far below your price they would be unreasonable. An agent must present them all to you, and can make recommendations. A serious buyer will usually offer earnest money ($500 or more) until you make up your mind, and to keep you from selling the house to someone else meanwhile. Very often a buyer will agree with you on a price, subject to his being able to get mortgage money. At the time you decide to sell your house it is a good idea to find out from your own mortgage company whether your loan arrangement can be transferred to the new buyer, whether the company might be willing to arrange an entirely new mortgage for him and at what interest rate, or whether you wish to handle the financing yourself. Real-estate agents are familiar with lending institutions and can often advise a buyer about a suitable agency.

Most buyers are short of cash and have less for a down payment than you would prefer. Whatever the situation you will have to be ready to work with the buyer to smooth out the financial arrangements or lose the sale. Your lawyer or banker are the advisers to go to if you are not sure the agreement is safe from your viewpoint.

Get a deposit. Once the deal is closed, the contract signed, and financing arranged, the buyer makes a deposit and the property goes into escrow, a period during which final transfer is completed, you move out and the new owner moves in.

Tax problems. Payment of tax on the profit you make when you sell can be postponed if you buy another home within a year. There are exceptions, however. Ask an Internal Revenue Service Office for assistance in understanding the law on sale of property. You can also get a free booklet titled "Selling Your Personal Residence" (IRS publication 523).

Do you need a lawyer? Unless you are a lawyer, or unless you are willing to take the time to do the research on buying and selling, you will probably do better to hire a lawyer you trust to handle your business or to get a recommendation from him for the name of a lawyer who handles real estate settlements. Such matters as title search, title insurance, appraisal fee, survey charges, recording fees, credit report on the buyer, property taxes, insurance premiums are a few of the transactions which are a part of a house sale. The buyer usually pays closing costs and the seller pays commission to the real-estate agent, lawyer's fees, a share of the year's property taxes, current bills on the property.

Selling the house yourself. You will need to create an appealing, eye-catching ad for the classifieds. You can get an idea of how to do this by noting which ads catch your eye and why. Your ad should definitely include: location of the house (or your phone number only if the house is hard to find and detailed directions are necessary); how many bedrooms and baths; price; and type of financing available. By stating a price you eliminate house shoppers who cannot come close to meeting your price. By giving a phone number only you can limit showing the house to convenient times for you.

The most tiresome part of the job is repeating certain basic facts and figures about the house many times a day. Solve this problem by typing out a comprehensive profile about every feature of the house: size of the lot; square footage of the house; number and kinds of rooms and their size; location and nature of the fireplaces; roof type; foundation; siding; type of wall finishes; kind of floors and their coverings; brand names of fixtures and built-in appliances; type of heating and names of furnace maker; kind of water heater; septic tank and its location; source of water; nature of fire protection; tax figures and utility bill figures for the previous year. A xeroxed copy given to each potential buyer to take along will make it easy for him to remember your home.

Do not assume that friendliness and a handshake mean the house is sold. Be ready, at least, with a *binder receipt* to give to any prospect serious enough to put up at least $100, with written declaration that he will show up at your lawyer's office to complete negotiations, and make a substantial deposit pending closing of the contract.

Selling your own home can be a discouraging business. Sentimentality tends to get in the way of business. Days and even months go by when no one seems interested, even when you think you have a great bargain to offer. Be prepared to earn that commission.

MOBILE HOMES

On the face of it, the mobile home is such an incredible bargain in today's market that it deserves to dominate it, and it almost does. More than half the single-family dwellings being sold in the United States today are mobile homes. Their annual rate of sale passed the half-million mark early in the 1970s, and today they represent virtually the only kind of new house that can be bought for under $20,000 almost anywhere. All this is true, in large part, because even as the cost of conventional home construction rose recently from an average of $15 a square foot to $20 and then kept right on going, mobiles were being built for $8 to $10, frequently with better space utilization and more equipment as well.

Another cost advantage — initially, at least — that the mobile-home dweller enjoys is that he need not buy both house and land. This is becoming an even more important consideration each year, as the cost of land rises. In many areas land costs have gone up faster than those of the other aspects of homebuilding, so that land cost frequently represents one-fourth or more of the value of a new house instead of the long-traditional 10 per cent. Of course, what the mobile owner saves by not buying land he must spend in paying land rent in some form, but at least he is only committed to this by the month. Actually, if you become a mobile-home owner, there is statistically only about a fifty-fifty chance that you will do so without owning land of your own. About half of all the mobile units now in use stand on their own individual small-town or country lots or acreages. In addition, a small, but growing, number stand on a new kind of residential land. This is the mobile-home subdivision, in which, if there is such a development available to you, you can buy a lot on which to put your mobile among other lots devoted to the same use.

Somewhat less than fifty per cent of mobile homes are placed in mobile-home parks. If this is what mobile-home living means to you, you will find yourself with a choice of about 25,000 such parks nationally. However, zoning that forbids both parks and the use of mobiles on individual residential sites is not uncommon; and many a hopeful builder of a mobile park has been turned down time and again by planning boards, country supervisors and similar governing boards.

A mobile home is not a trailer. Unlike a trailer, a mobile home is not intended to be moved frequently once it has made its first trip from the factory and moving it is a large and expensive undertaking. It should not be confused with a modular or factory-built or manufactured or prefabricated home. Although some of these arrive at their sites on wheels, the wheels don't stay and the house is not intended to be moved again, even once.

There is ample reason for the confusion. Manufacturing methods for the two are often similar, and both may be made in the same factory. Today's modular home looks like a house and usually is built of essentially the same kind of materials as other single-family dwellings. The mobile home necessarily retains a good bit of a trailer look, having quite a lot in common with trailers in its shape and materials. This rather barren look is one of the problems of the industry as well as of mobile-home owners. Some of the most successful efforts to solve it are in the form of landscaping and exterior additions. Many of the best reasons for buying a mobile home are financial ones and, oddly enough, so are some of the strongest arguments against buying one.

Quite a good new mobile home might cost you about $15,000. Only in areas where not many people want to live will you find any house at that price. These facts, plus the correspondingly lower down-payment required, may make this form of homeownership available to you years before you would be in a position to buy a conventional house.

It is partly for this financial reason that quite a

large percentage of people living in mobiles are young-marrieds. In fact, somewhat more than half of all mobiles are occupied by families including one or more children under 18. The percentage of mobiles occupied by retired people is not so large as it has often been assumed to be — possibly because so many of the mobile parks have many retired residents. Of all mobile homes, including those on individual lots and acreages, only about one in ten is occupied by people past 65.

What, as much as anything, makes the question of mobile *vs.* conventional home so controversial is that, in spite of the great difference in initial cost, there is no general way to compare the long-run costs. Mobile-home living, though it has proved a great bargain for many families, could turn out costly in the long run for others.

Assume you have shopped the mobile home market and decided that your preference is for a doublewide, which means a house formed by putting together two of the standard 12-foot-wide units together. These appear to be on the way to becoming the dominant kind since such a combination produce dimensions similar to those of the houses most people are familiar with.

You tentatively decide upon a model costing $15,000, a sum that buys quite a bit of mobile home even today. You can buy it for 20 per cent down and payments spread over the next seven years. You have investigated financing and discovered a bank or other source through which you get an FHA, or perhaps VA, loan. The interest rate is a relatively modest 10 per cent. Your payments will be just about $200 a month. (It makes sense, besides saving time and arithmetic, to stick to round numbers when making an estimate like this. You are not so likely to forget it *is* an estimate.)

You have shopped mobile-home parks and found one you like in which you can get space for $90 a month. This is not cheap, but it includes

many desirable features and the park seems extremely well maintained. From residents with homes like the one you're thinking of you learn that you can expect to pay the rather modest annual tax of some $300, vehicle (which is how your new dwelling will be classified for tax purposes) and personal property combined. While you were about it, you also obtained estimates of your probable utility bills and maintenance costs.

For comparison, the best buy available to you in a conventional house, comparable in size to the mobile home, is at $36,000. You guess that the lot constitutes $6,000 of this value. Assuming the same down-payment as for the mobile, $3,000, you'll need a $33,000 mortgage. You'll need this much even if you're able to bargain the seller down a bit, to cover extra furniture and closing costs you won't have if you buy the mobile home instead. At 7¹/₄ per cent for 30 years, the mortgage payments will be $225.

In a conventional home, your taxes will be much more than you would pay in a mobile. You own more house value, in dollars, for one thing, and you are paying taxes on land. (In reality, the mobile owner does, too but his are hidden in his monthly rent payment.) Also if your locality is like most, the tax you pay on your home as a vehicle is figured at a more modest rate than it would be as real estate. As a conventional householder you would get an annual tax bill of around $900. You find you should allow about $110 a month for utilities, insurance and maintenance, although $75 would cover these things in the mobile.

Now you're ready to add up, to make a direct comparison of monthly costs for the first seven years. That's a useful period because it is how long it will take you to pay for the mobile home and it is at least as long as the average family keeps a house.

For the mobile, you add payments of $200, rent of $90, taxes of $25 and maintenance-insurance-utilities of $75. Total: $390. For the regular house, you add payments of $225, no land rent, taxes of $75, maintenance etc. of $110 to get $410 a month.

The out-of-pocket difference is in favor of the mobile, but it is probably too small to consider significant. And there is one thing you haven't considered that may — or may not — be important. The money you pay in property tax and that part of your loan payment that represents interest are deductible for federal income tax purposes. That is, unless you take the standard deduction. For a more final comparison, then, if you will itemize your deductions on income tax, you must subtract from your monthly cost what this will save you. In a 25 percent tax bracket, your saving could come to somewhere around $20 a month as a mobile-home owner, but nearer $70 in the conventional house with its larger mortgage and larger tax bill. Now the monthly cost figure is reversed and favors buying the house.

Since month by month there may be little difference, a vital question becomes: how will you stand at the end of the seven years? You'll be the free and clear owner of the mobile home, with no further payments to make. Since such units have been found generally to depreciate rather like cars, though not quite as fast, losing half their value in a little less than seven years, what you will have to show for your payments will be worth about $7,000. What if you buy the house? With 23 years of payments still to go, what will your equity be worth? On past experience, the house will be worth quite a bit more than you paid for it. Whether your equity will be worth quite a bit more than $7,000, or somewhat less, is the gamble you will have to take.

If your own situation is sufficiently similar to these hypothetical figures to make the financial side of the decision a tossup for you, too, you will probably make your decision on personal grounds.

Many problems, that at first seem inherent in the mobile-home idea, are being conquered. Mobile interiors can be to the highest of standards and to almost anyone's tastes. Exteriors are improved not so much by decorating as by the addition of landscaping and storage facilities and various kinds of outdoor-living areas and buffers from neighbors and passers-by.

Purlin

A purlin is a horizontal beam used under rafters between the plate and ridge boards as an extra support. *SEE ALSO ROOF CONSTRUCTION.*

Push Drill

A push drill is a hand drill which is shaped much like a screw driver. It is held in one hand and, as the handle is pushed down, the drill revolves. When the pressure is released, a spring in the handle returns it to its original position. The push drill is used mainly for drilling small holes such as pilot holes for screws and nails or the initial indentation for larger drills. *SEE ALSO HAND TOOLS.*

Putty

Putty is a dough-like cement mixture used for filling holes or crevices in woodwork, and other similar purposes. Putty may be ready-mixed or powdered. The powdered type is combined with water for use. Two types of ready-mix putty are the plastic compounds, which are a combination of an adhesive and wood powder, and linseed oil putty, which is generally used to hold glass in a window sash.

The plastic compounds are quick-drying and ready to use straight from the can or tube. These materials are sometimes difficult to smooth out on the wood surface because they dry quickly and sometimes have a coarse texture. If the wood being repaired is to be stained, the stain should be applied prior to the compound, and the compound should be colored to match the stain. Factory-colored patching compounds are available from most manufacturers, or powdered pigments may be added to the natural-colored material.

The linseed oil putty is composed of approximately ten percent whiting and boiled linseed oil. It is easy to handle and economical. The putty is pressed onto the depressed area with the fingers or a putty knife. Paint may be applied immediately, and the putty is easily smoothed on. As with the plastic type putty, linseed oil putty should be tinted to match the wood, as it is not stain absorbent. Linseed oil putty has better sticking power if put on after a coat of paint or sealer has been applied. *SEE ALSO PASTE WOOD FILLER.*

Putty Knife

The putty knife is not actually a knife, but more a tool for scraping paint and pressing filler into holes. Putty knives are available with stiff or flexible blades; the flexible blade is better for scraping, while the stiff blade is better for applying putty, spackle and other material into dents, crack and holes. The most conventional putty knife for home repair should have a blade width of one inch and a wood or steel handle. Blade widths of putty knives used by carpenters in house construction can be as wide as 12- or 14-inches. *SEE ALSO HAND TOOLS.*

Quarry Tile

Quarry tile is unglazed, square, ceramic tile. A corruption of the French word *carre,* or square, the tiles are often confused with stone *quarried* tile. Quarry tiles are virtually fireproof and are used mainly on floors where traffic is heavy. *SEE ALSO FLOOR CONSTRUCTION.*

Quarter Round

Quarter round, as the name implies, is molding cut from a round dowel. The dowel is cut in four

quarters producing a strip of molding used for wall and ceiling joints, doors and sometimes picture moldings to conceal the edges. *SEE ALSO MOLDING & TRIM.*

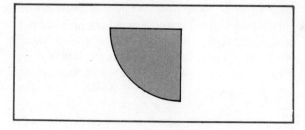

Quarter round molding.

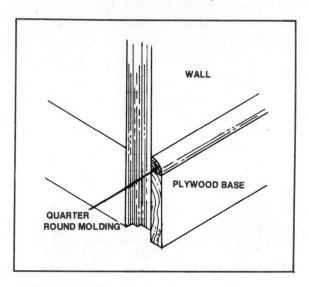

Quarter round molding used on plywood base to conceal edges.

Quarter-Sawed
[SEE LUMBER.]

Quill

A quill is the hollow sleeve in a drill press that holds the bearings and spindle. The quill is moved down by the feed lever and an automatic spring action smoothly returns the quill to its normal position without any jolts or shock. *SEE ALSO DRILL PRESS.*

Rabbet

A rabbet is a right angle groove, notch or channel either cut out of the edge or face of a surface or formed by nailing a smaller strip onto a larger strip. Rabbeted surfaces can be joined together.

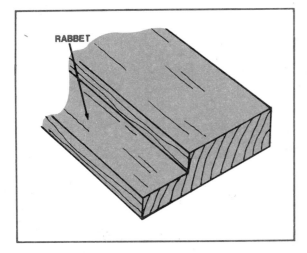

Rabbet Joint

A rabbet joint is formed by cutting a depression in one of the joining pieces. The alternate side mates with this recess and forms the joint. It can be cut either at the edge or at the end of the material. This joint is usually used in frame and box construction because its sturdy structure holds up under major stress. *SEE ALSO FURNITURE MAKING.*

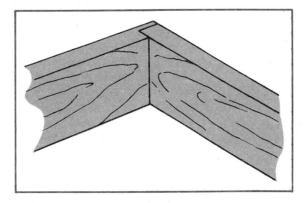

A common rabbet joint.

Rabbet Plane

A specialized type of plane, the rabbet plane is used to cut rectangular recesses or rabbets along the surface of a board at the edge. Since the cutter extends all the way to the edge of the plane on one side, each stroke of the plane deepens into the wood until the required depth of cut is obtained. This tool is guided by a fence, or a batten on the work, which is attached to it and can be adjusted to hold the rabbet to the width desired. For planing across the grain, a sharp spur attachment fitted on the plane is employed. *SEE ALSO HAND TOOLS.*

A typical rabbet.

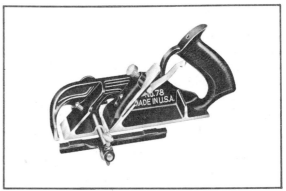

Courtesy of The Stanley Works

Rabbet Plane

Radial Arm Saw

USES

If you combine the rigidity of a large stationary tool with the flexibility of the portable circular saw, you get a fairly good picture of what a radial arm saw is. Of course, with this machine you always bring the work to the tool; but the fact that you can swing, tilt, raise and lower or adjust the cutting direction of the blade makes the tool-work relationship comparable to hand-held saw applications.

When the tool is ideally situated, it's easy to trim off the ends of 20′ long pieces of 2″ stock or to reduce such material to shorter lengths. This capability is a great feature of the radial arm saw and explains why the original model was generally a contractor's tool. The saw's table was extended to the left and the right to provide a total length of as much as 20′. Such support for long pieces that had to be crosscut, mitered, etc., made the tool ideal for people involved in house framing.

In modern versions, especially those designed for laymen's use, the tool still performs these basic applications well, but other features have been added and a wider range of applications devised so the inherent flexibility of the design is fully utilized. As a result, the radial arm saw enters the complete shop-in-one tool category.

With the more advanced models, you can mount dadoes and molding heads, do shaping and routing, accomplish many drilling and sanding chores, use it as a power source to drive flex shafts and, sometimes, complement tools such as a lathe or a band saw. Some versions have built-in mechanisms to drive more than one arbor at different speeds. One type also has a variable speed changer.

Such features extend the tool's application to a variety of uses other than just sawing. However, if the tool is limited to one arbor, one speed, and one direction of rotation, special adapters and cutting tools are usually offered as accessories.

As far as sawing is concerned, the big difference between the radial arm and the table saw can be demonstrated with a simple crosscut. On the table saw, you hold the work against the miter gauge and advance both the gauge and the wood past the blade to make the cut. On the radial tool, the work is set on the table and against a fence. The saw blade is pulled through to make the cut. Obviously, this procedure can have advantages in some areas — typically, on some angular cuts where a stationary workpiece can help achieve accuracy.

General Characteristics

Design details may differ, but generally the motor is cradled in a yoke of sorts which in turn connects to a carriage that moves to and fro along an overhead arm. This is a basic cut action. You pull the motor unit toward you to make the cut, away from you to complete the pass action. The motor, the yoke, and the arm are all adjustable, and each component can be locked in a particular position to situate the saw blade for any cut you wish to make. For a miter, you simply swing the arm. For a cross-miter, you tilt the blade. When you do both, you get a compound cut.

The rotation of the saw blade is away from you. In essence, its action is to hold the work down on

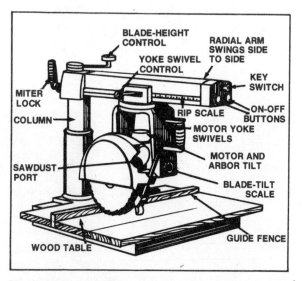

Nomenclature of the radial arm saw. Features may differ from machine to machine but they all include the basic components.

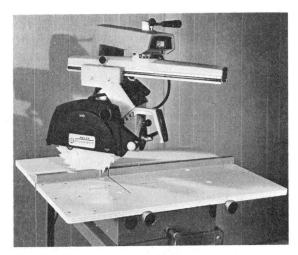

When the arm is swung (in this case the turret arm), miter cuts are set up. When the stock can be flipped, work in one miter position. If not, use both left- and right-hand positions.

the table and against the fence as you make the cut by pulling the blade toward you. If you feed too fast, the blade will tend to "walk," much like a tractor tread. So feed speed is critical. For smoother cuts and safety, it's better to feed a little too slowly than too rapidly.

The yoke can swivel 360°. A 90° turn will place the blade parallel to the fence; this is the rip position. For ripping, you secure the blade in a particular position and move the work for the cut. When you turn the blade 90° toward the column, you set up for "in-ripping". When you turn the blade 90° away from the column, you organize for "out-ripping". The latter position is used for extra-wide rip cuts.

On rip operations, you feed the work against the blade's rotation. Therefore, the blade tends to fight feed pressure. This can cause kickback if you neglect to use the anti-kickback "fingers". This safety item is mounted on a rod that is situated in the saw guard. The fingers do not interfere with normal pass direction, but they dig in if the blade tries to fight you. It only takes seconds to set them up regardless of stock thickness.

It's normal on the radial arm saw for the blade to cut into the table; it has to in order to get through the stock. Each time you change the saw-blade

position, for a miter or a rip cut or whatever, you make a new cut in the table. This shouldn't bother you since it's routine; but for a lot of experimental cutting that might distress the table

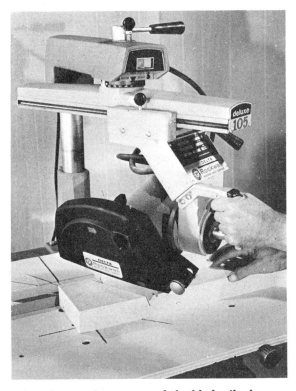

When the arm is swung and the blade tilted, compound-angle cuts result.

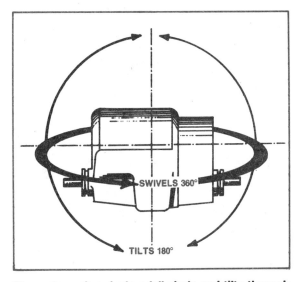

The motor unit swivels a full circle and tilts through 180°. It's this kind of flexibility that provides such an almost infinite number of tool-to-work positions.

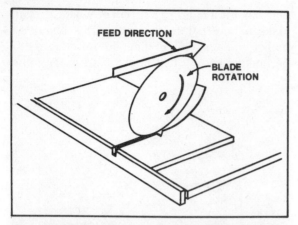

How the blade cuts. Its rotation is away from the worker and fed by pulling it toward you. Pushing the feed might cause the blade to climb.

beyond normal needs, you can cover the table with a thin material to take the beating. This covering can be a piece of plywood that you tack-nail to the regular table.

How much the saw blade penetrates the table is not critical; about $1/8''$ is sufficient for most cuts. Consider the fence an expendable item. If you did nothing but cross-cutting on your radial arm saw, one fence might last forever; but if you use the saw for all types of cuts, the fence will take a beating and should be replaced when necessary. However, it's nothing but a straight piece of

The guard covers about 50 per cent of the blade but may be tilted to cover more teeth on the operator's side. The rod supports anti-kickback fingers and it can be adjusted in relation to stock thickness.

wood, and you can quickly make a dozen as replacement parts or for use in particular applications.

Work Support

One of the great advantages of the radial arm saw is the ease with which you can make cuts on long pieces of material. But this feature must be developed to make it wholly operational. A work support is the answer whether the tool you own is on casters so you can move it about or whether you place it in a fixed position.

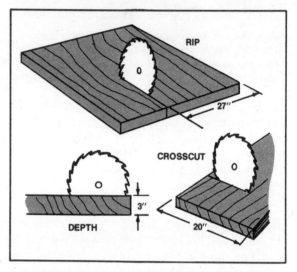

Capacities of the tool are listed as maximum crosscut, maximum rip, and maximum depth of cut. The smallest will cut through 2" stock at 90° and at 45°.

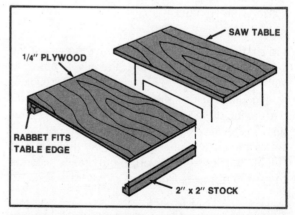

Make an auxiliary table that will slide over the regular table. It cuts down a bit on depth-of-cut, but can be used to preserve the original table.

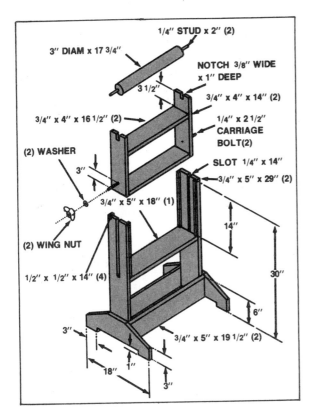

A roller top stand will provide good work support for crosscutting or ripping.

Flip-down extension table extends the work surface about 2¹/₂′, but the design includes a sliding action that nearly doubles the support length.

A common work support is a roller-top floor stand, much like the one that is usable with a table saw. When used with the radial arm, it can be placed in position to support long work for crosscutting or for ripping. Since its height is adjustable, the independent stand may be used with other tools.

Contractors, who normally set the tool up outdoors and have no space limitations, and lumber-supply people, who also have no space problems, usually use roller-type extensions. When the tool is so equipped, it's no chore to square off the ends of pieces that are 20′ or more long. That example may seem extreme, but it is a fact that you may need a similar setup even if the lengths you ordinarily work with are only 6, 8, or 10 feet long.

Alignment

To get the most out of your machine, check it immediately, and periodically thereafter, to be sure

In storage position, the extension table rests within the floor space required by the tool alone. Saw design and mounting determine the location of the attachment block.

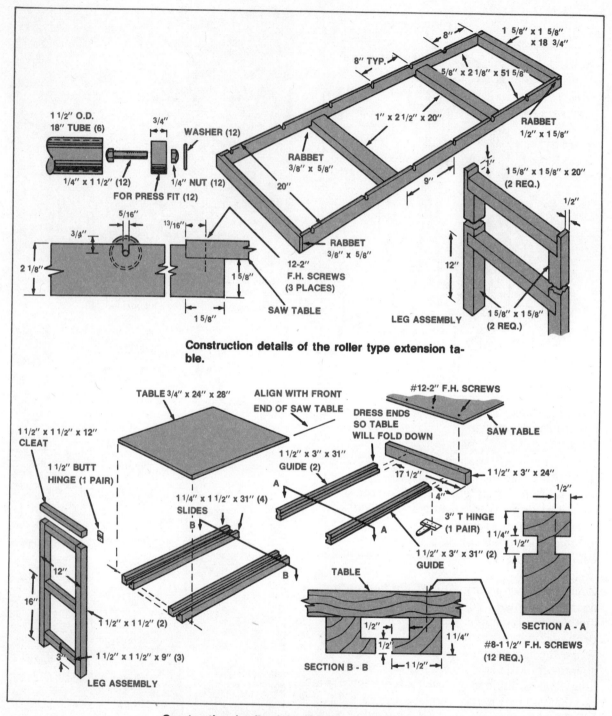

Construction details of the roller type extension table.

Construction details of the flip-down extension table.

all components are in correct relationship. All machines have built-in adjustment features so corrections can be made, when necessary, to maintain a high level of accuracy. How this is accomplished can vary from tool to tool, but the end result must be the same. Check your owner's manual for adjustment procedures to accomplish the following.

On a simple crosscut, the line of the blade must be 90° to the fence. Check by marking a wide piece of wood with a square and the cutting on the line. If the blade doesn't follow the line for the full length of the cut, you know adjustment is required. You can also check with a carpenter's square. Place the short leg against the fence and the long leg on the line of cut. Raise the blade to just clear the table and then, while pulling for a crosscut, see if the blade follows the line of the square.

To get square cuts, the saw blade must travel a line that is 90° to the fence. To check this use a wide board on which the cut line has been marked with a square.

In checking angle, you can move blade along the long leg of a carpenter's square placed as shown. With this method make sure that the machine is turned off.

To see if the blade is perpendicular to the table, use a square. Be sure the blade of the square rests between set teeth, then sight to see if the square is flush against the saw blade.

The cut must be square to the work edge placed against the fence, but it must also be square to adjacent surfaces. This will occur if the vertical plane of the saw blade is 90° to the table surface. Use a square to check for this after you remove the saw guard. Be sure to place the blade of the square between set teeth on the saw blade.

When the "back" teeth of the blade do not cut on the same line as the "front" teeth, you get an undesirable result called "heeling". Check for this by crosscutting a wide piece of 2″ stock; halt the blade just short of leaving the stock. Check at the back teeth to see if there are pronounced radial marks on the cut edge. If there are, then adjustment is required. Adjustment is simply a matter of pivoting the blade a bit to the left or to the right. Heeling is something you can feel and see during normal cutting. The blade will seem to drag and cut edges will not be as smooth as they should be.

"Heeling" is indicated by pronounced radial marks in the area indicated by the arrow. When this is a fault, kerfs will be wider than they should be and result in excessive splintering on plywood.

The cut on the left was made with a combination blade. The other was made with a special plywood cutting blade. Difference makes obvious the wisdom of using the right blade for the right job.

To check the angular settings — those for which the machine has auto-stops — work as you did for the crosscut. Mark the line on the work with a protractor and check to see if the blade follows the line as you make the cut. Actually, you could make gauge blocks from wide pieces of wood and keep them on hand for just this purpose.

The table surface should be parallel to the arm. Check by clamping or tack-nailing a large, flat board to the table. Adjust the saw blade to take a very light scraping cut, go through crosscut and miter passes, and swing the arm from one position to the other while the blade is turning. The shallow kerfs and coves you will make should be uniform in depth in all areas.

Check bevel-cut settings by making the cuts and checking the results with a protractor. Do this at each setting the machine has an auto-stop for.

You can and should check for all these factors as you work. Once in a while, put a square or a protractor on the cut you have made to assure yourself that things are as they should be. Machines do get out of alignment even during routine work sessions, and it's better to find out quickly when it does happen.

Saw Blades

Everything said about saw blades in the entry on table saws applies to blades for the radial arm machine, even feed speed as it affects smoothness of cut and choice of blade for a particular cut or material.

No matter what blade you use, forcing the feed will always result in a rougher cut than the blade will normally produce. If you want proof of this, make two cuts with the same blade. Feed as fast as possible on one without stalling the motor; feed easily and steadily on the second. When you compare the two cuts, the effect of feed speed will be obvious.

On the radial arm saw it's not possible to get the free projection normally recommended for a hollow-ground blade. You can get around this, when you feel it's necessary, by placing a wide piece of plywood on each side of the cutline. This will raise the work and provide clearance under it for the blade. Place the plywood "elevators" so the gap between them is not much more than the normal kerf width.

Crosscutting

When you start a crosscut, the saw blade should be positioned behind the fence. After you have placed the work snugly against the fence, you can turn on the machine and pull the blade toward you to make the cut. The total operation is not complete until you have returned the blade to the starting position.

It's usually a good idea to mark the cutline on the work. This gives you a point you can align with the kerf in the fence and provides a means for checking accuracy of the cut while you are working. Remember that the kerf has width and that it should occur on the waste side of the stock.

In most cases, you will use your right hand to do the feeding, your left hand to hold the work. Keep your left hand away from the cutline. If the workpiece is so small that holding it brings your hand close to the saw blade, nail or clamp the work to the table and keep your hand in your pocket. When the work is held by hand, keep

When the stock is so thick that it can't be cut in one pass, make conventional crosscut, then flip the stock and raise the arm so you can cut from the other side, following a cutline on opposite surfaces on the workpiece.

your hand in position until the blade has been returned to its starting position behind the fence. The right hand holds the saw handle.

For extra-wide cuts — those beyond the capacity of the machine with the fence in normal-use position — do a normal crosscut to the full travel of the blade. After you have returned the blade to the starting position and have waited for it to stop, relocate the fence to its "back" position and position the work so the saw blade sits in the kerf already formed. Then make a second pass to extend the first cut.

You can do extra-wide crosscuts by flipping the stock after the first pass and making a second cut to meet the first one. A good job results when you are very careful about placing the work for the second cut. When the cut length cannot be solved by either of these methods, then you should plan to make the cut by using a ripping setup.

Stock that is thicker than the maximum depth of cut of the saw blade can also be crosscut by making two passes. Your best bet is to use a square to mark the cutline on opposite surfaces of the work. After you have made the first cut, flip the stock, line up the saw blade with the cut mark, and make the second pass.

Good operator position is shown here. Use the left hand (well away from the saw blade) to secure the work — the right hand to pull the blade for the cut and to return it to its original position behind the fence.

Radial Arm Saw

When work size permits, you can do "gang cutting" to produce many similar pieces in one pass. Just butt the parts together and place them against the fence as if they were a solid piece. Then simply crosscut as you would normally.

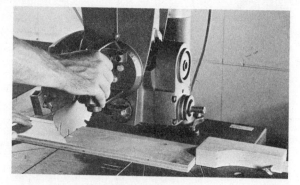

Make adjustable stop blocks that slide smoothly along the fence. These become permanent accessories.

Another way to produce similar pieces is to use a stop on the fence. To work, place the stop so it determines the length of the cutoff. Position the work against the stop and then cut. Avoid letting sawdust pile up against the stop, for the accumulation can reduce the accuracy of your setting.

On this kind of work, you'll probably leave the saw blade running as you position the work for each new cut; therefore, *be alert*.

With the blade set up for normal crosscutting, you can use a repeat pass technique to accomplish dadoes and rabbets. Elevate the blade above the table so the depth of cut will equal the depth of the dado or rabbet you need. When a lot of this work is required, it's best to use a dado assembly so you can accomplish the job faster and more accurately on similar cuts. But when you need just one or two, you can save setup time by staying with the saw blade and repeat passes.

Lastly, you can be guided by marks that you place on the work, or you can use stop blocks to gauge the outline cuts and then clean away between them.

Ripping

You do ripping by setting the saw blade parallel to the fence and locking it in position. Then you feed the stock against the direction of rotation of the blade. Adjust the anti-kickback fingers so they rest on the surface of the work; tilt the guard so the end nearest you covers a maximum amount of the saw blade. This is a safe position and one that will also capture most of the sawdust.

Because the motor unit can be rotated in either direction, you can set up for "in-ripping," which places the blade on the column side of the table,

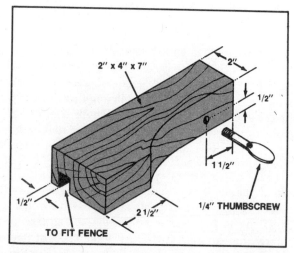

The stop block, made to these dimensions, is drilled for an undersize hole in which the thumbscrew is threaded.

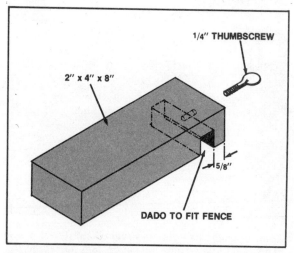

This type of stop block will extend farther out from the fence. On some types of cuts, it does a better job than the first one.

or for "out-ripping," where the blade is swung away from the column. The choice can be made according to the size of the work. The in-rip position is convenient for most work. If the width-of-cut range of the in-rip position isn't sufficient for the job, then set up for out-ripping. This allows you to get the maximum rip capacity from the machine.

The setup is made by measuring from the fence to the side of the blade that faces it. When the blade has set teeth, be sure to measure from the point of a tooth that is set toward the fence.

When the width of cut isn't sufficient to permit a safe hand feed, use a push stick. It's not a good idea to rely on a scrap piece as a push stick. The best push stick is designed to straddle the fence so it can't slip; it also should have a long handle so you can push work past the blade without endangering your hands.

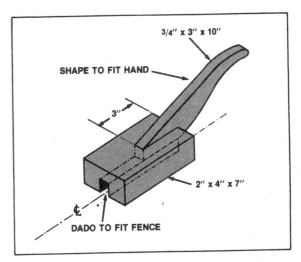

This push stick rides the fence so it can't slip. Cut the dado so the tool will slide easily.

A push stick should be used when working space is narrow and hands are too close to the cut area.

Use two passes to rip through a stock that is thicker than the maximum depth of cut of the blade. Raise the blade above the table so you get clearance between the bottom of the motor and the stock surface. Make a pass as you would for any rip cut. Then flip the stock and make a second pass. Since you are using a fence as a guide, the cut marks recommended for a similar operation when crosscutting are not needed here.

You can do a rip cut on stock that lacks a straight edge to ride the fence by tack-nailing a guide strip to its underside and then feeding so the guide strip rides the outboard edge of the table. The width of the cut is determined by the place-

ment of the guide strip on the work and the position of the saw blade on the table. In most cases, it is best to set the blade in an out-rip position. Be sure to keep the guide strip snugly against the edge of the table throughout the pass.

Horizontal Sawing

This feature is peculiar to the radial arm saw because of the many ways you can situate the saw blade. To set up for horizontal sawing, raise the blade well above the table, turn it to the in-rip position, and then tilt it parallel to the table surface. Its position in relation to the fence can be adjusted by using the arm, pivoting the motor, or altering the position of the fence itself. After you have made the setting, be sure that all components are firmly locked.

For horizontal cutting, it's often necessary to raise the work above the table surface. This can be accomplished by placing the work on a board that you move along with the work or by tack-nailing a piece of plywood to the table.

With this method and similar techniques discussed later, it's often a good idea to use a special, high fence through which the cutter protrudes. Your best bet is to lock the fence in place and make the opening for the cutter by pulling it through slowly while it is turning.

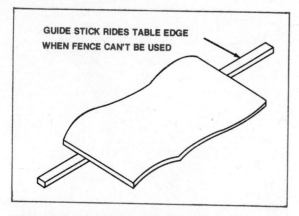

GUIDE STICK RIDES TABLE EDGE
WHEN FENCE CAN'T BE USED

When the work doesn't have an edge that can ride the fence, tack-nail a guide strip to its under side. Then make the pass so the guide strip rides the front edge of the saw table.

Special tables can be made for horizontal cutting operations. These tables are especially useful when you hold the work still and pull the blade through for the cut. Used in such a manner, these tables provide a means for you to elevate the work as well as supply a fence that positions the work for an accurate cut.

A typical operation, made possible by combining horizontal cutting on one of the special tables and simple cutting with the blade in normal crosscut position, is the shaping of a wide two-pass rabbet. The width of the rabbet is established by cutting with the blade positioned

A special table elevates the work for horizontal cutting.

horizontally and the work resting on the special table. The second pass, the shoulder cut, is done in normal crosscut position with the blade height set to meet the depth of the first cut.

Miter Cuts

A miter cut is accomplished with the saw blade in normal crosscut position but with the arm of the tool swung to the angle required. On most machines, common angles such as 45° will have auto-stops. Settings for angles between the automatic stops have to be gauged by using a miter scale usually situated at the top of the column. Since the joining of miter cuts in good fashion relates directly to how accurately the cuts are made, it's good practice to check the first cut with a protractor before you proceed to cut all the pieces. In a picture frame, for example, being "off" just a second or two will result in quite a gap when you try to assemble all four pieces.

Hold the stock firmly against the fence and make the pass even more slowly than you usually do. On the radial arm saw, you don't have the amount of movement from the cutline that you may have with a table saw. Even so, many professionals use a special fence as an aid in keeping the work stationary. This special fence is no more than a regular fence with nails or screws driven through from the back so the points protrude just a bit at the front. These protrusions help to hold the stock still as you pull the blade through.

Making miter cuts at each end of the stock is no problem when the material is flat and can be flipped for alternate cuts. This is not the case when mitering moldings. Then you must make both left- and right-hand cuts which means swinging the blade to achieve the positions. Therefore, you have twice as much room for error, which calls for being especially careful when setting up the machine and for making test cuts to prove the settings.

One possible method is to cut the frame pieces to overall size first and then miter the ends. This will waste some material, but you have to judge

A stop block on the fence can be a big help when cutting miters on similar pieces. The operation calls for cutting the parts to correct length first.

the cost of the waste in terms of better accuracy. The use of a stop block makes the procedure even simpler. Cut the first piece and use it as a gauge for setting the stop block on the fence. The stop then positions other pieces correctly so the cuts will be duplicated.

You can also make and use special mitering jigs. When you do a good job making them, the accuracy of the cut will be assured. Whether you use precut pieces where you just miter the ends or make consecutive cuts along the length of a single piece, the saw blade position is for normal crosscut work. Thus, work placement, assured by the jigs, establishes the accuracy of the cut.

Cross Beveling

The cross bevel is often called a miter (or the reverse, if you wish). Whichever, you accomplish it with the blade in a crosscut position but tilted to the angle required. Whenever it is necessary to tilt the blade, elevate it above the surface of the table and, after tilting, lower it as it is turning to take the 1/8″ bite in the table surface. When you run it through the fence, you get a kerf that you use like the one needed for crosscutting.

To cross bevel a number of pieces quickly, place them together as you would for a simple crosscut. Hold them firmly together in place and pull the blade across the whole batch.

Rip Beveling

The rip bevel is done with the machine in rip position but with the blade tilted to the angle required. Follow all the rip-cut rules about anti-kickback finger position, guard position and safe hand placement. Feed the stock through as you would for a rip cut but be even more careful about keeping it snug against the fence throughout the pass. Use the push stick when necessary and always feed against the direction of rotation of the saw blade.

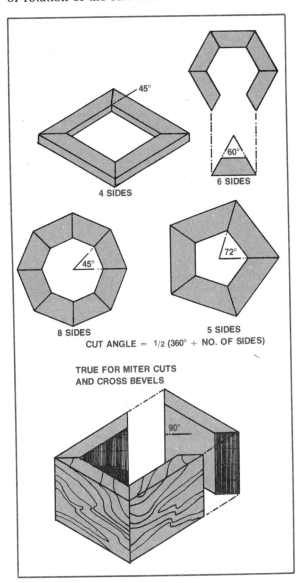

Miters and cross bevels are used as joints in multi-sided projects. The formula lets you select the correct cut angle for any number of sides.

Chamfer Cuts

The chamfer cut is just a partial bevel. You can make it along an edge or across an end. When working on an edge, set the saw up for a rip-bevel operation. However, since you won't remove the entire edge of the stock, keep the blade elevated above the table. When the chamfer is across an end, set up as you would for a cross bevel.

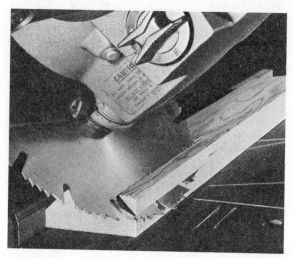

Do chamfer cuts the same way, elevating the blade so it removes just part of the edge.

V-grooves

Do V-grooves by setting up for a rip bevel but adjust the blade height to provide for the groove depth required. Two cuts are required for each groove. When the "V" is in the center of the board, you can turn the stock end for end to make the second pass. When it's located elsewhere, you must reset the blade in order to mate the second cut with the first cut.

Compound Miters

You cut a simple miter when you swing the arm but keep the blade in a perpendicular position. If you swing the arm and also tilt the saw blade, you get a compound angle cut.

Compound miters are probably the toughest kinds of cuts to make because of the perfect accuracy they require. Everything we said about

care when doing the simple miter has double emphasis here. Work slowly, doublecheck each setting before you make the cuts and test the setting by cutting first on scrap stock.

Sometimes, when you are cutting parts of similar length consecutively from one long board, you can use the first piece cut as a template for making the succeeding cuts. Flip the first piece over and place it on the board so you can mark the cut-line with a very sharp pencil. Place the stock so the next cut you make will just remove the pencil line.

Being able to flip the stock will allow you to work exclusively with right-hand cuts. Other times, you must change the settings and make half the cuts on the right side and half the cuts on the left side. This situation should make it more obvious than any number of words that care in setting up is the primary factor.

If you first establish the slope angle of the work by making bevel cuts on the edges, you can use the simple miter jig to do compound cutting. The work is put in position against the guide but resting on the bevel. The blade is set in normal crosscut position and pulled through in the usual fashion. The cut is compound simply because the work is tilted to begin with.

You can also use a height-block to establish the work angle. In this case, the blade is set up for a simple 45° miter. This method is not as accurate since the thickness of the height-block can be arbitrary. However, a few degrees in the work angle one way or the other shouldn't be that critical.

You can also work with a U-block jig. This is made especially for pieces of particular width and is clamped to the table at a 45° angle to the saw-blade path. The work nestles between the verticals of the jig and is held at a fairly close slope angle. Then you make what amounts to a simple crosscut, but you get a compound angle. Of course, both the height-block and the U-jig can be organized to produce a very specific work angle. Either one of these two methods might be used if you require a particular compound-angle frame in quantity.

Odd Angle Cuts

To cut angles you can't handle in the usual fashion — whether because the work is too large or too odd-shaped or the angle is too extreme — use a guide strip that can ride the outboard edge of the table. This is tack-nailed to the underside of the work and positioned so that it parallels the line of cut you want. Thus, you can handle the job like a simple rip cut.

If you own a turret arm radial arm saw, in this kind of situation the work can be clamped to the table and the blade pulled through for the cut. Naturally, the length of the cut will be limited by how far the carriage can travel along the turret arm.

Using the Dadoing Tool

The dadoing tool is not used to part the stock, so it is always elevated above the table surface to form a U-shape that is a "dado" when done across the grain, a "groove" when done with the grain. The cut depth can be gauged easily if you mark it on an edge of the stock and adjust cutter height to match the mark.

The dado assembly is used much like a saw blade. However, since it removes considerably more wood, the feed speed should be minimized. If you feed too fast, the dado will tend to "climb" and "walk" along the work instead of cut. While the normal feed direction is the same as for a saw blade, there are times when pushing

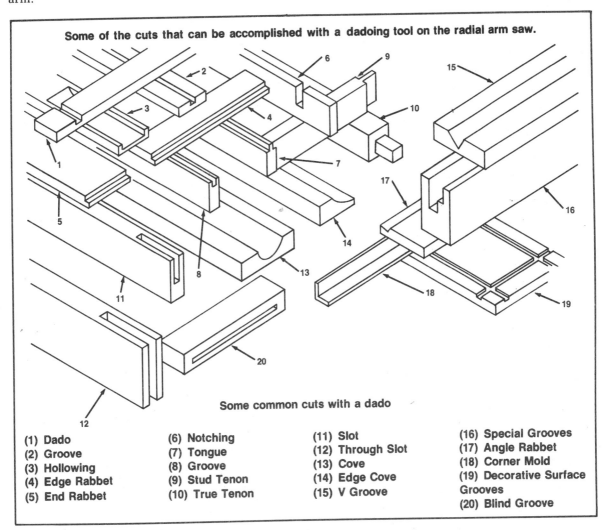

Some of the cuts that can be accomplished with a dadoing tool on the radial arm saw.

Some common cuts with a dado

(1) Dado	(6) Notching	(11) Slot	(16) Special Grooves
(2) Groove	(7) Tongue	(12) Through Slot	(17) Angle Rabbet
(3) Hollowing	(8) Groove	(13) Cove	(18) Corner Mold
(4) Edge Rabbet	(9) Stud Tenon	(14) Edge Cove	(19) Decorative Surface Grooves
(5) End Rabbet	(10) True Tenon	(15) V Groove	(20) Blind Groove

the cutter through instead of pulling it may be better. This means that you position the dado at the front of the table instead of behind the fence and, after the work is placed, push the dado toward the rear of the machine to make the cut.

No matter which way you feed, whether you are cutting across the grain or with it, make all dado cuts at a speed that will permit the cutting edges to do their job without clogging. As with all cutting tools, one rule concerning good feed speed and pressure is paramount: keep the tool cutting constantly but without strain.

When the same dado is required on many pieces, it's wise to use a stop block on the fence to gauge the position of the cut. This method is much better than marking the pieces individually and then gauging each cut by eye. If you require an extra-wide cut, such as a half-lap on wide pieces, the stop block can be used to set the work for the outline cuts. The material between is then removed by making repeat, overlapping passes.

A kind of "gang cutting" may also be employed to assure accuracy of dadoes on mating pieces. For example, in dadoing opposite sides of a bookcase for horizontal shelves, cut the first dado in the parts, butt them edge-to-edge and use a small piece of the shelf material in the dado already formed. This will keep the pieces in alignment for the following cuts. Often you can combine this kind of gang cutting with a stop block on the fence for faster, more accurate work.

The "stopped" dado or "blind" dado is a cut that does not go across the full width of the stock. This is done, for example, when you use the joint to hang a shelf but wish to conceal the cut at the front edge. All you have to do is draw a line on the work to indicate the length of the cut, then stop when the dado reaches that point. Since the cut so formed ends in a radius, you will have to clean it out by working with a chisel or shape the end of the shelf to match the radius.

To do groove shapes, you organize the saw for ripping and feed the stock into the cutter as if you had a saw blade mounted. To get the correct depth of cut, work as explained for dadoing. Use the guard and the anti-kickback fingers as if you were doing a normal rip cut.

Whenever possible, work with the machine in the in-rip position. Feed steadily but, since the dado removes more wood, a little more slowly than you would when ripping. To do extra-wide grooves, just make repeat, overlapping passes. To do stopped grooves, use a stop block on the fence to limit the length of the cut. After you hit the stop block, retract the work carefully until it is clear of the cutter. For angular cuts with a dadoing tool, situate the machine as you would for miters.

Cutting Rabbets

The dadoing tool is fine to use when you require a number of rabbet cuts that are too many to be done by the repeat-pass regular saw blade method. When the rabbet is required across the end of the stock, use the crosscut position; when it follows a long edge, use the rip position. Procedures are approximately the same as for dadoing; the difference is simply in the shape you produce. To do a "bevel rabbet," a shape that is handy when you wish to join two pieces at an angle, work with the machine set up for horizontal sawing but tilt the cutter to the angle you need.

Variable-Depth Cuts

You can use this technique on both dado and rabbet cuts when, for example, you want the side members of a bookcase to slope inward. How much slope you can get will depend on the thickness of the stock you are using. To do the job, tack-nail a strip of wood under one edge of the work or to the saw table so the top surface of the workpiece is no longer parallel to the table.

Since the cutting tool moves on a parallel plane, the cut will be deeper at one end of the stock. The difference in depth from one end of the cut to the other is controlled by the thickness of the elevating strip.

Some Decorative Cuts

When you do intersecting, shallow dadoes and grooves in the surface of the stock, you come up with a panel effect that can be simple or very fancy, depending on the number of cuts you make.

pletely across the stock with equally spaced cuts, you produce simple cove shapes. Such a part can be used as it is, or it can be strip cut to make many pieces with the same profile.

Working with the machine in crosscut position, but with the dado tilted, will produce "V's." Experimentation here will result in many intriguing effects. For example, if you stop the cuts, you get a knife-point design. When you form two of these back-to-back on a common center line, you create an arch.

To get faceted effects, use both crosscut and rip positions, but with the cutter tilted. Do the crossgrain cuts first. Be careful to make cuts meet perfectly.

If you want to extend the idea to the point where the results come close to resembling some intricate chip carvings, work approximately the same way but with the dado tool tilted. This requires that you make matching cuts to create facets instead of flat-bottom grooves.

It's also possible to hold the workpiece snugly against the fence while you pull the turning cutter toward you. When you stop the cut, the result is an arch plus a cove shape. When you go com-

Make a high fence through which the dado can extend to work more safely on many kinds of horizontal dado-cutting operations. This is the last pass of a four-edge rabbet cut.

Horizontal Operations

The dado tool can be used in a position that places it parallel to the table. For this kind of work, it's a good idea to make a special fence so the only part of the dado that will be exposed will be buried in the work. Plywood ($\frac{1}{2}''$) is fine for the fence; if you make the slot in it oversize, you'll have room for adjusting the dado position.

When used as previously described, the dado tool does a good job of producing scallop cuts. These can be individual cuts, equally spaced or one extended cut done by feeding the stock forward after you have made firm contact with the fence. In each case, you can be guided by marking the work or by using stop blocks to control spacing or cut length.

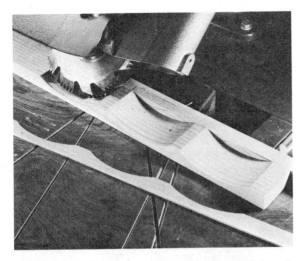

Keep the work very secure, by clamping it for each cut, for horizontal dado cutting with the tool tilted to produce matching coves. The part can then be ripped into thin strips like the one in the foreground.

Radial Arm Saw

Scallop cutting generally falls in the area of decorative cuts, but the horizontal dado setup can have more practical applications, such as grooves, rabbets and spline cuts.

Circular Work

To do a rabbet on the perimeter of a disc, use the horizontal dado position and work in one of the following ways.

Use a V-block setup with the special fence. The blocks that form the "V" can be tack-nailed to the table or secured to the fence. Set the width of the cut by the position of the blocks and by the projection of the cutter; set the depth of the cut by the height of the cutter above the table.

A second possibility is to use a piece of the waste, which is cut off when you form the disc, as a guide. This is clamped or tack-nailed to the table as a guide for the cut. It's assumed that cutting of the disc is done carefully enough so the waste and the work are fairly well matched.

In either case, to do the cutting, rest the work solidly on the table and ease it forward gently to make the initial contact. Then, rotate it slowly against the direction of rotation of the cutting tool.

Slots

To cut a slot by using the dado, set up in a rip position but place the work before you lower the cutter to make contact. Do this slowly and, after the cutter has penetrated the work, feed until you have the slot length you require. Such slots will begin and end in a radius. If you want those points to be square, finish up with a chisel.

Using a V-block

You can form notches across a corner post by using a V-block to situate the work and pulling the cutter across as you would for a simple dado. The block doesn't have to be more than a length of 2x4 with a "V" cut down its center. When you need such a cut on many pieces, it's a simple matter to tack-nail a strip across the "V" for use as a stop. In such cases, it's probably a good idea to secure the V-block to the table or to the fence.

Your concern will then be to hold the work still as you make the cut.

The Molding Head

The flexibility of the radial arm saw increases the usefulness of a molding cutterhead. When you consider the number of knives available, each one's capability of providing various shapes, and the positioning of the head vertically, horizontally or at an angle, you realize the infinite number of cut possibilities.

For a basic kind of molding-head work, organize the machine as you would for horizontal sawing. A conventional fence may be used as long as the center area is reduced to provide turning room for the knives. It's also possible to use a two-piece fence with the sections situated so the gap between them allows room for the cutter.

To establish knife height and projection for a particular shape, put the work in position and turn the cutterhead by hand until one knife butts against the edge of the work. In this way, you can actually see what the results will be.

To make the cut, hold the work flat on the table and snug against the fence. Move it slowly to engage the cutter and keep the feed action steady throughout the pass. Most molding cuts remove a

To get an idea of how the edge will look after the cut, set one blade flat against the stock's edge.

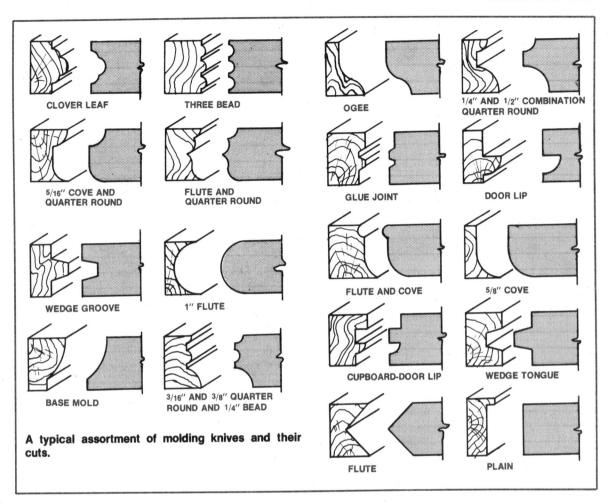

CLOVER LEAF

THREE BEAD

OGEE

1/4" AND 1/2" COMBINATION
QUARTER ROUND

5/16" COVE AND
QUARTER ROUND

FLUTE AND
QUARTER ROUND

GLUE JOINT

DOOR LIP

WEDGE GROOVE

1" FLUTE

FLUTE AND COVE

5/8" COVE

BASE MOLD

3/16" AND 3/8" QUARTER
ROUND AND 1/4" BEAD

CUPBOARD-DOOR LIP

WEDGE TONGUE

FLUTE

PLAIN

A typical assortment of molding knives and their cuts.

lot of material so don't force the feed. Try to work so that you are cutting with the grain of the wood. Cuts made in this manner will always be smoother than cuts made against the grain or across it. When you can't work with the grain, make the passes even slower than normal. This will let the knives take smaller bites, and they will pass over a given area of the wood a greater number of times.

For a partial cut, either a one-piece fence or a two-piece fence with the bearing surfaces in line will do. On a full cut, the work will lack support after it has passed the cutters so you must make some compensation. The easiest solution is to use a two-piece fence with the infeed section shimmed back an amount that equals the depth of cut. Cut the shim so it does not project above the table.

When a part requires cutting on each of its four edges or on two adjacent edges, do the cross-grain cuts first. The final with-the-grain cuts will

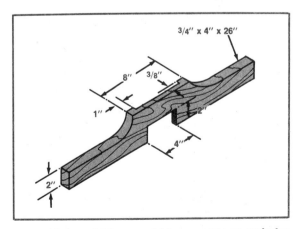

Make this special fence, which you can use as is for all straight-line cuts that do not remove entire edge of stock.

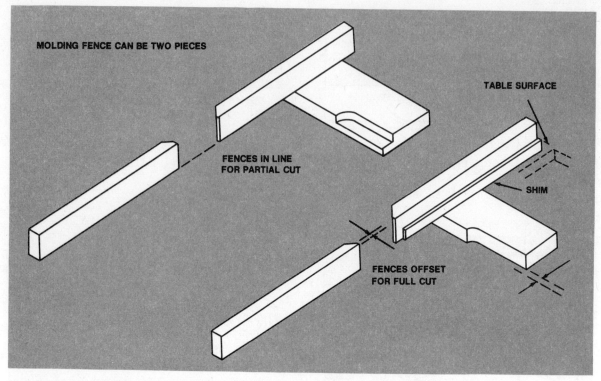

MOLDING FENCE CAN BE TWO PIECES

FENCES IN LINE
FOR PARTIAL CUT

TABLE SURFACE

SHIM

FENCES OFFSET
FOR FULL CUT

The difference between full and partial cuts. Use a shim to compensate for the stock that is removed on a full cut. This will provide support after the cut.

remove the end-area imperfections that are almost inevitable on cross-grain passes.

On any cut where the work is narrow, be sure to use a backup block to feed the stock across the cutter. This will keep the work square and allow you to complete the pass safely. It also helps to minimize the splintering that normally occurs at the end of a cross pass. Don't work on stock that is so narrow that even a backup block won't help. In such cases, it's best to do the job on a wide piece and then rip off the section you need.

Narrow Mouldings

When you need just one piece, you can work by shaping the edge of a wide board and then ripping off the width you want.

To turn out narrow moldings in quantity, it's best to pre-rip pieces to the size you want and then run them through a special fixture. This is no more than a long, heavy piece of stock in which you form a rabbet to suit the size of the basic strips. The block is clamped in place to cover the

cutter; the work is fed into one end (the infeed side) and pulled out the other. To avoid chatter as you make the pass, be sure the L-shaped cut in the block matches the size of the precut strips quite closely.

Circular Work

The V-block technique described for rabbeting discs with a dado tool can be used to shape the edge of circular pieces. For greater flexibility, you can attach each block to a half-fence. Thus, you have a two-piece arrangement you can situate to suit the size of the work.

Ease the work in slowly to make initial contact and, when the piece is firmly settled in the "V," rotate it slowly against the direction of rotation of the cutterhead.

Irregular Work

To work on irregular pieces, you need a special half-circle guide that is attached to a fence so that it can be situated under the molder. This guide does approximately the same job performed by collars on a shaper. Depth of cut is controlled by the relationship between the cutting knives and placement of the guide. Don't try to mold pieces that are too small to be held safely with your hands.

Angular Cuts

To increase the shapes you can get from an assortment of knives, try working in a horizontal cutting position with the cutter tilted. Because a setup like this presents an unusual knife angle, it may be difficult to visualize the shape and the depth of the cut. So use even more care than usual, starting with a very light cut and increas-

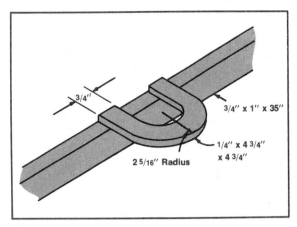

How to make the special molding cutter guide.

ing depth as you make repeat passes. When the cut you wish to make is a critical one, do the preliminary setting up and cutting on scrap stock.

Strip Moldings

With the machine set up in crosscut position, you can do a repeat-pass pattern across the stock's surface and then rip the piece into slim sections. This kind of cutting should be done very slowly with the stock held firmly. It's not a good idea to try to cut deeply in one pass. It's better to achieve full depth of cut by making repeat passes.

A special fence, drilled to take a nail stop, is almost a necessity for this kind of work. Using it, you have a mechanical means for work placement to gauge equally spaced cuts. Space the holes in the fence about ½" or 1" and drill them so they will be a tight fit for the nail you will use as a stop.

Coving

Coving cuts with a molding head are accomplished by setting up the machine in an in-rip position and feeding the stock against the direction of rotation of the cutter. Different types of knives may be used, but in all cases the basic procedure is the same. Achieve full depth of cut by making repeat passes.

The cuts can be made on the edge of the stock or somewhere along the surface. Variations are possible by tilting the cutter.

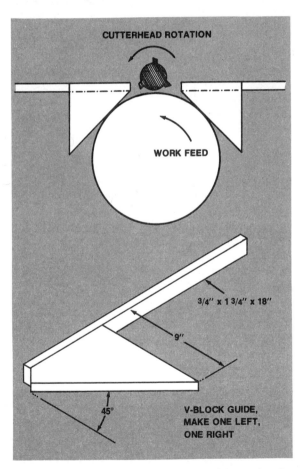

A V-block setup (top drawing) lets you shape the rim of circular pieces. The arrow indicates direction to turn after full contact with the cutter. The two-piece fence permits adjustment to suit the size of the work and minimizes the gap around the cutter. Bottom drawing shows dimensions of V-block guide. Make one left, one right.

1397

Taper Cuts

There are several ways to cut tapers on the radial arm saw, and each of them calls for a special arrangement that will position the work for the cut. You can make a step jig to suit the job or a variable jig that can become a permanent accessory for use on just about any tapering job.

The step jig can be a production tool, used when you require many similar cuts. It has an advantage in that the steps, which determine the taper, are fixed. Any number of pieces you cut will be exactly alike. When the taper is required on opposite edges or on all four edges of a piece of stock, the jig must incorporate two steps. For four edges, the first step in the jig will position the work for cuts on adjacent sides. The second step which doubles the first setting, sets the work for the two remaining cuts.

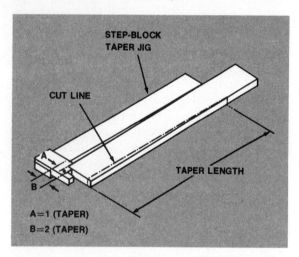

Here are construction details of the fixed taper jig. If the work is square and a taper is required on all four sides, two steps in the jig are needed.

With the variable jig, you work about the same way, setting the angle for the first cuts and then re-setting for the final ones.

Make taper cuts approximately the same way you do ripping. The work is snugged in the jig; both the jig and the work are moved past the blade for the cut. The distance between the fence and the blade should equal the width of the jig plus the width of the work where the taper begins.

Notched guides are also possibilities for taper cuts. Since these are used with the machine in crosscut position, the work length will have to be within the crosscut limits of the machine.

Pattern Sawing

Pattern sawing is a fast method of cutting any number of odd-shaped pieces. It's a good method because it sets up a mechanical means of gauging cuts; therefore, the size and the shape of the workpieces are determined by the pattern. All pieces will be exactly alike, since the pattern is a precise example.

Keep the jig snug against the fence as you make the pass. Set the guard down closer to the work than it is shown here — use the anti-kickback fingers. Note that the sawdust ejection elbow points away from the operator.

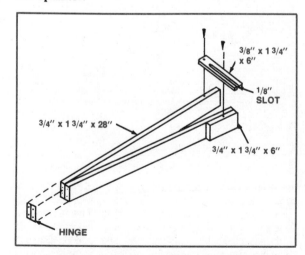

Construction details of the variable taper jig.

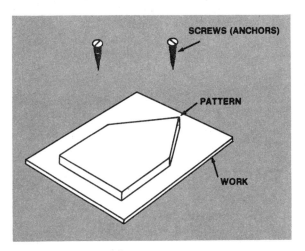

The work is tack-nailed to the pattern. Use screws just long enough to project through the pattern; then the work can be pressed down on the points.

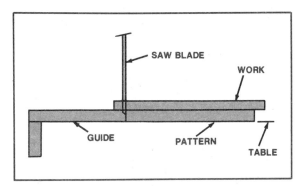

The basic setup for pattern sawing is shown here. The thickness of the pattern should be at least equal to the thickness of the guide for best results.

The stock is first roughly cut to approximate size and then, for the cutting, each piece is tack-nailed to the pattern. Feeding is done by guiding the pattern along a guide block that is secured to the table in line with the saw blade. The blade cuts the work so that it matches the pattern.

Kerfing on the Radial Arm Saw

Kerfing for Bending

Kerfing for bending is done with the machine in crosscut position but with the blade raised so it doesn't cut through the stock. Since many kerfs are required, usually equally spaced, it's best to make a special fence if a lot of work is to be done or use a nail-stop in a conventional fence for an occasional job.

Kerfed Moldings

The same kind of kerfs made for wood bending and variations of them can be used to produce many types of distinctive moldings. The idea is to strip cut the pieces after they have been kerfed to produce the design you have in mind.

Since you are not concerned with bending the wood, the depth and even the width of the kerfs can be varied arbitrarily to suit your design.

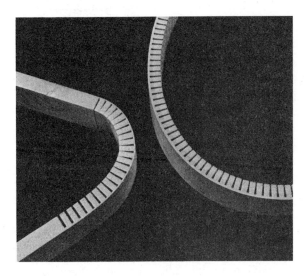

The kerfing method provides an easy way to bend wood without having to steam it. The cutting must be done carefully and evenly at just the right intervals to make sure the wood will bend easily and will not break.

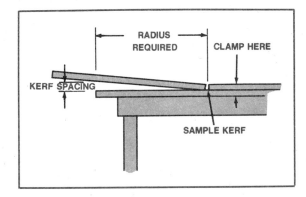

This method will help determine kerf spacing for the job being done. Lift the wood until the sample kerf closes, then measure from the bottom of the work to the table surface . . . not foolproof, but a good place to start.

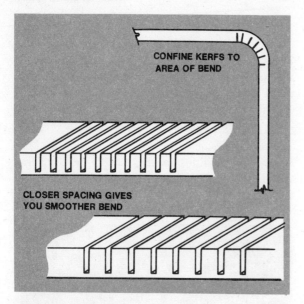

The closer the kerfs are, the easier it will be to bend the wood. Over-doing it, though, can weaken the wood too much.

A simple variation is to flip the stock for each cut or after each two cuts. You can use a dado for this kind of work, or you can combine saw kerfs with dado cuts.

Coving

For coving on the radial arm saw, organize the saw for crosscutting but tilt the blade to between 10° and 15°. Lock the blade over the center of the work and adjust its height to take a shallow bite (between $^1/_{16}$'' and $^1/_8$''). Feed the work slowly past the blade as if you were making a rip cut. Be sure to hold the work snugly against the fence throughout the pass. Repeat the procedure several times, lowering the blade a maximum of $^1/_8$'' for each pass. The cove will begin to take

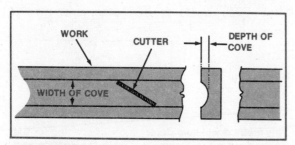

The angle at which the blade is set determines the width of the cove. Its depth depends on how many passes you make.

shape immediately, getting wider and deeper with each pass you make.

All cove cuts should be accomplished by making repeat passes. Remember that the action involves a lot of scraping by the saw blade; therefore, make passes slowly and keep depth of cut to a minimum. The final pass should be made with the saw blade barely touching; this will produce the smoothest end result.

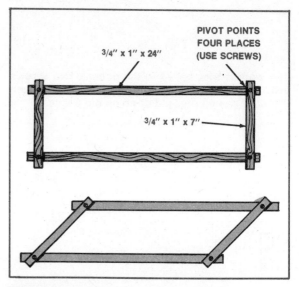

Making a parallel rule and using it will help you pre-determine cove size.

Circular Cuts

You can cut circles with an ordinary saw blade if you set the machine up for in-ripping and use a pivot-guide system so the work can be rotated against the direction of rotation of the blade. The cut you get is actually a small cove, so the cut depth on each pass should be limited to about $^1/_8$''.

The distance from the pivot point to the saw blade determines the radius of the circle. When the work is very large, you can set up the pivot off the saw table by using a sawhorse or some kind of improvised stand.

For some kinds of circular cuts, it's possible to clamp the work securely and move the cutting tool.

Form curved grooves and slots like this. Clamp the work to the table — don't cut too deeply — feed as indicated by the arrow.

Saucer Cuts

A saucer cut is a unique operation that is somewhat related to coving in that the blade is used more in a scraping action than in a cutting one.

To try a simple saucer cut, clamp the work to the table and raise the blade (while in crosscut position) until it is high enough to be swung through the full tilt range without hitting the work sur-

face. Lower the blade about $1/16''$ and swing it through the tilt while the blade is turning. Keep your hands well away from the cut area, be sure the work is firmly clamped and achieve full depth of cut by making repeat passes. If the saucer cut is to go completely through the work, be sure to use a scrap block between the work and the saw table.

Cutting "Diamonds"

Diamond-shaped pieces that can be assembled into many-pointed star shapes can be cut as follows:

First, bevel the stock so that a cross-section would be an isosceles triangle. Actually, any bevel may be used, but the given method that produces certain results is best to start with before you attempt variations. Once the stock is so formed, a series of compound angle cuts are made to form the individual pieces. If you swing the arm to 45° and tilt the blade to the same angle

Swing the blade through its tilt range and make repeated, slight scraping cuts in the stock. If the cut is to go through, use scrap between the work and the saw table.

Diamond-cut pieces can be assembled to make effective decorations. Proceed carefully with the cutting as explained in the text. Use a blade with little set, or a hollow-ground one.

used to cut the bevel, you'll get an eight-point star. If you want a specific number of points, divide the number required into 360° and set the arm to this figure.

Make the first cut on the end of the stock with the work positioned on the left-hand side of the blade. Then move the work to the right-hand side of the blade and make a second cut to mate with the topmost point of the first cut.

Return the work to the left-hand side and again make a cut; then return the work to the right side for the second cut. The piece cut off when the work is on the left side of the blade is scrap. Continue the procedure until you have the number of pieces you require.

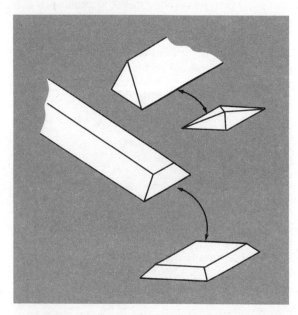

Two ways to prepare stock for diamond cutting. Experimenting can lead to infinite variety.

Saw-Blade Panel Raising

You can "raise" a panel with a conventional saw blade if you work in the horizontal position with the blade tilted up a few degrees. If the very tip of the cut is set to hit the surface of the work, you can do the panel raising in one pass. The disadvantage, however, is the angle on the shoulder that is the result of the blade tilt. To eliminate it, make slight surface cuts with the blade perpen-

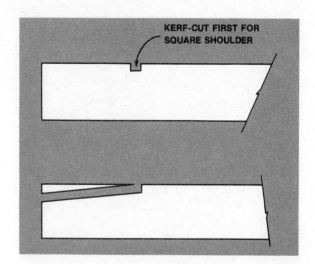

To get a square shoulder on the panel-raising job, cut a shallow kerf to meet the angle cut.

dicular to the table, either before or after you make the angle cut. Of course, the two cuts must meet exactly.

Multi-Blade Ideas

There are advantages in being able to mount two saw blades on the arbor. For example, using two blades in making kerfs for wood bending reduces the cutting time by 50% because you need just half the number of passes.

Of course, there are limits because the arbor is just so long. However, for kerfing and some similar operations, the double-blade idea works fine. You can also use blades with different diameters: for example, you could do a cutoff and form a shoulder cut for a rabbet at the same time. This technique can be applied when you need a number of similar drawer fronts. You can also work with a dado and a saw blade to do the same thing. In this case, the rabbet would be completely formed during the one cut.

Finally, remember that you do want to be careful about what you put on the arbor. You must always leave enough threads exposed so the lock nut can be tightened securely.

Rotary Planer

It's easy to use a rotary planer on a modern radial arm saw because most of these accessories have outboard spindles that rotate in a direction compatible with the cutting action. If they were to turn the other way, they simply wouldn't cut.

In addition, a rotary planer is handy to use on the radial arm saw because of the infinite number of ways you can position it in relation to the work.

Be sure to read the instructions that come with the accessory. Such matters as depth of cut and number of cutters can vary from tool to tool, and these factors will affect the number and scope of applications. Generally, a slow feed speed with shallow depth of cut works best. Cuts will always be smoothest when you feed the stock (or the cutter) so that the tool cuts with the grain of the wood.

Piercing

You can do piercing with a saw blade or a dado by making cuts on both sides of the stock. Depth of cut is a little more than half the stock thickness. Thus, openings through the work are created where the cuts cross each other. The shape of the openings is determined by how you do the cutting. You get squares when the cuts are of equal width and at right angles to each other, diamond shapes when they are angled, etc. The possibilities are infinite.

Dado "Turning"

There is a method of mounting work between the centers of a special jig so you can accomplish some jobs you would ordinarily do on a lathe. The system calls for rotating the stock by hand against the direction of rotation of a turning dado assembly.

You can use this system to form integral tenons on cylinders or square stock, round a square piece of stock for its full length or in a limited area or even do tapers.

The rear part of the jig is clamped in place of the fence. The forward part is secured to the table with clamps after the work has been mounted between the centers.

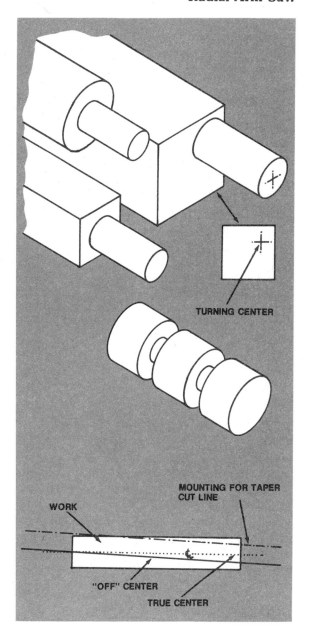

TURNING CENTER

MOUNTING FOR TAPER CUT LINE

WORK

"OFF" CENTER

TRUE CENTER

Here are cuts to make by doing dado turning. Also how to mount the work for turning a taper.

This kind of cutting calls for caution since it's natural for the cutter to try to turn the work. Make the initial contact between the cutter and the work very slowly and be sure to grip the work firmly with your hands well away from the cut area. Adjust the guard for maximum tool coverage and be sure to rotate the work very slowly when you are cutting.

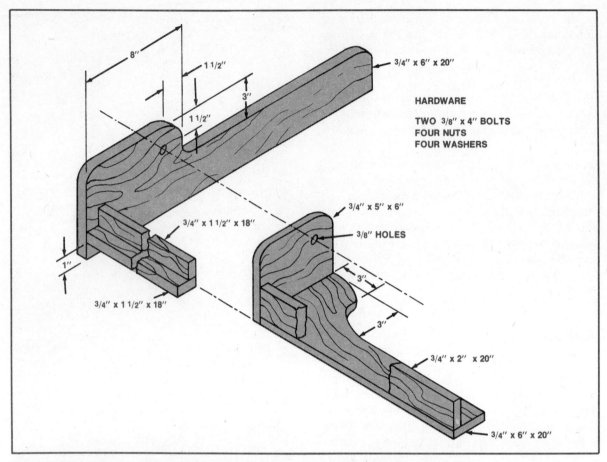

Construction details of "dado turning" jig. Be sure the ³/₈" holes have the same centerline. Both parts of the jig must be securely clamped to each other and to the table.

Don't try to make deep cuts in single passes. Instead, make repeat passes, lowering the cutter a bit after each until the job is finished.

Always check twice before starting to work to be sure that the stock is very secure between the centers and that the jig is tightly clamped to the saw table.

Drilling

You can do quite a bit of drilling on the radial arm saw, but there are factors to consider that might affect the kind and the size of the tools you can use. For example, if you have a single-arbor machine, its rotation won't be good for conventional tools. The solution is to use special cutters that are designed to function under those conditions. Some machines have an outboard arbor in addition to the saw arbor; for these you can buy special adapters and chucks for mounting conventional tools. You might be limited to one particular speed which means, of course, this is not an ideal setup for overall drilling operations. Because of these factors, be sure to read your owner's manual carefully. It will provide important specifics concerning the particular machine you own. Also, check the entry on drill presses for general information concerning drilling tools.

Simple Drilling

When work size permits, it's sometimes possible to place the work on the table and do the drilling by using the arm-raising crank. The fence can be used as a gauge to control edge distance when you require a number of holes on the same center line. When the holes must go through the stock, use a scrap block between the work and the saw table.

Horizontal Drilling

One type of horizontal drilling is done by organizing the machine so the cutting tool points to the rear. You do the drilling by feeding the power unit in that direction. Often, it's possible to secure the work itself in place of the regular fence. Other times, especially for edge drilling, it's better to work with a special platform-fence arrangement that elevates the work so the power unit will have clearance above the table. The vertical part of the platform provides for backing up the work and for securing the unit to the table as you would a regular fence.

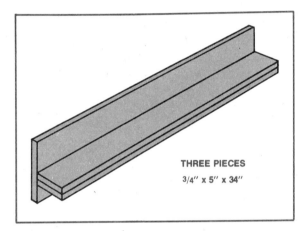

Details of the platform, which consists of three pieces of wood. If necessary, change dimensions to suit the measurements of personal equipment.

Actually, this arrangement functions as accurately as any horizontal drill. It's ideal for edge-to-edge dowel joints because you know that all the holes will have exactly the same edge distance. If you mark each piece of stock so a similar surface will be kept uppermost, it won't matter if the holes are not centered exactly.

Add a gadget that makes it possible to automatically position the work when you have a number of equally spaced holes to drill. To control hole depth, you can use a C-clamp on the arm of the tool to limit travel of the carriage. The same setup can be used to drill mortises merely by doing a series of overlapping holes and to form radial holes in round stock.

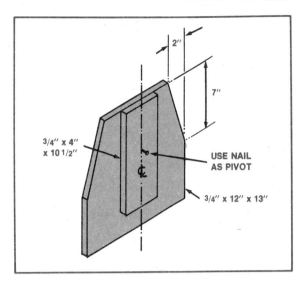

The vertical pivot jig is constructed this way. Clamp it to the backboard of the horizontal edge-drilling platform.

To drill radial holes on a surface, you can make a vertical pivot jig that is clamped to the vertical part of the horizontal drilling platform. This permits you to turn the work while it is in a position that is perpendicular to the saw table. Of course, your work size is limited by the maximum distance between the table and the arm.

For horizontal end drilling, you work with the drilling tool pointing to the left of the machine. The simple table you need takes the place of the

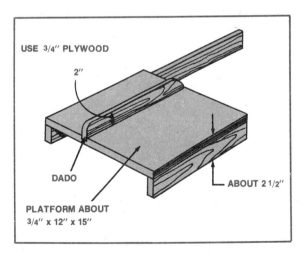

How to construct the table for horizontal end-drilling. It can be made out of ³/₄″ plywood. Cut the back piece long enough so it can be secured in place of the regular fence.

platform used for edge drilling. For these procedures, lock the position of the tool and feed the work to do the drilling. Be sure to keep the work flat on the table and snugly against the fence. To control the depth of the hole, clamp a stop block to the table. On this table, the fence is in a fixed position, so adjustments for hole location are done by situating the drilling tool. The setup is also usable for drilling into the ends of miter cuts. You do need guide blocks to hold the work at the correct angle.

Circular work that requires edge holes can't be fed along the fence. Therefore, for such work you make what amounts to a sliding table to which you can clamp the stock. Then, both the work and the table are moved forward to do the drilling.

Routing

Most manufacturers of radial arm saws list special chucks so router bits can be used in their machines. It's a good idea to use these chucks as opposed to the conventional three-jaw chucks because the bits develop considerable side thrust and are best held in the special devices. If your machine has spindles that turn at different speeds, use the highest available for routing jobs. When you are working at saw speed, which is all right but not ideal, use a slow feed speed so the cutting tool will have a chance to do its job.

Many routing operations can be done with the bit set in a vertical position. Adjust for depth of cut by using the arm-elevating crank. Routing a groove is simply a matter of placing the work on the table snugly against the fence and moving it forward against the cutter. The depth you can cut in one pass will depend on the material. Soft, grainless wood permits deeper cuts than hardwoods. But, if you must force the feed to get the cut done or if you feel excessive chatter in the work, you can be fairly sure that you are trying to do too much in one pass. It is better to achieve full depth of cut by making repeat passes.

To do cross-grain cuts, such as dadoes and end rabbets, use the machine as you do for crosscutting. The work stays put; the cutting tool is

moved. Cross-grain cuts are always a little harder to do simply because you encounter more resistance. Feed the cutter slowly.

A good deal of horizontal routing can be done by using the same platform you made for horizontal drilling. The difference in this situation is that you keep the tool locked and move the work. Forming tongues and grooves, round-end mortising and angular routing are examples of the jobs you can do.

The platform that was made for horizontal drilling can be used the same way for routing jobs. Here the cutter is locked in position and the work is fed to make a groove.

Pattern Routing

For pattern routing you need a guide pin that is the same diameter as the bit. The best way to set up is to tack-nail a sheet of $1/4''$ or $1/2''$ plywood to

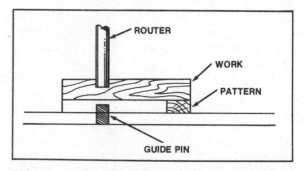

This is the setup for pattern routing. The guide pin must not project more than the thickness of the pattern.

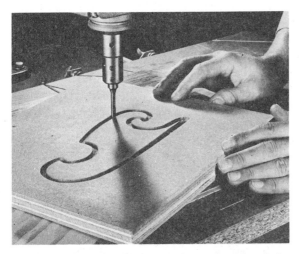

The pattern is tack-nailed to the underside of the work and the cutting is done by keeping the pattern in constant contact with the pin. The router then duplicates the pattern.

the saw table and then use the arm-elevating crank for the bit to form a hole in the plywood. Glue a dowel pin in the hole so it projects above the auxiliary table about $3/16''$. The pattern, which is the shape of what you wish to cut in the project, is tack-nailed to the underside of the workpiece and then placed over the pin. Position the router bit to the depth of cut required and do the cutting with the pattern in constant contact with the guide pin. Since the cutting tool is directly over the guide pin, the pattern design will be duplicated in the work.

Pivot Cutting

You can do circular grooves or rabbets on the edge of circular pieces if you use a nail as a pivot guide. All you do is drive a nail through the center of the work so the point can penetrate the saw table about $1/4''$. The distance from the nail to the cutter is the radius of the circle you will rout.

Decorative Cuts

Router bits offer many opportunities to make surface grooves for purely decorative purposes. A series of equally spaced, stopped grooves on slim stock will produce pieces that can be used as moldings. To limit the length of cut on operations like this, you can feed to a line on the work

or use a C-clamp on the arm to limit the travel length of the carriage.

Curved Grooves

You can rout grooves parallel to a curved edge if you use a triangular piece of wood as a guide. This is tack-nailed to the saw table with one point in line with the router bit but spaced away to equal the edge distance of the groove. Move the work so its edge bears constantly against the guide. As you make the pass, keep the work positioned so that a tangent to the curve at the point of cut will be perpendicular to the center line of the guide.

Freehand Routing

Since a router bit will cut in any direction, it's a logical tool to use for cutting intricate designs, house numbers, names, etc. Since a freehand operation has feed going in many directions, the results will depend on how well you follow the design. It isn't difficult but does demand careful feed and sharp tools. Success will come faster if you do some practicing in soft wood with minimum grain.

Shaping

The radial arm saw does a very efficient shaping job. Like the drill press, its drawbacks may be less than ideal speed and the fact that the spindle is situated over the work. However, slow feed will help compensate for lack of speed, and the overhead cutter position is not going to interfere with the bulk of the work.

How you put the cutters on your machine and what kind of adapters you need can depend on the design of the tool you own. So, again, check your owner's manual for pertinent details. Most tools provide an auxiliary arbor so the cutters can rotate in a conventional manner. Therefore, with the cutter set vertically and situated behind a fence, the feed direction would be from left to right as it is on a drill-press setup.

Straight Shaping

Chances are that most of the shaping you will require will be on straight edges so it can be done

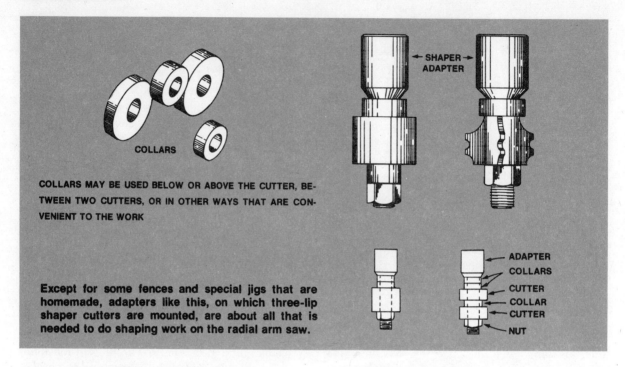

COLLARS

COLLARS MAY BE USED BELOW OR ABOVE THE CUTTER, BE-
TWEEN TWO CUTTERS, OR IN OTHER WAYS THAT ARE CON-
VENIENT TO THE WORK

Except for some fences and special jigs that are
homemade, adapters like this, on which three-lip
shaper cutters are mounted, are about all that is
needed to do shaping work on the radial arm saw.

SHAPER ADAPTER

ADAPTER
COLLARS
CUTTER
COLLAR
CUTTER
NUT

against a fence. On the radial arm saw this fence
can be two pieces of wood set in place on the
regular fence. Adjust the gap between the two
pieces to minimize the amount of cutter that is
exposed.

When the cut removes just a portion of the work
edge, the two pieces of the fence are in line.
When the cut removes the entire edge of the
stock, then you must compensate to provide support after the cut. You can do this by using a
shim against the outfeed fence. The thickness of
the shim should equal the depth of cut. The same
thing is accomplished when you use a shim between the table and the infeed fence.

You can preview the cut by placing the
workpiece flat on the table and against the fence
and turning the cutter by hand until the face of
the blade rests against the edge of the stock.

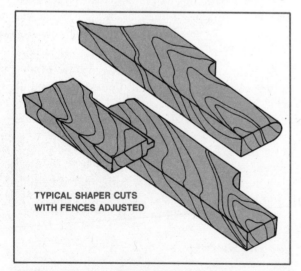

TYPICAL SHAPER CUTS
WITH FENCES ADJUSTED

On the left are partial cuts — some part of the
original stock edge remains after the cut.

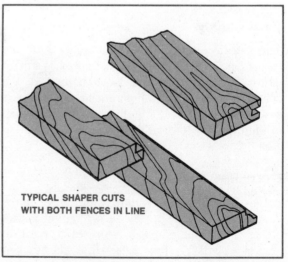

TYPICAL SHAPER CUTS
WITH BOTH FENCES IN LINE

On the right are full cuts that call for consideration to
support the stock after the cut.

Always feed against the direction of rotation of the cutting tool and keep your hands away from the cutting area.

To do cross-grain cuts on stock that is too narrow for good bearing surface against the fence, use a backup block as if it were a miter gauge. If you must shape all edges or two adjacent edges, do the cross-grain cut first. These will end with slight imperfections to be removed by the final with-the-grain passes.

Narrow Moldings

Never attempt to shape slim pieces of wood without taking special precautions. A spring holddown that you can make yourself is good to use for an occasional piece; but when you require many similar parts, it's better to make a special guide and holddown that is clamped to the fence so that the entire cutting area is enclosed. All you do is feed the pre-cut pieces of stock into one end and pull them out the other.

Stopped Cuts

To do stopped cuts, use stop blocks or clamps on the fence. To operate, place one end of the work against the stop on the infeed fence and swing it in slowly to engage the cutter. Then feed as you would normally until the work hits the stop on the outfeed fence.

Many decorative cuts can be accomplished using the stop-block technique. The idea is to brace the work against a stop on the infeed fence and swing the work in slowly to engage the cutter. This results in a semi-circular cut with its profile shape determined by the cutter you are using. The stop is positioned for each new cut. A special fence with holes drilled in it for a nail stop can be very useful in this kind of work.

Freehand Shaping

Circular work and work with curved edges can't be handled against a straight fence. Instead, make a special table and work against collars that are mounted on a shaper adapter. These control the depth of the cut and provide a surface against which part of the work edge can bear while you make the pass.

All the shapes shown here were made with the one cutter. Variations occurred when the position of the cutter in relation to the work was changed.

Whenever possible, feed so that the cutter works with the grain of the wood. This will give you the smoothest cuts. Also, it's a good idea to set up so that the cutter is under the work. Having the cutter under the work affords greater protection and avoids gouging the work should you accidentally lift it during the pass. It isn't always possible to work this way, but it's wise to do so whenever the operation permits.

In shaping, the following are general rules to keep in mind. Keep feed speed at a minimum but keep the tool cutting. Try to cut with the grain.

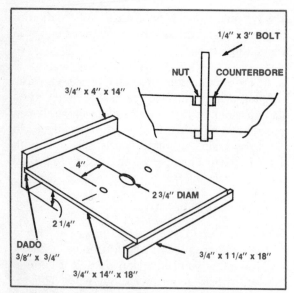

1/4" x 3" BOLT

NUT   COUNTERBORE

3/4" x 4" x 14"

4"

2 3/4" DIAM

2 1/4"

DADO
3/8" x 3/4"

3/4" x 14" x 18"

3/4" x 1 1/4" x 18"

Construction details of the special table for freehand shaping. Adapt dimensions, if necessary, to individual machines.

Since the collars turn with the cutter and bear on the work edge, it's necessary to keep them smooth and clean. Otherwise, they can con-

tribute to uneven cuts and burning of the wood. Making the initial contact when shaping against collars has an element of danger unless some means of support for the work is provided at the very start of the pass. The table should incorporate a left-hand and a right-hand bolt to serve as fulcrum pins. When you start the operation, you support the work against the infeed fulcrum pin and then move slowly to engage the cutter until the work rests solidly on the collar. Once the cut is full, you can bear against the collar only. At the end of the cut, take advantage of the outfeed fulcrum pin to provide work support.

Don't work in this manner when the pieces are too small to be safely held by hand. If you do require a slim, curved molding, do the shaping on the end of a wide piece and then cut off the part you need.

To do inside cuts, place the work before you lower the cutter to its correct position. Sometimes you can use the fulcrum pins, sometimes you can't. So extra caution is called for. Always hook your hands over the workpiece edges so it's

The radial arm saw can be a pretty efficient disc sander if set up for the job like this. Always place the work on the "downside" of the disc, keep the work moving steadily.

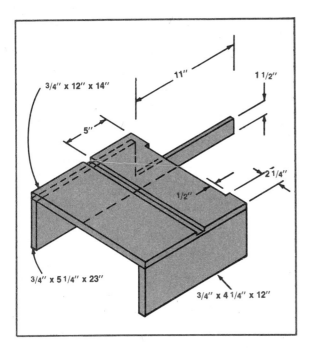

How to make the special table for disc-sander operations.

possible. As previously mentioned, it just isn't good practice to attempt jobs on pieces that are too small to be held safely.

The Radial Arm Saw Used As A Sander

Disc Sanding

Be sure to use a disc that is listed as an accessory for the machine you own. It will be designed to operate safely at the speed (or speeds) that your machine can provide. The best way to utilize it fully is to make a special table that imitates a conventional disc sander setup, incorporates a groove for a miter gauge and has a leg so the entire unit can be locked in place as you would a conventional fence.

Always operate so the work is placed on the table on the "down" side of the disc. Working the other way will cause the disc rotation to lift the work.

Drum Sanding

In working with a drum sander, use a special table designed for freehand-shaping operations, or one designed for disc sanding.

Other Uses

You can use your radial arm saw as a grinder as long as you check to be sure the wheel you wish to mount is designed for safe operation at the speed or speeds that are available to you. For more information on grinder use, check the entry on grinders.

If you consider the tool as a power source, then you can think in terms of using wire wheels, buffing wheels, even flex shafts. It is important that whatever you mount on the arbor of your radial arm saw be designed to operate safely at the speeds you must work with. It's wise to check your owner's manual carefully and work with accessories listed by the manufacturer for that particular tool. *SEE ALSO BAND SAW; BENCH GRINDER; DRILL PRESS; JIGSAW; JOINTER; LATHE; SHAPER; STATIONARY BELT & DISC SANDER; TABLE SAW.*

A grinding wheel renews and maintains the edges on tools. Lock stand securely to table. Adjust guard for maximum protection without obstructing visibility.

Radial System, Forced Warm Air

A forced warm air radial system is a type of duct heating that drives warm air through a building or home. The radial system has ducts which extend outward from the furnace and outlets for the air which are located on the outside walls of the room around the circumference of the home. This type of heating is easily installed and is economical. Generally, round pipe duct is used to run the air from the furnace to the warm air registers, so the entire layout resembles the spokes in a bicycle wheel. *SEE ALSO HEATING SYSTEMS.*

Radiators

Radiators are baseboard room-heating units. They transmit heat by passing boiling water through coils. There are three methods by which a radiator receives the hot water and returns the water to the boiler.

The first method is a series loop. This is the simpliest method of distribution. The water leaves the boiler and travels through all the radiators before returning to the boiler. Shutting off one radiator would shut off the entire system beyond that point. All radiators heat and cool simultaneously.

The one-pipe system allows individual radiators to be turned off at the shut-off valve inlet. When turned off, the shut-off valve inlet does not prevent water from flowing through the main valve to other radiators in the series. This system allows central control with individual room adjustment.

The two-pipe system is a gravity hot-water system with a pump that forces water from the boiler to the radiator and back again. Because the hot water traveling to a radiator is not mixed with the cooler water traveling from another

radiator, the first and last radiators have approximately the same temperature. Whereas, the series loop and one-pipe system has the water circulate the complete pipe line before returning to the boiler, the two-pipe system has the water sent to and returned from each radiator directly to the boiler. Every radiator has its own set of

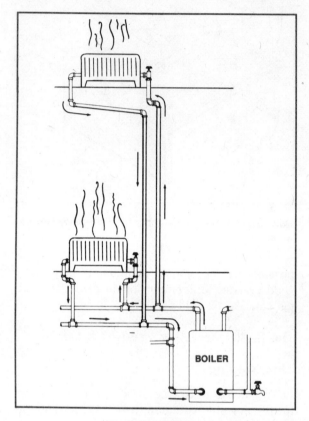

Two-Pipe System

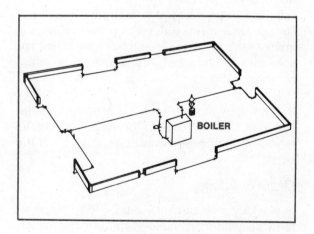

Series Loop

supply and return lines directly connected to the boiler. Because the two-pipe system provides individual water supply, there is less temperature change between the first and last radiator, as compared to the series and one-pipe systems where the water is considerably cooler from the first radiator to the last radiator. *SEE ALSO HEATING SYSTEMS.*

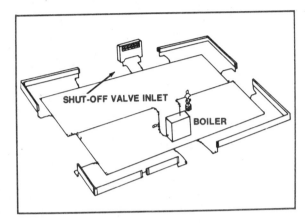

One-Pipe System

Radiator Bleeding

Radiator bleeding is a process for removing trapped air from radiator vents, thus allowing more thorough heating of an area. These air vents come from small pipes near the top of radiators and are opened by turning a small faucet attached to the pipe. If there is a large screw in place of a faucet, it must be loosened to release air. Water will begin to flow from the valves shortly after the vents are opened. They should then be closed immediately to prevent too much water loss. The bleeding process ideally takes place prior to each cold season. Begin with radiators located at the highest point in the house. *SEE ALSO PLUMBING REPAIRS.*

Rafter

A rafter is one of the framing members of a roof that is used to support the roofing materials. Common rafters, such as those used in a gabel roof, run perpendicular from the wall plate to the ridge. Hip rafters run at a 45 degree angle from the ridge to the plate. Valley rafters run diagonally from plate to ridge in the area left by two intersecting roof sections. Hip jack rafters are basically the same as a common rafter but intersect a hip rafter rather than a ridge. The valley jack rafter resembles the upper portion of a common rafter but intersects a valley rafter, not a

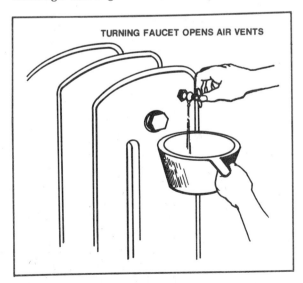

Radiator Bleeding

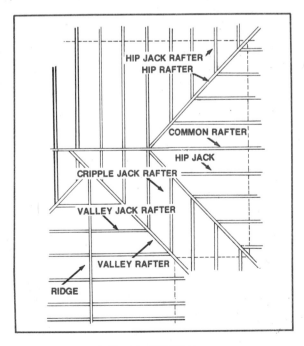

Types of Rafters

plate. The cripple jack rafter is stopped at each end by hip and valley rafters and does not intersect a plate or ridge. The cripple jack may also be called cripple rafter, hip-valley cripple jack or valley cripple jack. *SEE ALSO ROOF CONSTRUCTION.*

Rafters, Laying Out

Laying out rafters is the process of marking off rafters with a carpenter's square. In determining the length of the rafter, find one half of the building distance. Measure on the square the distance between 12 on the blade and 8 on the tongue; 12 is the unit of run and 8 is the hypothetical rise. The figure is $14^5/_{12}$ inches which represents the line length of a rafter with the total run of one foot and an eight inch rise. Because the run of the rafter is 10 feet, multiply 10 by the line length for one foot. The answer should be $144^2/_{12}$ inches or 12 feet and $^1/_6$ inch. Any overhang, usually one foot, is added to the figure making it 13 feet. Because 13 feet is an odd lumber length, 14 feet lengths are used.

Lay the timber across the sawhorses, using a straight piece for the pattern rafter. With the tongue of the square in the right hand and the body in the left, place the square at the upper end of the rafter keeping the figures 8 and 12 on the timber edge. Mark along the tongue edge of the square, which will be the plumb cut at the ridge. Measure the distance from the top of the plumb cut and mark it on the board. To measure the next plumb cut, hold the square with the 8 mark on the tongue over the 12 feet $^1/_{16}$ inch mark and draw along the tongue. Perpendicular to this mark, measure off the length of overhang along the timber and make a plumb cut mark as before. This makes the tail cut for the rafter. Using a try square, square lines down the sides from all level and plumb cut lines, then cut the rafter. *SEE ALSO ROOF CONSTRUCTION.*

Rafter Square

The rafter square (also called framing or car- penter's square) is a big, flat piece of L-shaped steel. Its body measures 24- by 2-inches, and the tongue is 16- by 1$^1/_2$-inches. Special tables and graduations are marked on both the body and tongue. The rafter square is used for measuring and cutting braces and rafters, converting timbers from squares to octagons, calculating proportions, finding the circumference and center of a circle, laying out hopper and miter joints and ellipses and figuring board measure. The rafter square is considered the most important and useful of all squares. *SEE ALSO HAND TOOLS.*

Railings, Porch

Porch railings not only act as a safeguard against accidents, but can complement the architecture of the home. Most railings today are made of aluminum, metal, iron or alloys and are used not only outside the home, but inside for decoration or to act as room dividers. Wood railing, when properly treated, will last as long as the metal varieties and, if they are unfinished or unpainted, give a rustic appearance to a home. Screened-in porches practically require porch railings to act as anchors for the screening material. *SEE ALSO PORCH CONVERSION & CONSTRUCTION.*

Rakes
[SEE LAWNS & GARDENS.]

Ranges & Ovens

RANGES

While the basic shape and size of many freestanding ranges conforms closely to the old wood range from which they evolved, there are also new shapes and new concepts in cooking. Modern features help to reduce cooking time and control temperatures more evenly to make today's range capable of producing more consistent results.

Despite its frequent usage, the range requires maintenance, and given proper care, will deliver good service over a long period of time. To get even better service and obtain better cooking results, it is necessary to understand how a range operates. Keep in mind before any inspections are made or before any panels are removed for servicing that the circuit to the range should be turned off and it should be unplugged as well. In the case of a gas range, the gas supply should be turned off and disconnected before moving the range for any reason. Electric ranges operate on a 230-volt power supply, making the risk potential even greater than it would be otherwise, particularly if you consider that all noncurrent carrying metal parts are connected to ground. There is no reason to expose any live electrical terminals on the range or on any other appliance.

The cooking surface of an electric range usually consists of four enclosed type heating elements, each made in a circular form. Many of these heating elements are divided into two sections, a larger outer coil and a smaller inner coil. These sections can be arranged to help change heat ranges.

Two types of switching arrangements are used to control heat levels and to give various ranges of heat input to the food. The first of these is a

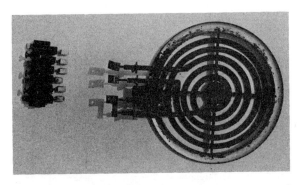

A surface unit for seven position switch is composed of two sections. The voltages are varied to provide different heat levels.

multi-position switch which has either pushbuttons or definite clicks between heat levels. This switch operates by varying the circuits and voltages into a dual-section element. For instance, on high heat ranges the switch would apply 230 volts across each of the two coil sections. On the next highest heat level, it would apply 230 volts across the large coil only; dropping another level, 230 volts across the small coil; at a still lower level, 230 volts across the outer limits of both coils and so on. There are seven combinations that can be arrived at with this system.

The second system used on many ranges is a cycling device. The switch on this element has a small heater built into it. One of the sets of contacts that controls the heating element is attached to a bimetal arm. The current passes through the arm when the switch is turned to the on position and the bimetal arm begins to bend from the heat of the switch heater. A certain amount of tension is set up against the arm, depending on the position of the switch. When the switch is in the highest position, the contacts are mechanically held together so that they constantly apply 230 volts to the single element. When the switch is turned toward the lower position, less tension is applied to this arm so that the on cycles become shorter and the off cycles longer. When the heating element is on, the switch heater is also on and current flows to the element. Once the bimetal has overcome the tension of the spring set up by the switch knob, it snaps open and breaks the circuit to the heating element and the switch heater. In a few moments the switch is cooled and again closes. The timing of current

Multi-position pushbutton switch is used to control input to surface units.

The surface unit for infinite heat switch is composed of only one section. Often these units unplug from range receptacle.

A cross section of the heating element shows how the wire is supported by manganese powder between the nichrome element and the outer shell.

input to the burner determines the heat. The advantage of this type switch is that an infinite number of heat ranges can be obtained anywhere between the low to high positions. There are usually no click stops between settings. A disadvantage is that on low heat levels some foods such as sauces and gravies may tend to boil during the short interval that the heat is turned on, then stop during the off cycle.

If it is necessary to obtain a replacement switch or element, be sure and get one specified for your particular model. Some switches depend upon the wattage of the element for the correct switch heater input. In others, the switch heater is wired across the line and the element wattage would have no effect.

Be certain to follow the wiring diagrams included with a replacement switch exactly. If no diagram is enclosed, connect the replacement exactly like the original. Switches that also control pilot lights can be damaged by connecting the lines to the wrong terminal.

Inside a typical surface unit element there is a small coil of nichrome wire that is insulated from the steel outer shell of the element by manganese powder. Many manufacturers make these elements as thin as possible to get maximum heat transfer and quick-heating capabilities from the element. On occasion the nichrome coil may reach a point where it can touch the side

of the heating element. Since the steel shell is grounded, this often causes a burn out which is very obvious and visible.

If this occurs, you'll have to replace the element. They are available from many servicing dealers and you should have no trouble replacing it. Simply turn off the power, and reconnect the wiring as the old element is removed or as shown in a diagram which might accompany the new element. The wires are coded in red, white, and black colors. If the terminals are burned and corroded be sure and clean them before installing them on the new element. If it is ever necessary to replace wire use only the heat resistance type wiring found only in electric ranges. Some elements simply unplug from the range.

You can prevent such burnouts. They are often caused by leaving the heating element on for a long period of time without a pan on the element to soak up the heat. This causes undue expansion and increases the likelihood of such a burn out. Never use the oven surface units to heat the kitchen during cold weather. Another possible cause of such a problem is a high-voltage surge from lightning. There are surge arresters which an electrician can install in your service entrance panel that will prevent such an occurrence. During a particularly severe storm, it is a good idea to unplug the range as well as other appliances.

One new innovation is the ceramic cooking surface. It utilizes heating elements under a special type of ceramic material. This presents a perfectly smooth top, usually with designs in the glass at the point where the heating element would normally be. Some of the first models required special utensils but many newer ones do not. As with any cooking surface, even the standard one, the utensil should fit flat against the top for maximum heat transfer between the pot and the heat surface. While these surfaces are put through special tests before they are released from the factory, they can be broken if a utensil is dropped on them. Be sure and follow manufacturer's instructions explicitly for cleaning and care of the cooking surface.

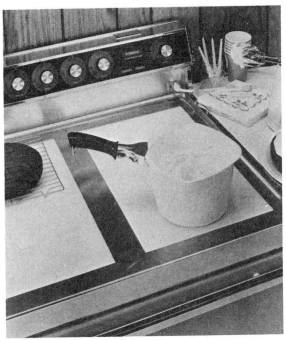

(Courtesy of Corning.)

Ceramic cooking surface has heating element located below. The easy to clean surface has appeal for large number of homeowners.

Electric ranges, except the counter top microwave units, are 230-volt appliances. On those that use a click position type switch, some heats on surface units may operate even if one fuse is blown or if one side of the line is interrupted. On any range it is possible that the surface units and oven might not heat, yet the lights and fan would operate even if one fuse was blown. If this occurs, be sure to check the fuses or the circuit breaker before blaming the range for the malfunction.

Most ranges have a fuse or small circuit breaker built into the cabinet which operates the 115-volt accessories such as the light, the timer, and the 115-volt outlet. If these devices fail to work, check this fuse or breaker. This will more than likely cure the problem.

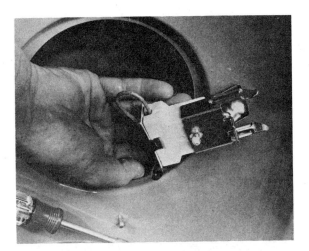

Check wiring on range receptacles when plug-in units fail to operate. Also, be sure that unit is in position. Use only specified wiring for repairs.

If a burner or an element fails to operate turn off the power and check to be sure that one of the wires feeding it is not broken or that one of the terminals is not loose where the wire connects to the burner. Any wire replacement should be made with high-heat resistant wiring of the type used in the range. The terminals should also be of the heat-resistant type. Be sure that all connecting portions are cleaned thoroughly and that no corrosion exists before replacing. The need for service can often be prevented by following a few simple rules: never use a range to heat a room, always be sure that pots are placed on surface units while thay are in operation, wipe away all spills immediately, and try to prevent any grease from entering the area around switches and surface units where it can be absorbed into the wires or electrical contacts. By keeping the range clean, you also help keep it serviceable and in good condition.

OVENS

The heating elements found in ovens are subject to the same potential failures as those of surface units. If an oven fails to heat, check to be sure that the timer (if the range is so equipped) is turned to the manual position. It's very easy to turn this switch when you wipe the range off after use and many service calls are made for just this reason. If the timer is set to a timed position, the surface units will work but the oven won't heat. Sometimes selector switches and thermostats are at fault when an oven fails to heat also. The continuity tester or volt-ohm-meter is necessary to check many problems, but some can be visible. Look closely on the switch for a charred or burned surface on the Bakelite

The heating element from oven can be removed after first loosening screws that hold it in place.

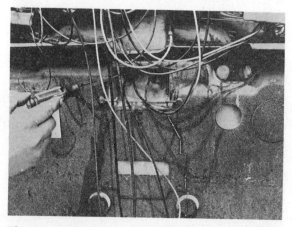

The terminals of oven elements are accessible after removing panel on back of range. If a wire or clip burns off terminal, be sure that the terminal is clean and shiny before installing new clip or refastening wire.

body. Also, inspect closely the heating element and the thermostat and selector switch for any loose or burned wire connections. Be sure that all connections are cleaned carefully before installing them on a switch. Special high-heat, quick-disconnect clips are available from servicing dealers to repair such failures.

If you feel that your oven isn't heating to the correct temperature, check the calibration of the thermostat by obtaining an oven thermometer (preferably of the mercury type) at a department store or at a servicing agency. First, check the accuracy of the thermometer by placing it in a pan of boiling water. The temperature should register close to 212 degrees. Next place the thermometer as near the center of the oven as possible. Turn the oven on and let it heat for five or ten minutes before taking a reading. Start at a lower temperature and work your way up. If the thermometer registers within 25 degrees of the setting on the dial, the oven temperature should be considered accurate.

If the temperature varies more than this, check to see if the sensing bulb is clipped into the proper place within the oven. Sometimes a pan or utensil can knock the tube out of place and this will affect the temperature range of the thermostat. If it is, the thermostat can often be calibrated from the front of the stove. After first unplugging the

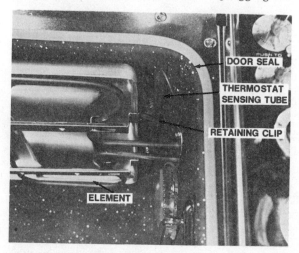

Thermostat sensing tube must be positioned correctly for correct temperature control. Be sure that it is positioned in clips and that they are securely fastened in place.

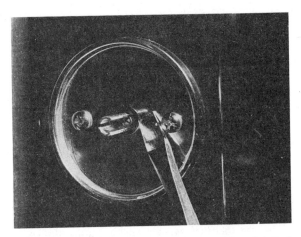

Calibration screws for thermostats are often located within the center of a hollow shaft. This is accessible after removing knob of thermostat shaft.

Some knobs have a calibration skirt within knob. Correct temperature after first placing an accurate thermometer near the center of oven.

stove, pull the knob from the thermostat and see if a calibration screw is located there. Sometimes these screws are located within a hollow shaft of the thermostat. At other times they may be reached through a separate opening. In most cases they will be accessible from the front, and will usually be marked with an arrow to show the direction of rotation to make the thermostat maintain a warmer temperature. Make only slight adjustments at a time and then recheck. An adjustment of only a quarter of a turn can make a 50 to 80 degree difference in the temperature of the oven.

Door seals affect the air circulation within the oven during use. They can have a great effect on the temperature that the oven registers. Most current ovens and ranges have a vent, usually located under the right rear or right front surface unit, from which the hot air of the oven is exhausted. At the front of the oven where the door closes there will be an opening in the seal. As the air within the oven cavity is heated, it tends to escape out the vent and cool air from the room is pulled in at the lower front of the oven to replace it. This convection current helps to provide even heat throughout the oven.

If a door becomes twisted in position or if the gasket fails to seal around the upper portion of the door, the air can escape near the front of the range rather than at the back. This not only increases the temperatures on the top surfaces near the front of the range, but the poor air circulation reduces the heating efficiency of the oven. To correct a door that appears to be out of position, first look for any openings or plugs that may conceal adjusting bands built within the oven door. If they are there, you can adjust the door by tightening the screw which controls the side that has pulled away from the oven body. If no bands are provided, the door is usually supported by the inner liner. In this case, loosen the screws around the inside of the door liner. Then gently position the door where it seals best, reopen the door carefully and tighten the screws firmly, but not so tight that they begin to chip into the porcelain. The door should now seal properly.

Door springs are often located within oven body. Adjustments are available to tighten or loosen springs as required to provide proper seal.

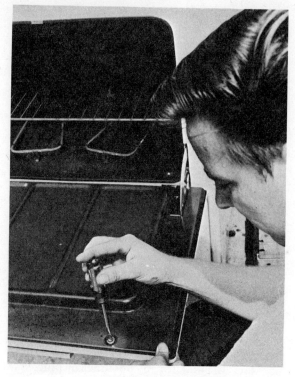

Screws on door panel should be loosened to allow door to be moved or aligned properly with cabinet. Snug screws up, but do not overtighten as this can chip porcelain.

Seals that are torn or broken should be replaced. Often these are held in place by small stainless steel clips and can simply be snapped into position. On some models it is necessary to loosen the oven liner, which is usually held in place by screws at the side and rear. Pull it forward slightly before the seals can be installed. Follow the manufacturer's instructions for seal replacement.

Sometimes the springs that pull the door closed lose their tension after being in use for many years.

Most ranges have notches or slots to help compensate by moving one end of the spring. If your range has a storage drawer or toe panel, remove it and look underneath the range at both sides. You will be likely to see these openings and be able to move the springs to a tighter position.

The oven should be level. If it is not, batter and foods placed within the oven on the racks will tend to run to one side. Check your oven and be sure the racks are in the proper position and that any guides are fully in place. Then, place a level in the center of the rack in the area you use the most. Level the range from side to side then change the position of the level and level it from front to back.

Self-Cleaning Ovens

Self-cleaning ovens operate on two principles. The first is the *pyrolytic* principle, where special controls and heating elements are used to heat the oven to a high temperature range (around 800 degrees) to burn away any food soils that may remain within the range. As these soils are slowly oxidized, the gases must pass through a special platinum-palladium coated screen at the outlet vent in the top of the oven. This screen, often incorporating a small electric heater, acts as an after burner to help to burn away any particles or smoke that would remain.

Pyrolytics do an excellant job of cleaning since the intense heat reaches into every corner. Although the energy consumption during cleaning is fairly high, the energy consumption during normal use is lower than a standard range due to the high-density insulation that is used. The only part of the job that remains to be done is simply to wipe away any smoke or food that may accumulate outside the door seal. This will be found around the outer edge or throat of the oven liner. Since this isn't subject to high heat during use, soil usually isn't baked on and can be easily wiped away with a damp cloth.

Problems with pyrolytics can often be traced to improper setting of controls at the beginning of the cycle. If the oven does not come completely clean, check to be sure that you are setting the time control for the proper length of time. Usually three to four hours are required for normal soil. Also, be sure to remove any heavy food particles or spills before the cleaning cycle is initiated. While the pyrolytic will take care of such soils, the high level of smoke can overcome the action of the smoke eliminator and this of course is undesirable.

Continuous clean ovens are standard ovens that

incorporate a special coating on the oven surfaces to help burn food soils away at low temperatures. This is a catalytic process and it does work so long as you do not expect it to do more than it was intended to do. Spills should be wiped away immediately. If they are heavy enough they can smother the action of the catalyst in the coating. Since catalytic ovens operate at normal temperatures, there is no cleaning effect on door glasses or any parts of the ovens that may be uncoated. The finish is fragile and commercial type oven cleaners or abrasives should never be used on it. Follow the manufacturer's instructions specifically for cleaning of particular soils.

Eye Level Ovens

Eye level ovens are now becoming quite popular. Many of these incorporate full glass doors and may have a standard oven or even a self-cleaning oven below the cooking surface with a smaller eye-level oven above. Another line incorporates a grill with a heating element located just under the grill and above special trays that contain stones. As meat fats drop upon the stones, the smoke passes across the food to a down-draft vent. The result is an excellent "charcoaled" taste, available indoors upon command both summer and winter.

Courtesy of Jenn-Air Corp.

Special purpose units such as this Jennair grill allow charcoal flavor to be imparted to grilled meats on demand.

Microwave Ovens

Microwave ovens, both counter top and free standing, are becoming increasingly popular. The microwave unit is best known for its ability to cook foods at very fast speeds. In addition, if prepared correctly some foods have been judged to be even juicier, more tasty than they are when cooked by standard means. Most manufacturers are promoting their microwaves as supplements, not replacements, for standard ovens. When used in this manner they are very convenient. One of the latest innovations is a new free standing range that combines the microwave oven and the self-cleaning pyrolytic oven.

Servicing a microwave is strictly for professionals and requires professional instruments to check for leakage after repairs are made. But you can be sure to use utensils that are recommended by the manufacturer and wipe away any spills or residue that accumulate near the gasket surface. Report any tears or breaks in the gasket to the servicing agent immediately. Never attempt to operate the oven with the door ajar or with damaged seals.

(Courtesy of Litton Industries.)

Counter top microwave ovens are becoming increasingly popular. Servicing must be done by qualified technician.

Rasps

[SEE FILES & RASPS.]

Ratchet

A ratchet is a gear with triangular-shaped teeth. These teeth are engaged by a pawl that allows rotation, while locking the gear against backward movement. When used in the spiral ratchet screwdriver, the ratchet provides the twisting motion. Special types of socket wrenches and hand drills also employ a ratchet. *SEE ALSO HAND TOOLS.*

Ratchet

Ratchet Screwdriver

Ratchet screwdrivers have several advantages over standard screwdrivers, as they have a sliding button that locks the blade in either a ratchet or non-ratchet position. When locked in the ratchet position, the blade rotates only in the direction in which the screw is being turned; when locked in the other position, the blade operates like a regular screwdriver. The ratchet action provides a continuous turning motion. Ratchet screwdrivers usually have interchangeable blades, a good, steady grip and are useful for working in tight areas because of their versatility. *SEE ALSO HAND TOOLS.*

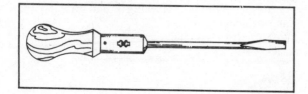

Ratchet Screwdriver

Rattail File

The rattail file, also called a round file, is round and tapers to a blunt point at one end. It is generally used to shape and smooth recesses and enlarge holes in both wood and metal work. *SEE ALSO HAND TOOLS.*

Rattail File

Receptacles, Outdoor

An outdoor receptacle is a single or duplex 15-ampere outlet housed in a weatherproof box. Whether the receptacles are flush or surface mounted, their housings will have snap, hinged or threaded disc covers. Outdoor outlets make electricity available for yard or patio, decorative and holiday lighting, power tools and fans. *SEE ALSO SWITCHES & OUTLETS.*

Outdoor Receptacles

Reciprocating Sander

Reciprocating sanders are designed for final sanding with the grain and roughing down work across the grain. The vibrator-driven sander makes $1/8$ inch strokes at an average rate of 14,400 per minute when working with the grain, but is relatively slow when sanding across the grain. Motor-driven varieties are operated and act much the same as the vibrator-driven except that the strokes are longer. But, this type, unlike the vibrator-driven models, also has bearings which wear out and require replacing. *SEE ALSO PORTABLE POWER TOOLS; STATIONARY BELT & DISC SANDER.*

Reciprocating Saw
[SEE PORTABLE POWER TOOLS.]

Recreational Boats & Boating

To make sure you will find the boat you want, form a clear idea of what you look forward to most: water skiing, fishing, cruising or boat camping, transportation, or making new friends. Maybe you can find a boat that does all things, but you will be more satisfied in the end if you decide on your priorities and keep these in mind when you start looking. This will also help you arrive at a budget for a boat, motor, and equipment.

EQUIPMENT YOU SHOULD HAVE

Certain boating equipment is extremely useful, and the man who sells you the boat will probably make sure it comes to your attention. Be on guard against over-equipping your boat. Everything you add counts against the boat's total load capacity. The more permanent equipment you have, the less capacity remains for passengers and sporting gear.

Courtesy of Stearns Manufacturing Co.

Basic safety equipment is specified by law, according to the size of the boat. You should have one life preserver, buoyant jacket or cushion for each person aboard; running lights; suitable anchor; a whistle, horn, or bell; fire extinguisher; backfire flame arrestor for an inboard engine; and at least two ducted ventilators for inboard engine and fuel compartment. Check with local boating authorities or write to the Coast Guard's regional office for safety requirements (now being revised) applicable to your boat, based on its length measured at the centerline. In addition, an experienced boatowner will include a bailing

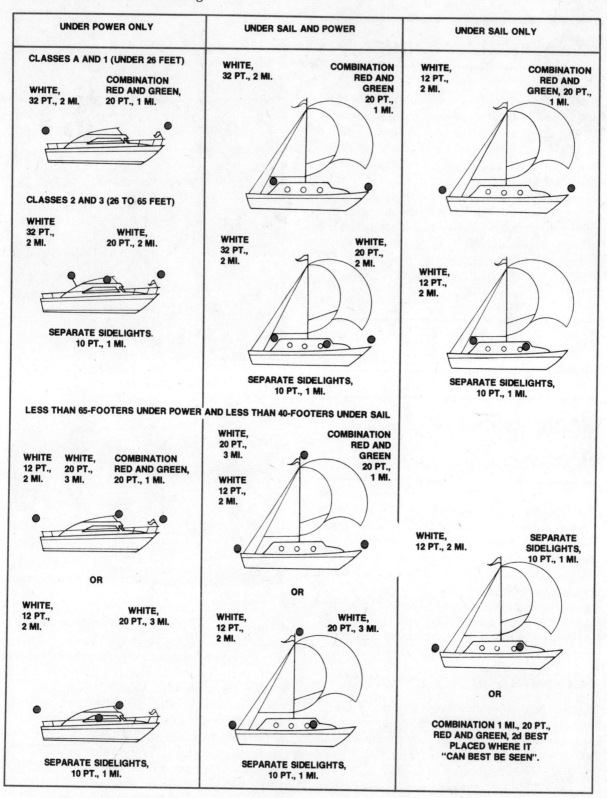

UNDER POWER ONLY	UNDER SAIL AND POWER	UNDER SAIL ONLY

CLASSES A AND 1 (UNDER 26 FEET)

WHITE, 32 PT., 2 MI.

COMBINATION RED AND GREEN, 20 PT., 1 MI.

CLASSES 2 AND 3 (26 TO 65 FEET)

WHITE 32 PT., 2 MI.

WHITE, 20 PT., 2 MI.

SEPARATE SIDELIGHTS. 10 PT., 1 MI.

WHITE, 32 PT., 2 MI.

COMBINATION RED AND GREEN 20 PT., 1 MI.

WHITE 32 PT., 2 MI.

WHITE, 20 PT., 2 MI.

SEPARATE SIDELIGHTS, 10 PT., 1 MI.

WHITE, 12 PT., 2 MI.

COMBINATION RED AND GREEN, 20 PT., 1 MI.

WHITE, 12 PT., 2 MI.

SEPARATE SIDELIGHTS, 10 PT., 1 MI.

LESS THAN 65-FOOTERS UNDER POWER AND LESS THAN 40-FOOTERS UNDER SAIL

WHITE 12 PT., 2 MI.

WHITE, 20 PT., 3 MI.

COMBINATION RED AND GREEN, 20 PT., 1 MI.

OR

WHITE, 12 PT., 2 MI.

WHITE, 20 PT., 3 MI.

SEPARATE SIDELIGHTS, 10 PT., 1 MI.

WHITE, 20 PT., 3 MI.

WHITE 12 PT., 2 MI.

COMBINATION RED AND GREEN 20 PT., 1 MI.

OR

WHITE, 12 PT., 2 MI.

WHITE, 20 PT., 3 MI.

SEPARATE SIDELIGHTS, 10 PT., 1 MI.

WHITE, 12 PT., 2 MI.

SEPARATE SIDELIGHTS, 10 PT., 1 MI.

OR

COMBINATION 1 MI., 20 PT., RED AND GREEN, 2d BEST PLACED WHERE IT "CAN BEST BE SEEN".

Running Lights Between Sunrise and Sunset

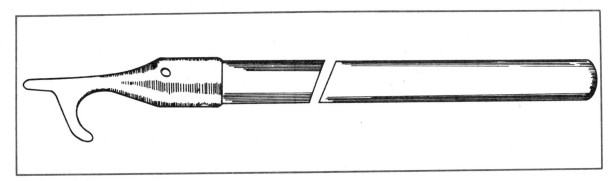

Boat Hook

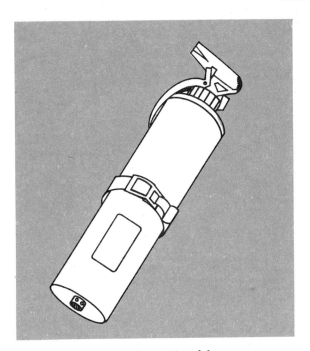

Marine Fire Extinguisher

Marine Bell

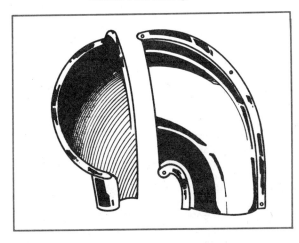

Side Vents

device, first-aid kit, waterproof flashlight, compass, oars or paddle, a map or chart for the waters you are on, at least a small transistor radio on which you can hear weather broadcasts, and a kit of hand tools and basic spare parts such as spark plugs and wires, gaskets, hoses, and clamps. Personal equipment should include deck shoes, rain gear, and spare food and drinking water.

BE A GOOD SKIPPER

Boat handling demands more than good driving. You must get used to reading danger signs both in the water and in the skies. Keep an eye out for shallows, swift currents, floating logs, and anything that will affect the safety of your boat and passengers. Pointers:

Fishing tackle, water skis, and other gear should be secured out of the way of people's footing. As you load, check off the safety equipment. Count the life preservers against the number of people aboard. Guard against overloading, looking at the freeboard and posture of the boat in the water before casting off. Vent the boat for at least one minute and preferably five minutes after fueling. Then sniff in corners before turning on the ignition. Watch your wake as you leave or approach the dock. You are responsible for any damage it does to other craft or the shoreline. Keep a sharp lookout when underway and ask another person to help watch for swimmers, skiers and floating debris. Wear your own life preserver, and make sure another person aboard knows how to operate the boat in case something happens to you. Learn to read weather signs (wind, cloud formation, wave action) early

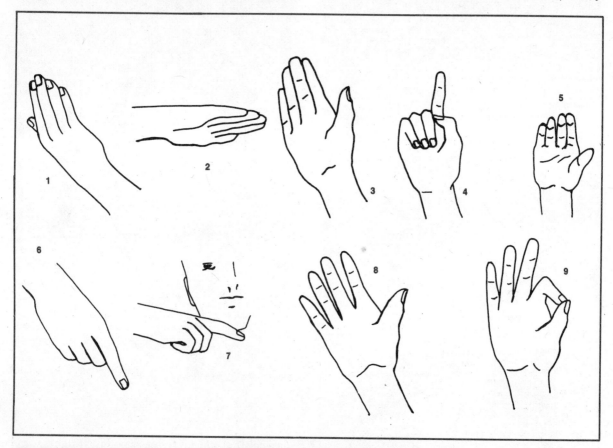

The **American Water Ski Association** has developed the hand signals above for communication between boat and skier. 1. **Speed up** — open palm up with arm sweeping upward. 2. **Slow down** — open palm down, with arm extended and sweeping downward. 3. **Turn** — with open palm, describe curve with hand in direction desired. 4. **Whip off** — point to direction and give circular motions with extended finger. 5. **Jump** — with open palm, signify soaring motion by sweeping hand forward and up. 6. **Back to dock** — with arm straight, bring extended forefinger sharply downward, or point downward with elbow bent. 7. **Cut motor** — move extended finger across throat with cutting motion. 8. **Stop** — raise hand with fingers outstretched. 9. **Everything OK** — the traditional signal "O" made with finger and thumb.

enough to seek safety before a storm breaks.
Learn the rules of proper boathandling and
follow them. Printed copies are available free
from the Coast Guard. You'll find that handling
your boat in a legal, considerate and watchful
manner will increase your enjoyment.

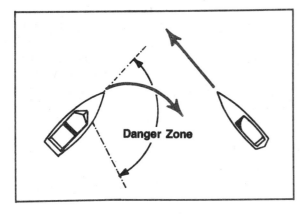

Crossing Situations

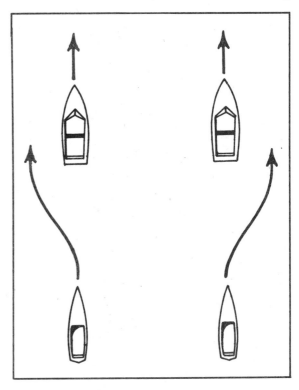

Overtaking Situations

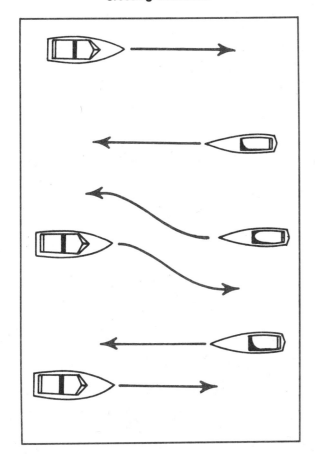

Passing Situations

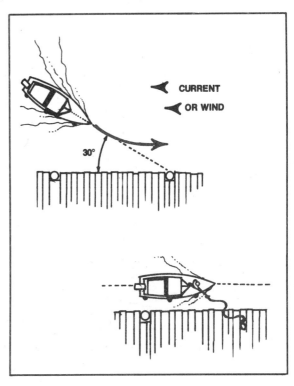

Docking Situations

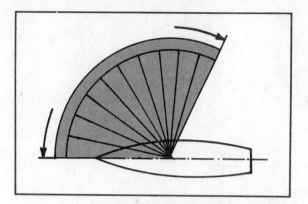

Ten Point Danger Zone

ANCHORS AND LINES

An anchor is basic safety equipment for a boat, although not required by law. It is necessary in order to hold your position in a blow. When your engine quits, instead of drifting into dangerous rock or reefs, it holds your boat in a safe position in harbor. You will also need it when using the boat as a swimming platform or when fishing. Fluke-type anchors, even for small open boats, are most reliable and easiest to handle. Make sure you have enough anchor line and that it is in good condition and securely fastened inside the boat.

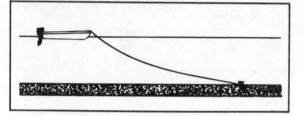

On quiet waters, the anchor line can be four or five times the depth of the water, but on open, windy waters it should be seven or eight times the depth. Anchorage security depends on the horizontal pull against the anchor flukes.

Making Fast To A Cleat

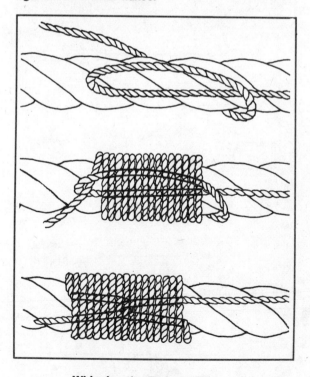

Whipping the End of A Rope

Clove Hitch

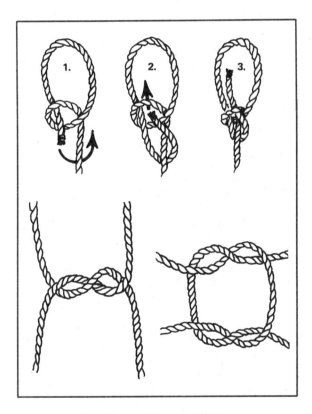

Bowline and Square Knot

TRAILERING YOUR BOAT

Any boat trailer should have enough supports, in the right places, to support your particular hull.

Critical points are where the hull is most heavily loaded with engine, tanks, and outfitting, and where the main overall hull weight rests, as in the broad area midship and toward the transom. Where the hull presents corners, as at the bow, keel, and transom, there should be no possibility of chafing or bumping. Tight, strong, padded tie-downs are important.

If you use the trailer for overnight trips to distant waters, make sure it has the weight capacity for not only your boat and motor, but the gear that you may have to stow inside. Weight should balance at a point just forward of the trailer axle to prevent fishtailing.

The trailer's critical running gear is at the hubs. Wheel bearings should be inspected frequently for good packing, and avoid immersing wheel hubs when backing the boat to the water.

HOW TO BUY A BOAT

Ask yourself some basic questions before you buy: Where will you use the boat — in lakes, streams, or salt water; in big waters or small? What size and type of boat do you really need for your uses? Where will you keep it during the boating season — and where will you store it over the winter? What hull type and material will serve your purposes best? How much power do you need; inboard or outboard? And, finally, how much will it cost?

New Boat or Used Boat

The warranty you get from a reputable builder is a big asset when it comes to making a large investment for a boat and motor. It gives you a definite right to return to the dealer or factory when something is unsatisfactory. When you have compared specifications, looked into the construction and characteristics, and assured yourself that you have found the boat you want, then having a new boat gives you reasonable assurance that there are no major defects. In buying either a new or used boat it is important to know the reputation of the maker and of the dealer with whom you are doing business.

You can find excellent buys in used boats, especially at the end of the season. The problem is to make sure you are getting what you pay for. If buying a larger boat, say over thirty feet, it is a good investment to pay a qualified boat surveyor to inspect before you buy, or make the sale conditional on a clean bill from a marine insurance surveyor. Here are some checks to make when you start looking: Determine if the boat has been maintained and used responsibly, or abused and neglected. Cracks, broken fittings, torn upholstery, a knicked or bent propeller will tell much. Has the boat been stored under cover, in the open or in the water? Look for signs of cracks caused by freezing, for instance at the transom corners; look for rot, corrosion or pitting.

If used in salt water, look thoroughly for electrolysis damage to metal hulls and fittings, propeller and lower motor unit; look for borer damage to wood hulls. You can expect to pay about 20 percent more for a boat used only in fresh water, other things being equal.

Inspect inside at the point of the bow, under floor boards, and in transom corners for signs of rot, neglect, or collision damage. Look carefully at hull fastenings and fittings to estimate how soon you will have to replace them. Color stains and cracks in a fiberglass hull are serious, while crazing of the surface gel coat may indicate mere age, not weakness.

Listen to the motor with the cover off and inspect the water pump, seals, fuel lines and carburetor. Look at the spark plugs and fuel filters as indications of upkeep. How much smoke is in the exhaust? Take it out for a spin long enough for the motor to get well warmed; open up the throttle for several minutes, then turn it down to trolling speed (about three mph) to see if it will perform without overheating and choking. Never buy a boat you have not tried on the water.

In choosing a powerplant for your boat the object is to customize your rig — a matched boat and motor — to perform best for your needs. If you enjoy water skiing, then you will need ample horsepower with fast acceleration, superior carburetion and exhaust porting. Husky outboards are most popular; inboard/outdrives or inboard-powered jet drives suit boats in the range over 20 feet.

Courtesy of Glastron

The fifteen-foot runabout with enough power to tow a skier is a favorite boat type across the country. About forty horsepower is needed, but choosing a lightweight hull of minimum length reduces gas consumption when ski-towing.

As the cost and supply of fuel becomes more of a problem, you will want to choose a motor for fuel-economy features. Read the manufacturer's literature and ask what features are incorporated to accomplish this. Efficient ignition systems, carburetion, and exhaust porting are signal factors.

Courtesy of MonArk

One of the best-selling and most talked about boats today, the fiberglass bass boat evolved from the old johnboat and the newer sled-type runabout. It has a narrow beam for operating in weed- and brush-filled waters, and this design factor reduces horsepower required. Swivel chairs enable you to cast and play the fish from any quarter while keeping a safe seat. A bow-mounted small electric trolling motor gives these anglers silent movement along the shoreline.

For fishing you need a motor that will get you there without wasting the day, and will then troll for hours if necessary or stop and start frequently, all without problems. A top-quality outboard with moderate horsepower, made for fishing, suits most serious anglers.

Don't overlook electric trolling motors for crawling silently and slowly along shorelines while you cast. This may be the only power you need for a canoe. For larger boats, it will help you find fish, and spare your outboard from overloading with carbon from too much slow running.

For fast runabouts a big outboard or an inboard/outdrive or jet is usually the choice. Power tilt to raise the lower unit or outdrive for beaching or shallows is valuable, with power trim to cant the propeller position to suit the load you have in the boat.

Jet power is the safest type of motor boat, able to stop in two boat-lengths or less by throwing the control into instant reverse, and having no prop to endanger people in the water. Jets are especially popular in man-made lakes where submerged tree-trunks abound.

A clear-cut safety rule is to power your boat adequately, but not to overpower it. Check the Boat-ing Industry Association plate attached to the boat's transom for recommended and maximum power rating for that particular boat.

Courtesy of Stearns Manufacturing Co.

Water skiing is a sport enjoyed by many recreational boaters. A personal flotation device (PFD) should be worn for safety.

RUNABOUT

This most versatile kind of boat includes a broad variety of hull designs ranging from about fourteen to twenty feet in length. In deck layout it is an open boat. The name runabout is really a catch-all for boats commonly used for water skiing, swimming, fishing, outings, friendly racing, and, of course, running about on the water for the fun of it or for a quick errand down at the

Dourtesy of Glastron

The speedboat with lounge deck is comfortable at any speed. You don't always have to go fast to enjoy this sport runabout.

Midget runabouts require less power but still give you speed thrills.

other end of the lake. Normally the runabout is used on calm waters, for the boat has low freeboard and is relatively light in weight and construction. It is easy to trailer a runabout for hundreds of miles on vacations. A folding or zip-on top is a useful accessory for protection from sun, wind and rain, and also for boat-camping. Well-upholstered lounge-recliner seats are some of the most popular accessories on runabouts.

Most runabouts have good speed. Both in-board/outdrive engines and outboards are matched to this type of boat; outboard power predominates because of its size, weight suitability and lower cost. A steering wheel and driver's seat, with companion seat opposite, is arranged much like an automobile's. However on well-designed boats the driver's seat is on the right, for the danger zone on the water, where you must give right-of-way to the other boat is from dead ahead to two points abaft the starboard (right) beam.

A versatile tri-hull runabout, the eighteen-foot Nor'Wester has a large forward deck for diving or casting, with comfortable lounge seats and roomy cockpit behind the steering console.

Many runabouts have a small bow deck with seat and platform for diving or fishing. Anchor, lines and other gear may be stored under the bow deck. Side and rear storage between the cockpit walls and hull is also provided. Water skis can be stored under the cockpit floor or in side racks on many boats.

UTILITY BOAT

The bare-hull aluminum or fiberglass boat from twelve to eighteen feet probably outnumbers all other boats afloat. It is simple to handle and care for, inexpensive and many can be cartopped. Seats are riveted or molded across the boat providing main structural bracing. The power is outboard, steering is done by the motor handle or by a wheel mounted on a midway steering console. You will see fishermen, hunters, and those with work to do on the water operating these boats in every part of the country. Necessary maintenance is practically nil.

Bare-hulled aluminum utility boat is inexpensive and will operate with under-ten-horsepower outboard. It's the most popular fishing boat and equally suits family outings or simple transportation.

Courtesy of Johnson

With covered bow, this sixteen-foot aluminum utility is used on big lakes. Extra length calls for a forward-facing steering position.

Ten-foot square-bowed dink will run you about the harbor and moves well with a two-horsepower motor.

Express cruisers are faster and more versatile than the bigger ones, able to run in more shallow waters and berth almost anywhere.

CRUISER

With bigger capacity and weight, heavier construction, and more equipment required for longer times on the water, the true cruiser has a cabin with galley, built-in seats, head (toilet) and overnight accomodations. A raised cockpit behind the cabin, with hatches to the engine bedded under the cockpit, has plenty of space for sitting or fishing in most layouts. The forward bow deck on many new cruisers is almost useless; styling curves the bow deck in a streamline down to the sides, and often is very slippery. It takes an agile sailor to handle the anchor and lines from the bow deck and he has to rely on the bow rail if the boat is equipped with one.

The pilot's station is on the starboard side or on a flybridge on the cabin roof. Power is usually inboard and often with outdrive to leave more deck space in the middle of the boat. Cruisers range from under twenty feet to forty-five feet or more; over that length, a pleasure boat is usually called a yacht. Daycruisers are powered with inboard/outdrives or husky outboard motors. A small sink, alcohol burner, and a small bunk or two tuck neatly into the cabin and bow.

HOUSEBOATS AND PLATFORM BOATS

The houseboat is the motorhome of the water. Sizes range from twenty to more than fifty feet, all with live-aboard facilities. You will see large ones fully furnished with convertible living-room furniture, a complete galley, and washer and dryer. Outside a walk-around deck is useful for fishing and swimming or when docking the bulky craft. Atop the cabin or house is a sundeck. The hull is a shallow V or tri-hull designed for maximum stability. Twin out-boards or inboard/outdrives are desirable for better maneuverability.

Houseboating is great fun for family-style living on the water and can give you the most relaxing vacation ever if you don't demand great speed and performance.

The twenty-four foot Poseidon house-trailer/cruiser affords camping overland and comfortable quarters on the water.

Platform boats are simply flat, open-deck boats with a rail all around and perhaps a flat canvas top. These are fun boats for swimming, fishing and entertaining. Ponton hulls with shallow draft make it easy to put ashore anywhere for a cookout or picnic. A single outboard motor is usually adequate.

SPORTFISHERMAN

Sturdily built fishing machines, these boats are designed and outfitted for tracking down and catching gamefish. The most important development in recent years is the inshore-offshore fishing boat of from seventeen to about twenty-four feet that handles well in fishing the tidal flats, reefs, and points, but that can also take off into big water for other game. The bow is usually a deep V, tapering to a shallow V midships and flat at the stern. This combination gives it shallow draft but wave-handling ability—an ex-

Courtesy of Kikhaefer Mercury

Most popular of sportfishing boats now is the inshore-offshore boat made in sizes from seventeen to twenty-four feet. A center steering console leaves walk-around space when the fishing action gets hot. This boat has a sun shade up but a storm cover can be zipped overhead quickly.

tremely useful and versatile design. An open boat with a center steering console with well-padded seats, the bow and stern are made with fishing platforms for freedom of action. Single or twin outboards are the rule. Many owners who previously had larger and heavier sportfishing boats with a cabin and flybridge top have found that the inshore-offshore boat helps them to find more fish with its easy handling, totally useful deck space and shallow draft. Fuel cost and maintenance are much lower than on the big sportfishermen.

Open-deck fisherman like this Trojan 25 can ably hunt the big game but affords bare comfort. Purchase price and fuel consumption are relatively low.

The big boats, with cabin, berths, and galley, are suited to all-weather and long-distance situations. A large, open cockpit is outfitted for rod-handling with padded fighting chairs and space to boat the catch. A flybridge and steering station atop the cabin provides a necessary vantage point for sighting the fish and maneuvering. Outriggers make it possible to handle several fishing lines. Sportfishermen range from 25 to 50 feet and more, and are generally inboard-powered with powerful engines to work in heavy seas when necessary. Initial outlay, fuel costs and maintenance run high.

MOTOR SAILER

This boat is built for comfortable, long voyages with both sail and motor power. The sail supplies all the power when there is adequate wind on the open water, saving fuel, smoke and noise. Diesel power is installed for rugged reliability and low fuel consumption over great distances. Sturdy construction and comfortable design help to weather all seas, and the boat is outfitted with complete facilities in ample space to make a long voyage a relaxing adventure. Lengths range from thirty-five to about seventy feet.

Courtesy of Pacemaker

The great sportfishing boats are built for the sea in any weather. Outfitted for the chase, outrigger poles keep several lines in the water without crossing, the bait skipping on the surface to attract billfish. This Pacemaker has twin engines and full comfort belowdecks.

You could sail around the world in this schooner. It's the Skipjack, built by Kenner. An auxiliary motor gives steerage in calm weather and close quarters.

Shell-like small sailboats are inexpensive and easy to sail, often race as a class in boating communities. This is the eleven-foot Sunflower, an improved version of the famous Sea Snark, with a 40-square-foot lateen sail. It can carry two adults, is easy to cartop or slip into the rear of a wagon, weighs only sixty pounds fully rigged.

AUXILIARY

A smaller sailboat with auxiliary power in form of a small outboard or inboard engine beats the doldrums when you are caught in a calm while cruising or need to maneuver in crowded moorings without the sail.

CANOE

The canoe is one of the most useful of all boat designs. It is lightweight and extremely easy to handle. It draws little water, so that it can be used on rivers, small lakes, and streams, and it is silent.

Canoes are among the easiest of all boats to use. Lightweight aluminum canoes respond instantly, are generally tough and maintenance-free. This Grumman can carry two or three adults with camping and fishing gear. Flotation can be added.

Courtesy of Stearns Manufacturing Co.

Personal flotation devices will increase the safety of any canoe trip.

Canoe sailing is blithe fun, for any breeze will move the craft. Daggerboards are slung athwart to hold headway in the lightweight, top-of-the-water hull. This is a seventeen-foot Aerocraft.

The small Sears raft can be tossed into the water anywhere, inflates in a minute or two, rides easily on a small car top, and stores in the closet ready for the weekend.

INFLATABLE

If you are short on storage space, perhaps this is the answer. The inflatable boat is made of neoprene or hypalon bonded to nylon fabric. It is an entirely safe fun boat that can be used as a swimming or scuba raft, for drift fishing, bouncing down shallow streams, or just playing about on the water. It can be carried in the car trunk and inflated at the water's edge with a foot pump or CO_2 cartridge.

DESIGN AND MATERIALS

How a boat is built has much to do with how and where you can use it. The basic factor is hull design; construction methods and materials must follow suit. Here are several popular types and what you can expect from them:

Deep-V bow design with hard chines running into the bow gives these Uniflite hulls a comfortable ride even in big waves. Such a hull must be well engineered and built to take pounding.

V-shaped hull

The V-shape boat bottom was the first step up from variously round-bottomed boats built for so many centuries. The point of the V at the keel from fore to aft slices through the water, pushing it away from the hull and reducing water resistance or friction, while the flat sides of the V raise the boat to the surface as more power is ap-

plied, allowing more speed as the area of surface in contact with the water is reduced. A simple, uncomplicated form, it is relatively cheap and easy to build. Modern versions tend to fit one of two types: A shallow V leveling off to a flat bottom at the stern gives good speed in addition to stability and comfort. The flat area at the stern provides a planing area that helps the boat stay on top of the water at somewhat lower speeds than the deep-V shape, and is a more stable platform for fishing and sitting on the water. The deep-V bottom is deeply pointed from bow to stern and permits very high speed and sharp control in turns. Many boats combine the best characteristics of both V types.

Tri-hull (Cathedral or Gull-wing)

Very popular in powered boats from 14 to 20 feet in length, the hull with three V points acts somewhat like a sled on the water, combining speed with outstanding stability and good control. Swimmers, fishermen, and the whole family can use any part of the boat. It represents a great stride in family-boat design, for the bow deck is wide and stable, making the entire topside useful, not just the cockpit. The drawback of the tri-hull is that it has more wetted surface than the simple V hull, and at slower speeds tends to

A modified V hull with longitudinal strakes molded in the fiberglass and sharp chines aft will be seaworthy, relatively fast, quick to respond to the helm, and stable when idle in the water, as when picking up a water skier or fishing.

Bow view of the tri-hull shows compound curves employed to give the boat great stability all around, with additional lift to get on top of choppy water, and deep-V center hull form for speed and good steering control. Level fore-to-aft posture of boat in the water is an operating safety factor and makes a comfortable ride.

Safe cruising in open water demands the use of personal flotation devices.

push the water before it, therefore, requiring more horsepower in relation to boat length. For this reason it is not used in bigger cruisers and sportfishing boats, where power requirements would be prohibitive.

Round Bottom

This hull rides *in* the water, even at top speed, not planing on the water's surface. Top speed is slow compared to planing hulls, but it can be built with great strength and load-bearing capacity. Since it rides lower in the water, the center of gravity is nearer to occupants' seats, making it more comfortable and safer in big waves and the open sea. Most "round-bottom" boats are actually variations of an hour-glass configuration, recurving to a keel of some sort. Many sailboats fit this description, and larger sailers have a deep keel weighted to prevent capsizing in a stiff wind.

Catamaran and Trimaran

One has two, the other has three slim, lightweight hulls connected by crossbars to make a boat that rests virtually atop the water and therefore is capable of both speed and stability with little power. The catamaran, with two hulls,

Catamaran sailing is one of the great thrills in water sports. Running on one hull, the Hobie Cat 16 can reach twenty-five miles an hour with two aboard. Catamarans are very shallow draft craft, drawing an average of ten inches of water. Asymmetrical hulls, curved on the inside and flat on the outside, eliminate the need for a centerboard.

is a popular small sailboat design, with a trampoline-style canvas deck stretched between the hulls. Trimarans are usually large sailers; the center hull is larger, with steering gear and cabin, the two outside hulls acting as outriggers for stability.

Fiberglass, Aluminum, or Wood?

Fiberglass is perhaps the most-wanted boat material, for it is easy to keep clean and requires little seasonal maintenance as far as the hull is concerned. In this respect, the quality of the gelcoat (the surface lamination) is important. Fiberglass is also a strong material, built with structural reinforcement where needed, depending on the hull type and size. However, fiberglass is not buoyant, and flotation material must be built in. It will also burn unless fire-retardant material is incorporated with the resin. Because fiberglass is molded, it can be built in any configuration, making complex curves such as the tri-hull possible. Price is usually higher than aluminum or wood.

Aluminum boats can be made cheaply and lightweight by comparison with other materials. They give good service, require little maintenance, and take a lot of abuse in relation to lightweight construction. Small aluminum boats such as cartop fishing boats and canoes can be made with welded or riveted plates, or a combination. Small cruisers and sailboats have welded main seams, at least. Aluminum is easy to repair (a pot mender can stop a small puncture), but flotation must be built in. Sound-deadening paint is used to make aluminum boats quiet.

Wood is beautiful, comfortable and naturally buoyant. However, it needs a lot of maintenance, with seasonal scraping and sanding, filling seams, and painting to keep it dry and the hull efficiently sleek. A good wood boat can be expensive to build, but the home craftsman can build a very satisfactory wood boat inexpensively from plans.

BOAT SYSTEMS

Your boating satisfaction and safety depend greatly on the fuel, engine cooling, and electrical

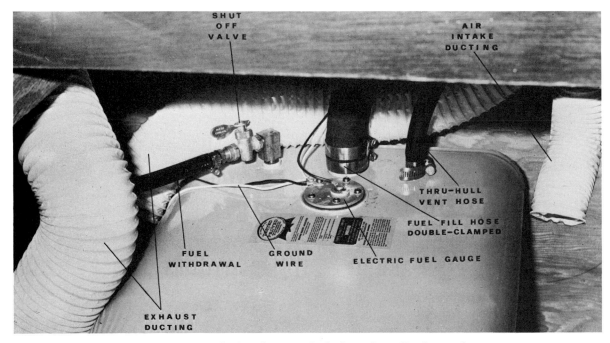

The proper installation of a permanent fuel tank system includes a shut-off valve on the fuel withdrawal line; double clamping on the fuel fill hose, a thru-hull vent, a grounded remote fuel gauge, an anti-siphon valve, and adequate compartment ventilation.

For positive protection against static electricity sparking, a bared end of the ground wire is fastened to the deck plate filler opening.

The other end of the ground wire is placed under the double clamps and a bared end of inserted between the hose and the tank fill neck.

systems. Here are key features to check:

Fuel system

Metal tank approved for marine use.

Copper fuel lines with flange connections for fixed fuel system, with a service valve and flexible section to the engine.

For outboards, flexible fuel lines made of approved material such as neoprene protected by bronze (not plated steel) mesh.

Check-valve at the tank.

Fuel-line filter for a permanent outboard fuel system. An inexpensive plastic fuel filter that can be inserted in the hose line of a portable outboard fuel tank is available.

Tank ground wire unless the fuel line from tank to engine connection is metallic.

Static discharge strip conductive hose at filler neck.

Screened overboard vent.

Insulation between tank and supports that is neither abrasive nor absorbent.

Air intake and exhaust venting with blower that will clear gas fumes from engine hatch, under decks, or wherever fumes can collect.

Flame arrestor for inboard-engine exhaust.

Cooling System

This maintains proper engine operating temperature; faulty functioning may cause serious overheating and major engine damage. Points to check are:

Water pump: Listen for whine and whistle in pump operation. Inspect the seals. Lubricate according to the manufacturer's directions. On an inboard engine, check the drive V belt and replace when it starts to wear, adjusting belt tension after the first hour of use.

Water hoses and clamps: Inspect for heat damage and cracks. Overheating during long runs can result from residue collected inside hoses; loosen clamps, remove hose and ream out with a dipstick. Replace faulty clamps with stainless-steel clamps. Keep the clamps tight.

Electrical System

The electrical system supplies engine ignition, lights, electric power controls and more sophisticated equipment on larger boats. The smallest outboard motors have simple magneto ignition with no need for a storage battery. Larger outboards and inboards have automotive-type battery ignition or capacitor-discharge (CD) ignition with an alternator. Internal ignition problems, certainly in the CD systems, should be taken to an expert because of precise settings and special equipment required. But most ignition problems are basically simple:

Check all connections to make sure they are clean and tight.

Check all exposed wires; look for cracks or rubbing damage.

Remove spark plugs and look for heavy carbon or burned electrodes.

Check the battery for a strong spark by grounding an insulated wire from a terminal to the engine block. If the battery is weak, you can try to start an electric-starting outboard by rope crank.

Check the ignition switch with a 12V test light at the input terminal. If it is out, use a jumper wire to get started.

Look at the fuse in the starter circuit.

Keep your fuse board and connections clean.

Remove and check the distributor or magneto cap and rotor. Look for cracks and burning. Use dielectric spray and try starting again.

Recreation Rooms

Remodeling a poorly used basement or garage area into a cheerful playroom for family use is one of the most rewarding home-improvement jobs. You need not duplicate any of these rooms but every one of them has at least one idea to offer that will help you plan your own procedure.

There is one thing that nearly all recreation-room projects have in common—a noise-transmission problem. Many a homeowner has transformed part of a dingy basement into a cheery family activity room, and then discovered too late that he has not protected the rest of his home from the noise generated in the new room.

Sometimes the homeowner deliberately ignores the problem when he builds, because one of the major misconceptions regarding noise control is that expensive, massive construction with dense materials is the only way to reduce the noise to

The home craftsman who designed this recreation room escaped the basement look by using outdoor siding material for walls, window-curtaining a pair of large artifical-light wells and including fluorescent fixtures in the suspended ceiling.

acceptable levels. Actually you can achieve acceptable noise control with economical frame structures surfaced with such readily available materials as softwood plywood, and easily built by home craftsmen. This type of construction lends itself easily to building two primary elements in noise control: motion-damping wall material combinations and isolated air spaces in floor and wall assemblies.

Plywood and gypsum board are useful in this type of construction because the large panels reduce the number of joints and cracks that can leak the airborne noises generated by voices, television and traffic. Plywood is a good foundation for acoustical tile ceilings and is an exceptionally good base for resilient floor coverings, such as carpeting, that muffle the impact noises of footfalls and fallen objects.

Recreation Rooms

Of course, no material can give good noise control if proper construction practices are not followed and details carefully watched. Sound leaks around doors can be sealed with weatherstripping. Piping that might carry structural vibrations can be caulked. Effective wall and floor assemblies can control airborne and impact noise. But all of this careful construction can be rendered ineffective if care is not taken to modify some common construction practices which create flanking sounds paths such as pass-through heating ducts, back-to-back electrical and plumbing outlets and joist spaces that are not blocked at partitions.

Family playroom takes advantage of above-ground location of one wall to provide a generous window. Room was floored, curtained, paneled for less than $200 by using tough but inexpensive vinyl-asbestos tile for floors, warm and woody looking prefinished hardboard (set off by decorative black-iron hinges) for all four walls.

Courtesy of Masonite

Courtesy of Western Wood Products Association.

If there's no place in basement, attic or garage for a new playroom, you may wish to convert a patio. This one was enclosed by the use of an impressive radial-beam system that preserves the original circular shape and western hemlock wood paneling. White paint renews the old patio corner fireplace.

As a playroom remodeler you will be especially concerned with sound transmission through the upstairs floor that serves as the basement room's ceiling. The basement partitions also will be a concern if there are bedrooms or a study in the basement. The typical unfinished basement ceiling with bare joists topped by the upstairs floor has a sound transmission classification of about 30, which as an acoustical engineer's measurement means that someone upstairs talking over the buzz of an electric razor can be understood fairly well in the basement. At that rate, a downstairs party would disrupt the sleep of anyone upstairs. An economical basement ceiling treatment that can help reduce sound transmission from above and help absorb the sounds created in the basement consists of simply nailing 1/4 inch plywood directly to the ceiling joists as a base for acoustical tile. The resilient plywood helps break up the sound path, and the acoustical tile helps absorb the sound that otherwise would bounce around the room. A number of treatments are possible when it is desired to isolate the upper floor from the basement. One system tested by the American Plywood Association is so effective that it can boost the sound transmission classification to 48, a level where loud speech is reduced to a point where it is barely audible at peak intensity, and heavy footfalls become muffled thuds.

This uncomplicated ceiling system is worth consideration by basement remodelers seeking to control the noise that will be generated in a new family room. The plywood panels and strips form the resilient base for other ceiling coverings, one of the essentials in good noise control systems. This one reduces the sound of loud voices to a barely audible level. Beginning with existing floor joists, sub-floor and finish floor, this system places a sound-blocking resilient layer between the bottom of the joists and the

basement room. Glass-fiber insulation is first stapled between the joists, then $1/4$ inch plywood panels are nailed on with the face grain parallel to the joist direction. Two-inch-wide strips of $1/4$ inch plywood are tacked or cemented to the panels parallel to the joists and mid-way between them, and a $1/2$ inch gypsum board is attached with screws that pass through both plywood layers. It is important that the two-inch strips be located between joists to take advantage of the sound-deadening resilience afforded by nailing the plywood panels with their face grain parallel to the joists. Additional noise control, especially sound absorption within the basement, can be had with this system by installing acoustical tile on the basement ceiling. Carpeting on the upstairs floor will greatly diminish impact noise.

Use of ground-floor space makes possible some features not available to basement remodelers: a door directly to outside, and dining space easily reached from the kitchen.

Courtesy of Masonite

One of the more efficient systems of reducing noise transmission through the walls of an activity room is an uncomplicated structure of staggered studs which reduces to a minimum the physical connections between two wall surfaces. Staggered studs of this wall system are the key to its noise control ability, creating a structural separation of wall surfaces that dampens sound waves. An ordinary wall system connects walls to both sides of the studs, creating a mechanical linkage that transmits noise from room to room. Loud voices on one side of the wall become whispers on the other side. Additonal noise con-

trol is possible with this system by weaving glass fiber insulation between the studs.

Constructing this wall starts with installing 2 x 6 inch top and bottom wall plates. Regular 2 x 4 studs are spaced 24 inches on centers and nailed flush with one side of the plates. Then a second row of studs is spaced 24 inches on centers between the studs of the first row and nailed flush against the other side of the plates. This study system effectively breaks the physical connection that occurs in standard walls where both surfaces are secured to the same studs.

Fireplaces are attractive additions to remodeled basements. This one which looks so much like brick is, like the "cork" beside it, a realistic Masonite hardboard reproduction.

Courtesy of Masonite

Recreation Rooms

BEFORE: Not quite a shop and hardly a lounge, this basement room was not worth the promising space it occupied.

Each row of studs is covered first with a lining of ³/₈ inch standard-grade plywood applied vertically with 6-penny common nails. The nails are spaced 6 inches on centers along the edges and 12 inches on centers along intermediate framing.

Nail heads are dimpled into the plywood to eliminate any possible interference with the next layer of material.

Over the plywood is installed a surface of ⁵/₈ inch gypsum board applied vertically, with joints offset 12 inches from those of the underlying plywood. No nails are used to secure the gypsum board; instead, it is laminated to the plywood with ³/₈ inch beads of panel adhesive applied with a caulking gun continuously around the perimeter of the gypsum panel and 16 inches on centers vertically. Joints are taped in the standard way.

A wall like this has a sound transmission classification of 47, and it can reduce loud speech to a barely audible level. It can be turned into an attractive finished wall (for which the accompanying photographs offer a multitude of ideas) by painting or by paneling with lumber, prefinished plywood or prefinished hardboard. *SEE ALSO WOOD PANELING.*

AFTER: Delicate details in decorating please the eye in this new room — but its most appealing assets are the soft, foam-backed carpet (easily laid by anyone, without need of adhesives or tack strips) and the Cushiontone ceiling, both of which help reduce noise.

Courtesy of Armstrong

Recreational Vehicles

All recreational vehicles offer their users a bed for the night and some way to carry and prepare food, that rolls along with them. RVs of all types free their owners from dependence upon hotels/motels and restaurants and save them from the bills that go with them. They all offer the pleasures of living close to the outdoors and of spending nights as well as days in the great national parks and other places of natural beauty. All recreational vehicles offer the pleasure of daily meeting with other RV owners.

PICKUP COVERS

Costing the least and, inevitably, offering the least in space and luxury are the little shells or caps that fit onto pickup trucks. For the camper-traveler who already owns a pickup truck, or has reason to acquire one, any one of these covers provides a conversion into a camping device at a fraction of the cost of most rigs. Since generally the covers are easy on and easy off, other use of the pickup truck is not hampered. In fact, many owners simply leave the covers on, removing camping equipment to turn their pickups into daily-use vehicles in which equipment or merchandise is protected from weather or casual theft. At least one model, a vinyl-coated metal framework, folds and pushes flat against the back of the cab, so you can still use the truck for hauling and have the shell ready for instant use.

Camping under a pickup cover is only a little better than sleeping in a tent. It is protection from snakes because it is off the ground, and neither rain nor snow will disrupt your sleeping comfort. It is nothing like having the comfort of a motor home or trailer or even a van conversion when night comes. For this reason use of pickup covers is mostly limited to sportsmen and persons taking short trips.

For many people, the biggest advantage of this setup is that you are driving a vehicle which can go into the roughest back country, and off the road into areas completely unavailable to all other recreational vehicles. A station wagon may provide the same basic contained shelter, but it is neither as rugged nor as economical. A pickup with shell, including some deluxe fittings, is still less than half the price of a station wagon.

The chief objection to the pickup-shell combination is that you cannot stand up, even in the ones having high-rise covers which go up four feet above side-height. Pickup-shell owners usually cook out of doors over a propane or gasoline stove during good weather and carry along a Sterno for use inside on bad days. A better arrangement might be to invest in one of the coffee-soup making containers which hooks over the window ledge and is plugged into a cigarette lighter while you drive.

Another objection to the pickup-shell combination is that with some models you have to climb over the tailgate. Look for one with a door much like one in your own home. It may not be more than 48 inches high, however, so you will have to watch your head. A few have double or offset doors. Before you buy one of these models give the door a good tryout to see how easily it works, whether you can get in or out in a hurry, and, if it is a liftup type which hinges at the top, whether you will have to hold it while you are crawling in or whether it has the necessary strong metal supports which keep it in place after it is up.

Do-it-Yourself with a Kit

You can draw your own plans and assemble materials from your own sources. You can buy plans for a few dollars; or you can buy a kit which will turn your truck into a home of sorts. Beware of the word "kit", especially if the price seems unusually low. Find out what it includes. Some include instructions, basic aluminum panels for the sides, and assorted hardware and glue, but they leave out all the expensive items such as insulation, lumber, window materials and electrical equipment which you will have to buy at the lumber and hardware store, bringing the cost to more than three times what you paid for the kit. Putting it all together can take a week or more of labor, something you have to count as part of the cost.

Recreational Vehicles

There are good kits, too, but they are not cheap, and they do require skill in assembling beyond that of the ordinary do-it-yourselfer. You might find you have invested several hundred dollars in a shell kit, plus your time, and you still have an unsatisfactory cover which cannot be sold when you sell your truck.

SLIDE-IN TRUCK CAMPERS

The descriptive word "slide in" makes this type of RV sound simple to use, but it is not all that easy. A slide-in is not a camping conversion which you casually push onto the back of your pickup when you want to take off for a vacation. It weighs well over a ton and requires special jacks plus quite a lot of skill to place the truck in exactly the right position so the slide-in unit settles snuggly and in perfect alignment with the cargo bed.

There are definite advantages to owning a slide-in rather than just a cover for a pickup. First, there is enough headroom and space for a fairly comfortable kitchen and sleeping quarters. Second, there is space for storage cabinets and closets. A few slide-ins even include bathroom facilities. Third, the over-cab extension (the reason why this type of RV has the nickname "turtle") gives additional sleeping, lounging, or viewing space for two people, usually children who enjoy watching the road through the high front window.

Truck plus slide-on camper make a rugged pair to go off the road to a scenic campsite such as this one.

Courtesy of General Motors Corp.

Slide-ins come in two types: one with a rear section that hangs beyond the back edge of the cargo bed; and another which extends only to the end of the cargo bed. This type has a rear door, feasible because of removal of the tailgate. The safer version of the two is the hang-over version which distributes the load more evenly, avoiding the more unstable top-heavy version which ends at the cargo bed. Even with the hang-over type, there is a problem. All that weight at the back puts a strain on the rear axle. One company has solved this problem by adding a special axle to take the weight imbalance. Equipped in this way, there is less tendency to sway or lean, and the vehicle will hold the road even if a tire blows out.

When you look for a slide-in, do a lot of comparison shopping, and talk to other campers who own them. Find out what features make for easy maintenance; whether there are special safety devices; which ones have the best insulation. For example, one slide-in now uses a lightweight nonbulky insulation which is more than three times as efficient as the older types still being used by most manufacturers. What is the interior like? Shag carpet looks elegant, but indoor-outdoor carpet that can be hosed off is easier to keep clean. What kind of mattress is on the bed? Lightweight polyfoam takes many pounds of load off the tires.

Is there an escape door in the cab-over? This is an especially important feature if children ride in that area. Two small children were asphyxiated by fire when a rear-end accident caused a camper to catch fire at the back, the only exit.

Readymade Covers

Look for fiberglass. It is resistant to almost every hazard which attacks and out wears the aluminum and wood-framed models. Rust, road tar and soil from weather changes do not affect it. There are no leaking seams, because a fiberglass cover is seamless. There is no repainting, because the color, if any, is inherent in the material. The only disadvantage is that fiberglass is heavier than aluminum, and, as with any material, there are good and bad qualities of fiberglass. It is better to pay a little more and buy from a reputable firm.

If you choose something other than fiberglass, it probably should be a heavy grade aluminum. Wood is attractive, but, just like the old wooden station wagon bodies, it requires a lot of upkeep and, in the long run, deteriorates until it can no longer be repaired or brought back to its original condition.

EXTRAS AND ACCESSORIES FOR A PICKUP-SHELL

Options are many, but some are almost essential, such as good sliding window with screens, a roof ventilation unit and an interior light. The smaller the cover, the more ventilation you will need. You are more likely to find roof vents on covers that go up four feet above side-height of the pickup.

Other extras include running lights, luggage compartments, decorative panels for exterior and interior, insulated side panels, white plastic ceiling and decorative trim. Safety glass in side and rear window should be a must, although it is not yet required by law.

You can also buy a conversion kit which will turn your pickup into a camper with stove, sink, table, storage cabinets, and foldup bunks. It would be better to go to some other kind of RV if you want these features.

CHASSIS-MOUNTED TRUCK CAMPERS

The chassis-mounted camper is basically a combination between a steel truck bed and a portable home. This is because the two are permanently welded together, unlike the pickup with a shell or a slide-on camping unit which can be disassembled.

A truck camper has several big advantages: It is a convenient vacation cottage wherever you can drive and park it. Two or more people who do not mind togetherness can enjoy a holiday for about the same cost as staying home. For a sportsman who uses it in all four seasons and takes it into rugged country, there is nothing more reliable than a sturdy truck-based unit. The camp is always ready to use, even if you arrive at your destination in the early hours of the morning or during a cloudburst. On a cold morning

Chassis-mount shown here is a sturdy chopped van and mini motor home with a 125-inch wheelbase.

Interior of these RV vehicles contains beds, cooking facilities, and storage facilities.

you can have a warm breakfast in a warm room before going out to hunt or fish in chillier temperatures. It is sturdy enough to carry extra equipment such as a bicycle, boat, motor bike or sports equipment.

If you already own a camping unit, then you must choose a truck with capacity to carry it. If you own the truck, its load-carrying capacity is set and it may take quite a bit of shopping to find a camping unit of the right size and shape.

Weight is the key word in solving the chassis-mount problem. Weight watching involves these three factors: load capacity of the truck, weight of the camper's body with gasoline and water tanks filled to capacity and the weight of everything you plan to put in the camper.

Neither the truck nor the camper manufacturer can be blamed if you overload and take the rig on the road. First, if you own the truck, you must know its weight capacity. Find this by looking for a label with Gross Vehicle Weight Rating. You will probably find it on the forward portion of the left-hand door opening. If, on the other hand, you own the camper and are buying a truck to be mated with it, you will need to know the weight of the camper. This you can get from a label on the unit, from literature you may have or by writing the manufacturer. You will also need to know what that weight means. A camping unit bought as a shell will have quite a different weight from one which you bought

with built-ins such as refrigerator, shower, water heater, stove, beds. Do not forget to add in such items as tools, spare tire and optional features such as rear step bumper, radio, air conditioner and extra springs.

Second, figure the maximum number of extras you are likely to carry at any one time. If you carry several bicycles on a family trip you might be adding only another couple hundred pounds. If you add a boat or motorcycle, at times, you could be putting on a thousand pounds. Should you go on a long trip you might be carrying several hundred pounds of food and water.

Third, how many people will you carry? If yours is to be strictly a family-used vehicle, and your family is a man, woman, and two small children, the weight might run a total of about 400 lbs. If you use the vehicle for your hunting gang, each one weighing in at about 200 lbs., the human load could jump to 1,000 lbs. or more.

Fourth, consider what you might add in the future: no one goes in more for accessories and those extra comfort features than the family which owns a camper. Here are a few items which truck campers often add: extra mirrors, a second battery, flares, fire extinguisher, intercom system between cab and camper, crawl-through boot from cab to camper, additional

Van conversion has a fiberglass top. It will not leak, adds little weight to the camper, and is easy to maintain.

water and gasoline tanks and emergency equipment. Chances are you will always be carrying a heavier load than you realize.

Matching up truck with camping unit and custom equipment means there is no such thing as a standard model or firm price on any chassis-mounted rig. There are not only choices among manufacturers, but each one has many sizes and models. In general, most people buy a ³/₄ ton truck which can safely handle the usual load. When it comes to extras, it is good to choose a rig with heavy-duty springs, heavy shock absorbers, larger than usual axles, large capacity radiator and oversize tires. A unit carrying five tons or more should have dual rear wheels.

A truck camper is no cinch to drive, especially when there are high winds and/or heavy traffic. If you are fond of desert travel, wind conditions can be so extreme at times that truck campers are grounded. But for rough country, you can not beat its adaptability to difficult terrain. And at least, as of now, no special license is required to drive a camper. Furthermore, passengers can ride in the coach, something prohibited to trailer owners.

VAN CONVERSIONS

Converting a van or microbus is an easy do-it-yourself project. For a few hundred dollars and quite a bit of labor you can have any kind of minihome you want. All that is really needed,

1461

Courtesy of Vanguard Industries

Low-profile camping trailer can easily be towed by a compact car. It backs easily, will not obstruct drivers vision through rear window, cleans and maintains easily, is small enough to be stored in a home garage.

Courtesy of General Motors Corp.

Camping trailer ready to go, no problem to a small car, because the lightweight trailer has almost no effect on the driveability of the car or the gas consumption.

Courtesy of General Motors Corp.

Interior of an RV is luxury living indeed. In addition to living, dining, and cooking areas, this one has a separate bedroom for a daytime retreat and privacy at night.

however, is a platform to hold a foam mattress (or a rear seat which unfolds to form a platform), a table hinged to a side panel, some storage cabinets, a dry sink, ice box, and camp stove. Most vans have no standup space, which is probably just as well, since it is safer to cook outside. A fold-down table attached to a door makes a good surface for the stove, and also can be used for a wash basin.

Most owners, of course, want headroom. This has led to a variety of conversions with pushup, popup and tiltup expandable tops, many of which can be lowered when the van is on the

Deluxe motor home shown here is a beauty, easy to maintain and drive, but it will cost upwards of $15,000 with all the luxury options such as the roof-mounted air conditioner. A home like this serves nicely for a retired couple who like to move from one climate to another, or for a young couple whose jobs change often.

move. It is a distinct advantage to own one with an expandable top, because it is then possible to park it in an ordinary garage.

Space of every kind is definitely so limited in a van that it is suitable for only a couple of people to camp in comfortably. Most vans have no in-sulation and no room for a heater, so thay can be damp and chilly, especially at night. A couple of people sleeping in an uninsulated van produce enough moisture to cause a steady drip of water from the ceiling during the night. If you are thinking about a van conversion, you would also be wise to take the claim "sleeps five or more"

Courtesy of General Motors Corp.

A van conversion of this type has a raised roof, fixed in place, so there is plenty of head room. The fiberglass top is leakproof and weather resistant, and adds little weight to the car.

with some of disbelief. Those people had better be either short or children, and should not mind sleeping in a small bunk or a hammock.

The van conversion does have one big thing going for it. It drives easily, is maneuverable in heavy traffic, and parks in a space smaller than that needed by an ordinary station wagon. It makes a good second car, and many families make do with one as an only car. If the conversion outfit is easily removable and there is a back seat that can be replaced, the van is an ordinary passenger car again.

You pay for what you get, and what you pay for is likely to be anywhere from $5,000 to $8,000. For a custom conversion job you could easily go to $15,000. Unless you plan to keep the van quite a few years, you will do better financially if you stick to a conversion with the necessities.

MOTOR HOMES

Essentially a motor home is a self-powered house trailer. It can be as short as 15 feet or as long as 36 feet, up to 8 feet wide, and contains every convenience you would normally have in an apartment or vacation house. A motor home can be a comfortable only home for a retired couple who like to summer in the north and winter on

the desert, or for a couple whose employment requires frequent moves. It is a good vacation vehicle for a family who wants the comforts of home in rather far-out spots. It does not make much sense financially for the family who will use it only a couple of weeks a year. Some families are sharing ownership, each signing up for the period wanted, and dividing repair and upkeep costs. The only thing wrong with this is that most people want to take their vacations at the same time, and the motor home might not be used in winter, especially in a harsh climate.

The problem of what to do with the motor home when it is not being used has become serious enough so one manufacturer is selling a prefab garage designed for a motor home. The price tag is $2500 erected on your land. The ordinary garage will not hold one, and some cities will not permit owners to park their vehicles on the street.

A Motor Home to Suit Your Family

In some ways choosing a motor home resembles planning a custom house. You decide what you can afford, choose an architect (in this case the manufacturer of the basic unit) and choose the builder (the dealer). The dealer is the one who helps you arrive at the kind of "package" you want to live in while you are on the road.

You can find out, in advance, of course, about such features as insulation. Sprayed on foam polyurethane $3/4$ inch thick has twice the insulation value of fiberglass. It also seals out road noise. What kind of rear suspension does it have and why? How much ground clearance? What kind of service can you expect when you are on the road and have a breakdown? What if you breakdown late at night or on a Sunday afternoon? Some dealers offer help through a toll-free number, where you will get the name and location of someone set up to give after-hour assistance.

In a motor home (as in all RVs) check interior fittings by opening and closing cabinet doors, folding and unfolding beds, try out the mattress, see whether the sink is large enough to hold a moderate sized pan, how easily can two people move past each other, how easy is it to get from front driving area to the back, if there are swivel seats in driving compartment, what kind of visibility through the windows and what kind of privacy and how good the ventilation is.

Courtesy of General Motors Corp.

A 23 foot integrally-designed motor home shown has such safety and convenience features as front wheel drive, independent rear suspension, six-wheel brake system and self-leveling device for parking on uneven terrain. Noise level is kept low on the road because there is a specially treated one-inch thick exterior grade plywood floor and the entire body is rubber-insulated from the chassis.

Courtesy of The Coleman Co.

A motor home is more than an RV. In an emergency, should electricity go out or a disaster strike, it is a self-contained living unit.

A deluxe motor home may be offered at a base price of around $15,000, but by the time you get some of the desirable special options, there will be another $5,000 added on. Do not be misled by the basic figure. Figure the extras from the start.

Motor homes are a parking problem in cities. If you plan to stop often in towns along your route, you would do well to park a half mile from the business district and walk the rest of the way. Residents of the town, and often the parking policeman, seem to have a built-in antagonism toward any vehicle which takes up two parking places and a part of the width of the street. Even with power steering, it is not an easy job to back a motor home into a tight space.

TENT TRAILERS

The typical tent trailer is a flat box lower in height than the vehicle towing it when it is on the road. The box and top, usually of aluminum or fiberglass, pops open and outward, providing beds with foam mattresses on opposite sides of the living and cooking space, all about a foot above the ground. Screened windows all around and screen doors, built-in kitchen equipment, and storage areas make a Tent Trailer comfortable and an inexpensive way to vacation. The tent itself opens almost automatically, sometimes with the release of a few catches, sometimes with a button and battery system.

When you travel with a tent trailer your vehicle is not a captive. You just fold out your home on wheels and drive off when you feel like it. Another advantage is that the whole rig is light enough so a couple of adults can maneuver it to a desirable site without hitching it again to the car which pulled it.

TRAVEL TRAILERS

The next step up from the tent trailer is the travel trailer. It can be either a two or four-wheeler, is a permanent living space, light enough in weight to be easily towable, usually less than 20 feet long, and is available in some models for less than a thousand dollars. It can be hauled easily on the highway, parked easily, and of course, is an independent structure which you can leave

Courtesy of General Motors Corp.

A good sized pickup can haul this rig. The cab is large enough for 6 to 8 passengers and the trailer large enough for a permanent home. Dual rear wheels on trailer add stability and the carrying capacity to use this combo under rough and off-road conditions. With the trailer, the pickup is a generous passenger vehicle plus small truck.

behind at a campground when you want to tour in your car.

Today's travel trailers are aluminum or fiberglass with lightweight foam insulation. With the trend toward more compact cars, a number of companies have come out with trailers easily towable by small vehicles. In other words, they do not carry a generator, large water supply, and have a complete bathroom. Self-containment adds to both the cost and weight.

One complaint often made against travel trailers is that their height blocks the view behind. A few companies have solved this problem with a hi-lo design. The permanent roof-ceiling (often fiberglass) is adjustable. On the road it drops down, giving a low silhouette which eliminates wind buffeting. In the up position at the campground, there is plenty of headroom. The chief lack in the hi-lo trailer type is storage space.

The hi-lo trailer has soft sides, which means not as much warmth and not as much protection against theft when walls are in the up position. The canvas deteriorates after a few years, especially if the vehicle is not cleaned carefully after each trip and stored inside a garage.

If you buy a telescoping trailer, be sure to check

out the raising and lowering mechanism carefully. The manual method is slow and somewhat difficult; a hydraulic lifting mechanism is fine provided it is foolproof. When you are on the road and want to stop for a rest or a meal, it could be just too much trouble to use the telescoping trailer if the raising requires much strength.

SAFE TOWING

Safe towing any RV begins with proper equipment. Whether you are hauling a 36-foot trailer or a 6-foot tent trailer you need the proper equipment. Car, trailer and hitch must be matched.

The class of a trailer is determined by its *Gross Trailer Weight,* which is the total weight of a trailer ready to roll. It includes the base weight of the trailer itself, plus drinking water, bottled gas, household equipment, personal and recreational equipment.

Tongue Load is the weight the trailer tongue adds to the rear of the car by pushing down on the hitch. It affects the stability and handling of your outfit. The combination of tongue load and trailer weight determines the type of hitch to be selected. Success and safety are determined by correct matching of load with hitch.

Recreational Vehicles

An over-loaded trailer is a safety hazard. If you already own a trailer, you can check its gross weight with a trip to the scales. Your dealer or the nearest Highway Patrol office can tell you where to take it.

To determine gross trailer weight, weigh both the trailer and your car. Weigh the towing vehicle separately. The difference between the two is gross trailer weight. To determine tongue weight, disconnect the trailer and place the tongue only on the scale with the coupler at hitch ball height. If the tongue load exceeds 15% of the gross trailer weight, shift extra gear and camping equipment rearward to the degree necessary to achieve recommended tongue load for your trailer class. If less than 10%, shift load forward.

Select Proper Hitch

A *Class I trailer* is one with a frontal area (width x height) up to 25 sq. ft. The static tongue load is 200 lbs. or less and fully loaded, the trailer weighs up to 2,000 lbs. Use a nonequalizing hitch. This is a simple ball-type mounted to frame or body. Ford Motor Company does not recommend the use of a hitch which attaches to the car axle. Use a multi-clamp hitch only on a rental trailer. It should be attached to bumper mounting brackets. A single point clamping type is not acceptable. A ball-type should be used only for light weight trailers such as tent trailers.

A *Class II trailer* is one with a static tongue load up to 500 lbs. Fully loaded, the trailer weight may be 2000 to 3500 lbs. Use a load-equalizing hitch to prevent front end lift and rear end sag on towing vehicle.

A *Class III trailer* is one with 700 lbs maximum and the fully loaded trailer weight is 3500 to 6000 lbs. This type of hitch is bolted to the underbody vertical frame section at several points, distributing the car trunk and trailer tongue load to the car front axle and trailer axle(s) allowing uniform weight distribution and easier handling.

Sway Control, provided by a special device on the equalizing hitch, is recommended for any trailer above 4000 lbs. Anti-sway devices, however, are not compatible with trailers equipped with surge-type brakes. An equalizing hitch requires tension adjustment to establish proper vehicle attitude. A trailer or hitch dealer can show you how.

TRAILER TOWING SAFETY TIPS

Select the right towing equipment. Electric or surge type brakes are best. A safety chain is essential. (The law requires it in most states.) Rear overload springs improve riding and handling a heavily loaded trailer. Dual mirrors are a *must* but should be disconnected and removed when your trailer is parked to avoid accidents.

Because trailer wheels will be closer than the car wheels to the inside of a turn, compensate by avoiding soft shoulders and driving beyond a normal turning point before starting your turn.

When another vehicle passes, hold a straight course, or your trailer might fishtail. When you are passing, signal well in advance, allow more distance than you actually think you need and make sure you have ample clearance before cutting back in.

Keep your rig a safe distance behind the vehicle ahead. For each ten miles an hour of speed, allow the distance of at least one length of your car and trailer combined.

Stopping distance is about the same for a car towing a trailer equipped with brakes as for a car without a trailer. If your trailer has no brakes, allow more time and distance. Stop smoothly and very gradually.

When climbing a hill, use a lower transmission gear to reduce engine overheating. If the engine overheats, pull off the road and run the engine at fast idle, but do not shut it off. Proceed up the hill in low as soon as the engine reaches normal temperature.

On a downgrade, shift to second gear for extra braking. On a very steep downgrade, come to a halt and shift into first before proceeding downhill.

1468

Courtesy of Turtle Top, Inc.

Maxi-van shown has been turned in a large camping vehicle by adding a "Turtle" top. There are four separate floor plans to allow you to customize your van to meet the needs of your own family. This top, constructed of plastic reinforced with fiberglass has an inner liner and large forward stoarge area of cab. Two bunks in top are available as options.

RVs and the Law.

Get a copy of the vehicle code for your state. Laws which apply to RVs of various sizes and weight are quite different from those which apply to passenger vehicles. Requirements for safety equipment differ, too. Since most RVs do a lot of roaming, it is not sufficient just to know the law in your own state.

Before each trip you had better get a rundown on the requirements of any state you will be driving through. Ignorance of the law will not protect you against a fine or arrest.

Find out, also, what insurance you will need. The policy on your passenger car does not extend to the trailer you may be hauling. If you are in a wreck it may not cover destruction of equipment you are carrying in or on top of your motor home. Liability insurance requirements also vary greatly throughout the United States. You need to be prepared for maximum liability in all states where you drive. A safe trip in an RV depends as much upon the owner as it does upon the vehicle itself. Here are a series of tips before you leave your driveway.

Check tires for proper inflation pressure (cold) and for possible signs of excessive wear.

Check the valves on the propane gas bottles to assure they are turned off for travel. (Make sure there are no open flames or pilot lights burning while traveling.)

Check all running, brake and turn signal lights for proper operation. If you have a trailer, do this after you hitch up since the electrical connector acts as a ground between the two vehicles.

Hitch the trailer to the car properly. This is essential for good towing. It is recommended that you have the hitch installation performed by a factory-trained installer familiar with your make hitch.

Connect the safety chains, breakaway switch and the electrical connector. Do not forget to crank up the front jackscrew and stow the jack wheel in a convenient location. As you start your trip, check to assure your trailer brakes are functioning and adjust them if necessary. If you have a friction type antisway device, do not lubricate friction surfaces.

Carry only essential items. Consider leaving those items at home which can be purchased as you travel (food, for instance). Before a trip, check your equipment and eliminate those items you never seem to use.

Place heavy articles, canned goods, tools, etc., as low to the floor as possible. This helps keep the center of gravity low so your rig is not top heavy, makes it more stable — especially on curves. Balance the load from side to side. Distribute heavy items so that one side does not carry more weight than the other.

Place lightweight items, bedding, clothing, etc., in high cabinets or in the cab-over section of your pickup camper. Secure all doors and drawers against opening in route. Nothing should be left loose in the living area, to cause damage or changes in weight distribution.

Keep emergency items, flashlights, flares, first aid kits, etc. in a place where they can be reached quickly.

Red Oak Wood

Red oak wood is a hard, stiff, highly shock resistant hardwood. It has a large amount of shrinkage during drying, and seasoning must be done quite carefully to avoid warping. Red oak wood is difficult to work with hand tools. The gray-brown heartwood has tints of red throughout the grain and also has a low resistance to decay. Although red oak has many of the same characteristics of white oak, red oak wood differs in the fact that it is extremely porous due to the lack of tyloses.

Red oak wood can be used for millwork, boxes, crates, caskets, coffins, boats, agricultural implements, woodenware and inside trim. Because of its durability, red oak wood can be used for flooring. And, if treated with a preservative, it can function as crossties, fence posts and mine timbers. *SEE ALSO WOOD IDENTIFICATION.*

Reducer

A reducer, which may be called by other names, is available for all types of pipes. It is used to

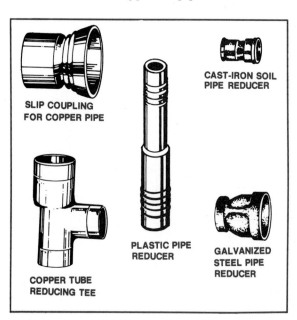

SLIP COUPLING
FOR COPPER PIPE

CAST-IRON SOIL
PIPE REDUCER

PLASTIC PIPE
REDUCER

GALVANIZED
STEEL PIPE
REDUCER

COPPER TUBE
REDUCING TEE

change the diameter in a straight run pipe, and as a fitting that joins the same type of differently sized pipe. *SEE ALSO PIPE FITTINGS.*

Reducing Tee

A reducing tee is a copper tube and galvanized steel pipe fitting. Besides joining different sized tubing in a straight run, it has a branch joining the straight run at a right angle. *SEE ALSO PIPE FITTINGS.*

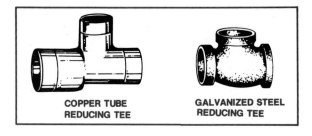

COPPER TUBE
REDUCING TEE

GALVANIZED STEEL
REDUCING TEE

Red Wood

Red wood is a decay and termite resistant, easily seasoned, even grained, fine textured hardwood. It shapes and retains the shape well. It is moderately hard as well as moderately strong and holds paint well. Red wood shrinks very little and is relatively free of knots and other defects. Probably the most distinctive feature of red wood is that it has no distinctive feel, taste or odor. Because of this feature, red wood can be separated from other woods that are very similar in appearance such as western red cedar with its distinctive odor. Red wood is also very durable and can be exposed to moisture and water. Another distinctive feature is that the uniformly deep, reddish-brown heartwood does not contain resin canals. Its sapwood is nearly white.

Red wood can be used for paneling, house siding, sash, blinds, doors, outdoor furniture, tanks and general millwork. It can also be used for heavy construction such as bridges, trestles and framing for industrial building and homes.

Native to a small area along the Pacific Coast of California from 100 miles south of San Francisco to just beyond the border of Oregon, one tree has produced as much as 300,000 feet of board measure. Over one million board-feet of lumber has been obtained from a single acre. *SEE ALSO WOOD IDENTIFICATION.*

Reeding

Reeding is a wood design of raised parallel lines in convex or beaded form. It usually appears on molding. *SEE ALSO FURNITURE MAKING; MOLDING & TRIM.*

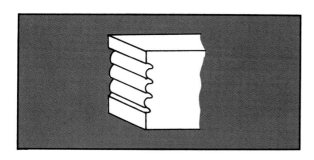

Reel Lawnmowers
[SEE LAWNMOWERS.]

Refinishing Floors

Refinishing a floor is necessary for an attractive appearance when the wood has become stained or scratched or if the present finish is blotchy. Paint remover, a strong solution of trisodium-phosphate and boiling water or a sander are the more common methods of removing a finish with sanding being the simplest and most popular. To achieve a clean surface, both a drum and disc sander are needed. Both may be rented along with the sandpaper from a hardware dealer. Drum sanders are not hard to operate, but do require careful controlling and constant motion to avoid uneven sanding and to keep the drum from grinding into the floor.

After the major areas have been sanded use the disc sander to get into corners and tight areas. Always work with the grain to prevent scratching or roughing the surface. Hand sand areas close to walls and under radiators where a disc or drum sander will not reach. When all sanding is completed, vacuum the floor thoroughly.

FLOOR STAINING

The staining or coloring of a floor is usually done first. The most common methods of wood staining are done with pigmented wiping stains, colored penetrating floor sealers, stains and colored varnishes. Each type of finish has its advantages and disadvantages. Both pigmented wiping stains and colored varnishes have some degree of resin. Water and nongrain-raising stains do not have a built-in finish. Colored penetrating finishes are a complete, one-coat system.

Pigmented wiping stains are applied with a rag and require additional drying time if they are finished with lacquer. Stain in cracks must dry completely or, when the lacquer is applied, the finish will flake and peel. Test the stain for the correct shade before rubbing it on the floor.

Colored penetrating sealers are usually available in a wide variety of colors. These sealers may be purchased or colors can be mixed with oil at home to form different shades.

Nongrain-raising and water stains give the clearest, most attractive permanent color without pigmentation in the wood. They work well under lacquer, shellacs, varnishes and penetrating finishes.

Experiment with colored varnishes before applying them to the floor. If dilution is necessary, use paint thinner or turpentine until the desired color is achieved. Use lacquer over this finish only after allowing it to dry for no less than three days.

After selecting the stain, apply it to the floor following the manufacturer's directions. Polish the floor with a buffer after it is dry. *SEE ALSO FLOOR FINISHES.*

Reflective Insulation

Reflective insulation, usually a foil-surfaced material or a metal foil, works by reflecting heat back into a room or to the outdoors. The value of reflective insulation is in the number of its reflecting surfaces, not in the material's surface.

Aluminum foil, an excellent conductor of heat, is available in sheets or corrugations on paper supports, in inexpensive rolls and in combination with gypsum board. The foil is laminated to the back of gypsum board so that the wallboard and insulation may be installed at one time. Multiple-spaced sheets of foil are effective as an accordion type of insulation. They come in flats which are opened to form spaces between surfaces during installation. Multiple layers of foil work on the principle of reflection and captive air space.

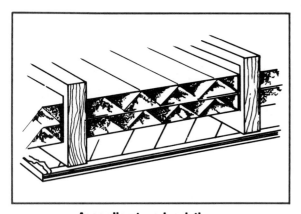

Accordion-type Insulation

Foil, as a reflective insulator, is mostly used between first-floor joists where there is no cellar, to prevent cold air at ground level from rising through the flooring. When used between wall studs, foil must form a tight seal where it is attached to framing members. For effectiveness, it should be recessed between framing in layers with air spaces, preferably $3/4$ inch or more in depth, between each layer. The installation of foil is similar to that of blanket insulation. However, foil has about $2/3$ the value of blanket, batt or loose fill insulation. One layer of foil is used in warm climates; two or three in colder areas. *SEE ALSO INSULATION.*

Refrigeration Appliances

The refrigeration appliances in a home differ widely in shape, design, and application, but basically they are all built around the mechanical refrigeration system. This system is a sealed unit which continuously makes use of the same material to move heat units which is powered by an electrical pump called a compressor.

Heat is a form of energy which cannot be destroyed, but we can move heat units from place to place. This is what the refrigeration system does. In the case of a freezer or refrigerator it moves the units from inside insulated compartments to the outside. You will feel this heat being displaced into the room through the warm air that flows underneath the refrigerator or freezer, or at the thin tubes that are located on the back of the unit. In the case of an air conditioner, when you walk by the outside of the unit and feel the blast of warm air coming out the outer unit, you are feeling the heat that is being removed from inside the room.

While these systems differ greatly in details that determine the temperatures at which they operate and the amount of heat that they are capable of removing, the principle is the same. By looking at the accompanying drawing you can see that the compressor is connected to two coils of tubing which are interconnected to form a complete closed circuit.

There is a negative pressure (vacuum) or low pressure on the side of the system known as the low side. On the opposite side of the system, high pressure exists and is known as the high side. Beginning at the point where the refrigerant enters the coil (known as the evaporator), the refrigerant enters this section as a liquid. Since this is a low pressure area, the boiling point is reduced from its normal level which is only 21 degrees below zero at atmospheric temperature and pressure. Most home refrigeration systems use a refrigerant known as dichlorodifluoromethane or refrigerant 12, most commonly known as R-12. Some systems, notably air conditioning systems, use a refrigerant known as R-22, monochloromonofluorethane, which has a boiling point of some 42 degrees below zero. In addition to their low boiling points, these refrigerants also have other desirable characteristics such as the fact that their boiling point is raised and lowered to a great extent by relatively low changes in pressure.

When the liquified refrigerant enters the low pressure area in the evaporator, it immediately begins to boil since the pressure is reduced below the normal level. As it boils, it evaporates and carries excess heat units with the vapor just as the steam does from a pan of water on the stove. As the evaporator coil becomes chilled, the liquid level moves farther along in the coil until the entire coil is frosted. The amount of refrigerant in the system determines the extent to which the evaporator frosting is carried with normal loads. The evaporator is the cold plate that is inside your refrigerator or freezer. If you listen very closely when the appliance is in operation, you will actually be able to hear the refrigerant boiling as it passes through this coil.

The vapor from the evaporate or coil now laden with heat units, comes into the compressor. Here it is pumped out again and into the condenser section. At the outlet end of the condenser, there is a tiny tube called a capillary tube which meters the flow of the refrigerant between the condenser and the evaporator. This tube causes a pressure differential to exist between the high and low sides of the system.

As the vapor travels through the condenser, two things begin to happen. First of all, the air circulating through and around the condenser coils tends to cool the refrigerant passing through. Second, the pressure is raised to a point that increases its boiling point to a level above that of the room temperature or that of the air flowing through the condenser. As these two factors begin to act upon the refrigerant, it begins to condense back into a liquid form. By the time it has traveled through the condenser, it has reached a point about a third of the way or so from the outlet end where the condenser tubing is full of liquid refrigerant. When the liquid reaches the capillary tube, it passes through the tiny opening and finally again enters the evaporator where it suddenly is exposed to the low pressure area and the cycle repeats itself.

Refrigerants don't wear out and in modern sealed systems (usually known as hermetic systems) even the compressors are welded shut and electrical terminals sealed with glass beads so that there is no possibility of refrigerant escaping. For this reason, unless a line is broken there is never any need to add more refrigerant. If refrigerant has to be added, there is a leak that must be found and repaired before the repair would be effective. All this is a job for a refrigeration technician. It takes special equipment with delicate gauges and vacuum pumps to remove all traces of moisture from the system to do this type of repair work.

Fortunately though, repairs within the system are the least likely type of problem that you might have with home refrigeration appliances. If you understand how a refrigeration system operates, you'll be better able to understand how each of these appliances operate and what you can do when something goes wrong with them.

Be sure to unplug the appliance before beginning any testing or inspection and watch out for sharp edges on cabinets. *SEE ALSO APPLIANCE REPAIR, MAJOR.*

Refrigerator Repair

The refrigerator is the most popular home appliance in existence. In fact, in America today there is slightly more than one refrigerator per household. Sales continue to increase, primarily because of new innovations and conveniences such as built-in automatic icemakers and frost-free systems.

The basic type of refrigerator is a single-door model that uses an evaporator to cradle or encir-

The drain pan on this single door refrigerator catches condesate water and also controls air flow within the refrigerator.

cle the food. The evaporator normally has a drip pan located below it to catch any condensate water when defrosting and to control the air currents that are within the refrigerator. A baffle is used on this drip pan which can be opened and closed to compensate for summer and winter temperatures. In the summer position the baffle is open and allows convection currents to flow more readily to the evaporator. In winter, the

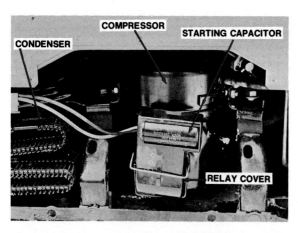

The compressor looks like a steel dome in this refrigeration compartment unit which has been removed from this refrigerator. The section of condenser on each side is the pre-cooler unit.

baffle can be closed to block some of these currents. The drip pan should never be removed since this tends to upset the balance of air circulation, causing the evaporator to run warm and the refrigerator section to run cold.

Some of the first automatic defrosting systems were made very much like this except they had a heater attached to the evaporator and a timer to turn the heater on and off. The heating element would sometimes melt or at least raise the temperature of some of the food within the freezer section, however, and soon it was apparent that some other type of system would have to be devised. This brought about the development of the split-evaporator system, where a plate was used in the refrigerator compartment to provide cooling for that section. The freezer compartment could then be insulated and set apart from the refrigerator section altogether. This evaporator was located toward the end of the freezer evaporator in the refrigeration cycle in most cases; that is, the liquid refrigerant would first flow through the freezer evaporator and then to the refrigerator compartment evaporator. The freezer compartment then often received its own door, and two-door refrigerators came into existance. In such systems the freezer is usually not a self-defrosting compartment; since doors are opened less frequently and less warm, moisture-laden air is allowed to enter, defrosting is not required so often.

The refrigerator evaporator may be defrosted by a timer and heater combination but the cycle-defrost method is much more common. In cycle-defrost systems a special thermostat is used. The

If a serpentine coil like this becomes iced in one particular area, clean it well using a solution of dishwater detergent (marked "safe for aluminum") and water. Oil from cans or waxed cartons can begin frost build-up.

sensing bulb is clamped near the end of the refrigerator evaporator.

This evaporator may take the shape of a serpentine coil across the top of the refrigerator, a fin and tube across the back wall or a flat plate with passage ways expanded into it to allow the refrigerant to pass. When the thermostat has reached the temperature determined by the setting on the dial, it turns the refrigerator compressor off just like any other thermostat. However, it will not restart the unit to begin another cooling cycle until the temperature on the evaporator plate has risen to 35 to 37 degrees. Since this is above the freezing point, it insures that all frost is melted from the evaporator. This defrost water or condensate water is carried away through a trough and often through a drain tube to a pan underneath the refrigerator in the motor compartment. In this pan air flow and heat from the condenser evaporates the moisture into the room air. Some food particles can remain, however, and the pan should be removed and cleaned about twice a year.

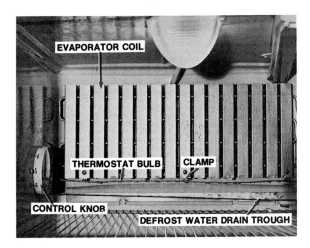

Thermostat bulb must be clamped tightly to the serpentine coil or flat coil on cycle defrost models.

The next big change to find favor with appliance owners was the "frostless" refrigeration system. This system isn't really frostless at all. It may be more accurately described as a hidden frost system. With the frostless system, the evaporator coil is located behind or under a hidden plate. A fan is then used to pull air from the refrigerator or the freezer section across this plate and cir-

culate it back into the cabinet after it's cooled somewhat like an air conditioning system. This also makes it possible to use a single evaporator to cool both sections. To accomplish this, thermostats are used to sense the air temperature rather than the temperature of the refrigeration coils as previous systems had done. A central evaporator coil can be used with ducts leading away from this coil to various sections of the refrigerator and freezer, and the air channeled through the ducts to meet the demands of the system.

A typical side-by-side refrigerator works like this: the air-sensing thermostat in the freezer compartment controls the compressor, turning the unit on and off as air temperature is maintained at the proper levels (usually around 0 degrees). When the refrigerator compartment calls for cooling, the thermostat simply opens a baffle in a duct leading from the freezer compartment. This allows the super-cooled air to enter the duct and flow into the refrigerator compartment. When the refrigerator compartment thermostat is satisfied, the damper closes down and shuts off the frigid air flow.

Condensate pan should be removed and cleaned twice a year. Hose off and wash out thoroughly to remove food particles.

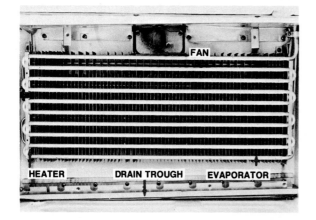

The evaporator section on frostless system shows how fin and tube arrangement allows air to circulate freely between coils.

In the meantime, the removal of this cold air from the freezer has caused the air temperature to rise within the freezer compartment itself, so the freezer thermostat simply turns the compressor on to again bring the temperature back down to the correct level.

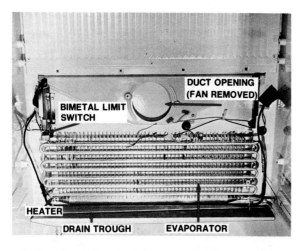

The heater on this model is not imbedded within the coil, but heat radiation allows complete defrosting of coil when heater is energized.

Frostless systems have certainly met with favor and with good reason. Since the freezer evaporator coil is actually separate from the freezer compartment, it is simple enough to shut the fans down and turn on an electric heater to evaporate the frost from the coil. Previously this had been practically impossible since applying heat to the freezer evaporator tended to thaw any food that

might be in contact with it. Now only a few degrees temperature rise occurs in a well-designed freezer compartment during defrosting. Also, it helps maintain temperatures throughout each compartment more consistantly than before, since the air is being circulated by the fan and flows into all corners of the compartment.

Some complications are a result of the continuous air circulation. It makes it even more important that food be well-covered and air-tight since the air flow tends to evaporate moisture much more quickly than before. Odors are transferred more readily as well. Even in the freezer compartment this becomes more important.

The entire principle of the frostless refrigerator is based upon a process we know as *sublimation*. In sublimation a substance can pass from one stage to another without going through an intermediate stage. In this case, it means that frost that forms in the freezer compartment of a refrigerator can pass through a gaseous stage and back to a solid stage without going through an intermediate liquid stage. Here's how it works. When frost forms on packages or the interior walls of a freezer, as it will when a door is opened, it forms a thin film of frost. Moisture will travel from a warmer to a colder surface. In the areas exposed to the freezer compartment, the evaporator is the coldest point in that system.

Loading is critical in frostless type refrigerators. Do not place packages in areas where they can block air flow.

Through sublimation the frost will travel to that point. This is what makes it necessary to keep all foods tightly covered and air-tight.

Space conservation is important in the modern kitchen, and appliance manufacturers keep this in mind when designing an appliance. Thin-wall insulation has come into wide usage in recent years and has increased the interior space of refrigerators and freezers greatly while keeping outside dimensions practically the same. Also to save space, the condensers on many models have been moved from the back and placed underneath refrigerators and freezers.

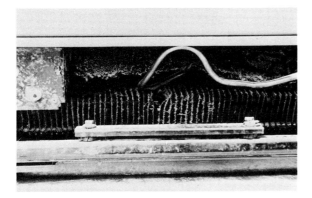

Condenser coils must be kept free of lint and dust. Vacuum at least monthly. Use care not to bend or damage any tubing in unit compartment. This condenser is located under refrigerator.

REFRIGERATOR MAINTENANCE

When the condensers were located on the back, there were no moving parts. They were called static condensers and a yearly cleaning with a vacuum brush to remove lint that had accumulated was all the maintenance that was necessary. With the condensers redesigned and placed under the unit, however, it was necessary to install a small fan to furnish the proper amount of air flow necessary to cool the refrigerant that was flowing through the tubing. This also increased the amount of lint buildup. If a condenser becomes blocked with lint, the hot vapor that passes through it can no longer be cooled and liquified. The condenser capacity reaches an extent that warm vapor flows back into the refrigerator and inside temperatures increase sharply. It can lead to even more serious results, as it can cause the compressor motor to operate at higher than normal temperatures. Even with the protection offered by the overload protector, this can cause windings to become so hot that insulation can be released into the system and blockage of the refrigerant flow results. Even worse, the compressor itself could be damaged to such an extent that it would have to be replaced.

All of this is avoidable by simply cleaning a condenser on a regular basis. Every thirty days is not too often. To do this, simply remove the grille on the front of the refrigerator and vacuum with a dusting brush attachment. Gently brush all lint

On static condensers (those located on back of refrigerators) a yearly vacuum with dusting brush attachment is usually all that is necessary.

from the front of the condensing unit. Use care not to bend or kink any tubing that may be attached to this part of the condenser. Turn off all power to the refrigerator before beginning this operation.

Refrigerators run more often than they used to because they are cooling more area and also cooling two separate sections. In the case of frostless systems, either compartment calling for more cooling could cause the compressor to operate. Reduce running time by keeping door openings to a minimum. Second, don't place a large amount of warm food into the appliance all at one time. If possible have food prefrozen before it goes into the frozen compartment. Third, be sure that all the gaskets and seals are doing their job properly.

Door gaskets prevent warm air from entering the refrigerator. Care of these gaskets is very important. If a gasket is torn, the only recourse is to replace it. The life of a gasket can be prolonged by keeping wax off it when the cabinet of the refrigerator is cleaned and by not touching the gasket with the hands. The oily film that is left can hasten the deterioration of the material.

Most modern refrigerators use magnetic gaskets that are designed to seal with a minimum of

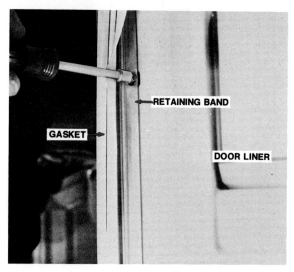

Door gaskets must be replaced when broken or damaged. A gasket can be replaced without removing door by first removing upper half of gasket. Install the gasket in place and tighten screws loosely. Then remove the remaining section of gasket on bottom and tighten screws. The retaining band need only be loosened, not removed, to remove gasket.

force applied to the door. This is necessary because the amount of door force is regulated to a level well below that which a child could overcome if he were trapped in it. Keep this in mind when discarding old refrigerators. Be sure that the door is removed and the latch mechanism is jammed so that there is no possibility of a child entering.

To replace a gasket, first obtain a new one from a

distributor or servicing dealer for the model of the refrigerator that you have. Most gaskets are held in place by screws that are located under the edge of the gasket. Lift the gasket from the inside of the door and you will see these screws in the outer edges of the liner or the inside liner of the refrigerator door. You may find it easiest to take the door off and place it on a quilt or other protective surface to remove the entire liner. Fit the new gasket in place and reinstall the screws, but not tightly.

You may prefer to change the gasket with the door in place. Remove or loosen those screws on the upper half of the door panel. This will allow enough leeway to pull the gasket free and fit the upper portion of the new one in place. Then reposition the screws and partially tighten them. Remove or loosen the screws from the lower section and fit the remaining portion of the gasket over that. Install those screws loosely.

Using a strip of paper or dollar bill, insert it behind door and pull. You should feel resistance when door is sealing properly.

Regardless of the method used to replace the gaskets, the door should now be back on the refrigerator, the gasket in place and the liner in position, but the screws not tightened firmly.

This allows you to obtain some flexing of the door from corner to corner. Now align the door by pushing it closed and note any edges that may not line up with the cabinet itself. Simply twist the door to get the edges into correct position and then tighten the screws snugly, but not firmly. The liner in most refrigerators serves as a support for the outer door panel. By following this method you not only install a new gasket but align the door as well. To test the alignment procedure, try the "dollar bill test." Simply insert a dollar bill at a number of points along the edge between the gasket and cabinet, close the door on the dollar bill, and pull it away. A firm resistance to the pull should be felt at each point. If not, this is a sign that the door needs to be pulled closer to this particular point.

After replacing a door gasket, it is often necessary to apply some outside force to the door until the gasket seals properly. This force can be a large piece of duct tape or masking tape or simply a chair placed against the door. It is not unusual for it to take the gasket several weeks to seat itself, but once seated, it will provide a good

firm seal against air and moisture entrance into the cabinet.

Measure freezer temperatures by inserting thermometer between packages, then taking a reading. This stabilizes temperatures so that they are not affected radically by door openings.

Measure the temperature in a refrigerator section by placing thermometer in a glass of water and letting it stay for 24 hours.

Automatic and manual damper controls are used to control flow of cold air in frostless refrigerators and freezers. The adjusting knob in the refrigerator section baffles the air duct leading to freezer and provides control of freezer temperatures in this unit.

Reduce appliance running time by observing the exact temperatures that are being obtained by the present thermostat settings. Start by placing a thermometer in the freezer section. It should be around 0 degrees. In the refrigerator compartment, 38 to 40 degrees here is considered normal. If it is substantially colder, around 34 degrees or less, you will not only add to the running time of the unit but will overcool some products, particularly vegetables. Adjust the control until the proper temperature is obtained.

Any frost built-up in a frostless system will block the cooling effect because it will tend to keep air from flowing across the evaporator coils. If you notice a frost buildup or if water is spilled in a freezer compartment near the hidden coil, try to rid the freezer of frost as soon as possible. Often a door being left open can cause frostless evaporators to ice up quickly. In this event, shut off the refrigerator and move the food to a separate unit or a neighbor's refrigerator. Leave your refrigerator standing open all day if possible, because *all* the hidden frost must be removed. If it should build up again there is a problem within the defrosting system, probably

A frosting condition is critical. Be sure to remove all traces of frost after the problem has been repaired. Often this is caused by inadvertently leaving the door open. Hose from hair dryer speeds front removal.

with the heater or timer motor. It will take a continuity test or a volt-ohm-meter to pin down problems in this area. Of course, when inspecting such conditions, be sure that all power is turned off before removing any plates or covers.

If your refrigerator fails to operate at all, first check to see that it is plugged in and that power is reaching the receptacle. Do this by simply

plugging a table lamp into the outlet, or checking to see if the light is burning in the refrigerator. Next, listen for any unusual noises. An overheating compressor, for instance, might make itself known by a buzz or click from time to time as the overload protector tries to cycle it on. In this case, look for a clogged condenser or a slow-turning or stalled condenser fan motor. Other possible causes are a defective relay or capacitor on the motor compressor or a defective thermostat. These require a volt-ohm-meter or continuity tester to verify. Caution! The capacitor must be discharged before being handled or tested.

If a refrigerator runs but doesn't cool, check the condenser to see if it's warm. If so, chances are good that the hermetic refrigeration system is doing its job. Look for exterior causes such as an evaporator blocked by ice on frostless models or improper loading of food.

AUTOMATIC ICEMAKERS

Automatic icemakers are becoming very popular. They are actually an appliance within an appliance. If you are familiar with some of their principles you can often pinpoint a problem that

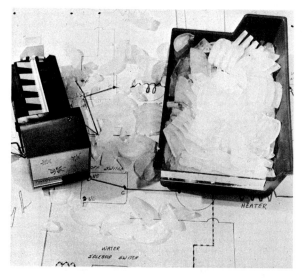

Automatic icemakers such as this provide approximately one mold per hour under normal conditions. If the ice maker seems to be taking significantly more time than that, check temperature of freezer compartment first.

arises with an icemaker. You will usually find the problem is not the icemaker at all.

An icemaker is a mold that may be provided by an aluminum casting or by a plastic mold, often formed in the shape of a tray. A timing device, controlled by a thermostat, turns on a switch that opens an inlet valve and allows water to flow into the icemaker. Exposed to the cold temperatures of the cooling compartment, it quickly solidifies into ice. A thermostat in contact with the mold senses this temperature. When it reaches a certain level (usually 15 degrees) it turns on a motor which initiates the ejection cycle. During this cycle a heater comes on to begin to melt the ice from the mold when aluminum molds are used. When plastic molds are used, the motor may turn or twist the mold in such a way that ice is forced away from it. The ice then leaves the mold by lifting it with an arm or by dumping it into a tray. A feeler arm or photoelectric cell senses the amount of ice in the tray and turns off the icemaker when the tray is full.

The inlet valve on the automatic icemaker is very much like the one on a dishwasher. It has a flow washer that controls the rate of flow. It is a single port type valve, since it is connected only to the cold water line. If no water flows into the icemaker, listen for a low buzzing sound. If you hear it, it means that the solenoid on the valve is operating. If not, the switch or the wiring from the icemaker to the valve may be open or the solenoid coil itself may be open. Check this with a volt-ohm-meter or continuity tester. If you do hear the buzzing sound and no water goes into the icemaker, look to see if a tube between the valve and icemaker is frozen and blocked or check the filters at the water line where the valve attaches to the line. The valve is located outside of the cabinet, usually at the back or bottom of the refrigerator, to protect it from the freezing temperatures. If a tube is blocked with ice it's usually caused by water dripping past the valve. This is often due to a piece of sand or other foreign object lodged in the diaphragm of the valve. The remedy is to take the valve apart and clean it under running water, just as you would a valve in a dishwasher or washing machine. Be sure to unplug the appliance and turn off all power to the refrigerator before servicing the icemaker in any way.

Since the icemaker unit is temperature actuated, it follows that any condition that causes a temperature rise in the freezer compartment would slow down the cycling action of the icemaker. If it rises above 15 degrees the icemaker may stop operating altogether. If you encounter this condition, look first for things that would cause the temperature of the refrigerator to rise. A door left ajar, an evaporator coil that has iced, or a large amount of warm food that was placed in the refrigerator shortly before can cause this problem. To increase the cycling time of the icemaker and increase ice production, turn the freezer to operate at a colder temperature. It makes a noticeable difference.

Ice picks up taste and odors from other foods very quickly. For this reason it is advisable to

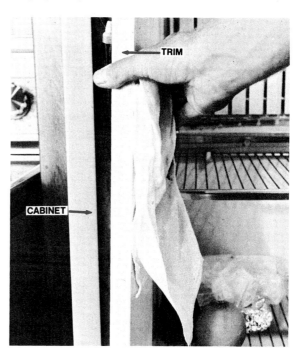

Cracked trim around the edge of the refrigerator can be a source of problems. To replace it, first warm the trim with a damp cloth that has been soaked in hot water. Next, pull the front lip of the trim away from the cabinet, then pull forward releasing trim from cabinet liner. Reverse the procedure to install new trim.

Light switch also controls fan operation in many new models; if it fails, the fan will not operate and cooling capacity is lost. Often these can be snapped out of trim for replacement.

empty the container every couple of weeks and make a new supply of ice. If you notice a peculiar taste in the ice, check first to be sure that nothing has spilled in either the freezer or refrigerator section and that all foods are covered well. Even exterior sources such as brown paper bags (which often have a high sulfur content) can transfer tastes to ice.

The modern refrigerator has many more components than its predecessors. All in all, it can give you good care. Keep the condenser clean and airflow passages clear. Wipe up any spills immediately. Keep foods covered and operate the system at normal temperatures. Keep door openings to a minimum. These practices can add years to the life of the equipment and reduce operating costs greatly. *SEE ALSO APPLIANCE REPAIR, MAJOR.*

Registers

Registers are metal, rectangular plates with louvered vents that control the flow of heat. Registers are designed for use in both gravity and forced warm air systems with different locations for each.

In the gravity system, registers are generally installed next to or in the baseboard on the inside walls. The fit between the wall and the register should be tight to prevent dirt from streaking the wall.

Diffusion-type registers are commonly used in forced warm air systems. With these registers warm air is distributed without drafts, so they may be placed close to the floor or ceiling. Careful register mounting is required in order for the air to be dispersed properly. Installed upside down or inside out, the register may deflect warm air in the wrong direction. *SEE ALSO HEATING SYSTEMS.*

Courtesy of Leigh Products, Inc.

Register

Reinforced Concrete Construction
[SEE CONCRETE, REINFORCED.]

Reinforcing Bar

A reinforcing bar is a steel rod which is embedded in poured concrete or in the mortar between courses in brickwork. This adds strength to the framework of a structure and makes it virtually indestructable. *SEE ALSO CONCRETE, REIN-FORCED.*

Relative Humidity

Relative humidity is the ratio of the amount of water vapor present in the air to the total amount it could hold at the same temperature.

Relay Unit

A relay unit or remote-control relay is the heart of remote-control switching, which takes the place of three- and four-way switches and their complicated wiring. The relay unit is the size of a small radio tube and is mounted in the knockout of the outlet box of each light fixture or receptacle that it controls. The 115-volt household wires are connected to the large end of the relay, which contains a 24-volt coil. A transformer, located in a convenient part of the house (attic, basement, etc.), steps down the 115-volt household current to 24 volts. The 24-volt current which operates the unit can then be transmitted through small, inexpensive low-voltage wire that is run from the transformer and connected to the low-voltage or small end of the relay. From there, the wire is run to surface-mounted push button switches mounted in a convenient place.

The relay unit permits flexibility in household wiring because the 115-volt wires connect to it, avoiding long runs of expensive 115-volt wiring to convenient switches and outlets. Low-voltage wire can then be run from a push button switch to the light fixture (containing relay unit in its outlet box). Remote-control switching with relay units and low-voltage wire makes remote control of one or more light fixtures possible from push button switches throughout the house. In addition, a master control switch with push buttons to control lights or appliances all through the house can be installed near the front door or in the bedroom. *SEE ALSO SWITCHES & OUT-LETS.*

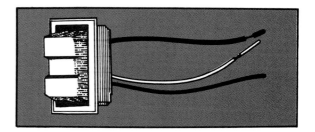

Push Button Switch

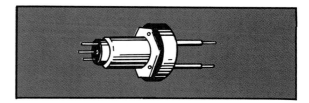

Relay Unit

Relief Valve for Hot Water Tank

A relief valve, which has a pump-type handle about four to seven inches long, should be attached to a hot water tank. When the temperature of the water is near boiling or the

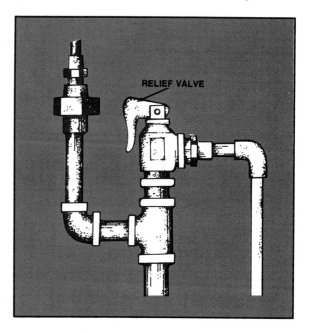

Relief Valve for Hot Water Tank

Courtesy of The Masonite Corporation

A comfortable country home with a great deal of character has a great need for complete remodeling.

Courtesy of The Masonite Corporation

New siding, new additions and new paint make the country home once again a warm, inviting place to live.

pressure is above normal, this valve will open, releasing water to a drain. Once the pressure and temperature are back to normal, the valve will close. Some valves respond only to pressure while others respond to both pressure or temperature. Damage to the hot water system, such as burst tanks, can be prevented by having a relief valve. *SEE ALSO DRAINAGE SYSTEMS.*

Remodeling

Remodeling an existing home to make it more liveable has become very important to many peo-

ple. Remodeling does have certain advantages: it can add room to an existing house in a desirable neighborhood, it can bring an old house up to modern living standards and it can offer an opportunity to obtain more house for less money than purchasing a new house.

With the exception of kitchen remodeling, bathroom remodeling and adding a room (all of which are discussed in other entries), remodeling projects usually involve four areas: the basement, the porch, the garage or the attic. In any of these areas, three processes are usually involved: laying floor tile, installing wall paneling and installing ceiling tile.

BASIC PROCEDURES FOR
Laying Floor Tile

Before laying floor tile, a smooth even subfloor must be obtained. Plywood underlayment may be used to obtain a smooth surface. If the tile is being laid on a concrete slab, a thin layer of latex underlayment may be trowelled over the slab.

Courtesy of Azrock Floor Products

The centerlines of the room must first be found before any tile can be laid. To locate the center of the room, fasten a chalkline to the midpoint of facing walls and snap a chalk line on the subfloor. These chalk lines will allow the room to be squared so that the tiles can be laid parallel to the walls.

Courtesy of Azrock Floor Products

Next lay a row of loose tiles down the chalk lines, starting at the midpoint of the room and moving to the end wall and the side wall. Measure the distance between the last full tile and the wall. If this distance is less than half a tile wide, the spacing must be adjusted. Move half a tile width toward the opposite wall and snap a new chalk line. Check the right angles. Then repeat the process with the other row of tiles.

Courtesy of Azrock Floor Products

A thin coat of adhesive should be brushed, troweled or rolled on the subfloor. Do about one fourth of the room at a time, making sure that adhesive covers, but does not obscure, the chalk line. Keep the coating thin so adhesive will not push up between the tiles. If self-stick tiles are being used, this step may be omitted.

Courtesy of Azrock Floor Products

Work on one fourth of the room at a time. Begin by placing one tile at the center point of the room, where the chalk lines cross. Place each tile firmly and tightly against the preceding tile, so there are no cracks or open joints between them.

1485

Do not slide the tiles together, such sliding may force adhesive up between the tiles.

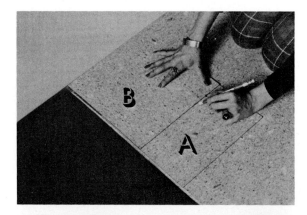

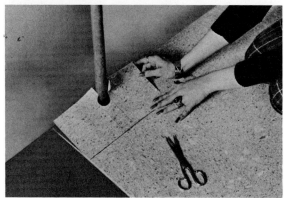

Courtesy of Azrock Floor Products

Cutting and fitting tiles at the edge of the room or around pipes is a simple task. To fit border tiles, first place a loose tile (A) precisely on top of the last full tile before the wall. Place a third tile (B) on top of this stack, then slide it over until it butts against the wall. Using the edge of B as a guide, make a cutting line on A with a pencil. Cut A to fit, using a pair of household shears. Place the tile in the space with the cut edge against the wall. To fit a tile around a pipe, jog in the wall or other obstruction, make a paper pattern that fits the space exactly, using a loose tile to form the basic shape. Trace the outline of the special cuts onto the tile, and cut with household shears. Fit the cut tile in place.

Applying Wall Paneling

Wall paneling may be applied in two basic ways: with nails or with adhesive. The paneling may be applied directly to the existing wall surface if it is dry and solid, or wood or metal furring strips may be used. Specific directions of the paneling manufacturer will state which method is preferred. A typical installation process is described below.

Four feet from one corner of the room, using either a carpenter's level or a plumb bob, establish a true vertical line on the wall. If the corner is markedly out of plumb (more than $1/8$ inch), place the sheet of paneling so that either the top or bottom corner is touching the adjacent wall, and the panel is plumb. With a pair of dividers (a child's school compass is an acceptable substitute), mark a pencil line down the edge of the panel indicating the actual shape of the corner, much like fitting a border floor tile. Cut the paneling to fit the corner.

Courtesy of Marlite Paneling

Courtesy of Marlite Paneling

After cutting and dry fitting the panel, apply adhesive to the back with a comb-tooth spreader. (Note adhesive applications may vary with manufacturer.) Position the panel and press firmly to the wall to achieve a secure bond. Apply matching molding to cover the edge of the panel. Fasten by nailing through the exposed flange. (Note: Grooved plywood paneling may not require such molding, as the joints are concealed by the grooves.) Fit the next panel, apply adhesive and press to wall.

Wall paneling resembling wood planks provides a quick way to give a room a completely different appearance.

Applying Ceiling Tile

One of the most obvious ways a home may be remodeled is with the application of a new ceiling. Several manufacturers have developed suspended ceiling systems, which permit the home craftsman to not only change the appearance of the ceiling, but also the change its height. General procedures of establishing wall moldings, hanging main runners, installing cross members and placing tiles or panels are relatively similar in most ceiling systems.

Courtesy of The Armstrong Cork Company

Installation begins with the wall molding. Nail the molding to the walls at the desired ceiling height.

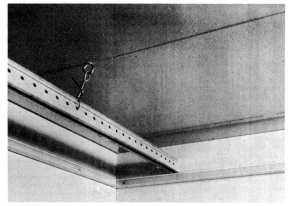

Courtesy of The Armstrong Cork Company

The main runners are next installed using hanger wires as shown. (The length of wire used depends upon the change in ceiling height planned.) This system locates the first runner 26 inches from the side wall, and all remaining runners 48 inches on center, perpendicular to the joists.

Courtesy of The Armstrong Cork Company.

When the main runners are in place, begin installing the ceiling tile in a corner of the room. Lay the tile on the wall molding, snap a cross tee on the main runner, and slide the tee into a concealed slot on the edge of the tile.

Courtesy of The Armstrong Cork Company

Install the remaining tiles in a similar manner. When a tile must be cut to complete a row, use the leftover length to begin the next row. Note how suspension members are concealed in the completed ceiling.

Courtesy of The Armstrong Cork Company

In situations where no change in ceiling height is needed and the joists are exposed, as in a basement, the joists may serve as the main runners, with the cross members fastening to spring clips placed on the joists. One clip and one cross member will support four square feet of ceiling tile.

Courtesy of The Armstrong Cork Company

The completed ceiling has no readily visible joints.

BASEMENT REMODELING

For many people, the basement is the obvious area to convert to additional living space. The principal problem with most basements is making what is often a somewhat dark, underground concrete box into one or more liveable rooms. Modern paints, modern floor coverings, and ceiling tiles have done much to make the home craftsman's task easier.

Courtesy of The Armstrong Cork Company

When most remodeling projects begin, a basement is a place of usually unorganized storage, a "downstairs attic." This basement has an advantage because insulation has been installed between the floor joists, which will provide some measure of sound control between the two levels.

Courtesy of The Armstrong Cork Company

Selection of easy-to-install ceiling and floor tile hastened the remodeling process. Ceiling planks in a woodgrain pattern are stapled to the joists; self-stick floor tile is installed straight from the carton.

Courtesy of The Armstrong Cork Company

The new ceiling and floor are complemented by the white walls and furniture. Bright colored accessories complete the conversion of a dark "downstairs attic" into a bright, welcome addition to family living space.

Courtesy of American Olean Tile Company

Ceramic tile in earth tones and handcrafted shapes can be used to create an attractive floor that is impervious to spills and resists wear.

Courtesy of The Armstrong Cork Company

Bright, light colors make a basement remodeling job effective. Accessibility to plumbing connections often makes adding a bar or wet sink a simple process. A thematic decorating scheme often adds to the effectiveness of a remodeling job by bringing the various areas of a room together. Notice the card symbols on the table, the face card wall hangings, and the playing card wall border, all of which serve to unify the area.

Floor tile can be used to separate as well as join areas. In this basement recreation room, the stairway entered the basement at a central point. The remodeling divided the space into a conversation area and a game area, with the stairs serving as the division point. The floor tile also marks the division, with a forceful diamond pattern in the games area contrasting with the unobtrusive pattern of the tile in the conversation area.

PORCH REMODELING

Enclosing a porch, either with window or with a standard framed wall, is a relatively inexpensive way to gain additional living space.

Courtesy of Marlite Paneling

Porches often provide space for needed bedrooms for growing children, for elderly relatives, or for guests. Colorful hardboard paneling provides a bright yet economical way to decorate. Fabric wall covering, also used as curtains, and washable shag carpeting on the bed provide easily changed color and pattern.

Courtesy of The Masonite Corporation

Courtesy of The Masonite Corporation

A dormitory bedroom for three boys was made from an upstairs porch. Moveable pegboard dividers provide each youth with a private sleeping area. Paneling, acoustical tile, and carpeting effectively mask the original purpose of the area.

A screened porch, added after the house was built, was usable only during the summer months, and added little to the appearance of the house.

Courtesy of The Andersen Corporation (Wood Casement Windows)

When the area was remodeled into an all-purpose room, it provided the family with an attractive, useful year-round area for relaxed entertaining.

Courtesy of Mid-State Tile Company.

**Easy-care tile surfaces can often recapture the open effect of a porch while providing
the comfort of year-round use. A touch of nostalgia can be added with a four-bladed
ceiling fan.**

Courtesy of American Olean Tile Company

**Installing a tile floor in a converted porch will provide easy-care maintenance for what
is often used as an all-purpose area.**

1494

Courtesy of Andersen Corporation (Beauty-Line Windows)

Porch conversions often provide year-round usefulness for an area. If the windows added contain insulating glass, the need for storm windows is eliminated. An easy-care carpet adds warmth underfoot.

Second floor porches of older homes often provide needed expansion areas. Upstairs sitting rooms and additional bedrooms can easily be created from these spaces. For example, the above sitting room is such a conversion. Hardboard paneling covers the walls, and an oak parquet floor covers the original pine flooring. An adjacent chimney provided a flue for the Franklin stove. An eclectic mixture of new and old furniture contributes to the comfort of this new living space.

Carpet tiles offer the home craftsman an easy way to obtain an attractive floor in a remodeled area.

Another view of the upstairs sitting room. The rich-looking hardboard paneling adds to the comfort of the remodeled area.

GARAGE REMODELING

The garage, like the basement, offers the home craftsman an area that may be converted to living space with minimal structural rearrangement. Providing an attractive floor over a concrete slab is often a major problem in a garage conversion. No-wax, self-stick floor tile provide an economical solution to this problem. Thorough cleansing of the garage floor is necessary to remove all imbedded grease and grime. Plywood subflooring on sleepers may be necessary if the floor is seriously stained.

Courtesy of The Armstrong Cork Company

As with ordinary floor tile, the first step in laying self-stick tile is to strike chalk lines from the midpoints of opposite walls, dividing the area into quarters.

Courtesy of The Armstrong Cork Company

The adhesive backing of each tile is protected by a paper covering. Peel off the protective covering and place the tile in position. Do not try to slide the tile into place.

Courtesy of The Armstrong Cork Company

Complete one section of the room at a time. Cut border tiles to fit, using household shears. Mark the tiles for cutting by the same process used for regular floor tile. Do not remove the protective backing while measuring.

Courtesy of The Masonite Corporation

In garage conversions, sufficient natural lighting is often a problem. Some possible solutions include the following: use light colored furniture. White or blond finish furniture brightens a room. Cover the walls with bright, rather than dark paneling. Avoid curtains and drapes. Use attractive filigree lattices across the window to transmit as much light as possible.

**The remodeled area now boasts a wall of wood-finished paneling, and a wall covered
in a siding that resembles stucco. Beams on the ceiling and translucent plastic
resembling Venetian glass at the window add to the effect of the remodeled room.**

Dark-toned ceramic tile and mellow wood paneling provide an inviting home environment. The imaginative use of home-improvement products conceals the origins of this converted garage.

Courtesy of The Sikes Corporation

In many garage conversions, the large open space formerly occupied by the garage door often becomes a window wall. If an informal style of decorating is used, featuring light colors, a pleasant, cheerful room such as this may result.

Courtesy of American Olean Tile Company

Sliding glass doors may also be used in a garage remodeling. Ceramic tile provides a colorful, maintenance-free floor that will stand up under hard wear.

Carpet squares can be used in many areas of the house. With plywood underlayment fastened to attic joists, carpeting can be used in the attic area.

ATTIC REMODELING

In many older homes, room may be found in spacious attics that can be converted into living space. In newer homes, dormers or shed dormers may be added to an attic area to obtain needed living space.

Courtesy of The Ozite Corporation

A dormer window, plus bright decorating makes this attic remodeling job an inviting bedroom for a teenager.

Courtesy of Ethan Allen

Any ceiling in the house may be resurfaced with tile. In addition to suspended ceiling systems, ceiling tile may be used as a finish ceiling glued or stapled directly to the old ceiling. Ceiling tile applied directly to the roof sheathing can contribute to an unusual decorating scheme.

Courtesy of The Armstrong Cork Company

The first step in cementing tile to an old ceiling is applying the cement to the back of the tile. Place the cement on about five places on the back of the tile, keeping away from the edges so that when the tile is pressed against the ceiling, the cement will spread across the back.

Courtesy of The Armstrong Cork Company

Beginning in a corner of the room, place the tile against the ceiling. After the first tile, the tongue and groove edges of the tiles will interlock and make the joints virtually invisible.

Courtesy of The Armstrong Cork Company

To hold the tile in place while the cement hardens, staple the exposed flanges to the ceiling.

Courtesy of Georgia-Pacific

As a supplemental heater, a Franklin stove offers welcome and safe heat on a cold day.

Remodeling

Courtesy of The American Plywood Association.

Remodeling is one way the home craftsman can obtain maximum value from the housing dollar. Home improvement products have made it possible for even the less-experienced person to do a creditable job in remodeling their home. *SEE ALSO BARS; BATHROOM DESIGN & PLANNING; BAY WINDOW; BRICK & STONE WORK; CONCRETE; CONCRETE BLOCK; DECORATING; FINISH FLOORING; FIRE-PLACES; HOUSE DESIGN; KITCHEN DESIGN & PLANNING; PAINTS & PAINTING; PORCH CONSTRUCTION & CONVERSION; RECREA-TION ROOMS; ROOM ADDITIONS; WALL & CEILING CONSTRUCTION; WOOD PANEL-ING.*

Remote Control

A remote control operates appliances or other devices from a distant point. Remote controls enable the homeowner to open his garage door, start his coffeemaker and change the channel on his TV set at the push of a button.

One type of remote control consists of a unit connected to an appliance and plugged into an outlet. A portable control wand operates the unit from a distance by ultra-sound. Some units are available which control the appliance through the wiring from anywhere in the house.

Another type of remote control uses a sensitivity device. This device is often used in swimming pools to detect motion such as splashing. *SEE ALSO AUTOMATION.*

Replacing Electric Switches
[SEE SWITCHES & OUTLETS.]

Resilient Flooring

Laying a resilient floor has been so simplified and the results are so satisfactory in improving the appearance of a home that it has become one of the best ways to upgrade an older house or help finish and decorate a new one.

Large flooring companies which sell sheet and tile flooring materials report that more than half their business now comes from homeowners who do their own flooring jobs. Rising labor costs make do-it-yourself jobs one of the best ways of fighting inflation.

WHAT IS RESILIENT FLOORING?

Resilient flooring can be any of a number of materials: pure vinyl, vinyl-asbestos, asphalt, cork, vinyl-cork, rubber or linoleum. Most of it is available in 9 x 9 inch or 12 x 12 inch tiles. Recently, however, major flooring companies introduced first quality sheet flooring in 9 and 12 foot widths which can be either loosely laid or permanently installed with a mastic recommended by the manufacturer. A few years ago only a professional could install big-sheet flooring. Now flooring companies encourage the homeowner to do his own job and help him get a professional result by supplying instruction sheets, diagrams and the correct installation supplies.

KINDS OF RESILIENT FLOORS

Vinyl

A first choice for flooring is vinyl, either in tile or seamless roll type. It can be used in a basement or on a concrete subfloor as well as above ground. Usually it can be placed over an older floor without removing the existing material, provided the floor is still in fairly good condition.

Vinyl is easily laid on an adhesive, but has recently become available in a cushioned roll type which is loose laid and requires only that the installer be accurate with his measuring and fitting. In the peel-stick tile form all that is necessary is to buy the correct number of tiles, cut with scissors when necessary, remove a thin sheet of paper from the back of the tile, and press it in place.

Vinyl needs almost no maintenance. Most of it comes with a factory wax finish which, with

Wallcoverings, fabrics and floors are all styled to go together. You can lay your own flooring and be your own decorator in expert fashion now that one large flooring company is offering this service in larger cities.

care, lasts for years. Vinyl comes in hundreds of designs and sun-resistant colors to fit any decorating scheme.

The homeowner who likes the look of tile, but does not want the bother of putting down individual pieces, can now get vinyl tile floor that is not a tile floor. It is a sheet flooring designed to look like tile.

Vinyl has begun to replace hardwood floors which are becoming prohibitively expensive. Sheet vinyl comes in a wood look-alike, a process achieved by taking a photograph of an actual wood floor and transferring the image to the vinyl. It is available in parquet, random-width

planks and in a wide range of mellow wood tones with decorative peg markings.

Linoleum

This is an older type of flooring, still available and moderate in cost. It is especially durable in a type called "battleship linoleum" which never seems to wear out. Linoleum is not difficult to maintain, does not absorb grease, and, if it's gouged or burned, the hole can be repaired merely by taking a scrap of the original material, grinding it into a coarse sawdust-like mixture, adding plain lacquer and mixing a thick paste to fill the hole. After it's dry, smooth with a sanding block and re-wax. The chief disadvantage of linoleum is that it cannot be used below grade or on a concrete slab nor does it come in as wide a variety of patterns and colors.

Courtesy of GAF Corporation

Named Karachi, this cushioned vinyl flooring has all the rich color of the Far East. It comes in 6′ and 12′ widths, although it looks like individual tile at first glance.

Asphalt Tile

Where moisture and price are primary considerations, asphalt tile might still fit your flooring needs. It is highly resistant to alkalis and dampness, and is the least expensive of all flooring materials, except paint. Unfortunately, asphalt tile is extremely brittle and it can chip or crack and corners sometimes snap off. Other disadvantages are that sounds carry when you walk on it, and stains cannot easily be removed.

Asphalt tile comes primarily in dark colors with marbelized patterns. The darker colors can be a problem because soil shows easily on them. Asphalt tile could be a first choice for a basement recreation room, shop, utility area or vacation house, where you want something inexpensive to cover concrete.

An amateur can lay it in a mastic recommended by the manufacturer. The brittle tiles should be warmed before and during the job so they can be handled and cut without breakage. A heat lamp, a lukewarm oven or a heating pad will render them pliable.

Cork and Vinyl-Cork

All-cork tile makes a luxurious, warm, cushioned and handsome floor, however it is expensive. It goes down easily in a mastic. If damaged, a mixture of ground-cork and glue can be pressed into the damaged area and will blend in so well it is not noticeable. The type with a plastic surface finish resists stains and is easy to mop.

Cork cannot be used where there is dampness or alkali such as on a concrete slab floor. It is very subject to abrasion, especially when sand or coarse soil is tracked in. It shows footprints and always seems soiled, especially when used near an outside entrance.

If you still prefer cork, a better choice may be a cork-vinyl type which looks and feels almost the same as pure cork, but wears better, retains its gloss and cleans easily. Stains do not soak through the vinyl shield surface.

Rubber Tile

Before the vinyl age, rubber tile was more popular because it gives a cushion feel and is durable. It is still available in some stores, but there is not much choice of color or pattern. It should not be used in a kitchen, game room or shop because it absorbs grease and stains.

Selecting a Floor Covering

Consider where the floor will be installed, and determine the nature of the subfloor and its condition. Decide whether the subfloor must be treated, repaired or removed. Decide the amount and kind of traffic the floor will have. If it must stand up to heavy tracking and daily abuse from cooking, play, outdoor soil or water, vinyl flooring would be the best solution as it rarely wears out. Often it is only replaced to change the color or decorating scheme. A design which extends completely through the thickness is a safer choice than one with a thin surface effect.

If this is a first job for you, tile is a better choice than sheet flooring. It goes down quickly and the job can be done a little at a time. If you make a mistake, you ruin only a tile or two. In a small

Resilient Flooring

room, or in one with a lot of area, but no complicated cabinets, corners or appliances, you should have no trouble with sheet flooring, but you must be more careful.

Recently developed sheet flooring materials with cushioned backing cut readily with a linoleum knife or scissors and go down without being glued. A beginner should choose a patterned design which need not be matched perfectly.

Flooring should complement the furniture, the size of the room and the general design of the house. Patterns and styles come in a wide variety such as these: sheet vinyl in a French parquet design; a vinyl reproduction of authentic Dutch delft ceramic tile; a red-white-and-blue sheet-tile to complement an Early American setting; an ornate Spanish filigree tile pattern. There are also fine reproductions of natural materials: brick, flagstone, slate, marble.

Vinyl flooring looks every bit as dramatic and colorful as the expensive ceramic tile which it duplicates in appearance. It's glamourous enough to use in any room of the house.

Courtesy of Mannington Mills

Light or medium colors reflect light back into the room, show footsteps, heelmarks, spills and stains less than dark colors. Maintenance is easier if you choose an all-over, or mottled pattern, which conceals lint and crumbs. Embossed patterns catch more soil than smooth surfaces.

You may tire of very bright colors more quickly than you would neutral tones.

Is the shining finish a semi-permanent one? All new samples shine. Ask if the gloss is a no-wax surface or whether it must be renewed each time

Area rugs plus a no-wax resilient floor make for easy cleaning but elegance and comfort in sitting areas, a good solution where there are small children and wall-to-wall carpet would be impractical.

Courtesy of The Armstrong Cork Co.

it is thoroughly cleaned. Even a no-wax type will require re-waxing after a few years heavy use.

Courtesy of Mannington Mills

This isn't a brick floor. It's vinyl, but it's hard to distinguish from the real thing. However, it's warm, easy to clean, and non-porous — three characteristics which real brick does not have.

Take home a sample of the material and test it with spills and soil. Try washing it carelessly, then carefully. How does it look? Rub the sample with a piece of steel wool or sandpaper to simulate the action of shoes carrying sand or gravel, and you will get some idea of what the floor will look like after it has been in use. If you live near a beach, this is especially important. A beautiful and expensive cork floor in a beach house can be ruined in less than a year's time by tracked sand, even though the floor is swept and mopped frequently.

Flooring manufacturers say most homeowners wash floors too often. Cleansers, abrasives, and detergents which are not rinsed off, can be as harmful to patterns and colors as traffic. Too much wax, or too frequent waxing, will darken or yellow flooring and trap dirt. Daily sweeping and immediate wipe-up of spills, with a wash job once a month, is all that a good floor requires.

A local dealer (one who has been in business a long time) can show you a full line of materials from more than one manufacturer, will lend you samples and can help you decide which types suit your needs and your budget. If he supplies the labor, the work should be guaranteed. He can give you instruction booklets, help you measure and supply advice if yours is a do-it-yourself job. Don't skimp on quality. Time and effort in laying the material is worth more than the actual cost of the flooring.

How to Lay Resilient Flooring

Careful preparation is of utmost importance. Fill cracks and holes of a new, as well as an old, floor. If the subfloor is concrete, use a patching material made for the purpose. When the patch is thoroughly dry, sand it smooth.

If yours is a concrete floor which has previously been painted or waxed, it is safest to remove these materials, especially if you plan to lay the flooring in mastic, as wax could keep the floor from adhering. If concrete seems to be dusting, put down a seal coat (consult a dealer for the type). Wax and paint can be removed easiest by renting a floor sanding machine.

If you're working on a rough wooden floor, you may need to cover it with plywood or 1/2 inch

Courtesy of GAF Corporation

A jagged edge made by your scissors will be hidden by the molding strip.

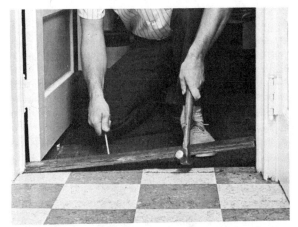

Courtesy of GAF Corporation

Take up door stops. It will make the job easier and give a neat finish when you put it down again after the job is complete.

Courtesy of GAF Corporation

Thoroughly clean the area to be covered. Old tile or linoleum may be left in place if not seriously damaged or loose. Remove quarter-round molding.

Courtesy of GAF Corporation

Pry up and remove any seam covering strips such as this one. The seam of your new floor — if any — may not come in the same place, and the slight irregularity of this strip will show through the new floor material.

Courtesy of GAF Corporation

Use a damp mop, as sweeping is not enough. Tiny pieces of gravel or debris may show through your new floor.

hardboard underlayment. If the floor is made of boards, check each board for rough areas and loose spots. Sand and smooth irregularities, and nail down the loose places. You may need to cover an unevenly laid, old wooden floor with lining felt to cover individual board joints.

Pry up moldings along floor edges before placing either plywood, underlayment or lining felt. Felt should be installed by gluing it to the floor with linoleum paste. Smooth it and don't leave wrinkles or lumps, as they might show through

your new floor.

Sweep

You may even need to damp mop the floor to be sure every bit of grit, wood silver or debris is removed. Professionals sometimes skip this important feature. Tiny bits of debris will not show through when the floor is newly laid, but after a few months of wear a new floor could have pock marks and bumps. Once they are under the flooring, they are there until the flooring is changed. As you work, keep a whiskbroom and

Resilient Flooring

damp sponge handy to keep each area immaculate before placing the flooring.

Check to see if the walls are straight. Few are, and it is sometimes difficult to make a tile job come out with straight rows. Solve the problem by starting in the center of the room and lay tile toward the sides. Stretch a chalk line down the middle of the room in both directions, then snap it against the floor to mark it.

Courtesy of GAF Corporation

Unroll sheet flooring in a large room, porch or the driveway and rough cut it to size with a craft knife (linoleum knife) or scissors. Allow several inches extra in length and width.

Courtesy of GAF Corporation

Match and cut patterned material carefully. In a room wider than the flooring used, it will be necessary to have a seam. In this case the direction of the second piece should be reversed. Then lap the sec-

ond sheet over the first (arranging the second sheet to obtain a pattern match) and cut through both sheets of flooring at once with the knife. Use at least two inches of adhesive on both sides of the seam. With "loose lay" flooring you should still glue, or paste down seam edges with a recommended adhesive or the edges will come up and soon be damaged.

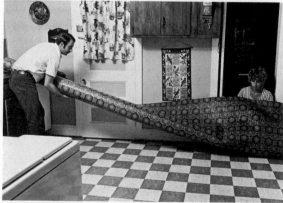

Courtesy of GAF Corporation

Place the sheet material in the room to be covered. Start unrolling with the longest or most irregular wall (one which needs cut-outs for pipes, cabinets, door irregularity). Allow the flooring to gently cove up the other walls.

Courtesy of GAF Corporation

Position the flooring as close to the edge of the wall as possible. You may have to do some cutting if the wall is not straight.

Make sure lines are square by measuring 3 feet from the intersection of one line and 4 feet on the other. When these points are exactly 5 feet apart the lines are square. Check to see if this leaves borders that are less than half a tile wide. If it does, move the line half a tile. Now you are ready to work from the intersection of the chalk lines, work outward. Place tiles tightly together without sliding them. If you are laying them in an adhesive, this is especially important, or you may cause adhesive to ooze up between tiles. When working with adhesive, spread only a small area at a time.

Courtesy of GAF Corporation

Handle the material gently, especially in a difficult spot such as this one. You may start a tear if you use force. Where the cuts are complicated use first a piece of heavy paper, cutting it to follow the walls, door area, or cabinets. Then trace the outline on the flooring material and cut it with your knife.

Courtesy of GAF Corporation

Linoleum knife technique shown here makes a quick clean cut.

Courtesy of GAF Corporation

The job is done. Molding and heat register are back in place with raw edges concealed.

Courtesy of GAF Corporation

Nail door strip back in place to hold flooring edge firmly. Use the same nail holes or you'll have a patching job.

Courtesy of GAF Corporation

Self-stick tile make for an easier flooring job. It can be done by one person, a little at a time if desirable. If a mistake is made in placement or cutting, only one tile is wasted. Start by squaring off the room with chalk lines and work from the center. Position tile for fit and any cutting, before peeling off the protective paper from the self-stick back.

Courtesy of GAF Corporation

It only took a few hours to do this job. The design of this tile is Spanish, and the finished effect is so smooth you'd have to look carefully to see that it isn't all one sheet.

When laying sheet flooring the best remedy for crooked edges, or imperfections of cutting, is to cover the edges with molding. Vinyl cove molding-baseboard is often used if the house is new or if the old molding is shabby.

Cabinets and pipes can usually be accommodated by cutting and fitting the material using a few tricks. In really difficult places, as around the base of a toilet, cut out a pattern from a piece of heavy paper and place it on the tile to help you get a good fit, when you are doing the cutting.

When possible remove fixtures or cabinets and replace on top of the flooring after the job is done. Small irregularities around pipes and fixtures can be filled with a patching compound. When working with adhesive, wipe up spills immediately and you will not need to use a solvent which could destroy the finish or color.

Start with a simple job such as a closet, a square room with no cabinets or irregularities, or a shop where a beginner's minor mistakes will not be obvious.

Walk on the floor as soon as the job is complete. If the flooring has been placed in adhesive, walking or other pressure will assure a better bond. Try rolling it firmly with a rolling pin if some areas do not seem properly in contact with subflooring.

Resins

Resins are available in natural or synthetic substances. Natural resins are the yellow or brown sticky substance found oozing from trees such as fir and pine. The two natural resins are spirit-soluble and oil-soluble. Although most natural resins can be used in varnishes, the majority of the spirit-soluble resins are used in oils for turpentine. Oil-soluble resins incorporate the term rosin and are used in varnishes and Oriental lacquers. Amber, an oil-soluble resin, is the hardest of the natural resins.

Synthetic resins possess the majority of the physical characteristics of the natural resins in addition to their own unique qualities. The synthetic resins are used for coating and adhesives.

There are ten coating resins. Phenol-formaldehyde resin is used in dry oils such as china wood oil. Alkyd resin can be used as a varnish and to coat metals. Polyester resin is used to saturate glass and fiber and is used in plastic armour, trays, luggage, radar housing and lightweight boats. Epoxy resin is used for textile finishing. Urea-formaldehyde resin provides a hard, marproof, good color gloss but, unfortunately, is not expandable.

Melamine-formaldehyde resin provides a porcelain appearance, is abrasion resistant, and is used for automobile coating and industrial finishes. Polyethylene is mainly used in self-supporting films and moldings. Courmarone-indene resin is used to coat concrete. Silicones are used as a coating for electrical insulation, in high temperature paints and enamels and as a varnish. Silicones also help provide water repellency when it is baked on glass and ceramics. Fluorine resins are useful in reducing friction on metal bearings.

Synthetic resins are also used in adhesives. They are classified as plywood, wood impregnation and other adhesives. The classification plywood is divided into cold and hot adhesives with many resins used for a wide variety of jobs. Wood impregnation is achieved by subjecting the wood to a reduced atmospheric pressure to eliminate occluded air. Then, the wood is impregnated with resins. After the wood is dry and the temperature has been raised, the resin will cure inside the wood making it harder, stronger and resistant to moisture. Phenol-formaldehyde, urea-formaldehyde and a mixture of its resins are employed for wood impregnation.

There are many other resinous compositions that are used to adhere materials such as rubber, leather, cork, brickwork and metals.

Resistor

A resistor provides electrical resistance in an electric circuit for protection and to regulate current and voltage. It is a device that dissipates electrical energy by converting it into heat. Resistors are usually small cylinders or rectangles consisting of a resistance element wrapped inside a protective case with metal leads attached to both ends. The resistor's resistance value is measured in ohms and determined by the resistance element's composition and size.

Retaining Wall

A retaining wall, made of strong material such as concrete, is a wall built to resist lateral pressure other than wind pressure such as an earth slide or flooding water. A retaining wall should be built with an accurately engineered design because it has to hold back tons of pressure from one side. When a retaining wall is built with *batter,* this means its face slopes slightly inward instead of in a vertical position. The gradual slope is due to lessening the wall's thickness from top to bottom. In a three-foot wall, the slope may be as much as six inches inward.

Retaining walls should have adequate drainage since water collects behind them. Drains should be located about every ten feet. *SEE ALSO CONCRETE BLOCK.*

Reverse Pitch Roof

Reverse pitch roof is the inverted order of conventional slope in roof design. This order is used when the basic roof line of a house is altered by an extension such as an upper garage deck enclosure. In this case, the new roof should be pitched from the far end of a room down towards the back so that the new roof line meets the present line in a valley. Water which collects in the valley is then flashed into a drain. *SEE ALSO ROOF CONSTRUCTION.*

Reversible Screwdriver

The reversible screwdriver has one blade with two tips — one with which you are working and the other concealed in the handle. To change tips, pull out the blade, reverse it, push the tip you were working with up into the handle. This leaves the second tip free for turning the screw. A good reversible screwdriver combination would have a standard tip at one end and a Phillips at the other. For working with tiny parts, there is a small reversible that comes with a pocket clip and protective pouch. Another type is triple purpose. It is a reversible screwdriver with a $1/4$-inch nutdriver built into the handle's dome. There is one reversible set that contains four double-end blades that fit into a single cushion-grip handle. *SEE ALSO HAND TOOLS.*

Ribbon

A ribbon is a narrow board attached to the studs or other vertical members which support the ceiling or floor joists. *SEE ALSO FLOOR CON-*

STRUCTION; WALL & CEILING CONSTRUCTION.

Ridge

The ridge is the horizontal line which intersects at the top edges between opposite sloping roof surfaces or sides of a roof. It is also called ridge board, ridge piece and ridge beam. The rafters on both sides are nailed at the ridge. When constructing a roof, continue checking the ridge to make sure it remains straight. *SEE ALSO ROOF CONSTRUCTION.*

Ridge Cap

A ridge cap is the continuous wood or metal strip fitted over the roof peak to keep water out and to keep shingles or tiles in place.

Ridge Ventilator

A ridge ventilator provides a uniform air flow from the soffit or underside of house roofing to the ridge and protects against build-up of condensation. It may be installed over a 1½ inch gap in the sheathing at the ridge.

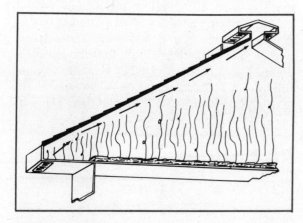

Ridge ventilator maintains the air flow from soffit to ridge.

Ridge Vent

Rifflers

Wood and metalworkers use rifflers in the smoothing and shaping of irregular features in hard-to-reach areas. These small files have a rasp end for rough cutting and a file end for finishing. The bent riffler is available in triangular, half-round, flat and round styles. *SEE ALSO HAND TOOLS.*

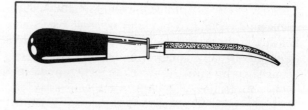

Bent Riffler

Rigid Copper Tube
[SEE COPPER PIPE & TUBING.]

Rigid Insulation

Rigid insulation, or rigid board insulation, is made of polystyrene plastic or compressed mineral wool and used on concrete, on walls and ceilings and inside the foundation before the concrete slabs are poured. For use in a basement or attic, some of these panels come with decorative finishes so they serve as finish paneling as well as a form of insulation. Rigid board insulation does not work as well as the bulkier insulation that is installed inside the wall. *SEE ALSO INSULATION.*

Rip Blade

The rip blade is used in circular saws for cutting large amounts of both soft and hardwood with the grain. It has larger teeth than a combination blade that form deep gullets which provide quick removal of sawdust. The rip blade, like others used in circular saws, should be adjusted to the proper height for even cutting and used in connection with a rip fence for accurate work.

Ripping is done by setting the work down flat at the front edge of the table against the rip fence. With the left hand holding the work and the right hand fingers hooked over the fence, feed the work forward. The work should be fed until the rear table overhang makes the back end of the board tilt up. Then, lift the work clear of the rip blade. When making narrow cuts and the fingers are six inches or less from the rip blade, use a push stick to finish feeding the lumber.

Ripping work on a radial arm saw may cause a kick back since the work is fed against the rotation of the blade. Therefore, a special feature called "fingers" is needed to dig into the work if the blade begins fighting.

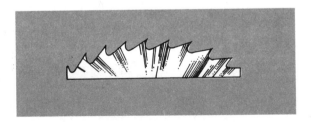

Rip Blade Configuration

Rip Fence

A rip fence is an adjustable guide used with a rip saw. *SEE ALSO TABLE SAW.*

Ripping Bar

A ripping bar is used for prying and ripping boards apart, opening wooden crates, getting under a log and pulling out large nails. The ones most commonly used are the gooseneck and straight ripping bars and offset ripping chisel. *SEE ALSO HAND TOOLS.*

Courtesy of The Stanley Works

Ripping Bar

Ripping Chisel

A ripping chisel is a type of bar which has at one end a nail-slot and a tear-shaped hole used for pulling nails. At the opposite end, a ripping chisel may have a gooseneck or the shaft may be straight for striking with a hammer. It is used to pry, drive under nailheads, pull up flooring boards or take out partitions. The ripping chisel is commonly 18 inches long and is made of a lightweight flat steel. *SEE ALSO HAND TOOLS.*

Courtesy of The Stanley Works

Ripping Chisel

Ripping Hammer
[SEE CLAW HAMMERS.]

Ripsaw

The ripsaw is designed to cut with the wood grain rather than across it. The leading edge of its teeth are almost perpendicular to the cutting edge, have no bevel and are slanted at 90° for cutting as well as ripping wood fibers. Because of the ripping action, the teeth leave small shavings rather than sawdust. The average ripsaw blade will have five and a half teeth per inch with one extra tooth (six and a half) at the tip. Therefore, cutting is started at the tip instead of the butt end. Alternate teeth are bent outward to widen the cut, prevent crimping and reduce friction.

The top edge of the ripsaw slants to the square tip and has a straight cutting edge. When cutting boards of average thickness, the angle between the cutting edge and blade should be approximately 60°, 45° on thin material. A sharp ripsaw will cut 10 feet per minute. *SEE ALSO HAND TOOLS.*

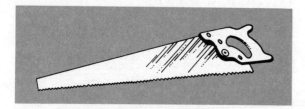

Ripsaw

Rise

Rise is the vertical distance anything rises, such as the rise of stairs or a roof. Rise is also the distance or elevation of one point above another.

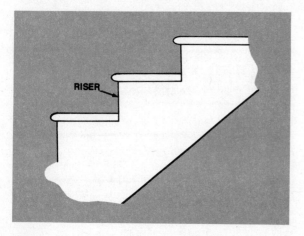

RISER

Riser

The riser is the vertical part of the step between two stair treads. *SEE ALSO STAIR CONSTRUCTION.*

Roaster Oven Repair

Courtesy of General Electric Company

Toast-R-Oven

Roaster ovens consist of a cabinet which encloses one and sometimes two heating elements. These elements are arranged to provide even heat throughout the unit and are often controlled through the action of a thermostat. In some cases this thermostat is a capillary-tube-type similar to those found on ordinary electric range ovens, rather than a bimetal type.

Most problems arising with roaster ovens will be due to electrical connections or cords. If the oven doesn't work, check the receptacle with a table lamp. If this produces no results, unplug the oven and check the cord at the plug and the entrance to the appliance. Next, remove the appliance covers and look closely for broken or damaged wires. This most often occurs around terminals where the appliance plugs or fastens to the heating element or thermostat.

The thermostat contacts may not be visible. If

they are accessible and are burned, they can be cleaned with an automotive point file and then polished. If they are not visible, it will take a continuity test to determine if they are closed to complete the circuit to the heating element.

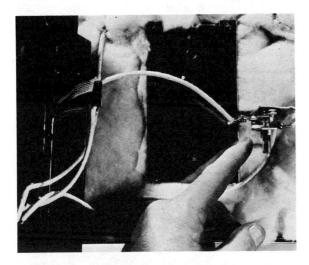

Thermostat in this roaster oven is of the bimetal type. It's adjustable by knob on control panel to give accurate range of heat levels.

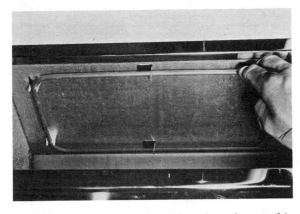

Heating element is held in place by tabs on this oven. It can be removed by springing away from metal tab.

Elements in most roaster ovens are of the enclosed-sheath-type. Again, the VOM is necessary to make an accurate diagnosis. Since you can't see the nichrome wire itself when you are testing an element for continuity, be sure to make ground tests on it as well.

The wiring used in a heating appliance such as this is a special heat-resistant type, and this must be used in any repairs involving the wiring. If a terminal should become corroded or should "burn off", the terminal must be cleaned and should look shiny and new when the connection is re-made. A tight connection will seldom give any problem. If a roaster oven should overheat, the thermostat contacts may be stuck or "welded" or the thermostat may be out of calibration.

To test the thermostat setting, obtain an oven thermometer at a department store. It's a good idea to test its accuracy with a known accurate thermometer of another type around the house before using it in the oven. Do this by placing the two side by side to see if the readings correspond. Lacking this, if the oven thermostat is the sealed-glass type, you can immerse it in a pan of boiling water and see if it indicates approximately 212 degrees.

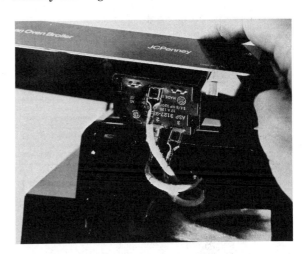

Elements can be switched in and out of circuit by pushbutton switch on this model. It's tested after removing control panel. Terminals such as this must be shiny and tight when being put back into position.

Some thermostats can be calibrated by a small screw located adjacent to and sometimes within the shaft of the thermostat, or in the case of the bimetal type, on the movable arm. If a thermostat continues to wander away from calibration it should be replaced.

If the contacts are pitted to the extent that they stick, it is sometimes possible to clean them and put them back into operation. Chances are, however, that the repair will be short-lived. The best bet is to replace the control once this condition is discovered. Test the roaster oven with a VOM set to the highest resistance scale before putting it back into use. Remove the appliance from service immediately if any user complains of a shock.

Rock Wool

Rock wool is mineral wool made by blowing a jet of steam through molten rock or slag. Used chiefly for heat and sound insulation, rock wool is resistant to moisture and rotting and is undigestible by insects. It comes in ready-to-pour bags and is placed in between joists underneath flooring in house construction. Also used inside walls, it can be machine-blown into walls of a house already built. Rock wool is not good for walls, however, because of its tendency to settle. *SEE ALSO INSULATION.*

Roof Construction

Roof construction involves the cutting and erecting of rafters and trusses and the application of sheathing, underlayment and shingles or tile. The layouts and procedures require careful following and the proper materials should be used to produce a strong, watertight roof that will last many years with only minor repairs.

Most roofs fall into the category of being constructed in either a butterfly, flat, gable, gambrel, hip, mansard or shed style. A butterfly roof drains water toward the center but can accumulate snow and ice in the valley which would eventually damage the roof. Flat roofs may be completely level or have only a slight pitch to provide water drainage. A gable roof is

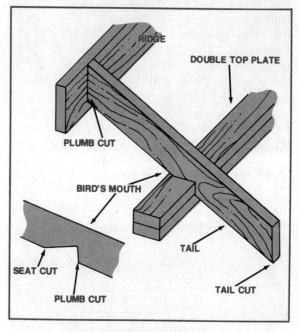

Parts of a Rafter

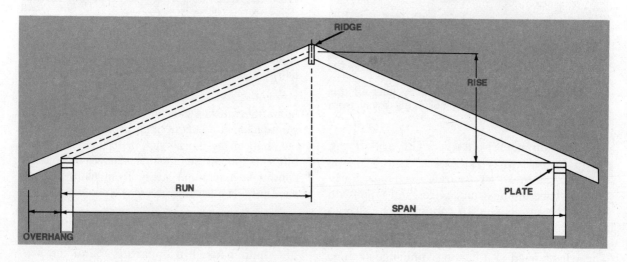

Basic Terms in Rafter Layout

built opposite from the butterfly in that it slopes from the center down. The slopes of the gambrel roof break near the center of the slope. The hip roof has four sloping sides; one at the back, front and at each side. Mansard roofs resemble hip roofs except that the slope is broken in two places. Shed roofs are slanted from the front to the back.

RAFTERS & RAFTER PARTS

Common rafters are used in practically all roof construction. These are the rafters that run from the wall plate to the ridge. Hip rafters run at a 45 degree angle from the plate to the ridge. Valley rafters extend diagonally from ridge to plate in the area left by the intersection of two roof sections. Hip jack rafters intersect hip rafters and extend to the plate. A valley jack rafter bisects a valley rafter. A cripple jack rafter runs from a hip jack to a valley rafter.

Rafters are made by laying out and cutting lumber. In the common rafter, a ridge cut permits the upper portion of the rafter to fit snugly against the ridge. A bird's mouth is made by the intersection of a seat cut and the plumb cut. The extension of the rafter beyond the plate is called the overhang or tail.

A bird's eye cut seats the rafter on the wall plates.

BASIC LAYOUT PRINCIPLES & TERMS

Roof construction is based mostly on the format of a right triangle with the base being the horizontal distance, the vertical distance being the altitude and the hypotenuse being the rafter length. To find the length of the rafter, use the formula that the base squared plus the altitude squared equals the hypotenuse squared. However, the scales on the carpenter's square provide a more rapid method of arriving at mathematical answers.

The run of the rafter, which is the base of the right triangle, is measured from the center of the ridge to the outside of the plate. The altitude, called the rise, is the length the rafter runs above the plate. The overhang is the distance from the plate to the farthest point on the rafter. The span is twice the length of the run.

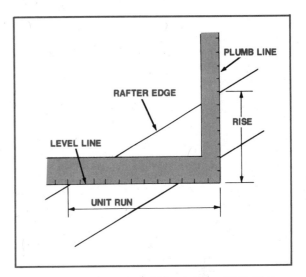

Laying Out Horizontal and Plumb Lines With Units

PITCH & SLOPE

Roof pitch is the slant of the roof as a ratio of the perpendicular rise to the span and is written like a fraction. If the rise of the roof is 6 feet and the span is 24 feet, the pitch is $1/4$.

Slope is the ratio of the rise to the run and is shown as X in 12. If a roof rises six inches for each foot or run, it has a 6 in 12 slope.

UNIT MEASURING & FRAMING

The carpenter's square is used to measure and lay out rafters. The face of the square is the side which has the maker's seal while the other side is called the back. This square cannot measure the rafter layout at one time, so units are used. The standard unit for the horizontal run is 12 inches with the unit rise being based on that distance. The unit rise and run are used in laying out rafter tails and level and plumb cuts.

A framing plan should be drawn to depict the tail, ridges and all the rafters so there is a clear picture of the roof to be constructed. Maintain accurate spacing and draw hip and valley rafters at 45 degree angles.

ESTIMATING MATERIALS

The length of a rafter may be determined by forming a scaled layout with a carpenter's square. Using the unit run and unite rise of the roof slope, draw a triangle with the back side of the square up and interpret the inches as feet and the divisions as inches. Extend the base and

hypotenuse length if the total run is greater than 12 feet. Move the square along the base line until the total run and acute angle are aligned and mark the point where the sloping line and the tongue cross. Use the tongue or blade to determine the length of the rafter. Make sure if any extra materials are needed that they are added in with the overhang requirements.

LAYING OUT RAFTERS

The step-off method or calculation on the tables of a carpenter's square are the two most common ways of laying out common rafters. Most carpenters will use the step-off method and then double check the work with the special tables.

For the pattern rafter, use a piece of true, straight lumber and place it across two sawhorses. Set the square on the lumber and line up the unit run on the body and the rise on the tongue with the

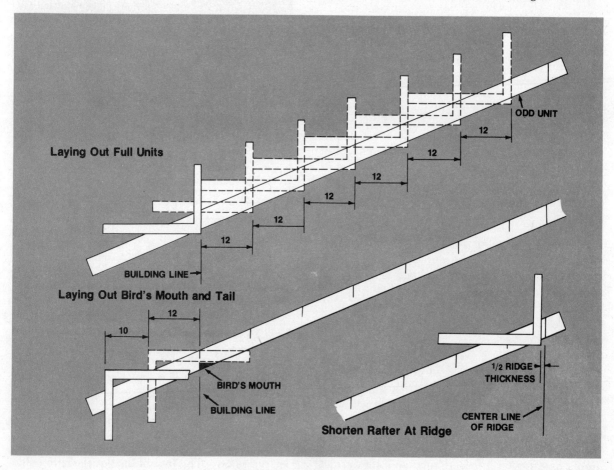

Laying Out a Common Rafter

top edge of the rafter. For example, the rise is 5 and the run is 12.

Beginning at the top of the rafter, position the square, draw the ridge line and then mark the odd unit length of 8 inches. Slide the square along the rafter edge until the 8 inch mark and the tongue are even and draw a line along the tongue. Mark the 12 inch spot on the blade and the first full unit is made.

Keeping the square evenly aligned, move it to the just made 12 inch point and duplicate the marking process. Repeat until all necessary units are laid out.

To make a bird's mouth, turn the square over and draw a horizontal line, called the seat cut, to the building line so that the width of the plate and the surface will be about equal.

Tails cuts may be square, plumb or both level and plumb. Cornice details in the architectural plans should be consulted for exact specifications.

Shortening the rafter is the last step in rafter lay out. Position the square and draw a plumb line horizontally spaced one half the thickness of the ridge back from the ridge. Make all the cuts and label each rafter and to which roof section it belongs.

It is considered good practice to layout rafters and ceiling joists at the same time. Choose straight stock for the ridges and layout the rafter spacing by transposing the marking from a layout rod or the plate. Ridge joints should fall at the center line of the rafter. Cut the ridge pieces and place them across the ceiling joists to where they and the rafters will be assembled. Have temporary bracing, ridge boards and rafters nearby. Nail one end of the straight rafter to the plate and another rafter on the opposite side with a support at the ridge. Put the ridge between the rafters and temporarily nail them in place. Move down five rafter spaces and set up another pair of rafters. Plumb and brace the structure and make any necessary corrections in

the first rafter nailing. Framing anchors may be used for additional rafter-plate support.

Temporary bracing supports the ridge until the alignment is correct.

To install the intervening rafters, secure the rafter to the plate and the ridge with 16d nails. Toenail the rafters on the opposite side of the ridge. It will be easier to keep the ridge straight if a few rafters are put on one side of the ridge before placing the matching ones on the opposite side. Add ridge sections and assemble rafters until the roof area is covered and install extra bracing if necessary to keep the ridge straight and level.

The end frame of the gable roof is made by first squaring a line across the wall plate end immediately below the gable center. If the house is to have a ventilator, measure one half of the size opening on each center line side and mark for the stud. Then, lay out the remainder of the spacing. At the first space, stand the stud upright, plumb and level it and mark across the stud edge at the rafter underside. Repeat the process at the second space. The common difference between the two studs may be used to layout the rest of the stud lengths. However, the carpenter's square may also be used to determine the common difference of stud lengths. Place the square on the lumber, set it for the unit rise and run and draw along the body. Move the square along the line until the stud spacing is even with the edge. The common difference will be the measured distance along the tongue of the square.

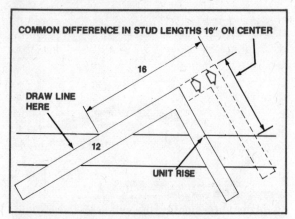

Using Carpenter's Square to Find the Common Difference in Stud Lengths for a Gable

HIP & VALLEY RAFTERS

Common, cripple, valley, hip and jack rafters are all used in hip roof construction. The common rafter and ridge boards are cut and framed first. The hip roof ridge is cut the length of the building minus twice the run plus the rafter stock thickness. This should intersect the common rafter at a right angle. From the building corners, layout one-half span's distance along the sidewalls; this is the center of the leading common rafters. The two roof surfaces that slant upward from the adjoining wall will intersect on the hip. The hip rafter is the one that supports the two and it runs at a 45 degree angle from the ridge to the wall plate.

The unit run of a hip rafter is the diagonal of a 12 inch square which is 16.97. The figure is rounded to 17 and is used to layout hip rafters. Follow the same method as used with common rafter layout with the exception of the 17 inch mark on the body being used instead of the 12 inch. The odd unit length is found by measuring the diagonal of the square with the sides being equal to the odd unit length.

Valley rafters are also the diagonal of a square with sides that are made by the ridges of com-

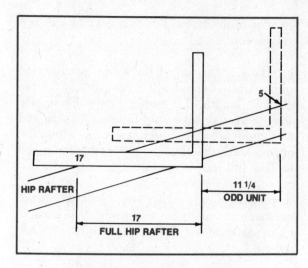

Beginning Hip Rafter Layout

mon rafters. Lay this out the same as hip rafters. Use the tables on the carpenter's square to figure the line length of the hip and valley rafters.

In order that hip and valley rafters fit the right angle of the ridge-common rafter intersection, a 45 degree angle half the thickness of the ridge must be cut in the rafter. The tail cuts are made by cutting at a 45 degree angle half the thickness of the rafter from the rafter end inward.

When the ridge and rafter meet, the rafter runs slightly above the center and should be planed down or have the seat cut deeper so the entire rafter is lowered. Trim the plumb cut of the bird's mouth so it will fit into the corner made by the walls. To provide sufficient space for the intersection of the cornice and fascia board, the tail cut must be shortened. The simplest method of doing this is to move the plumb cut toward the rafter tail a horizontal distance that is equal to the 45 degree thickness of the rafter. The hip and valley rafters may now be applied to the roof.

JACK RAFTERS

Hip jack rafters intersect hip rafters so their length from the point of intersection to the bird's mouth will vary. The common difference in hip jack rafters is the consistent variance of the equally spaced rafters along the plate. This common difference may be obtained from the rafter tables on the carpenter's square or by manipulating the square on a board. The latter is done by holding the square on the edge of a smooth piece of lumber according to the unit rise and run. After drawing a line along the body, move the square along the line to a point the same as the rafter spacing. This distance along the edge of the board is the necessary difference in length.

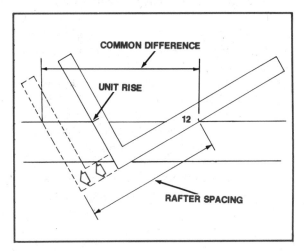

Determining the Common Difference of Jack Rafters

Jack rafters are made by choosing a straight piece of lumber and laying out the overhang and bird's mouth as is done with common rafters. Then lay out the distance from the center line of the ridge to the plumb cut of the bird's mouth. Measure the common difference in length for the first jack rafter down from the ridge. Shorten the jack rafter one half the 45 degree hip thickness and square this line across the rafter top and label the center point. Layout the side cuts through this point by marking two side cuts the same as in hip rafters but the thickness of a jack rafter on opposite sides of the lumber. Slide down the rafter the length of the common difference and make the next cutting line for the following hip jack. Use the pattern for marking the additional jack rafters. The hips in the roof require a matching set of jack rafters that are the same length and have side cuts in opposite directions.

Valley jack rafters are generally laid out beginning at the building line and moving toward the ridges. Except for the bottom side cuts, the longest valley jack is the same as a common rafter. Extend the plumb cut of the bird's mouth to the top edge of the common rafter pattern. The

side cut may be laid out with the fifth scale on the carpenter's square or by horizontally marking one half of the 45 degree thickness of the rafter.

The procedure for determining the common difference for valley jack rafters is the same as for hip jacks. After laying out the lengths, carefully cut them in pairs like hip jacks.

INSTALLING JACK RAFTERS

Secure all the different jack rafters with 10d nails and space the nails close to side cut heels. To prevent pushing the hip and valley rafters out of line, erect jack rafters in pairs. Place a pair approximately midway between the ridge and the plate while sighting the valley or hip straight; this purpose may also be served by temporary braces. Before erecting jack rafters, make sure all outside walls running parallel to the ceiling joists are securely fastened to the ceiling frame. After nailing all rafters, check the frame for any bowing. If bowing is present, sight each rafter, adjust as necessary and nail them to a strip of lumber. Remove the strip when it is reached during sheathing.

The roof framing, like the wall framing, provides a skeleton for the covering materials.

ANCHORING THE ROOF

Rafters that sit only on the outside walls of a building lean against each other, so mutual support is provided. This produces an outward thrust along the plate that demands consideration in the framing design. Side walls are usually secured by the ceiling joists which are fastened to several rafters. However, end walls are parallel to the joists and require additional support. Metal straps, framing anchors and stud joists may be applied for extra strength.

COLLAR BEAMS

Collar beams are ties which connect rafters on opposite sides of a roof and can later serve as ceiling supports if properly spaced. Collar beams are designed to brace the ridges and rafters, not support the roof. Typical collar beam application is 1 x 6 board placed at every third pair of rafters.

PURLINS

Additional support must be provided if the rafter span exceeds the maximum allowed. A purlin which is generally a 2 x 4 is secured to the underside of the rafter and is then supported with 2 x 4 bracing which rests on the plate over the outside wall. The under bracing for the purlin may be positioned in different angles to carry from the rafter mid point to the lower support.

FLAT & GAMBREL ROOFS

A flat roof is constructed much the same as a floor with roof joists supporting both the roof and ceiling. This double load generally requires 2 x 10's or 2 x 12's spaced 16 inches on center. However, the building code should be consulted for accuracy.

All methods and procedures used in floor framing may be used in flat roof construction. Overhang, cantilevered rafters and corners are all exceptions which may be used on a roof.

The gambrel roof is similar to the gable roof and the procedures for constructing both are close. The gambrel has two individual roof surfaces on each side of the ridge. The upper portion usually forms a 30 degree angle with a horizontal plane while the lower section is a 60 degree angle. Purlins are used where the two surfaces meet and the rafters are notched for the purlins. When constructing a gambrel roof, a full size sectional drawing of the intersection of the two slopes may be necessary to fully visualize the framing plan.

ROOF TRUSSES

A roof truss is the triangular-shaped framework which carries the roof and ceiling surfaces. It sits on the exterior walls, runs the full width of the building and requires no load-bearing partitions. Roof trusses allow larger rooms without additional supports and beams and can reduce labor costs since surface materials may be applied before partitions are built.

Roof trusses are made of sound lumber and should have carefully fitting joints. Spacing of 24 inches on center is used most frequently, however different spacing may be necessary in

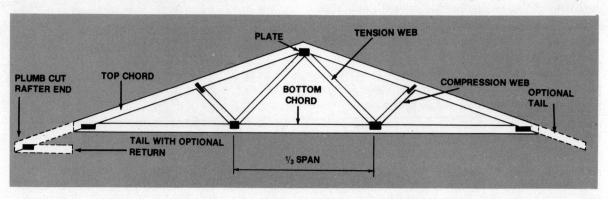

Fink Truss

some designs. After the truss is constructed and mounted, there will be a slight sag which is alleviated by raising the bottom chord during fabrication of the unit. Camber is the name for this adjustment and is measured midway of the span. A 24 foot long truss will generally need $1/2$ inch of camber.

Joint slippage in trusses must be limited and typical nailing patterns are not satisfactory. Plywood gussets, truss plates, truss connectors, bolts and washers and split ring connectors are easily applied and provide the support necessary.

In situations where the roof truss pieces are small, the truss can be laid out and assembled in a clear floor area. Make an entire layout on the floor, snap chalklines for long line lengths and use straightedges for shorter ones. Line up the lumber with the layout and cut the pieces working with the top and bottom chords and then the web pieces. Cut sufficient material from straight lumber for one truss and an extra of each piece for a pattern. Align the members and check the fit. Bore holes for ring connectors if they are to be used. Tack the joints together, apply the connectors and then finish the opposite side. Check it carefully and nail it to the floor. After cutting the pattern pieces, assemble each truss individually by using clamps to keep them in position. Use extra clamps on warped pieces and be sure all joints are held tightly together. Apply the connectors, unclamp the truss, turn it over and install fasteners.

To erect the trusses, place each one upside down at the point of installation on the wall, turn the peak up and revolve it into position.

SHEATHING

Sheathing is the plywood, shiplap or common boards that provide a nailing base for the shingles or shakes. A scaffold will be necessary for installing sheathing along the lower edge of the building and to do cornice work after the roof surface is finished.

If asphalt shingles or other composition materials are to be used, the sheathing must be

Tongue and groove decking is used with exposed beams. The roof surface is attached to the decking.

solid. For metal sheets, tile or wood shingles, board sheathing may be spaced according to the arrangement of the courses. Secure the board with two 8d nails at each rafter and locate the joint at the center of the rafter.

Joints may be made between the rafter if end-matched boards are used. Boards that are not long enough to cross over two rafters should not be used and joints in adjacent boards must not take place in the same rafter space.

Fit the boards carefully at hips and valleys and nail them in place. Boards should have a $1/2$ inch clearance from the masonry around chimney openings.

When working with plywood sheathing, lay it with the face grain at a right angle to the rafters and end joints formed directly over the rafter center. A plywood thickness of $5/16$ inch is recommended for wood or asphalt shingles with 16 inch rafter spacing. Use $3/8$ inch thickness for 24 inches. Asbestoes shingles, tile and slate need $1/2$ inch plywood for 16 inch rafter spacing and $5/8$ inch for spacing of 24 inches. Plywood should be spaced six inches apart on the edges, 12 inches in other areas and secured with 6d nails. When less than ¹/₂ inch thick plywood is used for wood shingles, 1 x 2 inch nailing strips should be nailed to the plywood and spaced according to the desired shingle exposure.

UNDERLAYMENT

The underlayment is installed to provide extra protection for the sheathing against wind, rain and snow. Underlayment is usually an asphalt-saturated felt or other material with a low vapor resistance. It should be applied with a two inch top lap at horizontal joints and a four inch side lap at the end joints. Lap underlayment at least six inches on each side of the center line of hips and valleys.

FLASHING

Flashing is sheet metal or other material that is used at eaves, valleys and walls to protect them from rain, snow or wind. Eave flashing is placed over the underlayment and drip edge. The flashing material may be either smooth or mineral-surfaced roll roofing and should extend from a point approximately 12 inches inside the wall line to the edge of the roof.

Valley flashing is usually done with a 90 pound mineral roll along the intersection of two slopes. This type flashing is done by centering a strip of roll roofing no less than 18 inches wide over the area to be flashed, mineral surface down. Nail the strip down and nail another strip 36 inches wide over the first one with the mineral side up. If joining is necessary with any of the strips, lap them at least 12 inches and secure with plastic asphalt cement. Nailing should be done so that before the second edge of material is secured it is pressed into the valley to follow the shape of the valley. Fasten the second edge of roll roofing.

Wall flashing is applied where the roof joins a vertical wall. Metal flashing shingles are used most and should be approximately six inches long and two inches wider than the exposed area of the shingle. Bend the metal shingle so that two inches run horizontally and the rest extends along the vertical wall. Secure the metal shingles at the same time the regular shingles are laid with one nail in the top corner. The finished sid-

ing is installed over the flashing allowing enough clearance for painting.

Outside edges are finished to provide an attractive appearance.

Roofing Materials

Roofing materials include a broad spectrum of items used for completing and protecting a roof on a home or building. The materials listed will give the homeowner a general idea of the types of sheathing, underlayment and roofing materials available, but the roofing contractor will generally know which materials are best to use.

SHEATHING & UNDERLAYMENT

Sheathing is the boards that are placed over the roof frame in preparation for the underlayment. Spaced and solid sheathing are two of the most common forms of covering. Spaced sheathing may be matched or unmatched one inch boards, plywood or shiplap. Solid sheathing adds to insulation and resists infiltration of air and dirt since the boards are basically all one size.

Underlayment is various types of tar paper used for insulation and waterproofing. Low vapor resistant building paper or asphalt-saturated felts are most commonly used. Coated sheets and heavy felt cause condensation and are not recommended for roofs.

SHINGLES, SHAKES & TILE

Before purchasing shingles or shakes, consider their durability, weight, versatility (colors, patterns and textures), cost and the color scheme of the home. Shingles are weighed in 100 square feet areas. Shingles weighing 290 or more pounds per 100 square feet are classified as heavyweights. Standard weights, which are used on most homes, weigh 235 to 240 pounds per 100 square feet. Heavyweight shingles are thicker and provide a more textured appearance and better protection, but the roof deck must provide adequate support before they can be installed. Heavyweight shingles also cost more than the standard weights.

Shingles are available in a wide range of colors, patterns and textures to suit the home and the homeowner. Black shingles make a house look smaller and attract heat. White roofs reduce air-conditioning costs by reflecting heat. Neutral, "earth" and forest tones blend well with wooded areas. The texture and pattern should be chosen according to the construction of the house and the effect desired.

Underwriter's Laboratories test shingles for fire resistance, making a safe choice easier. A Class A rating indicates extremely good resistance to fire under severe conditions. Class B roofing provides protection from moderate fires. Class C coverings are not readily flammable, but are effective only against light fires. Most wood shakes and shingles, when treated, are given a C rating. Look for the Underwriter's seal and rating before purchasing shingles and shakes.

Asphalt shingles are the most popular form of roofing because they are not only durable, extremely fire resistant and practically maintenance free, but are also available at reasonable prices in a wide variety of colors, patterns and textures. Quality asphalt shingles will be comprised of four layers — a back coated with asphalt to prevent weathering underneath, a felt base saturated and coated with asphalt, another coating of asphalt and an asphalt covering on the top that is embedded with hard mineral granules. Plain-barbed, annular-threaded and spiral-threaded nails are primarily used for installing

asphalt shingles. Eleven or twelve gauge galvanized steel or aluminum nails with head diameters of $3/8$ to $7/16$ inch are recommended for asphalt shingle installation. The nail should be long enough to penetrate the full thickness and driven straight to avoid cutting the shingle with the head. In some shingle installation a pneumatic-powered stapler is used.

Mineral fiber shingles are made of asbestos fiber and cement and are molded under high pressure so they will resist decay, salt air, snow, ice and fire. Because of their thickness, these shingles have prepunched nail holes and usually require a special cutter for shaping them around pipes and chimneys.

Fiberglass shingles are light and may not provide as much protection as asphalt or mineral fiber shingles. They are made of inorganic materials so they are less affected by weather and are extremely fire retardant.

Wood shingles and shakes are popular for their decorative features but provide little resistance to fire. Available in different lengths, widths, thicknesses and colors, wood shakes give a home a rustic appearance.

Clay tile is one of the more common roofing tiles. It is durable, unglazed and available in many shapes and textures. Clay tile can be used for reroofing if the old covering is in reasonably good condition and if the present roof frame provides adequate support for the additional weight.

METAL ROOFING

Galvanized sheet metal roofing is primarily used in the construction of plants and foundries. These sheets can also be laid on slopes as low as $1/8$ pitch and should not lap less than eight inches if an additional piece is needed to reach the roof top. They should be fastened with lead-headed nails or galvanized nails and lead washers.

Corrugated aluminum is long lasting and can withstand salt corrosion, if not directly exposed to it. Aluminum alloy nails are used in corrugated aluminum construction.

Terne metal roofing is made of copper-bearing steel that is coated with an alloy of 80 percent lead and 20 percent tin. This makes Terne metal retain a high level of resistance to weathering.

GUTTERS & DOWNSPOUTS

Gutters and downspouts are essential in roof maintenance for providing proper water drainage. Wood gutters are usually made of red cedar or Douglas fir, and when correctly installed and cared for, can last as long as the metal varieties.

Metal gutter and downspout systems are generally made of galvanized iron or aluminum. They should match the roof areas from which the water runs and be assembled with soft pop rivets or sheet metal screws. When primed or prefinished, metal gutters and downspouts may be painted to correspond with the colors of the house.

FLASHING

Flashing is tin-coated metal, galvanized metal, lead, copper, asphalt shingles, aluminum or roll roofing cut to fit around or into certain areas to make them watertight. Install flashing at the joints between chimney and roof, two roof sections or wherever two surfaces intersect.

Roof Pitch

Pitch signifies the amount that a roof slants. Units, or amount, of pitch are expressed as ratios. There are two methods of indicating pitch. In the first method, the pitch is indicated as a ratio of the rise to the span of a roof. This ratio is stated as a fraction. The units of span and rise must be the same (inches or feet), and the fraction is reduced to its lowest common denominator.

With the second method, pitch is stated as the ratio of rise (in inches) per foot of span. Using this method, 4, 6 or 8 inches rise per foot of span would give a pitch of 4-12, 6-12 or 8-12. *SEE ALSO ROOF CONSTRUCTION.*

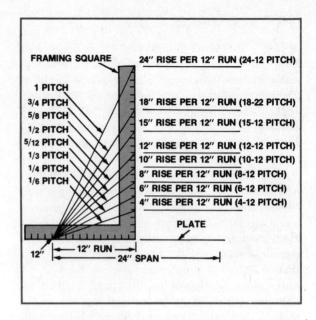

Roof Repair

Even small damage to a roof can cause serious damage inside the house. Anticipating problems before they begin depends on periodic inspection since roofing materials do deteriorate, some faster than others.

ROOF DETERIORATION

Basically there are three stages of roof deterioration. If the damage is caught in time, just a few shingles can be repaired or replaced. If not, it may still be possible to give an older roof new life as both wood shingles and those made of asphalt composition can be rejuvenated through the use of wood preservatives and high-grade acrylic house paint. When it becomes necessary to replace the entire roof, it is best to call in a professional roofing contractor to do the job.

Composition shingles, those formed of asphalt and fiber, deteriorate rather slowly. The base gradually wears away and the surface granules loosen and wash away. Composition shingles have a tendency to become brittle with time and will break away from the roof in small pieces or tear loose in high winds. The fastest deterioration usually occurs on the southern and western exposures and since composition shingles tend to deteriorate uniformly, all the shingles on one side of the roof usually need replacing if any of them do.

Wooden shingles change color in a set pattern from the day they are laid. The shingles fade from their original color to a silvery gray and then begin to darken, taking on an increasingly deeper gray color until they finally look black when wet. If one section of the roof stays darker after a rain, there is usually an accumulation of moisture under these shingles.

As a roof made of wooden shingles begins to age, the owner should also watch for cupped or dished shingles which dry faster on the outside and cause the wood to shrink and splits in shingles which may be caused by too much space between them, improper nailing and widths that are too great. Wooden shingles will also become worn and weathered with age.

DISCOVERING THE DAMAGE

There are several things to remember when climbing on a roof for repairs or for examination. The roof can be damaged seriously when walked on after the shingles have aged enough to be brittle. Since shingles also become slippery with age, wear soft-soled shoes to prevent falling. Keep the ladder directly below where you are working and make sure that it is well secured. Most important of all, stay off the roof in bad weather.

Locating a leak in a roof can be a frustrating experience because the leak is rarely found directly over the evidence (usually a wet spot on a ceiling or under an eave). To find the leak examine the roof uphill from the evidence since the water has to run down a few rafters and along the underside of some roof sheathing and so forth, before it comes to light. If the leak is discovered during a storm, it can be temporarily repaired by applying a sealer of caulking compound to the hole, working it well into and around the area.

REPAIRING THE ROOF

Composition shingles usually come in strips

rather than as individual shingles, and it is rarely necessary to replace more than an occasional flap. If a flap is raised, but not detached, use roof cement to fasten it back down. If there is a little separation at the crease, smear some cement along the crack. Even if the flap is completely loose, it can be replaced by cementing it in place and filling the crack. Small breaks in composition shingles can be patched with a spread of roofing asphalt.

If it is necessary to replace an entire composition shingle unit, do so on a hot day when the shingles are flexible and less likely to crack. Since shingles are applied from the lower edge of the roof surface upward in an overlapping pattern, it will be necessary to lift the shingles above the damaged ones, taking care not to crack the good ones. After removing the damaged shingles, along with their nails, slip the new shingles in place and nail down. Be sure to use special roofing nails with broad heads. Cover the nailheads with roof cement, and finish up by cementing down the flaps.

Cracks in slate shingles can be sealed with a plastic roof cement. If the shingle is broken, it can be removed by inserting a slate nail puller under the shingle, hooking the tool over the nail and driving it out with a hammer. To put a new shingle in place, first mark the locations of the required nail holes (two will be needed), and then make holes in the slate with a nail set or an electric drill. Apply roof cement to the vacant area of the roof and to the back of the new slate. Push the new slate up under the upper slates and drive in the two roofing nails, covering the heads with roof cement.

To replace a damaged wood shingle, use a chisel to split it in narrow strips. This will make it easier to dig out since only two of the strips will be held in place by nails instead of the whole shingle. When all of the damaged shingle has been removed, push the new one in place, making sure the thin end hits the nails. Give it a sharp tap so the nails make two marks on the end of the shingle. Remove the shingle and saw a kerf *parallel to the edges* where each of the nails made a mark. This lets you push the new shingle in place, the slats riding up the nails. With the new shingle in place, drive a nail through it in the center, one or two inches up from the butt. Make the nail weatherproof by covering its head with roof cement or other caulking material. Another method of securing the shingle is to spread the bottom of the shingle with a mastic-type adhesive. Keep the butt elevated as it is pushed in place, then press the shingle down to bring the mastic in contact with the roof.

If a large area of wooden shingles are damaged, only the top row must be removed by the method described. The remaining shingles can be torn off in any manner, being careful not to damage the roofing felt. If the felt must be replaced, slip the new material under the edge of the good felt at the top and edges.

To begin replacing the shingles, start at the bottom. Fit a row of new shingles across the lower edge of the patch, *making sure that one joint is not put over another.* Use two nails for each shingle, placing each one a little less than one quarter of the shingle's width in from both edges. These nails go in a row crosswise and will be covered by an inch or two of the next row of shingles. To keep the new shingles lined up, use a pencil or chalk to mark a straight line across the repair area, placing the butts of the new shingles along this line.

Repairing a flat roof is relatively simple. The cause of a leak will generally be found right over the damaged section in the ceiling below. These leaks will usually develop around chimney areas and at low spots where water can collect. Potential trouble is indicated by blisters, or bulges, in the roofing material which will eventually crack.

To repair a blistered area, cut through the middle with a sharp knife, being careful not to cut through the lower layer. Using a putty knife, force some roof cement under both sides of the cut. Nail down both sides of the cut with wide-headed galvanized or copper roofing nails. Cover the cut and nails with roof cement and apply a tarpaper or shingle patch over the cut. Nail this down and cover with cement.

If a large area of the roof needs repair, cut out the damaged section, making the cut in a square or rectangular pattern. Apply roof cement to the exposed area and under all four edges, lifting gently to avoid tearing. Cut a piece of new roofing felt large enough to extend about two inches over the exposed area. Nail this to the cemented area. The last step is to make a second oversized patch to cover the first. Nail this down and cover the nailheads and edges with roof cement. If the entire roof needs to be redone, cover it with black asphalt roof paint, not roof cement. Work in 5 x 5 foot sections, making sure the surface is free of dirt and pebbles.

Roof Truss Construction

Roof trusses are roofing timbers joined in triangular units and used to provide wide, unobstructed floor space over large spans. They are supported by bearing walls, posts or other trusses. The trusses are connected to the walls or posts by knee braces. Trusses are laid out on a workbench placed on a level spot of ground. The truss members are sized according to blueprints of the structure and nailed together temporarily in truss formation to determine the location of all holes to be bored. The holes are bored perpendicular to the face of the timber using a brace and bit or a woodborer. Refer to the blueprints to determine the size of the holes. The truss is then dismantled and the nails withdrawn. For the final assembly of the truss, timber connectors are used where the different members of the truss join. The truss is again assembled as it was for boring holes, and the bolts are placed in the holes and tightened, a washer being placed at the head and nut ends of each bolt. *SEE ALSO ROOF CONSTRUCTION.*

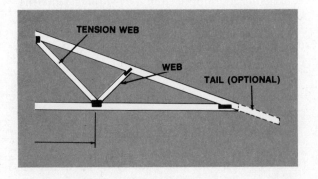